d by G. Goos, J. Hartmanis, and J. van Leeuwen

*rlin
*eidelberg
*ew York
*rcelona
*ong Kong
*ndon
*ilan
*ris
*ngapore
*kyo

odular
ogramming Languages

t Modular Languages Conference, JMLC 2000
ich, Switzerland, September 6-8, 2000
ceedings

erhard Goos, Karlsruhe University, Germany
ıris Hartmanis, Cornell University, NY, USA
ın van Leeuwen, Utrecht University, The Netherlands

ɔlume Editors

ırg Gutknecht
ГH Zentrum, Institut für Computersysteme
)92 Zürich, Switzerland
-mail: gutknecht@inf.ethz.ch

ʼolfgang Weck
beron microsystems Inc.
ːchnoparkstrasse 1, 8005, Zürich, Switzerland
-mail: weck@oberon.ch

ataloging-in-Publication Data applied for

ıe Deutsche Bibliothek - CIP-Einheitsaufnahme

odular programming languages : proceedings / Joint Modular Languages
ɔnference, JMLC 2000, Zurich, Switzerland, September 6 - 8, 2000.
ırg Gutknecht ; Wolfgang Weck (ed.). - Berlin ; Heidelberg ; New York ;
ırcelona ; Hong Kong ; London ; Milan ; Paris ; Singapore ; Tokyo :
ɔringer, 2000
(Lecture notes in computer science ; Vol. 1897)
ISBN 3-540-67958-8

R Subject Classification (1998): D.3, D.2, D.1, D.4, F.3

SN 0302-9743
BN 3-540-67958-8 Springer-Verlag Berlin Heidelberg New York

ringer-Verlag Berlin Heidelberg New York
ınember of BertelsmannSpringer Science+Business Media GmbH
Springer-Verlag Berlin Heidelberg 2000
ınted in Germany

pesetting: Camera-ready by author, data conversion by PTP-Berlin, Stefan Sossna
ınted on acid-free paper   SPIN: 10722581   06/3142   5 4 3 2 1 0

Preface

The circle is closed. The *European Modula-2 Conference* was originally launched with the goal of increasing the popularity of Modula-2, a programming language created by Niklaus Wirth and his team at ETH Zürich as a successor of Pascal. For more than a decade, the conference has wandered through Europe, passing Bled, Slovenia, in 1987, Loughborough, UK, in 1990, Ulm, Germany, in 1994, and Linz, Austria, in 1997. Now, at the beginning of the new millennium, it is back at its roots in Zürich, Switzerland. While traveling through space and time, the conference has mutated. It has widened its scope and changed its name to *Joint Modular Languages Conference (JMLC)*. With an invariant focus, though, on modular software construction in teaching, research, and "out there" in industry.

This topic has never been more important than today, ironically not because of insufficient language support but, quite on the contrary, due to a truly confusing variety of modular concepts offered by modern languages: modules, packages, classes, and components, the newest and still controversial trend. "The recent notion of component is still very vaguely defined, so vaguely, in fact, that it almost seems advisable to ignore it." (Wirth in his article "Records, Modules, Objects, Classes, Components" in honor of Hoare's retirement in 1999). Clarification is needed.

The JMLC 2000 featured four distinguished speakers: Ole Lehrmann Madsen, Bertrand Meyer, Clemens Szyperski, and Niklaus Wirth and 20 presentations of high-quality papers from 9 countries, a careful selection from 54 papers initially submitted to the refereeing process. Perspectives comprised parallel and distributed computing, components, extensions and applications, compilers, and runtime environments. A tutorial prelude taught by international experts shed light on commercially available component systems, including COM, JavaBeans, CORBA, Component Pascal, and Eiffel, and a special Oberon event provided a forum for Oberon developers from industry and academia to present their latest creations.

I would like to thank Springer-Verlag for publishing these proceedings and Wolfgang Weck for his editorial assistance. My thanks also go to the program committee members and to the referees whose competence assured the quality of this conference. Last but not least I thank all the helpful people at ETH and in particular Eva Ruiz, Patrik Reali, Marco Sanvido, Michela Taufer, and André Fischer for their work and dedication.

June 2000   Jürg Gutknecht

Organization

JMLC 2000 was organized by the *Institut für Computersysteme* at the Swiss Federal Institute of Technology (ETH) Zürich.

Organizing Committee

Program and Tutorial Chair	Jürg Gutknecht (ETH Switzerland)
Organizing Chair, Finance, Registration	Eva Ruiz (ETH Switzerland)
Public Relations, Advertising, Sponsoring	André Fischer (ETH Switzerland) and Niklaus Wirth (ETH Switzerland)
Logistics, Website	Patrik Reali (ETH Switzerland)
Publishing	Wolfgang Weck (Oberon microsystems, Switzerland)
Social Events	Michela Taufer (ETH Switzerland)
Oberon Exhibition	Marco Sanvido (ETH Switzerland)
Administrative Support, Volunteers	Hanni Sommer (ETH Switzerland)

Supporting and Sponsoring Organizations

ETH Zürich

SI — Schweizer Informatiker Gesellschaft
GI — Gesellschaft für Informatik e.V.
IFIP — International Federation for Information Processing

Atraxis
Microsoft Switzerland
McKinsey & Company, Inc.
Mettler Toledo

Program Committee

Jürg Gutknecht	ETH Zürich, Switzerland (Chair)
Frans Arickx	University of Antwerp, Belgium
Ralph Back	Åbo Akademi, Turku, Finland
Laszlo Böszörmenyi	University of Klagenfurt, Austria
Andreas Borchert	University of Ulm, Germany
Jim Cooling	Loughborough University, UK
Günter Dotzel	Modulaware, France
Mohamed Fayad	University of Nevada, Reno, USA
Cecilia Fischer Rubira	Unicamp, Sao Paulo, Brasil
Michael Franz	University of California, Irvine, USA
Jean-Luc Gaudiot	University of Southern California, USA
Gerhard Goos	University of Karlsruhe, Germany
John Gough	Queensland University of Technology, Brisbane, Australia
Thomas Gross	ETH Zürich, Switzerland
Dominik Gruntz	Oberon microsystems, Zürich, Switzerland
Mehdi Jazayeri	Technical University of Vienna, Austria
Chris Jesshope	Nassey University, New Zealand
Helmut Ketz	Fachhochschule Reutlingen, Germany
Brian Kirk	Robinson Associates, UK
Herbert Klären	University of Tübingen, Germany
David Lightfoot	Oxford Brookes University, UK
Ole Lehrmann Madsen	Aarhus University, Denmark
Hanspeter Mössenböck	University of Linz, Austria
Hausi Müller	University of Victoria, Canada
Libero Nigro	University of Calabria, Italy
Gustav Pomberger	University of Linz, Austria
Igor Pottosin	Institute for Information Systems, Novosibirsk, Russia
Kees Pronk	Delft University of Technology, The Netherlands
Peter Rechenberg	University of Linz, Austria
Martin Reiser	GMD Bonn, Germany
Roland Rüdiger	University of Applied Sciences, Braunschweig/Wolfenbüttel, Germany
Beverly Sanders	University of Florida, Gainesville, USA
Vladimir Safonov	St. Petersburg University, Russia
Peter Schulthess	University of Ulm, Germany
Gabriel Silberman	IBM Toronto, Canada
Alfred Strohmeier	EPFL Lausanne, Switzerland
Clemens Szyperski	Microsoft Research, Redmond, USA
Pat Terry	Rhodes University, Grahamstown, South Africa
Elena Trichina	PACT München, Germany
Pieter de Villiers	University of Stellenbosch, South Africa
Wolfgang Weck	Oberon microsystems, Zürich, Switzerland
Andrew Wendelborn	University of Adelaide, Australia
Niklaus Wirth	ETH Zürich, Switzerland

Referees Other Than PC Members

Mats Aspnäs	Markus Leypold	Michael Sperber
Martin Büchi	Stefan Ludwig	Joe Wigglesworth
Nelson Fonseca	Luigia Petre	Jongwook Woo
Spyros Lalis	Andreas Speck	Fan Xiaocong

Table of Contents

Extensions and Applications

Compilers and Runtime Environments

The Development of Procedural Programming Languages Personal Contributions and Perspectives

Niklaus Wirth

Abstract. I became involved in the design of a successor of Algol 60 in the years 1962-67. The result was Algol-W (66), and later the Algol-style Pascal (70), Modula-2 (79), and Oberon (88). In turn, they introduced the concepts of data structuring and typing, modular decomposition and separate compilation, and object-orientation. In this talk, we summarize these developments and recount some of the influences and events that determined the design and implementation of these languages. In the early 60s, CS was much influenced and concentrated around programming languages. Various programming paradigms emerged; we focus on the procedural branch, directed toward system programming and forming the backbone of engineering and data processing methods and tools. I conclude with some remarks about how the gap between methods taught and methods practiced in software design might be narrowed.

1   Algol (1960)

I entered the field of programming in 1961 as a graduate student at UC Berkeley, being interested in computer design as an electronics engineer. I met a group of people working on a compiler, a large program converting program text into machine code. Particularly intreaguing was the fact that the compiler was described in the same language (Neliac) that it accepted as input. This was the basis of the bootstrapping technique, the gradual development of language and compiler. The program was outrageously complicated by the standards of the day, and in effect a single person held the keys to it. For a student seeking a thesis topic, this project appeared as ideal with its evident need for disentangling the maze. Structure, building rules, a scientific approach was called for.

In 1960 the Report on Algol 60 had appeared [1]. It offered a promising basis for introducing a scientific approach due to its mathematically defined syntax. It is well known that in those years much effort went into the development of syntax analyzers. I designed my first compiler for a subset of Algol 60 for the IBM 704 computer, which was ill-suited for the implementation of an important feature of Algol: the recursive procedure. This, and more so my work on generalizing Algol came to the attention of the IFIP Working Group 2.1, and thus I became involved in language design along the line of Algol. What made Algol so interesting?

J. Gutknecht and W. Weck (Eds.): JMLC 2000, LNCS 1897, pp. 1–10, 2000.

1. Its precise, formal definition of syntax. For the first time, it was possible to derive the scaffolding of a translator from the definition of the language systematically. The syntax constituted the contract between programmer and compiler.
2. Its close adherence to traditional, mathematical notation. In particular, expressions followed longstanding tradition and could be used in their full generality independent of their place in the program, for example as indices and parameters.
3. Its block structure, providing the possibility to choose identifiers with limited scope independent of identifiers declared in other parts of the program, appeared as particularly important for introducing order into programs.
4. Its procedures with typed parameters provided a flexibility superior to that of the then common subroutine. Recursion opened the door to new ways of reasoning about programs, and it was a welcome challenge for implementors. On the other hand, Algol's name parameter was, as some suspected, a too high-flying mathematical notion to be appropriate for programming tasks.

But Algol also had its deficiencies, and remedies were necessary if Algol was to have a future at the side of Fortran. The argument of efficiency was everpresent, and some of Algol's features were definitely an obstacle in the competition with Fortran. The three main shortcomings were

1. Some ambiguities in the syntax of expressions and statements. At the time they gave rise to long debates, and were proof of the benefits of a precise, formal definition.
2. The field of application was too narrow in view of new emerging areas of computer usage. Languages like Cobol and Lisp (1962) had opened new paradigms and concepts, like records, files, dynamic data structures.
3. Some of its constructs were unnecessarily general, forbidding an efficient implementation. Primarily the For statement, name parameter, and Own variables were subjected to scrutiny and heated critizism.
4. The absence of facilities for input and output. As they were left to individual implementations, the concept of a standard language was severely compromised for practical purposes.

The outcome of WG 2.1's effort consisted of two languages: Algol W [2], implemented at Stanford in 1967, and Algol 68, [3] implemented by 1972.

2 Pascal (1970)

In search of a language suitable for teaching programming in a structured fashion, and for the development of system software, I designed Pascal (1968 -1972), free of conflicting demands from a large committee and with a clear purpose in mind

[4,5,6]. A Pascal compiler was available by 1970, and beginning in 1972 I used it in courses at ETH Zürich. The language report followed the example of Algol closely, and the language can truly be said to retain the "spirit of Algol". The highlights of Pascal were

1. Simple, structured statements for conditional (If, Case) and repeated execution (While, Repeat, For).
2. The user definability of scalar data types. Apart from standard types Boolean, Integer, Real, and Char there were enumerations.
3. The application of structuring principles to data type definitions. Structured types were records, arrays, files, sets, and their nesting provided the freedom to construct complex data structures.
4. Strict, static typing. Every constant, variable, function or parameter had a type that could be determined by a mere scan of the program text.
5. Dynamic data structures could be built with the aid of pointers, opening the field of list processing. According to Hoare, pointers were bound to objects of a fixed type, thus subjected to strict compile-time type checking as well.
6. Procedures can be used recursively. The controversial name parameter was replaced by the reference (VAR) parameter, appropriate for structured objects and for passing results.

In short, Pascal embodied the ideas of *Structured Programming*. Our first compiler (for the CDC 6000 computer) was programmed in Fortran with the idea to hand-translate it to Pascal for further bootstrapping. This turned out to be a failure. A second compiler project was launched, starting by programming in Pascal itself. The initial bootstrap was preceded by a hand-translation into the low-level language Scallop, which was much like the later C. Many other implementation efforts were undertaken at various universities. The first was a compiler for the ICL 1900 computer at the Queens University at Belfast. But the genuine breakthrough occurred years later with the advent of the micro-computer around 1977. With it, computing became available to many at school and at home, and the teaching of programming advanced to a subject of "general education". As the market grew, industry became interested. The distribution of compilers was significantly helped by our Pascal-P system: The compiler, written in Pascal itself, generated P-code for a virtual stack computer. The recipient's task was thereby reduced to program an interpreter of P-code in the local assembler language. The notable Pascal products were UCSD Pascal and Borland Pascal, low-cost programming tools affordable by everyone. By 1980 the competition had shifted from Algol vs. Fortran to Pascal vs. Basic. Pascal subsequently influenced other language designs, notably Concurrent Pascal and Mesa. A comprehensive account of Pascal's development and influence has appeared in [7].

3   Modula-2 (1979)

Of course, Pascal also had its shortcomings, particularly in view of the growing power of computing equipment and consequent increase on expectations on software. After 10 years of use of Pascal, some features and their importance appeared in a different light. For example, one had learnt to program without the controversial goto statement. In hindsight, several of the "concessions" made to tradition in Pascal were recognized as ill-advised. The handling of input and output in Pascal was considered as inadequate and inflexible. It was time for a successor to appear. Instead of Pascal-2, it was named Modula-2 [8,9].

The goto statement, one of the concessions mentioned, was eliminated. To cater for situations that could be foreseen where a goto facility would be missed, the collection of repetitive statements was enlarged. In addition to the while, repeat, and for statements, a general loop statement containing explicit exit statements was offered. So, one concession was replaced by a milder one. In practice the loop statement was merely a facility for increased efficiency in rare cases.

On the syntactic level, the open-ended if, for, and while statements of Pascal, giving rise to syntactic ambiguities, were adapted to the general rule that every structured statement not only has a unique starting symbol, but also an explicit closing symbol (END).

```
Pascal                            Modula
IF P THEN S                       IF P THEN S END
IF P THEN BEGIN S1; S2 END        IF P THEN S1; S2 END
IF P THEN IF Q THEN S1 ELSE S2    IF P THEN
                                      IF Q THEN S1 ELSE S2 END
                                  END
                                  IF P THEN
                                      IF Q THEN S1 END
                                  ELSE S2
                                  END
```

The most significant innovation of Modula with respect to Pascal, however, was the module concept. It derived from the concepts of *abstract data types* and information hiding, and was pioneered in the language Mesa, designed at the Xerox Palo Alto Research Center in 1976. Whereas in Pascal every program is a single piece of text, Modula facilitates the construction of large systems consisting of many modules, each a separate text, separately compilable. In contrast to customary independent compilation, separate compilation guarantees complete type checking across module boundaries at compile-time, an indispensable requisite for any truly typed language implementation. It requires that module interfaces be specified, and that the compiler must have at its disposal type information about module A, whenever compiling any client module B referring to A. This led to the technique of symbol files, invented with the implementation of the language Mesa. Modula generalized the concept of modules to nested modules, in analogy to nested procedures (procedures declared local to another procedure). It later turned out that nested modules are rarely of much benefit and complicate qualified notations.

An immediate and beneficial consequence of the module facility was that several language issues could be omitted from the language proper if it was possible to express them in the language itself in terms of more elementary constructs. In this case, they would be programmed and excapsulated in a module, possibly declared as a standard component belonging to every implementation. For example, the entire subject of input and output could be delegated to a module in a standard library. Another example was the file system, possible because access to peripheral devices could be expressed in Modula and be properly encapsulated in driver modules. This was the first step in a continuing trend towards standard program libraries.

Another significant new facility was the *procedure type*. It lets procedures be assigned to variables, and is a generalization of the (function) procedure used as parameter to another procedure. This is one of the two pillars of object-oriented programming. Complete parameter type specifications were considered as indispensable, as they constituted a remaining trouble spot and pitfall in Pascal.

Modula was designed with the goal to program the entire software for a workstation Lilith exclusively in this high level language. As a consequence, certain features had to be added, allowing to access special hardware facilities and to breach the rigid type system. These additions were made in the firm hope that they would be used only in rare instances in the construction of lowest level software, such as device drivers and storage allocators. Such parts were to be specified as modules safely encapsulating the dangerous statements. It turned out to be a misguided illusion! In particular, the so-called type transfer functions for breaching the type checker became very heavily misused by inexperienced programmers. It became obvious that a language is characterized not so much by what it allows to express, but more so by what it prohibits to express.

All these well-meant additions resulted in Modula growing into a fairly sizeable language, inspite of several features being delegated to a module library. Nevertheless, it had been demonstrated that entire systems could be programmed efficiently without resorting to error-prone assembler code, and that static type checking was an invaluable asset for large system design. Modula exerted its influence on later languages, including Ada. Although only few commercial implementations emerged, the use of the language spread, and Modula proved its suitability also for embedded applications.

Our first Modula compiler was for the DEC PDP-11 computer. Due to its small store (32 Kbyte), a 5-pass solution was chosen, with intermediate codes stored on the 2 Mbyte disk. It served as tool to implement the compiler for the actual target, out Lilith. With its 128 Kbyte store it allowed for a single pass compiler, resulting in astounding speed compared to the PDP-11. The output was M-code, a byte code directly interpreted by the microprogrammed Lilith hardware. Like in the case of Pascal, several implementation efforts were subsequently made elsewhere [10].

4   Oberon (1988)

As in the case of Modula, the seed to Oberon was laid during a sabbatical leave of the author at Xerox PARC. The goal was to design a modern multi-tasking operating system appropriate for powerful workstations. The example was Cedar, and as Mesa was considered too baroque, leading to Modula, Cedar led to the much simpler Oberon [11,12]. The author, together with J. Gutknecht, embarked on the project in early 1987 with the intention to use Modula as our implementation language, but quickly decided to extend our quest for simplicity to the language too. Applying the principle "Make it as simple as possible, but not simpler", we radically discarded several perhaps convenient, but not essential features, such as nested modules, enumeration types, variant records, sets and with statements.

The wave of object-orientation in full swing, we wanted to use these techniques wherever they were appropriate (for example in the window (viewer) system, and later in the graphics editor), without escalating into making everything an object. We rejected the view that a new programming paradigm would have to replace everything known and proven, and instead showed that object-oriented programming relies on features that mostly are available in existing languages, although presented under a new terminology:

Object-oriented	Conventional
Object	Record, accessed via pointer
Class	Record type
Method	Procedure, bound to record
Message	Call of bound procedure
Subclass	Record type extension

With the exception of the last, all concept were present in Modula, and therefore a single extension sufficed to cater for object-oriented programming in Oberon: Type extension. In the following example, a type *Element* (of a list or tree representing a graph, and in OO-terminology called an *abstract class*) is the basis of two (concrete) types called *Line* and *Circle*:

```
Element = POINTER TO RECORD
                x, y, w, h: INTEGER;   (*rectangle covering
                                        the element's area*)
                handler: PROCEDURE (e: Element; VAR m: Message)
            END ;
Line    = POINTER TO RECORD (Element) END ;   (*null extension*)
Circle  = POINTER TO RECORD (Element)
                width: INTEGER
            END
```

As a result, the powerful technique of object-oriented programming was obtained with a single, quite easy to implement language feature. We note, however, two differences to "conventional" OO-languages:

1. Methods (procedures) are bound to individual records, objects, also called class instances, rather than to classes. Oberon is object-centered instead of class-centered.
2. A call of a method m of an object x with parameter p is denoted by x.m(x, p) rather than x.m(p), because the object itself must be identified as a parameter too. The first x identifies the type to which m belongs, the second x the object (variable) to which m is applied. (Typically the two identifiers are the same).

Along with the introduction of type extension and type inclusion, the latter relating numerical types into a family, went the discarding of various features that were deemed of lesser importance in the light of past experience in programming with Modula. Hence, Oberon may justly be called a trimmed-down version of Modula, described in a report of a mere 16 pages, and implementable by a small and fast single-pass compiler. Together with the basic system modules, it made a radical departure from the traditional concept of batch processing system possible. It marks the

1. departure from batch processing, activating one program after another, one at a time,
2. departure from files stored on disk as the sole interface between one task and later ones,
3. departure from the strict separation between operating systems and user programs, and
4. departure from the notion of a program being the unit of computation.

Instead, the module represents the unit of separately compilable program text with explicit interface, whereas the unit of execution is the *command*. Modules are linked on demand when loaded (without prelinking). There occur no duplicates of modules, resulting in a most commendable storage economy. Any exported (parameterless) procedure can serve as a command to be activated by mouse-click in any visible program text. This concept represented a break-through in the way computers were used: Several tasks may coexist, typically displayed in the form of viewers, and the user applies commands to them in any order desired. For increased user convenience, pop-up menus, buttons and panels were later added through optional modules, programmable without additional features, the basic command facility covering all needs. Thus it became possible to create a full operating environment, programmed by two people with two years [13]. It gave evidence that a few simple and powerful concepts, distilled to the essential, led to an efficient and economical implementation. Like Modula, Oberon influenced the design of later languages, notably Java.

The first Oberon compiler was available by 1986 for the Ceres computer, a workstation built around the NS 32000 processor. Subsequently, several implementations were completed at ETH Zürich, among others for the PC, the Apple Macintosh, and the Sun workstation. Emphasis was given to avoid differences between their source languages. Indeed portability was achieved almost to perfection. The basic operating system, including the file and viewer (tiled windows) system, text editor and compiler required less than 200 Kbytes of store, a small fraction of the space occupied by commercial systems of comparable capability. This was considered as a powerful, existential proof that modern design and structuring techniques lead to a significant economic advantage. Dramatically reduced program size led to dramatically improved reliability [14].

5   Concluding Remarks

The last four decades of research have produced the methods of structured programming, supported by languages such as Algol and Pascal, data typing (Pascal), information encapsulation and modularization (Modula, Ada), and object orientation in the sense of associating specific operations to specific objects in heterogeneous data structures (Oberon, Java). Hierarchical structuring is recognized as the key to reasoning about program properties and the prerequisite for applying the techniques of assertions and loop invariants. Inspite of these remarkable achievements in the discipline of programming, we are often confronted with software products that give rise to complaints: Lack of reliability, frequent breakdowns, horrors of complexity, incomplete and inconsistent descriptions, and similar blessings. What has happened?

Today's software industry is still largely working with methods and languages that were acceptable 30 years ago, but are blatantly outdated and inadequate for designing complex software today. In many places, this state of affairs is recognized; but a remedy is not in sight. There exists a vast amount of legacy code, and customers demand and depend on new software being compatible with the past, including its mistakes. This request makes new designs impossible, because the specifications of the old designs lie in their code, the inscrutable, intertwined, unstructured code fraught with tricky constructions and hastily made fixups. In particular, complex programs, such as operating systems, compilers, data base and CAD systems are subjected to this plight. More isolated systems, such as embedded control and sensing applications, are somewhat less afflicted. Designers had been more anxious to avoid complexity that escapes their mastery, and customers are more likely to give security and reliability a higher priority than convenience and generality.

It is indeed difficult to see a way to break the vicious circle where industry delivers what customers want, and customers buy what industry offers. One possibility might be to introduce the notion of liability for malfunction. It rests on the assumption that customers are willing to pay for higher quality. As the price increase would be significant, there is little hope that liability concerns will enter the software market at large. However, in a modern world where everything has its price tag, also quality will not come for free.

It is equally difficult to envisage the breaking of another vicious circle, namely the one in which industry practices the methods taught at schools, and schools teach what is currently practiced in industry. Radical shifts of paradigms rarely occur. More likely is progress in small steps, preferably steps that are not noticeable individually. Industry is gradually becoming aware that old methods simply will not do much longer, and hence welcomes small steps. Examples are the use of simple annotations and assertions in programs, even if they are not checked automatically, or the use of the constructs of a higher level language, even if coding must be done with C or C++ and no compiler checks the rules, or the gradual enforcement of the rule of module ownership, although no compiler checks against violations.

This brings us to the role of universities. It is here that small cuts into vicious circles must be prepared, where modern methods, discipline, and languages expressing them appropriately must be taught, where students not only learn to program, but to design, to structure their programs. This is infinitely more important than teaching students the rules of C and C++, although students demand this, because it secures them a good income after graduation. Universities must return to take their responsibilities seriously, which demand that universities be leaders instead of followers. Unfortunately, current trends do not favour such a return. Universities too must look for income, and it is much more readily available for research, useful or esoteric, than for "teaching the right stuff". This is deplorable in a field where the methods available are far ahead of the methods practiced, and where therefore the promulgation of the existing new ideas is much more important than the creation of even more new ideas.

I hope I have clearly expressed my opinion that programming, programming style, programming discipline, and therewith programming languages are still not merely one of many issue in computing science, but pillars. Our society depends to an ever increasing degree on computing techniques. Let those who are tomorrow's designers receive an excellent education, and let them enjoy excellent tools instead of crutches. The mentioned vicious circles will be broken, when universities are consciously striving to be leaders rather than followers, as was the case some 40 years ago.

References

1. P. Naur, (ed.): Revised report on the algorithmic language Algol 60. *Comm. ACM 3*, 299 - 316 (1960), and *Comm. ACM 6*, 1 - 17 (1963)
2. N. Wirth and C.A.R. Hoare: A Contribution to the development of ALGOL. *Comm. ACM 9*, 6, 413 - 432 (June 1966)
3. A. van Wijngaarden, (Ed.): Report on the algorithmic language Algol 68. *Numer. Math. 14*, 79 - 218 (1969)
4. N. Wirth: The Programming Language Pascal. *Acta Informatica 1*, (Jun 1971) 35-63.
5. K. Jensen and N. Wirth: *Pascal - User Manual and Report.* Springer-Verlag, 1974.
6. International Organization for Standardization, Specification for Computer Programming Language Pascal, ISO 7185-1982.
7. N. Wirth: Recollections about the development of the programming language Pascal. *Proc. 2nd Intl' Conf. on the History of Programming Languages* (HOPL II) Addison-Wesley, 1993.
8. N. Wirth: History and goals of Modula-2. *BYTE*, Aug. 1984, 145-152.
9. N. Wirth: *Programming in Modula-2.* Springer-Verlag, 1982. ISBN 3-540-50150-9
10. P. H. Hartel and Dolf Starreveld: Modula-2 Implementation Overview. Journal of Pascal, Ada and Modula-2, July-August 1985, 9 -23.
11. N. Wirth: The Programming Language Oberon. *Software - Practice and Experience*, 18, 7, (July 1988), 671- 690.
12. M. Reiser and N. Wirth: *Programming in Oberon: Steps beyond Pascal and Modula.* Addison-Wesley, 1992, ISBN 0-201-56543-9
13. N. Wirth and J. Gutknecht: *Project Oberon.* Addison-Wesley, 1992, ISBN 0-201-54428-8
14. N. Wirth: A Plea for Lean Software. *IEEE Computer*, Feb. 1995, 64-68.

Composable Message Semantics in Oberon

Markus Hof

Johannes Kepler University Linz, Computer Science Department,
A-4040, Linz, Austria
hof@ssw.uni-linz.ac.at

Abstract. Most object-oriented languages offer a limited number of invocation semantics. At best, they define a default mode of synchronous invocation, plus some keywords to express additional semantic attributes, e.g. synchronisation. The very few approaches that offer rich libraries of invocation abstractions usually introduce significant overhead and do not support the composition of those abstractions.

This paper describes a pragmatic approach for abstracting invocation semantics with emphasise on remote invocations. Invocation semantics, such as synchronous, asynchronous, remote, transactional or replicated, are all considered first class citizens. Using an elegant combination of the *Strategy* and *Decorator* design patterns, we suggest an effective way to compose various invocation semantics. We completely separate the class definition from the invocation semantics of its methods and we go a step further towards full polymorphism: the invocation of the same method can have different semantics on two objects of the same class. The very same invocation on a given object may even vary according to the client performing the invocation. To reduce the overhead induced by the flexibility underlying our approach, we rely on *just-in-time* stub generation techniques.

Keywords: Distributed objects, programming languages, middleware, design patterns, abstractions, remote invocations

Technical areas: Adaptive Communication Systems, Distributed Systems Architecture

1 Introduction

Object-oriented languages usually offer rich libraries for sequential programming, together with various abstractions for expressing and controlling concurrency. Most modern object-oriented languages offer, for example, several forms of collection interfaces, e.g., *sets*, *bags*, *arrays*, etc. They usually also support *processes* and *semaphores* or some alternative built-in concurrency constructs. Composing various abstractions to build effective frameworks and applications has been an active area of investigation and has given birth to some interesting compilations of good practices [10].

In the last decade, many object-oriented languages have been extended towards distribution, and new object-oriented languages have been designed from scratch with distribution in mind [1, 2, 3, 5, 8, 17 19]. The objective is to provide the developers of distributed applications with higher level abstractions than what operating systems usually offer. For instance the CORBA approach to distributed programming goes along these

J. Gutknecht and W. Weck (Eds.): JMLC 2000, LNCS 1897, pp. 11-25, 2000.

lines [15]. It replaces the low-level socket-based communication model with a higher level construct: *remote method invocation* [16]. The latter can be viewed as a reproduction of the RPC abstraction in an object-oriented context. It basically aims at providing the programmer with the illusion of a centralized (i.e., non-distributed) context. For several applications, having distributed entities interact through (synchronous) remote method invocations is very acceptable. For many others, it is not. The reason is mainly twofold. First, remote invocations mean encoding (marshalling) and decoding (unmarshalling), behind the scenes, the name of an operation and its arguments into some standard format that could be shipped over the wire. Added to the latency of remote communication, the marshalling and demarshalling time is a strict overhead with respect to the time taken to perform a local invocation. For many time-critical applications, pretending that the overhead is negligible is simply impossible. Some form of asynchronous communication model is more adequate. Second, and in particular for large scale applications, the crash of a remote host and communication failures can simply not be ignored. More complex replication and transactional schemes are needed.

In short, remote method invocation has its own most suitable domain of applications but can hardly be considered as the single communication construct to fit all kinds of applications. The same reasoning applies to alternative communication paradigms such as asynchronous or atomic invocation [14, 16, 19]. In fact, even the parameter passing mode can be subject to variations and there is no best scheme (deep vs. shallow copy) that fits all applications.

We explore a fully object-oriented approach where invocation semantics are themselves viewed as first class abstractions [12]. Just like there are extensible libraries of data manipulation abstractions, we suggest an approach where various forms of invocation semantics are classified within a (interface) class library. The programmer can use various classes of that library to express different models of communication within the same application. Following the Strategy design pattern [9, 10], we de-couple algorithms from protocols, and hence promote the reuse of the code underlying the invocations. We also use the Decorator design pattern [10] to help composing several semantics for the same invocation (e.g., replicated plus asynchronous plus passing by reference). Specific semantics are viewed as filters that decorate the invocations.

Our approach shares some similarities with so-called reflective distributed object-oriented languages (e.g., [1, 19]). The underlying goal is the same: promoting system level abstractions (e.g., remote communication) to the rank of first class citizens. However, reflective approaches mainly focus on building Meta-Object Protocols (MOPs) that transparently intercept object interaction. A MOP enables the programmer to plug together specialized invocation semantics. We ignore transparency issues and address the question of how to represent invocation abstractions in such a way that they can be composed in a flexible and effective manner. It is pragmatic in the sense that the programmer is very aware of the communication semantics that are used in a given program: choosing the right communication model is not the task of a specialized meta-programmer. This enables us to use a very effective technique to reduce the overhead of our flexible approach: just-in-time stub generation [11]. We describe some performance measures obtained from our Oberon implementation and we point out the very fact that the cost of our flexible yet pragmatic approach is negligible.

The rest of the paper is organized as follows. Section 2 gives an overview of how to program with first-class invocations in our approach. Section 3 describes the way the invocation library is organized and the rational behind our combination of the Strategy and Decorator design patterns. Section 4 discusses implementation issues and Section 5 the performance of our just-in-time stub generation technique. Finally, Section 6 summarizes the contribution of the paper and gives some concluding remarks about the general applicability of the approach.

2 Programming with Composable Message Semantics

This section gives an overview of our library with the help of the "Dining Philosophers" problem [6]. This problem is well suited to show the advantages of our framework.

The message semantics of common object-oriented environments are fixed. The system either enforces one fixed semantics, or allows the choice between a small fixed set of semantics, each associated with some pre-defined keyword. Our invocation abstractions offer an open way to create arbitrarily many new kinds of semantics. For every method one can define the semantics that handles the invocation of that method: this is done by creating an instance of the invocation class and assigning it to the desired method. While doing so, two sets of semantics must be supplied: caller and callee side invocation semantics (see Figure 1).

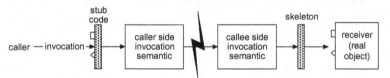

Figure 1: Overview of intercepted invocation

The chosen client-side semantic is executed on the host of the stub object while the server side semantic executes on the host of the real object. This distinction has two advantages. First, the programmer can decide, individually for each part of the invocation semantics, where it should be executed, i.e., on the client or on the server. Second, when several hosts have a stub of the same server object, a client-based modification is executed only when the corresponding stub object is invoked. A server side modification is executed whenever a method is invoked on the real server object, i.e., regardless of the stub that initiated the invocation.

Our first approach to the dining philosophers is a straight forward implementation that ignores all synchronisation concerns and is – of course – not correct.

```
MODULE Philosophers;

IMPORT Threads;TYPE    Eater* = POINTER TO EaterDesc;    EaterDesc* = RECORD
(Threads.ThreadDesc) END;        PROCEDURE (me: Eater) Think*; (* me denotes the receiver of the
method Think *)END Think;PROCEDURE (me: Eater) Eat*;END Eat;
```

```
PROCEDURE Start;VAR t: Threads.Thread; self: Eater;BEGIN      t := Threads.ActiveThread(); self :=
t(Eater);      LOOP      self.Think; self.Eat      ENDEND Start;  PROCEDURE Dinner*;VAR i: INTEGER;
p: Eater;BEGIN      FOR i := 0 TO 4 DO          NEW(p); Threads.Start(p, Start, 10000)          ENDEND
Dinner;END Philosophers.
```

To correct this faulty behaviour we have to insert synchronization code. The straight forward solution is to insert synchronisation mechanisms, e.g. a semaphore for every fork, before and after the invocation of *Eat*. However, this intermixes application code with code responsible to guarantee synchronisation constraints.

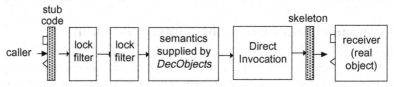

Figure 2: Semantics for *Eat* using *DecObjects*

Using our composable message semantics (CMS) we circumvent this mix-up. We use the module DecObjects to modify the invocation semantics of the method *Eat* (see Figure 2).

```
PROCEDURE Dinner*;
VAR
        i, res: INTEGER; t: Eater; first, second: Locks.Lock; c: Invocations.Class; m: Invocations.Method;
        forks: ARRAY 5 OF Locks.Semaphore; left, right: INTEGER;
BEGIN
        FOR i := 0 TO 4 DO
                NEW(forks[i]); forks[i].Init(1)
        END;

        FOR i := 0 TO 4 DO
                NEW(t);
                c := Invocations.GetClass(t);
                m := c.GetMethod("Eat");
                IF i#4 THEN left:=i; right:=i+1 ELSE left:=0; right:=4 END;
                first := Locks.New(forks[left]); second := Locks.New(forks[right]);
                first.next := second; second.next := DecObjects.Invocation();
                m.SetCallerInvocation(first);
                DecObjects.SetSemantics(t, c, phils[i], res);
        END;

        FOR i := 0 TO 4 DO
                Threads.Start(phils[i], Start, 10000)
        END
END Dinner;
```

As we changed only the initialising procedure *Dinner*, we included only this procedure. First we initialise the necessary forks, i.e. forks. Afterwards we initialise our philosophers in a loop. The procedure *GetClass* returns a *Class* object for the passed object instance. This *Class* object contains all information about all methods (including inherited ones). In particular, it contains the necessary information to change the invocation semantics. One can scan this information and change it according to the current necessities. We assign the new caller-side invocation semantic *first*. Afterwards, we assign the modified semantic information to the corresponding philosopher *phils[i]* by calling *SetSemantics*.

In *first* we define the semantics to be used for the method *Eat* of the different philosophers. The semantics consist of two locking filters and the invocation abstraction *DirectInvocation* (see Figure 2), which is part of the CMS framework and actually invokes the method. A locking filter first acquires its assigned semaphore (a fork in this example) and then passes the invocation on. The above example shows very well the separation of application and synchronisation code. The code necessary for the synchronisation is concentrated within the module body. The actual application code stays as it was before we introduced synchronisation into the example.

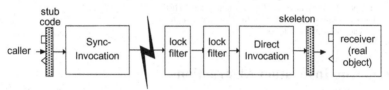

Figure 3: Semantics for *Eat* using *DObjects*

Using the distributed objects package we can increase the flexibility even further: we allow the philosophers to reside on different hosts, i.e. only when calling *Eat* they access the table in order to ensure correctness. We decorate *Eat* with an appropriate semantic (see Figure 3). On the client we choose *SyncInvocation* which executes the invocation as a synchronous remote invocation. On the server we choose the same semantics as we already used for our previous version. We omit to define a semantic for *Think*. However, we are free to choose whether it should execute on the server or on the client. We marked the code that we had to modify in order to distribute our dining philosophers implementation. We split the program into a server and a client part. The server *ServerInit* prepares the philosopher objects, assigns the correct semantics and exports them on the network. The client *Client* imports the remote object and invokes its method without caring about the used semantics.

```
PROCEDURE ServerInit*;
VAR
        i, res: INTEGER; l, r, first: Lock.Lock; c: Invocations.Class; m: Invocations.Method;
        forks: ARRAY 5 OF Lock.Semaphore;
        left, right: INTEGER;
        si: Invocations.Invocation;
        name: ARRAY 6 OF CHAR;
```

```
BEGIN
        FOR i := 0 TO 4 DO NEW(forks[i]); forks[i].Init(1) END;

        si := DObjects.SyncInvocation();
        FOR i := 0 TO 4 DO
                NEW(phils[i]);
                c := Invocations.GetClass(phils[i]);
                m := c.GetMethod("Eat");
                IF i#4 THEN left:=i; right:=i+1 ELSE left:=0; right:=4 END;
                l := Lock.New(forks[left]); r := Lock.New(forks[right]);
                l.next := r; r.next := DecObjects.Invocation();
                m.SetCalleeInvocation(l);
                m.SetCallerInvocation(si);
                name := "PhilX"; name[4] := CHR(i+ORD('0'));
                DObjects.Export(phils[i], Network.DefaultHost(), name, c, res)
        END
END ServerInit;

PROCEDURE Client*;
VAR
        name: ARRAY 6 OF CHAR; res: INTEGER; p: Philosophers.Eater;
BEGIN
        In.Open; In.Int(i); name := "PhilX"; name[4] := CHR(i+ORD('0'));
        DObjects.Import(Network.ThisHost("..."), name, p, res);
        Threads.Start(p, Start, 10000)
END Client;
```

3   Composing Invocation Abstractions

This section discusses the extensibility of our approach. We first describe our classification model and then how the invocation models can be composed and extended.

3.1 Combining the Decorator and Strategy Design Patterns

We use a flat class hierarchy, which allows us to change the behaviour combinations dynamically. To do so, we combined two design patterns: the *Decorator* design pattern and the *Strategy* design pattern [10]. The Decorator pattern is basically used for the static composition and the Strategy pattern for the dynamic one (see Figure 4).

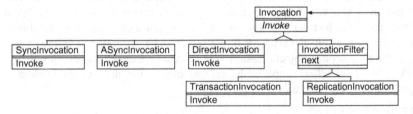

Figure 4: Type hierarchy of the CMS framework

An invocation abstraction can be decorated with arbitrarily many additional decorators. We distinguish between extensions of *Invocation* and extensions of *InvocationFilter*. Extensions of *InvocationFilter* are just decorators. We call them *filters*. They may be cascaded in an arbitrary order (some actual implementations may impose required ordering). They extend the semantics of the invocation, i.e., add functionality, but do not implement the invocation themselves. They forward the invocation to their decorated object. On the other hand, extensions of *Invocation* actually invoke the chosen method.

These are the actual *abstractions*. An actually used composition of a set of *filters* and one *abstraction* is called a *semantics*.

This structure is flexible in two directions. First, one can add arbitrary new filters, e.g., for logging, visualization, synchronization, authentication, etc. Second, one can add new invocation abstractions, e.g., best-effort, at-most-once, delayed, etc. The structuring also promotes arbitrary combinations of the different invocation abstractions and filters.

We use the Strategy design pattern in our system at run-time. All currently used semantics are held in an array where they are stored at a known index. The stubs only see an array of strategies on how a method may be invoked (Section 4 gives more details on this aspect).

3.2 Composition

The current library of invocation abstractions and filters is relatively small. However, the principles governing composition stay the same, when new abstractions or filters are implemented and added to the framework. Whenever one modifies the model with which a method is invoked, two semantics need to be supplied: one for the client, and one for the server. They will execute on the designated host.

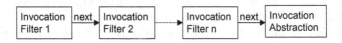

Figure 5: Chain of invocation filters

A semantics consists of exactly one invocation abstraction and of arbitrarily many invocation filters (see Figure 5). A filter never handles an invocation directly, but after some filter specific work, forwards it to its decorated object. Only the invocation abstraction actually executes the invocation. Server side abstractions actually start the execution of the method on the real object, i.e., it is located were the actual work occurs. Client side abstractions are responsible for transporting the invocation to the real object, in order to trigger the execution of the server side invocation semantics. Typically, this includes some kind of network traffic.

3.3 Extension

To extend the framework with new kinds of invocations, one has to distinguish between abstractions and filters. Writing a filter is much simpler. It requires implementing a new type that extends *InvocationFilterDesc*, and overriding the method *Invoke*. Consider the following example:

```
MyFilter = POINTER TO MyFilterDesc;
MyFilterDesc = RECORD (Invocations.InvocationFilterDesc)
END;

PROCEDURE (inv: MyFilter) Invoke (obj: PTR; id: LONGINT; s: Stream): Stream;
BEGIN
        SomePreprocessing (obj, id, s);
        result := inv.next.Invoke (obj, id, s);
        SomePostprocessing (obj, id, s, result);
        RETURN result
END Invoke;
```

Invoke receives the receiver object *obj*, an identifier *id* that denotes the called procedure, and a stream *s* that contains the marshaled parameters (The exact mode used for marshalling may also be changed along with the invocation semantic. For further information see [12]). As a return value, it supplies the stream containing the marshaled result of the invocation. Before and after the invocation is forwarded to the next abstraction, the filter can do its specific work. With the help of meta programming facilities, it can even scan the parameter stream and react to its contents.

4   Implementation Issues

Intercepting ordinary method invocations with minimal overhead is a key issue underlying our approach. In our case, this is done by cloning the actual object on which the methods are invoked. Methods invoked on the actual object are still handled as in any traditional object-oriented language. Those invoked on the clone are intercepted and handled as specified by the class information. The interception is done with the help of automatically generated code pieces: *stub* and *skeleton* (see Figure 1). In this section we describe the generation of the stub and the skeleton with their adaptation to the chosen semantics.

The code generation mechanism is generic. However, one normally will not access it directly but only indirectly through another API (e.g., distributed object system). Methods invoked on the clone (stub object) are handled by the generated stub code. The stub has the same interface as the actual method and replaces it transparently. It marshals the parameter and activates the appropriate client invocation semantics. Simultaneously, the skeleton code is generated. The skeleton is the counterpart of the stub on the server. It unmarshals the parameters and calls the actual method.

In typical applications, one does not have to care about these low-level abstractions, but one will see a higher level one, e.g. the distributed objects package. In this case, the Import and Export procedures automatically generate the necessary code. The application programmer sees nothing of these details.

One of our main goals was – from the beginning – that the delay, introduced by the increased flexibility of arbitrary invocation semantics, is kept as small as possible. In particular, this means that the delay introduced is constant with respect to the number of managed objects and the number of different semantics. Achieving that goal requires the stub code to know exactly where its semantics is. This, and the adaptable parameter passing modes, force the code generation to be done after the semantics have been defined. It also requires that the stub and skeleton code is generated at *run-time*: hence our *just-in-time* stub generation approach.

The actually assigned semantics are stored in an array. All used invocation semantics are in this array and are identified by their index. Each newly defined semantics is assigned a slot within this array, i.e., it receives a unique number. It is possible to use this knowledge and access the correct semantics directly through an array access. As this index is – at stub compilation time – a constant, it is even possible for the compiler to calculate the offset during compilation. This reduces the actual overhead on the client side to a negligible size. Consider the following class *Object* which defines a single method *Dec*.

```
Object = POINTER TO ObjectDesc;

ObjectDesc = RECORD
        PROCEDURE (o: Object) Dec (n: INTEGER) : INTEGER;
END;
```

The generated code below consists of two procedures: one for the stub object and one for the skeleton. The generated procedure *Dec* of the stub object is used to intercept invocations. It mostly deals with marshalling and unmarshalling of parameters. The actual call of the assigned semantics (bold line in the following listing) is a simple method invocation. In this example, the client side semantics is stored at index 10. The index is constant and therefore the compiler can calculate the offset into the array, which reduces the delay even further. The corresponding skeleton *DecSkeleton* has the inverse task. It unmarshals the parameters, invokes the actual method, and marshals the output values.

```
PROCEDURE (o: Object) Dec (n: INTEGER): INTEGER;
VAR lin: Linearizer; s: .Stream; retVal: INTEGER;
BEGIN
        lin := NewWriter();
        lin.Integer(n);
        s := lin.Stream();
        s := Invocations.inv[10].Invoke(o, 2, s);
        lin := NewReader(s);
        lin.Integer(retVal);
        RETURN retVal
END Dec;

PROCEDURE DecSkeleton (receiver: Object; VAR stream: Stream);
VAR lin: Linearizer; retVal, n: INTEGER;
BEGIN
        lin := NewReader(stream);
        lin.Integer(n);
        retVal := receiver.Dec(n);
        lin := NewWriter();
        lin.Integer(retVal);
        stream := lin.Stream()
END DecSkeleton;
```

The code, as shown above, is actually never generated. Our implementation directly generates compiler intermediate code, i.e., it builds an abstract syntax tree. This approach is portable, as we use a portable intermediate language with suitable back-ends for different platforms. This mechanism allows extremely fast code generation (as depicted by our measurements below). The code generator needs the meta information of the intercepted class to generate the necessary code pieces. This hence does not introduce any loss in speed with respect to an ad hoc approach where invocations do all have the same semantics. Even the amount of data transferred from client to server has not been increased by introducing flexible invocation semantics. The only overhead is actually the one introduced by the distributed lookup technique, as we discuss below.

5   Performance Measurements

In this section we describe some performance figures we obtained from our Oberon prototype. Although it has not been optimised, our prototype enables us to draw interesting conclusions about the cost of our flexible approach. Basically, we compare that cost with the cost of an ad hoc approach derived from our prototype, which uses always synchronous remote invocation.

5.1 Overview

As our test environment, we used a Pentium 200 MHz computer running Windows NT Version 4.0 (Build: 1381: Service Pack 3). To measure the time, we used a special register of the Intel architecture that always contains the cycles since the latest reset. This allows for extremely accurate timing. To cope with differences introduced by the garbage collector, we run all measurements three times in sequence with 100, 1000, and 10000 invocations. We also repeated all measurements ten times omitting the fastest and the slowest measurements. To have our measurements independent of the installed network and its current load, we used local TCP loop-back. In other words, client and server were running on the same machine and communicated via the TCP loop-back host (127.0.0.1).

Our marshalling mechanism is neither time nor memory optimised, i.e., it allocates a considerable amount of memory. This results in several runs of the garbage collector during the measurement. If not noted otherwise, the time spent collecting garbage is included in the measured intervals.

Our measurements use different situations to compare our flexible approach with an ad hoc approach. This ad hoc approach is a modified version of our flexible approach. It is modified in two ways. First, all parts allowing for arbitrary semantics have been removed, i.e., the ad hoc version always uses synchronous remote invocation. Second, we optimized the ad hoc version wherever a simpler solution was possible by the introduction of a fixed invocation semantics. The main differences between the flexible and the ad hoc approach can be seen in the following source sniplets.

fixed semantics server:
 	
    s := Objects.Call(obj, mID, s);
	fixed semantics client stub:
	
	    ...
	    s := DObjects.SendCall(obj, mID, s);
	    ...

arbitrary semantics server:
 	
    WHILE m.id # mID DO
        m := m.next
    END;
    inv := m.GetServerInvocation();
    s := inv.Invoke(obj, id, s)
	arbitrary semantics client stub:
	
	    ...
	    s := Invocations.inv[10].Invoke(obj, mID, s);
	    ...

As one can see, on both server and client side, additional work is done. The most expensive operation is the server-side lookup for the correct server-side semantics. This lookup is included in our measurements.

```
TYPE
    Object* = POINTER TO ObjectDesc;
    ObjectDesc* = RECORD
        ctr: LONGINT
    END;

    PROCEDURE (o: Object) Next* ;
    END Next;
```

We used the above class definition as our test environment. This definition declares a class *Object* with one method *Next* that has an empty body. Depending on the test we added parameters and/or a return value to the interface of *Next*. The server simply allocates an instance *o* of this class and exports it on the default host under the name "TestObject".

```
NEW(o); o.ctr := 0;
DObjects.Export (o, Network.DefaultHost(), "TestObject", NIL, err);
```

In the standard test case we use no invocation meta information, i.e. the default semantics (NIL), i.e., we use synchronous remote invocation. Depending on the test we add here customized meta information.

```
DObjects.Import (Network.ThisHost("TestServer"), "TestObject", o, err);
o.Next;

(* start measurement *)
FOR i := 1 TO n DO
        o.Next
END;
(* stop measurement*)
```

The client implements mainly a loop that repeatedly calls the method *Next*. The loop repeats n times depending on the current test. Our implementation needs some additional time to build data structures whenever an object receives its first invocation. Therefore we call *Next* once before we start the actual measurement (the code generation needs less than 2 milliseconds and can be further reduced by maintaining a persistent pool of already generated code snippets).

5.2 Measurements

On our test configuration, it takes about 990 microseconds to echo a TCP packet containing one byte of user data from user space to user space. This includes the overhead introduced by our generic network interface as well as the additional TCP layer introduced by the Oberon environment.

To compare the dependency of the invocation duration on the amount of passed parameters, we measured three times with different amounts of parameters. We made the measurements with the following interfaces:

```
PROCEDURE (o: Object) Next* ;
PROCEDURE (o: Object) Next (i: LONGINT) : LONGINT;
PROCEDURE (o: Object) Next (VAR buf: ARRAY 1024 OF CHAR);
```

In every case, the same amount of data is transferred back and forth over the network (0, 4, 1024). The results are shown below in milliseconds per invocation (see Figure 6).

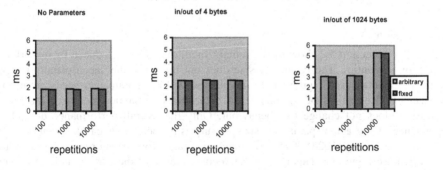

Figure 6: Measurements depending on parameter size

Next we tried to determine the additional overhead introduced by other invocation semantics. To test this we decorated the invocation of the method *Next* with either a server-side and/or a client-side filter (see Figure 7). Both filters have an empty body. We took the first version of *Next* without parameters. These measurements were, of course, only done on the version with arbitrary invocation semantics.

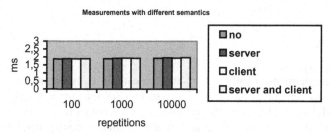

Figure 7: Measurements depending on additional filters

Finally, we split up the invocation time to determine where exactly the time is spent (see Figure 8). These measurements were only done on the version with arbitrary invocation semantics. We split the time into five parts: transport, server-side semantics, client-side semantics, stub, and skeleton, and compare in percentages.

	100	1000	10000
transport	94.6	93.2	92.3
server semantics	0.5	0.0	0.5
client semantics	0.0	0.0	0.0
skeleton	2.4	3.6	4.4
stub	1.8	2.4	2.2

Figure 8: Measurements split into smaller units

5.3 Discussion

The figures in section 5.2 show the extremely small overhead introduced by our arbitrary invocation semantics. The parameter size does not influence the speed penalty of using arbitrary semantics (see Figure 6). An invocation with no parameters needs around two milliseconds. Regardless of whether fixed or arbitrary semantics are used. Introducing parameters does not change this behaviour. Only the overall performance degrades in dependence of the actual parameter size. A surprising behaviour can be seen when the parameter size is big (1024). The performance is much worse if we repeat the invocation more often(see Figure 6). This is probably a consequence of the garbage collector, which has to run more often.

The second measurement was made to show the performance loss by introducing invocation filters (see Figure 7). It shows that it is quite cheap to introduce another invocation filter. This was to be expected, as an empty filter introduces nothing but an additional method invocation. The measured differences are actually almost too small to get meaningful results.

Finally, we split the invocations in five parts: transport, server-side semantics, client-side semantics, stub code, and skeleton code. We compared the different parts on how many percent of the whole invocation is spent to execute them. The results show that server and client semantics never use more than half a percent of the time spent for the invocation (see Figure 8). The main part of the invocation time is spent in transit from the caller to the callee or vice versa. Optimisation efforts will find many things to ameliorate. Another potential for further optimisations is in the marshalling done in the skeleton and the stub. But however good one optimises these parts, the mechanism of arbitrary invocation semantics is never the real bottleneck for remote method invocations.

With all these comparisons, one has to remember that the CMS framework is tuned for distributed applications. For strictly local applications one has to implement another scheme, which, e.g. , does not marshal parameters.

6   Conclusions

It is tempting to assume that all distributed interactions of a given application can be performed using just one (synchronous remote) method invocation abstraction, just like in a centralized system. In practice, this uniformity usually turns out to be restricting and penalizing and the myth of *"distribution transparency"* is very misleading. It is now relatively well accepted that the *"one size fits all"* principle does not apply to the context of distributed object interactions [18]. Most *uniform* approaches to object-oriented distributed programming have recently considered extensions to their original model in order to offer a more flexible choice of interaction modes. For example, the OMG is in the process of standardizing a messaging service to complement the original CORBA model with various asynchronous modes of interaction [15].

Several object-oriented languages offered, from scratch, various modes of communication. Each is typically identified by a keyword and corresponds to a well defined semantics. For example, the early ABCL language supported several keywords to express various forms of asynchrony, e.g., one-way invocation, asynchronous with future, etc [19]. Similarly, the KAROS language supported several keywords to attach various degrees of atomicity with invocations, e.g., nested transaction, independent transaction, etc. [7]. The major limitation of these approaches is that one can never predict the need of the developer, and coming with a new form of interaction means changing the language. Other approaches, e.g. composition filters [4], focus on the possibility to define arbitrary semantics. However, they use a class-centric approach, that is not suited for distribution and one pays a large penalty regarding the necessary execution time.

Our approach is different in that we focus on how to structure a extendable library of interaction abstractions in a pragmatic and effective way. By combining some good practices in classifying abstractions using the Decorator and Strategy design patterns, we suggest a composition model that promotes the reuse of invocation implementations (we go a step further than in [9]). We reduce the overhead, inherent to the flexibility of our approach, by giving up transparency and relying on just-in-time stub generation.

We illustrated our approach by building a distributed extension of the Oberon system and we demonstrated it on a simple example. The very same approach could be applied to other languages and environments. The actual requirements are easily fulfilled. The basic requirements are: (1) Run-time access to a compiler; (2) Dynamic code loading; and (3) Meta information. The only problematic implementation part is the support for run-time type generation. We solve this problem by patching the corresponding type descriptor. In order to validate the claim that our composable message semantics can be applied to other languages and platforms, we implemented another prototype in Java. This prototype offers similar functionality but uses another implementation technique to offer the desired flexibility. Whenever an object is either imported or exported, our run-time system generates the necessary code snippets with help of the standard Java compiler 'javac'. This means that we generate Java source code and load the class file that is generated by the compiler. This approach is quite time consuming (0.2 – 0.4 seconds for stub generation). A more efficient implementation of our composable message semantics has to use another technique, e.g. a custom class loader that generates the needed class files by instrumenting the original files at load-time. Keller and Hölzle [13] describe such a class loader that allows load-time instrumentation of class files. Using this technique it is possible to achieve performance comparable to our Oberon implementation.

References

[1]   G. Agha, C. Hewitt, P. Wegner, and A. Yonezawa (editors). *Proceedings of the OOPSLA/ECOOP'90 Workshop on Object-Based Concurrent Programming.* ACM OOPS Messenger, 2(2), 1991.

[2]   G. Agha, P. Wegner, and A. Yonezawa (editors). *Proceedings of the ACM Sigplan Workshop on Object-Based Concurrent Programming.* ACM Sigplan, 24 (4), 1989.

[3]   G. Agha, P. Wegner, and A. Yonezawa. *Research Directions in Concurrent Object-Oriented Programming,* MIT Press, 1993.

[4]   L. Bergmans. Composing Concurrent Objects. ISBN 90-9007359-0.

[5]   J-P Briot, R. Guerraoui and K-P Lohr. *Concurrency and Distribution in Object-Oriented Programming.* ACM Computing Surveys, September 1998.

[6]   E. Dijkstra. *Hierarchical Ordering of Sequential Processes.* Acta Informatica, 1(2): 115-38, 1971.

[7]   R. Guerraoui, R. Capobianchi, A. Lanusse, and P. Roux. *Nesting Actions through Asynchronous Message Passing: the ACS Protocol.* In proceedings of the European Conference on Object-Oriented Programming (ECOOP'92), Springer Verlag (LNCS 615), 1992.

[8]   R. Guerraoui, O. Nierstrasz, and M. Riveill. *Proceedings of the ECOOP'93 Workshop on Object-Based Distributed Programming.* Springer Verlag (LNCS 791), 1994.

[9]   B. Garbinato and R. Guerraoui. *Using the Strategy Design Pattern to Compose Reliable Distributed Protocols.* In proceedings of the Usenix Conference on Object-Oriented Technologies and Systems (COOTS'97), Usenix, June 1997.

[10]   E. Gamma, R. Helm, R. Johnson, and J. Vlissides. *Design Patterns: Elements of Reusable Object-Oriented Software.* Addison-Wesley, 1995.

[11]   M. Hof. *Just-in-Time Stub Generation.* Proc. Joint Modular Languages Conference '97, Hagenberg, March 1997, LNCS, ISSN 0302-9743.

[12]   M. Hof. *Composable Message Semantics in Object-Oriented Languages.* PhD Thesis University of Linz, 1999.

[13]   R. Keller and U. Hölzle. *Binary Component Adaptation.* In proceedings of the European Conference on Object-Oriented Programming (ECOOP'98), Springer Verlag (LNCS 1445), Brussels, Belgium, July 1998.

[14] B. Liskov and R. Sheifler. *Guardians and Actions: Linguistic Support for Robust, Distributed Programs*. ACM Transactions on Programming Languages and Systems, 5(3), 1983.

[15] The Object Management Group. http://www.omg.org.

[16] A. Tripathi and T. Noonan. *Design of a Remote Procedure Call System for Object-Oriented Distributed Programming*. Software-Practice and Experience, Vol. 28(1), 23-47, January 1998.

[17] M. Tokoro, O. Nierstrasz, and P. Wegner (editors). *Proceedings of the ECOOP'91 Workshop on Object-Based Concurrent Computing*. Springer Verlag (LNCS 612), 1992.

[18] J. Waldo, G. Wyant, A. Wollrath and S. Kendall. *A Note on Distributed Computing*. Technical Report, Sun Microsystems Laboratories, Inc, November 1994.

[19] A. Yonezawa and M. Tokoro (editors). *Object-Oriented Concurrent Programming*. MIT Press, 1987.

Derivation of Secure Parallel Applications by Means of Module Embedding[1]

Atanas Radenski

Computer Science Department, Winston-Salem State University, P. O. Box 19479
Winston-Salem, North Carolina 27110, USA
radenski@computer.org

Abstract. An enhancement to modular languages called *module embedding* facilitates the development and utilization of secure generic parallel algorithms.

1 Introduction

We have designed and implemented a strictly typed modular language framework that supports the specification of generic parallel algorithms and the derivation of specific parallel applications from such generic algorithms. The focus of our research is on *message-passing* parallelism and cluster computing applications.

A *generic parallel algorithm* encapsulates a common control structure, such as a master-server network, a pipeline, a cellular automaton, or a divide-and-conquer tree. Such a generic algorithm can be used to derive parallel solutions for a variety of problems. The key idea is that the generic algorithm must provide complete coordination and synchronization pattern in problem-independent manner, while its clients must provide only problem-specific *sequential* code in order to derive specific parallel applications.

In our language framework, generic parallel algorithms and their applications are specified as modules. A particular application can be derived from a generic algorithm by means of *module embedding,* a code reuse mechanism that enables the building of new modules from existing ones through inheritance, overriding of procedures, and overriding of types [11].

We have incorporated module embedding in the experimental language *Paradigm/SP*. Our language is an enhancement of SuperPascal, a high-level parallel programming language developed by Hansen [5]. In addition to embeddable modules, the language provides standard message-passing parallel features, such as *send, receive, for-all*, *parallel* statements, and *channel* types. We have developed a prototype compiler, which generates abstract code, and an interpreter for this abstract code.

---

[1] This work has been supported by NASA grant NAG3-2011.

J. Gutknecht and W. Weck (Eds.): JMLC 2000, LNCS 1897, pp. 26-37, 2000.
© Springer-Verlag Berlin Heidelberg 2000

We use Paradigm/SP to specify general parallel paradigms and to derive particular parallel applications from such general paradigms. We use the Paradigm/SP compiler and interpreter to test such paradigms and their derived applications. Once we have established the validity of a Paradigm/SP program, we convert it into efficient C code that runs on top of a cluster-computing library, such as PVM.

We agree with others [3] that „...for a parallel programming language the most important security measure is to check that processes access disjoint sets of variables only and do not interfere with each other in time-dependent manner". We have adopted in Paradigm/SP an interference control scheme that allows *secure* module embedding in above sense. The Paradigm/SP compiler guarantees that processes in derived parallel applications do not interfere by accessing the same variable in time-dependent manner.

In this paper, we introduce the concept of embeddable module and show how a generic parallel algorithm can be specified as an embeddable module. We demonstrate how module embedding can be employed to derive specific parallel applications from generic algorithms. We also explain how module embedding guarantees that processes in derived applications do not interfere by reading and updating the same variable.

2 Specification of Generic Parallel Algorithms as Embeddable Modules

An *embeddable module* encapsulates types, procedures (and functions), and global variables. *Module embedding* enables building of new modules from existing ones through inheritance, and through *overriding* of inherited types and procedures. An embedded module inherits entities that are exported by the embedded module and further re-exports them. A principal difference between module embedding and module import is that an embedded module is contained in the embedding module and is not shared with other modules, while an imported module is shared between its clients. Another difference is that a client module cannot override types or procedures that belong to an imported module, while an embedding module can override types and procedures that belong to an embedded module.

Type overriding allows a record type that is inherited from an embedded module to be redefined by the embedding module by adding new components to existing ones. Type overriding does not define a new type but effectively replaces an inherited type in the embedded module (i.e., in the inherited code) itself. In contrast, type extension, and similarly, sub-classing, define new types without modifying the inherited ones. Further details on module embedding and type overriding can be found in [11].

We demonstrate the applicability of module embedding to generic parallel programming with a case study of a simplified master-server generic parallel algorithm. The master-server generic algorithm (Fig. 1) finds a *solution* for a given *problem* by means of one *master* and *n* *server* processes that interact through two-way communication *channels*. The master *generates* a version of the original problem that is easier to solve and sends it to each server. All servers *solve* their assigned problems in parallel and then send the solutions back to the master. Finally, the master *summarizes* the solutions provided by the servers in order to find a final solution to the original problem.

The generic parameters of the master-server algorithm (Fig. 2) include the type of the *problem* to be solved, the type of its *solution*, and three sequential procedures:

- a procedure to *generate* an instance of the problem that is to be solved by server *i*;
- a procedure to *solve* a particular instance of the problem;
- a procedure to *summarize* the *set* of solutions provided by the servers into a final solution.

The generic master-server algorithm provides its clients with a procedure to *compute* a solution of a specific problem. The *compute* procedure incorporates the master and server processes, but those are not visible to the clients of the generic algorithm.

In Figure 3, all components of the master-server generic algorithm are encapsulated in an embeddable module, *MS*. The export mark '*' [3] designates public entities that are visible to clients of module *MS*. Unmarked entities, such as *master* and *server*, are referred to as private. The types of the problem and the solutions are defined as empty record type (designated as double-dot, „ .. „). Clients of module *MS* can (1) extend such inherited record types with problem-specific components, (2) provide domain-specific versions of procedures *generate, solve* and *summarize*, and (3) use procedure *compute* to find particular solutions.

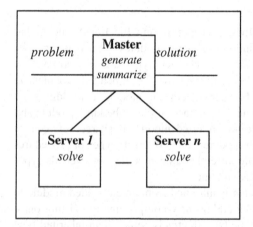

type *problem* = ..;
   solution = ..;
   set = **array[1..n] of** *solution;*
procedure *generate(i: integer;*
   p: problem; **var** *p0: problem);*
procedure *solve(*
   p0: problem; **var** *s: solution);*
procedure *summarize(p: problem;*
   b: set; **var** *s: solution);*
procedure *compute(*
   *p: problem;***var** *s: solution);*

Fig. 1. Generic master-server algorithms   **Fig. 2.** Generic parameters

```
module MS;                              procedure master(c: net;
const n = 10; {number of servers}          p: problem; var s: solution);
type                                    var  i: integer;
  problem* = ..; solution* = ..;           p0: problem; b: set;
  set* = array[1..n] of solution;       begin
  channel = *(problem, solution);         for i := 1 to n do begin
  net = array [1..n] of channel;            generate(i, p, p0);
                                            send(c[i], p0);
procedure solve*(                         end;
  p0: problem; var s: solution);          for i := 1 to n do
begin end;                                  receive(c[i], b[i]);
                                          summarize(p, b, s);
procedure generate*( i: integer;        end;
  p: problem; var p0: problem);
begin { default: } p0 := p; end;        procedure compute*(
                                          p: problem;  var s: solution);
procedure summarize*(                    var  c: net; i: integer;
  p: problem;                           begin
  b: set; var s: solution);               for i := 1 to n do open(c[i]);
begin end;                              parallel
                                          master(c, p, s) |
procedure server( c: channel);            forall i := 1 to n do
var p0: problem; s0: solution;              server(c[i])
begin receive(c, p0);                     end;
  solve(p0, s0);                        end;
  send(c, s0);
end;                                    begin end. {MS}
```

Fig. 3. Embeddable module *master-server*, *MS*. Public entities are marked by '*'.

3 Derivation of Specific Parallel Algorithms by Means of Module Embedding

A parallel generic algorithm is a common parallel control structure (such as master-server) in which process communication and synchronization are specified in a problem-independent manner. Clients of the generic algorithm can derive particular applications from the generic algorithm by extending it with domain specific sequential algorithms. When the generic algorithm is specified as a module, the derivation of specific applications can be achieved by means of module embedding. An application module can embed the generic master-server module and override relevant entities that are inherited from the embedded module, giving them more specialized meaning. This is explained in details in the next section.

3.1 Derivation of Parallel Integration Application

Consider, for example, the problem of deriving a simple parallel integration algorithm based on the trapezoidal method. This can be achieved by extending module *MS* into a module *TI* (Fig. 4). The *embedding module, TI,* inherits the components of the *base module, MS* and *re-exports* all inherited public entities. Besides, module *TI* introduces a new generic parameter *f,* the function to be integrated that should be supplied by clients of *TI.*

The embedding module, *TI,* overrides the inherited type *problem,* so that the new *problem* definition incorporates the lower and upper limits *a, b* of the integral to be calculated. Similarly, *TI* overrides the inherited type *solution,* so that the new *solution* definition incorporates the integral value *v.* Note that *problem* and *solution* were originally defined in module *MS* as empty record types. Overriding of non-empty record types is also permitted, as illustrated in the next section.

The embedding module also overrides the inherited default version of procedure *generate* and the inherited 'null' versions of procedures *solve* and *summarize.* The newly declared version of *generate* divides the integration range into *n* equal parts, one for each server. Procedure *solve* is defined in *TI* to be trapezoidal integration. Procedure *summarize* sums-up the partial integrals provided by the *n* servers.

```
module TI(MS);                          ...complete implementations of
type problem* =                         procedures generate and
   record  a*, b*: real; end;           summarize...
   solution* = record v*: real; end;    ...
                                        end. {module TI}
function f*(x: real): real;
begin end;                              module IA(TI);
                                        var p: problem; s: solution;
procedure solve*(p0: problem;
   var s: solution);                    function f*( x: real): real;
begin s.v := ((p0.b - p0.a) / 2) *      begin f := x * sin(sqrt(x)); end;
           (f(p0.a) + f(p0.b));
end;                                    begin compute(p, s) end. {LA}
```

Fig. 4. Derived modules *trapezoidal integration, TI,* and *integration application, IA.*

Module *TI* can be embedded on its turn into a specific *integration application* module, *IA,* that defines a particular function *f* to be integrated. Module *IA* serves as a main program by invoking procedure *compute* that is provided by the generic *MS* module (Fig. 4).

3.2 Derivation of Parallel Simulated Annealing and Traveling Salesperson Algorithms

A variety of specific parallel algorithms can be derived from the same general parallel generic algorithm. For example, we have derived a generic algorithm for approximate optimization that is based on *simulated annealing*, organized as module *SA* (Fig. 5). Note that the definition of type *annealingPoint* contains a component, *dE*, that is needed for all possible application of simulated annealing..

The generic *simulated annealing* algorithm can be used to derive approximate algorithms for different intractable optimization problems. For instance, we have derived a parallel algorithm for a particular *traveling salesperson problem* (module *TSP* in Fig. 5). Note that the inherited definition of type *annealingPoint* is overridden in *TSP* by adding two new problem-specific components, *i, j*, to the inherited component *dE*.

```
module SA(MS);                          module TSP(SA);
type                                    ...
  problem* = record                     type
    ...annealing parameters...            city = record x, y: real end;
  end;                                    tour = array [1..m] of city;
  annealingPoint* = record                solution* = record t: tour; end;
    dE*: real;                            annealingPoint* = record
  end;                                      ...field dE inherited from SA...
                                            i, j: integer;
...procedures select and change           end;
declared as generic parameters...
                                        var p: problem; s: solution;
procedure solve*(
  p0: problem; var s: solution);        ...complete implementations of
...complete implementation that         procedures select, change,
performs simulated annealing            summarize...
using the generic parameters select
and change...                           begin compute(p, s) end. {TSP}
end. {SA}
```

Fig. 5. Derived modules *simulated annealing, SA*, and *traveling salesperson, TSP*.

4 Interference Control for Embeddable Modules

When a parallel application is executed *repeatedly with the same input*, the relative speeds of its constituent parallel processes may vary from one execution to another. If one parallel process *updates* a variable and another process *updates or reads* that same variable, the order in which those processes access the variable may vary from one execution to another, even when the input for the parallel application do not change. Such parallel processes are said to *interfere* with each other in a time dependent manner due to a *variable conflict*. Interfering parallel processes may update and possibly read the same variable at unpredictable times. The output of an application that contains interfering parallel processes may vary in an unpredictable manner when the application is executed repeatedly with the same input. Such an application is said to be *insecure* due to a *time-dependent error*. A secure parallel programming language should allow detection and reporting of as many time-dependent errors as possible. The implementation may efficiently detect time-dependent errors through process *interference control* at compile time and, less efficiently, at run time.

Hansen [4] advocated the benefits from interference control and developed an interference control scheme for the parallel programming language SuperPascal. The SuperPascal language is subject to several restrictions that allow effective syntactic detection of variable conflicts, i.e., detection at compile time. These restrictions apply to a variety of language constructs and assure that a variable that is updated by a parallel process may be read only by that process. Note that parallel processes are allowed to read-only shared variables.

For each statement belonging to a SuperPascal program, the compiler determines the target variable set and the expression variable set of that statement. The *target variable set* consists of all variables that may be updated during the execution of the statement, while the *expression variable set* consists of all variables that may be read during that statement's execution. In SuperPascal, processes are created by *parallel* and *forall* statements. A parallel statement **parallel** $S_1 \mid S_2 \mid \ldots S_n$ **end** incorporates n *process statements* $S_1, S_2, \ldots S_n$ such that the target variable set of S_i is disjoint with the target and expression variable sets of $S_1, \ldots S_{i-1}, S_{i+1}, \ldots S_n$, $i = 1, 2, \ldots n$. A forall statement **forall** $i := m$ **to** n **do** S incorporates a single *element statement* S which generates $n-m+1$ processes and, for this reason, is required to have an empty target variable set.

It should be noted that the above restrictions on target and expression variable sets are very natural for parallel applications running in a cluster computing environment. Processes that are generated by a *forall* statement will run on separate cluster nodes. If such processes were to share a target variable, it could be quite hard and inefficient to synchronize that shared access over a network. At the same time, it is easy to make these processes efficiently share read-only variables by broadcasting those variables values just once to all processes. Similar considerations apply to processes that are generated by a *parallel* statement.

A SuperPascal parallel application consists of a single main program, exactly as in the standard Pascal language. The interference control scheme of SuperPascal [4] guarantees that single-module parallel applications do not contain time-dependent errors, i.e., they are secure in this sense. The Paradigm/SP language has been designed as an extension to SuperPascal that introduces separately compiled embeddable modules [11]. We have extended the single-module interference control scheme of SuperPascal to serve the specific requirements of Paradigm/SP.

In SuperPascal, procedures are never overridden. Therefore, the target and expression variable sets for procedure statements can be determined during the compilation of SuperPascal's single module parallel applications. This is not the case in a language with embeddable modules, such as Paradigm/SP: procedures that are defined in an embeddable module *M0* can be overridden in an embedding module *M1*. The overriding procedures that are defined in *M1* may have different target and expression variable sets from those in *M0*. Therefore, procedure statements in the embedded module *M0*, a module that has already been separately compiled, may have their target and expression variable sets changed by procedure overriding in *M1*. Thus, restrictions on target and expression variables sets that have been validated during the compilation of *M0* may be violated later, when *M0* is embedded in *M1*.

---

module *M0;*
 procedure *p*(j: integer);*
 begin end*;*
begin
  forall *i := 1* **to** *10* **do** *p(i);*
end. *{M0}*

module *M1(M0);*
 var *k: integer;*
 procedure *p*(j: integer);*
 begin *k := j* **end***;*
begin *k := 0* **end**. *{M1}*

Fig. 6. Modules *M0* and *M1*.

Consider, for example, module *M0* from Fig. 6 that defines and exports procedure *p*. Module *M0* contains a statement **forall** *i := 1* **to** *10* **do** *p(i)* that generates processes by executing the procedure statement *p(i)*. The procedure statement *p(i)* has an empty target variable set; therefore, its generated processes do not interfere due to variable conflicts.

Assume now that module *M0* is embedded in module *M1* and that *M1* overrides the inherited procedure *p*, as illustrated in Fig. 6. The overriding body of *p* may have access to a global variable, *k*. Therefore, the target variable set of the procedure statement *p(i)* in the separately compiled module *M0* will now actually contain the variable *k*, and will, therefore, be non-empty.

The main difficulty to interference control in a language framework with module embedding comes from the possibility to change, through procedure overriding, the target and expression variable sets in embedded modules that have been already separately compiled. We remedy this problem by introducing additional restrictions that make it impossible to modify variable sets during procedure overriding. More precisely, we exclude the so-called unrestricted procedures (and functions) from *parallel* and *forall* statements, as explained below.

A procedure that is declared in a module can be marked for export with either a *restricted mark* "*" or an *unrestricted mark* "-". A procedure exported by a module *M0* can be overridden in an embedding module *M1*, provided that the procedure heading in *M1* is the same as in *M0* (in particular, the export mark, "*" or "-", must be the same).

A *restricted procedure* is a procedure exported with a restricted mark, "*".

An *unrestricted procedure* is:
- a procedure that is exported with an unrestricted mark, "-", or
- a private procedure that invokes an unrestricted procedure, or both

A restricted procedure is not permitted to use global variables (directly or indirectly), and invoke unrestricted procedures. In contrast, an unrestricted procedure can use global variables and invoke unrestricted procedures.

Overriding an unrestricted procedure *p* in an embedding module *M1* may change target and expression variable sets in a separately compiled embedded module *M0*, because the overriding procedure is allowed to access global variables. This is why *parallel* statements and *forall* statements are *not* permitted to invoke unrestricted procedures. This requirement is in addition to the limitations on target and expression variable sets in *parallel* and *forall* statements, as defined earlier in this section. Restricted procedures are not excluded from *parallel* and *forall* statements because, in contrast to unrestricted procedures, they cannot modify target or expression variable sets in separately compiled embedded modules,

There are also procedures that are neither restricted nor unrestricted, such as, for example, private procedures that use global variables but do not invoke unrestricted procedures. This category of procedures may participate in *parallel* and *forall* statements as well, as far as they comply with the limitations on target and expression variable sets, as discussed earlier in this section.

Consider again the example modules in Fig. 6. Procedure *p* is declared with a restricted mark, „*". Therefore, accessing a global variable such as *k* in *M1* is a syntax error. Procedure *p* would be allowed to access a global variable if *p* was declared with an unrestricted mark, „-". In such a case, however, the use of *p* in a *forall* statement like as the one in *M0* would be a syntax error..

The exclusion of unrestricted procedures from *parallel* and *forall* statements permits syntactic detection of variable conflicts in separately compiled modular parallel applications. The Paradigm/SP compiler guarantees that a variable that is updated by a process cannot be used by another process, while sharing read-only variables is permitted. Paradigm/SP parallel applications may not be insecure due to variable conflicts.

Is the exclusion of unrestricted procedures form *parallel* and *forall* statements a serious practical limitation? Technically, it means that if an exported procedure is used to generate a process, and if it needs to access global variables, it must do so through explicit send/receive statements or through parameters, rather than directly. We are convinced that this restriction is quite natural in the domain of message passing cluster algorithms, because parallel access to global variables from different processes must be implemented through send/receive, anyway. Programmers who are forced to implement access to global variables through explicit send/receive statements are more likely to be aware of the underlying inefficiency of such access, in contrast to programmers for whom implicit message passing is generated by the implementation. Our experiments with four generic algorithms and several derivatives from each of them make us believe that the exclusion of unrestricted procedures form parallelism is not a serious practical limitation.

5. Conclusions

This paper outlines module embedding, a form of inheritance that applies to modules and that permits overriding of inherited types. Embeddable modules have been incorporated in a parallel programming language called *Paradigm/SP*. A prototype implementation of Paradigm/SP has been developed and documented [12]. Paradigm/SP has been used to specify generic parallel algorithms and to derive concrete parallel applications from them by means of module embedding. Paradigm/SP has been used as a higher-level prototyping language in order to conveniently test the validity of derived parallel applications before finally converting them into efficient C code that runs in a cluster-computing environment, such as PVM.

We have specified several generic parallel algorithms as embeddable modules, such as a probabilistic master-server [10], a cellular automaton [9], and an all-pairs pipeline [8]. Though module embedding, we have derived diverse parallel applications from such generic algorithms. Despite of the use of generic parallelism, most of the derived applications have demonstrated very good performance in cluster-computing environments, and a couple of derived applications have achieved super linear speed-up [8].

We have adopted interference control scheme for embeddable modules. This scheme guarantees that processes in derived applications do not interfere by reading and updating the same variable. That derived algorithms are *secure* in this sense is what makes module embedding unique in comparison to traditional object-oriented techniques supported by C++, Java, Corba, etc., where no static control helps programmers to avoid time-dependent errors in derived algorithms. For example, it has been recognized that Java multithreaded applications are inherently insecure because nothing prevents different threads from invoking unsynchronized methods [3]. A related insecure feature of Java is that data members are by default *protected* and that protected data members can be accessed from all classes that belong to the same package. For these reasons, it easy to gain access from different threads to protected data members by adding new classes to a package and to create applications that are insecure due to time-dependent errors.

Others have proposed dynamic load-time class overriding through byte-code editing [6]. This technique is justified by the so-called adaptation and evolution problems that appear when sub-classing is used to build software components. Our approach has the merit of integrating type overriding within the programming language and its compiler.

In traditional modular object-oriented languages, such as Oberon-2, Ada-95 and Modula-3, modules are not embeddable, while classes are represented by means of extensible record types [15]. What is different in our approach to classes is that record type extension overrides an existing type (both in the new embedding module and in the existing embedded module) and does not introduce a new type. A disadvantage of embeddable modules as compared to classes is that modules do not introduce types, and therefore cannot be used to create multiple instances. Furthermore, inherited type overriding imposes additional run-time overhead on the implementation. It has been recognized [7], [13] that both modules and classes support necessary abstractions, which should be used as a complementary techniques.

A collection of object-oriented language features that support the development of parallel applications can be found in [1], [2]. Parallel programming enhancements of a mainstream language, C++, are presented in [14]. A survey of earlier object-parallel languages is contained in [16]. An example of template-based genericity is contained in [17]. We do not know of a traditional object-oriented language that performs static analysis in order to guarantee that parallel applications are free of time-dependent errors. The main benefit of module embedding is that it guarantees at compile time the lack of such errors and that its static interference analysis scheme eliminates the overhead of run-time synchronization.

Paradigm/SP is a specification and prototyping language and as such is simpler than production languages and environments. Algorithm developers may focus on what is essential in their developed parallel control structures and application methods without being burdened by the complex details that are required for efficient practical programming. Simplicity and ease of use are advantages of Paradigm/SP as an algorithm development and validation language in comparison to production languages and environments.

As a continuation of this project in the future, we envision that it would be possible and beneficial to develop an interference control scheme for multithreaded Java applications. A Java source code analyzer may be used to discover variable conflicts between threads and to help eliminated time-depending errors due to such conflicts.

If algorithms are to be published on the web, they can be shaped as multimedia web-pages. A separately compiled module can be shaped as a source html file that can be fed into a compiler in order to produce executable code. Module import and embedding can be designated by means of hyper-links. Source modules that comprise an application can reside on different servers. These same servers can host corresponding distributed executable objects. The design of adequate language and compiler support is another possible continuation of this project in the future.

References

1. G. Agha, P. Wegner, and A. Yonezawa, editors. *Research Directions in Concurrent Object-Oriented Programming*. MIT Press, 1993.
2. J.-P. Briot, J.-M.Geib, and A. Yonezawa. *Object-Based Parallel and Distributed Computation*. Lecture Notes in Computer Science 1107, Springer, 1996.

3. P. B. Hansen. Java's Insecure Parallelism. *ACM SIGPLAN Notices*, Vol. 34, No 4, April 1999, pp.38-45.
4. P. B. Hansen. *Studies in Computational Science: Parallel Programming Paradigms*. Prentice Hall, 1995.
5. P. B. Hansen. SuperPascal - A Publication Language For Parallel Scientific Computing. *Concurrency - Practice and Experience*, 6, No 5, 1994, 461-483.
6. R. Keller, U. Holzle. Binary Component Adaptation. *ECOOP'98 Conference Proceedings* (E. Jul, editor), Lecture Notes in Computer Science 1445, Springer, 1998, pp.307-329.
7. H. Moessenboeck. *Object-Oriented Programming in Oberon-2*. Springer, 1993.
8. A. Radenski, B. Norris, W. Chen. A Generic All-Pairs Cluster-Computing Pipeline and Its Applications. *Proceedings of ParCo99, International Conference on Parallel Computing, August 17-20, 1999, Delft, The Netherlands*, Imperial College Press (under print).
9. A. Radenski, A. Vann, B. Norris. Development and Utilization of Generic Algorithms for Scientific Cluster Computations. *Object Oriented Methods for Interoperable Scientific and Engineering Computing* (M. Henderson, C. Anderson, and S. Lyons, editors), SIAM, 1999, 97-105.
10. A. Radenski, A. Vann, B. Norris. Parallel Probabilistic Computations on a Cluster of Workstations. *Parallel Computing: Fundamentals, Applications and New Directions* (edited by E. D'Hollander et al.), Elsevier Science B.V., 1998, 105-112.
11. A. Radenski. Module Embedding. *Intl. Journal Software - Concepts and Tools*, Vol. 19, Issue 3, 1998, 122-129.
12. A. Radenski. Prototype Implementation of Paradigm/SP, http://www.rtpnet.org/~radenski/research/, 1998.
13. C. Szyperski. Why We Need Both: Modules And Classes. *OOPSLA'99 Conference Proceedings*, ACM, 1992, pp.19-32.
14. G. Wilson and P. Lu, editors. *Parallel Programming using C++*. MIT Press, 1996.
15. N. Wirth. Type Extensions. *ACM Transactions on Programming Languages and Systems*, 10, 1987, 204-214.
16. B. Wyatt, K. Kavi, and S. Hufnagel, 1992. Parallelism in Object-Oriented Languages: A Survey. *IEEE Software*, 9, No 6 (Nov.), 1992, 56-66.
17. L.-Q. Lee, J. Siek, and A. Lumsdaine, 1999. The Generic Graph Component Library. *OOPSLA'99 Conference Proceedings*, ACM, 1999, pp.399-414.

Mianjin: A Parallel Language with a Type System That Governs Global System Behaviour

Paul Roe[1] and Clemens Szyperski[2]

[1] School of Computing Science,
Queensland University of Technology, Australia
p.roe@qut.edu.au

[2] Microsoft Research,
Redmond, USA
cszyperk@microsoft.com

Abstract. For the past few years we have been working on a parallel programming language, Mianjin, suitable for writing parallel programs for non-dedicated networks of workstations. This paper reviews an innovative feature of the language, a type system that statically enforces global system behaviour. This is achieved by typing the behaviour of commands, thereby differentiating commands that may admit communication from those that do not. Doing this guarantees safe asynchronous communications; in particular it prevents deadlocks caused by exhaustion of system-level communication resources (such as buffers) which are beyond an application programmer's control. These command types propagate though client and library code thereby simplifying some problems associated with constructing software components. The type system is semi-formally described using type rules, and some further applications of the idea to software components are discussed.

1 Introduction

For the past few years we have been researching and developing a parallel language called Mianjin[1], for programming non-dedicated networks of workstations (the Gardens project [5]). Since the original publication describing Mianjin [4] the language has been refined and improved. We have come to realise that its control of global system behaviour by typing the behaviour of commands is particularly innovative and useful, and may be applicable to other situations. This paper describes this feature semi-formally, and how it might be applicable to controlling other forms of global system behaviour which complicate the development of large software systems.

Mianjin is an object oriented language in the Pascal tradition; it is based on Oberon-2, with some extensions. It is designed for parallel programming so the efficient control of tasking and communication is vital. For this reason

---

[1] 'Mianjin' means place of the blue water lilies; it is an Aboriginal name for Gardens Point, where QUT is located.

J. Gutknecht and W. Weck (Eds.): JMLC 2000, LNCS 1897, pp. 38–50, 2000.

Mianjin supports distributed objects for communication, these have some similarities with Java RMI. Notable differences from Java RMI are its efficiency, asynchronous remote method call and atomicity typing; the latter is the subject of this paper. Atomicity typing statically controls object reentrance. This prevents deadlocks caused by exhaustion of system-level communication resources (such as buffers) which are beyond an application programmer's control. Note, this approach does not aim at reducing the computational power of the language; application-level deadlocks are not excluded, only implicit system-level ones. Other related languages and systems include CC++, Charm++, Orca, pSather, SplitC, CORBA, and DCOM. SplitC [2] is closest in that its communication model is also based on asynchronous send combined with non-selective synchronous receive, but it is not type safe. Note in this paper we only describe and formalise a simplified version of Mianjin.

The main contribution of this paper is to show how the global behaviour of a system, in particular certain forms of object reentrance, may be statically controlled through a type system, and to present a semi-formal description of Mianjin's type system, which does this.

The next section overviews Mianjin's support for distributed objects. Section 3 discusses general issues of object reentrance. Section 4 introduces atomicity typing and justifies the overall design decisions underpinning the aspects of Mianjin as presented in this paper. Section 5 presents a semi-formal description of Mianjin's type system, which controls object reentrance – a global system property. Section 6 describes how these features may be used to solve other problems, and the final section concludes.

2   Distributed Objects in Mianjin

Communication in Mianjin is realised via asynchronous global (remote) method calls, c.f. Java RMI [6]. Like some other languages Mianjin differentiates local from potentially global objects. Global objects are ordinary local objects which have been exposed globally. Through such global references, objects are subject to a restricted set of operations: tests for equality, locality tests/casts and invocation of global methods. Global methods are ordinary methods, again subject to constraints. Locally, objects support a superset of these global object operations including direct field access.

Here is a simple example of a local object which may be exposed globally. Note we use the syntax and semantics of our toy mini-Mianjin language, formalised in Section 5. In particular all objects are heap-allocated and object types, records in Oberon terminology, are reference types, as in Java [7]. The full Mianjin language has syntax and semantics based on Oberon-2. The example declares an object type that supports a single method **Add** and has two fields **count** and **sum**. An **Acc** object represents a form of accumulator to which other tasks may contribute values via **Add**. The client code uses the object remotely.

```
RECORD Acc(ANYREC)                  (* a record = class *)
   count: INTEGER                   (* a field          *)
   sum: INTEGER                     (* another field    *)
   GLOBAL METHOD Add (s:INTEGER)    (* a global method  *)
   BEGIN
      THIS.sum := THIS.sum + s
      THIS.count := THIS.count - 1
   END Add
END

VAR gsum: GLOBAL Acc                (* client code      *)
   ...
   gsum.Add(42)
```

For an object like gsum to be used remotely its type must be labelled GLOBAL. The GLOBAL type annotation enforces that only global methods such as Add may be invoked on gsum, the record fields and any non-GLOBAL methods (of which there are none) are not supported.

Local objects, the default, are always located locally. Global objects may be either located remotely or locally. Thus an implementation of the call gsum.Add(localval) will result in a communication if gsum is not local. In Mianjin global method invocations are asynchronous. However since synchronous invocation is just a special case, a Mianjin implementation is free to invoke global methods on local objects synchronously. In the example, if gsum happens to refer to a local object, then gsum.Add can be executed as a normal synchronous call.

Thus Mianjin supports location-transparent communication via global objects and their associated global methods. Global object references are valid across machines and hence are location independent. They can therefore be communicated freely among tasks running across a distributed system. In general local objects are compatible with global ones but not vice versa, other than through an explicit (and checked) runtime type cast.

Issues such as tasking are system-specific. Other issues such as returning values from global methods to implement efficient read operations are beyond the scope of this paper and discussed elsewhere [4]. Here we focus on the core issue of controlling object reentrance, and, to a lesser extent, local versus global objects.

3   Object Reentrance: A Global System Property

Reentrant calls into state-based abstractions introduce a number of well-understood problems [8]. These problems, fundamentally, are all rooted in the abstraction's implementation being in some intermediate state when it made the outcall that eventually led to the reentrant call. Designing and implementing object-oriented programs in a way that such reentrancy does not lead to errors is known to be difficult. Matters get worse when the state held by a reentered object is not actually managed by that object itself. Since object reentrance may occur through complex call sequences involving third party code it must be controlled globally within a system; it is not a local property.

Let us consider what happens in the case of an unconstrained language with asynchronous messaging similar to Mianjin. Assume that the underlying communication mechanism needs to allocate a buffer whenever a method is called and can only release the buffer once that method returned (methods are asynchronous). If such buffers are allocated out of a system-managed buffer pool, then the limit on the number of available buffers is not controlled by the application. If the communication system runs out of buffers, it blocks and waits for buffers to become available. However, if recursive remote method invocations are allowed, then such waiting for buffers can easily lead to a deadlock.

It might seem that this form of reentrancy is a special case of the more general situation of concurrent calls. Therefore, it would seem that traditional concurrency control and synchronisation mechanisms can be used to solve this problem. Unfortunately, this is not true and concurrent invocations and reentrant invocations are two different problems entirely. To see why, assume that some form of locking was used in an attempt to control reentrant calls. Since the reentrant call is logically made by the same thread that entered the now-locked section in the first place, an immediate deadlock would follow. To break this tie of "self-inflicted" deadlocks, languages such as Obliq [1] and Java allow for repeated granting of a lock to the same thread. More generally, techniques for handling concurrent calls are *in principle* unable to handle reentrant calls.

Another solution to problems caused by reentrant calls is to not allow them. For such an approach to work, reentrancy must be ruled out statically, or else a very hideous form of run-time-detected error results. A straightforward static approach would be to simply disallow any method call on another object from within a method's body. This is clearly not useful, since objects would not be able to call on other objects at all. However, only a slight modification of this approach leads to a scheme that proved to be useful and practical in the context of Mianjin.

4   Atomicity Typing

In Mianjin we prevent the problems mentioned in the previous section of unconstrained object reentrance by typing the atomicity of commands. We sort methods into three types: *atomic, global,* and *polling* methods. Atomic methods perform no communication and accept no messages (do not poll), global methods represent methods which may be implemented remotely and hence their implementation must not accept other messages nor communicate. Polling methods may perform communications and poll. Given this categorisation of methods we type commands in Mianjin, e.g. method calls, by their atomicity behaviour: either atomic or polling. This results in the following typing for method declarations: atomic methods can only call atomic commands; global methods can only call atomic commands; polling methods can call polling, or atomic commands. The only other similar system we know of is the restriction in C++ and Java that a method can only call methods with declared exceptions, if it itself either handles these exceptions or declares to throw a superset of them.

Mianjin assumes a model that enables an implementation of global method calls over message passing networks. Code that calls a global method and code that polls for incoming requests must therefore adhere to policies that prevent deadlocks caused by mutual waiting for network buffer resources. Atomicity typing statically guarantees that Mianjin code follows one such policy. Since global methods can neither call other global methods nor cause the polling for incoming calls, a global method cannot cause further pressure on network resources while it is executing. Deadlocks are thus statically prevented.

A global method can only call atomic code (code that does not communicate), but could post a continuation action that could communicate on its behalf. Once the global method returns, some scheduler can call pending continuation actions. For the sake of allowing (deferred) communication to follow incoming messages, the problem of network-resource pressure has thus been converted into one of application-resource pressure (to hold on to pending continuations). In the end, this is unavoidable for applications built using a partially recursive computational model can never be statically kept from running out of resources or deadlocking. However, deadlocks must not be caused by resource pressure that the application itself cannot control.

The Mianjin model opts for a remote method invocation model that *enables* an asynchronous implementation, but is carefully balanced to not *require* asynchronous invocation. This is most important when aiming for a flexible distribution of objects across networked machines. Asynchronous communication naturally masks the potentially significant latency of remote calls without requiring the use of additional threads at the calling end. At the same time, local calls are much more efficiently executed synchronously.

Potentially asynchronous calls need to be part of an appropriate communication model. Besides restricting signatures of methods that are to support potentially asynchronous calls (no out, inout, or return values), the receiving end also needs attention. Synchronous receive is required to avoid heavy use of multiple threads. To avoid deadlocks, receive operations must not wait for a specific call or else the automatic creation of threads would again be required. The Mianjin polling mechanism synchronously requests delivery of all pending calls, but does not block the system if there are no calls pending. It therefore enables a model that keeps threading orthogonal to asynchronous computing. (At a library rather than language level, this approach was pioneered by Active Messages [9].)

Requiring programmers to think in terms of abstractions that may and those that definitely will not communicate introduces a new burden. The same is true for the requirement to use continuations when trying to communicate from within a non-communicating abstraction, such as a message receiver. However, besides static safety gains, there is a significant gain as well: since abstractions are now statically classified, a programmer can rely on non-communicating abstractions not causing unexpected reentrancy as a result of communications hidden by an abstraction's implementation. Thus, the programmer now knows when exactly it is necessary to reestablish invariants over task-global data structures before calling on some abstraction. Doing so is required exactly if the called abstraction may communicate, i.e. poll, since system-level deadlocks can only be avoided if every attempt to send a message is paired with a promise to be able to receive a message.

In combination, the resulting Mianjin model is much simpler and cleaner than strictly synchronous models, including CORBA[2], Java RMI, and DCOM.

5 A Semi-formal Description of Mianjin

The previous sections introduced Mianjin, its distributed object system and the idea of preventing object reentrance through atomicity typing of commands. This section semi-formally describes the core concepts of Mianjin: distributed objects and atomicity typing via a cut-down version of the Mianjin language.

Mianjin proper is essentially an extension of Oberon-2. Note that in Mianjin and Oberon object types are termed records; here we use the two terms interchangeably. Mini-Mianjin as described here omits the following features from the full language:

- Pointers (all records are heap-allocated and reference-based as in Java)
- Constants, arrays, functions, procedures, modules, type aliases
- VAR parameters, projection on subtyped values
- Method overriding and super calls

Only a limited set of commands and expressions are described, others follow quite naturally. In addition some of the syntax has been changed to simplify formalisation, e.g., implicit "this" records are used for the receiver object in methods and methods are defined inside records (object types). The abstract syntax is described in Figure 1. It shows the syntax categories and identifiers used in rules to range over those categories, for example a variable t always represents a type.

The following wellformedness criteria apply to programs (we informally state these here to avoid cluttering rules):

- All record names in types must exist in the environment.
- All records must directly or indirectly extend ANYREC.
- Records may not add new methods or fields with the same names as ones defined in super types.
- All record names in the environment must be distinct.

---

[2] CORBA supports "oneway" methods, but their semantics in the case of an asynchronous implementation is rather unclear. Commercial ORBs all implement "oneway" synchronously.

$$
\begin{array}{ll}
\text{Program} & = \text{Record*} \\
r \in \text{Record} & = \text{RECORD Ident (Ident) Fields, Method* END} \\
fs \in \text{Fields} & = (\text{Ident : Type})* \\
m \in \text{Method} & = \text{Attrib METHOD Ident (Params)} \\
& \quad \text{VAR Locals BEGIN Cmd* END} \\
at \in \text{Attrib} & = \text{Atomicity} \mid \text{GLOBAL} \\
a \in \text{Atomicity} & = \text{ATOMIC} \mid \text{POLL} \\
\text{Params} & = (\text{Ident : Type})* \\
\text{Locals} & = (\text{Ident : Type})* \\
c \in \text{Cmd} & = \text{NEW LExp} \mid \text{LExp := Exp} \mid \\
& \quad \text{LExp.Ident (Actuals)} \mid \cdots \\
\text{Actuals} & = (\text{Ident : Type})* \\
e \in \text{Exp} & = \text{Exp = Exp} \mid \text{LExp} \mid \cdots \\
le \in \text{LExp} & = \text{Ident} \mid \text{LExp.Ident} \mid \text{THIS} \mid \text{LExp (Type)} \\
t,u,v,pt,lt \in \text{Type} & = \text{Ident} \mid \text{ANYREC} \mid \text{BasicType} \mid \text{GLOBAL Type} \\
f,p,l,id,b \in \text{Ident} &
\end{array}
$$

Fig. 1. Abstract syntax

- All field and method names in each record must be distinct.
- All parameters' and locals' names in each method must be distinct.

In all contexts global annotations are idempotent and only effect records:

$$
\text{GLOBAL (GLOBAL } t) = \text{GLOBAL } t
$$
$$
\text{GLOBAL BasicType} = \text{BasicType}
$$

We use two environments in our rules, one maps record names to records, R, the other maps variables to types, V:

$$
R : \text{Ident} \mapsto \text{Record}
$$
$$
V : \text{Ident} \mapsto \text{Type}
$$

The following relations extract a record's name from a record declaration (recname), assert that a type is a valid defined record (isrec), and assert that one record extends another (extends).

$$
\begin{array}{ll}
\text{recname(RECORD } id \ (\_) \ \_, \ \_ \ \text{END)} & = id \\
\text{recname(ANYREC)} & = \text{ANYREC}
\end{array}
$$

$$
\begin{array}{ll}
\text{isrec}(R, \text{GLOBAL } t) & = \text{isrec}(R, t) \\
\text{isrec}(R, id) & = \text{isrec}(R, R(id)) \\
\text{isrec}(R, \text{BasicType}) & = \textit{false} \\
\text{isrec}(R, \text{RECORD } id(b) \ fs, \ ms \ \text{END}) & = (\text{RECORD } id(b) \ fs, \ ms \ \text{END}) \in \text{range}(R)
\end{array}
$$

$$
\text{extends(RECORD } \_(b)\_, \_ \ \text{END)} = \text{RECORD } b(\_)\_, \_ \ \text{END}
$$

We now come to two key relations which define Mianjin. The atomicity relation (atomicity) governs the atomicity of method invocations given a method with a given attribute and object of a given type (local or global). The global relation represents the projection of the global type attribute across all parameters of a global method (global). That is, the record formal parameters of a global method are all implicitly globalised.

$$\text{atomicity} : (\text{Attrib}, \text{Type}) \leftrightarrow \text{Atomicity}$$
$$\text{atomicity}(\texttt{GLOBAL}, t) = \texttt{ATOMIC}, \texttt{local}(t)$$
$$= \texttt{POLL}, \text{otherwise}$$
$$\text{atomicity}(\texttt{ATOMIC}, t) = \texttt{ATOMIC}, \texttt{local}(t)$$
$$= \text{undefined}, \text{otherwise}$$
$$\text{atomicity}(\texttt{POLL}, t) \quad = \texttt{POLL}, \texttt{local}(t)$$
$$= \text{undefined}, \text{otherwise}$$

$$\text{global} : (\text{Attrib}, \text{Type}) \leftrightarrow \text{Type}$$
$$\text{global}(\texttt{GLOBAL}, t) \quad = \texttt{GLOBAL}\ t$$
$$\text{global}(\texttt{ATOMIC}, t) \quad = t$$
$$\text{global}(\texttt{POLL}, t) \quad = t$$

$$\text{local}(\texttt{GLOBAL}\ t) \quad = \text{false}$$
$$\text{local}(t) \quad = \text{true}, \text{for all other } t$$

Given the previous abstract syntax and relations we can now define the type rules for our mini-Mianjin. For the various categories of syntax the type rules have the following forms:

program and record declarations $R \vdash \text{Program}$ $R \vdash \text{Record}$
method declarations $RV \vdash \text{Method}$
commands $RV \vdash \text{Cmd} : \text{Atomicity}$
expressions $RV \vdash \text{Exp} : \text{Type}$

The type rules for program, record and method declarations are shown in Figure 2. Note, we use underscore for the wildcard "don't care" pattern, elipses to denote sequences, and "•" to denote mapping extension. The rule for methods is of particular interest; it states that:

- If the method is declared to be global or atomic all its constituent commands must be atomic i.e. only a method declared as poll may invoke polling commands. (In the case of a global method its server side code must be atomic although the actually method invocation on a global object will not be - see the rule for method invocation.) This simple analysis is conservative, c.f. Java definite assignment.
- All constituent commands must type check, within an environment extended with the parameters and local variable bindings. The parameters are implicitly globalised if the method is labelled as being global.

$$\text{Program}$$
$$R = \{\text{recname}(r_i) \mapsto r_i\}_{i=1\ldots n} \bullet \{\text{ANYREC} \mapsto \text{ANYREC}\}$$
$$\frac{R\vdash r_1, \ldots, R\vdash r_n}{r_1 \ldots r_n}$$

$$\text{Record}$$
$$R\{\text{THIS} \mapsto id\}\vdash m_1, \ldots, R\{\text{THIS} \mapsto id\}\vdash m_n$$
$$\frac{}{R\vdash \text{RECORD } id\ (\_)\ \_,\ m_1 \ldots m_n \text{ END}}$$

$$\text{Method}$$
$$V' = V \bullet \{p_i \mapsto \text{global}(at, pt_i)\}_{i=1\ldots m} \bullet \{l_i \mapsto lt_i\}_{i=1\ldots n}$$
$$RV'\vdash c_1 : a_1, \ldots, RV'\vdash c_o : a_o$$
$$\frac{at \in \{\text{GLOBAL}, \text{ATOMIC}\} \Rightarrow \forall_{i=1\ldots o} : a_i = \text{ATOMIC}}{RV\vdash at\ \text{METHOD}\ \_\ (p_1:pt_1 \ldots p_m:pt_m)\ \text{VAR}\ l_1:lt_1 \ldots l_n:lt_n\ \text{BEGIN}\ c_1 \ldots c_o\ \text{END}}$$

Fig. 2. Rules for program, method and record declarations

The type rules for commands are shown in Figure 3. The rule for method calls is of particular interest. It expresses the following:

- The atomicity of the call depends on the attribute of the method being called and locality of the receiver object, as defined by the atomicity relation.
- The method called must be declared in the receiver object's type or super-type.
- The method's actual parameters must be subtypes of the formal parameters.
- The formal parameter types are implicitly global if the method is global.
- The receiver object and actual parameters must all be type correct.

$$\frac{RV\vdash le : t \quad \text{isrec}(t) \ \& \ \text{local}(t)}{RV\vdash \text{NEW } le : \text{ATOMIC}}$$

$$\frac{RV\vdash le : t \quad RV\vdash e : u \quad R\vdash u \prec t}{RV\vdash le := e : \text{ATOMIC}}$$

$$R\vdash t_1 \prec \text{global}(at, pt_1), \ldots, R\vdash t_n \prec \text{global}(at, pt_n)$$
$$RV\vdash e_1 : t_1, \ldots, RV\vdash e_n : t_n$$
$$at\ \text{METHOD } id\ (p_1:pt_1 \ldots p_n:pt_n)\ \_\ \text{END} \in \{m_1 \ldots m_o\}$$
$$R\vdash t \prec \text{RECORD}\ \_\ \_,\ m_1 \ldots m_o\ \text{END}$$
$$\frac{RV\vdash le : t \quad a = \text{atomicity}(at, t)}{RV\vdash le.id\ (e_1 \ldots e_n) : a}$$

Fig. 3. Rules for commands

The type rules for expressions (including left expressions) are shown in Figure 4. Notice how only the fields of local objects may be accessed. Our simplified type cast is like Eiffel's: if the cast fails, `NIL` is returned. It may be used to cast global records to local ones; in which case the cast succeeds if the record genuinely is local.

$$\frac{RV\vdash E_1 : t \qquad RV\vdash E_2 : u \qquad R\vdash t\prec u \vee R\vdash u\prec t}{RV\vdash E_1\texttt{=}E_2 : \texttt{BOOL}}$$

$$\frac{V(id) = t}{RV\vdash id : t}$$

$$\frac{\begin{array}{c}(f : t) \in \{f_1 : t_1 \ldots f_n : t_n\}\\ R\vdash u\prec\texttt{RECORD}\ _(_)f_1 : t_1 \ldots f_n : t_n, _\ \texttt{END}\\ RV\vdash le : u \qquad \text{local}(u)\end{array}}{RV\vdash le.f : t}$$

$$\frac{V(\texttt{THIS}) = t}{RV\vdash \texttt{THIS} : t}$$

$$\frac{\text{isrec}(R, u) \qquad \text{isrec}(R, t) \qquad RV\vdash le : t}{RV\vdash le(u) : u}$$

Fig. 4. Rules for expressions

The relation $\prec$ denotes subtyping; it is defined in Figure 5. Subtyping applies to both explicitly defined subtyping of records and to local/global attributes of objects: local objects may be substituted for global ones but not vice versa.

6 Further Applications

The notion of atomicity typing can be generalised to *reentrancy classes*. The idea is simple: allow for any number of command types subject to a partial ordering (subtype relation). The default command type is at ground-level, i.e., cannot invoke code with any non-default reentrancy type—this corresponds to the atomic type in atomicity typing.

The observer pattern permits clients to attach to an object and to be notified when the object changes state. Often a synchronous notification is required i.e. all objects are informed of each state change, before subsequent state changes are permitted. A simple example is shown below, in pseudo code:

```
ABSTRACT RECORD Oberver
  PROCEDURE Notify
END
```

$$\frac{\text{isrec}(R, t)}{R \vdash t \prec \textbf{ANYREC}}$$

$$\frac{\text{extends}(t) = u \quad \text{isrec}(R, t) \quad \text{isrec}(R, u)}{R \vdash t \prec u}$$

$$R \vdash t \prec t$$

$$\frac{R \vdash t \prec u \quad R \vdash u \prec v}{R \vdash t \prec v}$$

$$\frac{R \vdash t \prec u}{R \vdash t \prec \textbf{GLOBAL } u}$$

$$\frac{R \vdash t \prec u}{R \vdash \textbf{GLOBAL } t \prec \textbf{GLOBAL } u}$$

Fig. 5. Rules for subtyping

```
RECORD Value
    val: INTEGER
    obs: ARRAY OF Observer
    numobs: INTEGER

    PROCEDURE Get(): INTEGER
    BEGIN
        RETURN THIS.val
    END Get

    PROCEDURE Set(newval: INTEGER)
    VAR i: INTEGER
    BEGIN
        THIS.val := newval
        FOR i := 0 TO numobs-1 DO THIS.obs.Notify END
    END Set
END
```

Problems can arise if an implementation of Notify calls Set since observers may no longer be synchronously informed of each state change. The key to solving the problem is to prevent Notify or any routine in its implementation from calling Set. It may however call Get. This is similar to Mianjin's insistence that ATOMIC code may not call POLL. We can envisage a system which supports the control of the contexts in which method calls may be made. Consider the following example:

```
ABSTRACT RECORD Oberver
  PROCEDURE Notify, RESTRICTION(Value.Set)
END
```

Similar to the **GLOBAL** attribute in Mianjin, the **RESTRICTION** attribute states that any implementation of **Notify** must not, directly or indirectly, call **Value.Set**. There are a number of issues with this approach:

- Restrictions (intentionally) interfere with procedural composition. It is thus important to pick a default that allows the coding of restriction-agnostic procedures/methods.
- The restriction must be declared when method is declared, and cannot be done afterwards. In the above example it would therefore be better (more general) to restrict **Notify** from calling a more general mutation interface and then to declare that **Value.Set** implements this mutation interface.
- Restrictions (intentionally) go against abstraction. Retaining the necessary restriction conditions across abstraction boundaries is the whole purpose of such annotations. Refinements, such as discussed in the previous point, can help in reducing the unnecessary impact on abstraction.
- Like most simple type-system approaches, restriction annotations affect all objects of a given type, rather than specific instances involved in some scenario. For example, it might be perfectly acceptable for a notifier to modify some other **Value** instance. For a finer-grained level of control, dependent types or alias-controlling type systems could be used [3].

A simple restriction system, as introduced above, goes a long way in addressing some of the pressing reentrancy problems of object-oriented programs. However, much work remains to establish the classes of reentrancy that can be covered with such systems and to formulate practical type systems that, at reasonable levels of annotational overhead, deliver static reentrancy control in practice.

7   Conclusions

We have described how the Mianjin parallel language uses a type system to enforce global system invariants. Namely to prevent reentrance of remote objects which could have unbounded buffer requirements in an asynchronous setting. Our experience with an implementation of Mianjin has been that such typing is extremely useful. It enables the development of software components which have an important aspect of their global system behaviour documented and checked as part of their type. We have also eluded to how the type system may be generalised to solve other problems of enforcing global system invariants by statically restricting certain forms of reentrancy.

References

1. L Cardelli. Obliq, a language with distributed scope. Technical Report TR-127, Digital Equipment Corporation, Systems Research Center, Palo Alto, CA, 1994.
2. D E Culler *et al.* Parallel programming in Split-C. In *Proc., Supercomputing '93 Conf.*, November 1993.
3. P Roe. An imperative language with read/write type modes. In *Proc Asian Computing Science Conference (ASIAN'97)*, number 1345 in Springer LNCS, Kathmandu, Nepal, 1997.
4. P Roe and C Szyperski. Mianjin is Gardens Point: A parallel language taming asynchronous communication. In *Fourth Australasian Conference on Parallel and Real-Time Systems (PART'97)*, Newcastle, Australia, September 1997. Springer.
5. P Roe and C Szyperski. The Gardens approach to adaptive parallel computing. In R Buyya, editor, *Cluster Computing*, volume 1, pages 740–753. Prentice Hall, 1999.
6. Sun Microsystems. Java RMI. http://java.sun.com/products/jdk/rmi/.
7. SUN Microsystems. The Java language: A white paper, 1995.
8. C Szyperski. *Component Software: Beyond Object-Oriented Programming.* Addison-Wesley, 1998.
9. T von Eicken, D Culler, S C Goldstein, and K E Schauser. Active messages: A mechanism for integrated communication and computation. In *Proceedings 19th International Symposium on Computer Architecture*, May 1992.

A Design Pattern and Programming Framework for Interactive Metacomputing

Spyros Lalis

Institute of Computer Science, Foundation for Research and Technology Hellas,
P.O. Box 1385, GR-71110 Heraklion, Greece
lalis@ics.forth.gr
Computer Science Department, University of Crete,
P.O. Box 1470, GR-71110 Heraklion, Greece
lalis@csd.uoc.gr

Abstract. This paper presents ADIOS, a system for the development of interactively controlled metacomputations. In ADIOS, coarse grain distributed computations, involving several different program components, are structured according to a distributed Model-View-Controller architecture. Design support is offered via interfaces and a base class, through which the fundamental behavior of program components is established within a concrete framework. In addition, appropriate communication mechanisms are provided to back up the data exchange between the various components. Consisting of only few Java classes, ADIOS is lightweight and promotes disciplined prototyping of metacomputations while allowing for the integration of legacy code.

1   Introduction

Thanks to advances in parallel programming platforms and mathematical libraries, scientists are more than ever able to seamlessly exploit special-purpose hardware, multiprocessors and clusters of workstations to speed up individual computations. Now, as scientific work gradually focuses on more complex phenomena, involving the interplay of processes that have been studied in isolation, a new challenge arises: to connect several different scientific modules in 'computational grids', spanning several regions or even countries. This coarse-grained distributed computing is also known as *metacomputing*. For example, the description of an ambitious project on the integration of combustion and airflow programs to build an advanced simulation of a jet engine can be found in [12].

Although metacomputations may run as 'silent' background tasks, interactive visualization and control can play an important role. One reason is debugging, i.e. to facilitate the detection of programming flaws, data exchange incompatibilities and performance bottlenecks. It may also be desirable to display the results of a computation at runtime, adjust parameters and restart the computation with different initial conditions to experiment with various "what if" scenarios. Taking a more futuristic perspective, users could immerse themselves in artificial spaces as these are being calculated via powerful computational grids. Direct on-line collaboration between multiple users wishing to jointly control a metacomputation from distant

J. Gutknecht and W. Weck (Eds.): JMLC 2000, LNCS 1897, pp. 51-61, 2000.

locations could also be supported. Notably, the technology for supporting interaction in virtual reality environments has made remarkable progress in the past years [19].

From a software engineering perspective, interactive metacomputing yields a transition from monolithic, stand-alone, command-line driven, batch-oriented code towards a network of remotely controllable programs. Each program is a component provided by a different team of scientists, and which, while performing calculations, can communicate and coordinate its execution with other components of the network. Metacomputations can also include additional components, providing control and visualization facilities. It is therefore important to identify the interactions among the various parts of a distributed computation and capture them in a pattern in the spirit of [10]. Providing conceptual guidance as to how this is done can be valuable for multi-disciplinary computing where, in practice, only a few persons involved in the development are likely to be computer experts.

In this paper, we present ADIOS – A Distributed Interactive Object System – intended to support the development of interactive metacomputations. In ADIOS, a computation consists of several different components integrated within a distributed Model-View-Controller architecture. The rudimentary interactions between these components are supported by appropriate communication mechanisms. Application programmers are thus able to design and implement metacomputations in a straightforward way. The system is implemented in Java and can easily be adapted to work with popular component models such as Microsoft's DCOM, OMG's CORBA or JavaSoft's JavaBeans.

The rest of the paper is structured as follows. Section 2 gives an overview of the ADIOS architecture. In section 3, the process of application development in ADIOS is sketched. Section 4 compares with related work. Finally, section 5 concludes the paper and sets future directions.

2   Architecture of ADIOS

The ADIOS architecture, depicted in Figure 1, is based on the Model-View-Controller paradigm [17]. In a nutshell, a computation is divided into three main component types: code that performs a calculation and manipulates local data structures (*Model*), code that forwards user commands to a model to control its execution (*Controller*), and code responsible for receiving and visualizing the state of a model (*View*). In ADIOS, view and controller are combined into a single entity called *Observer*. Each computation also includes a *Directory* used to register the addresses of components. Since metacomputations are de facto distributed, these components are located on different machines and communicate over the network. The role and the interactions between these components are described in the next subsections.

2.1 Components

Directory: The directory is a catalog holding the addresses (locations) of the computation's components. Additional properties of components, e.g. functional description, access control information, etc, could also be kept with the directory.

Each computation maintains a separate directory, hence has its own, private naming scope. The directory must be initialized prior to other components of a computation.

Model: Models embody programs performing calculations, thus are intrinsic parts of the computation. A metacomputation typically comprises several models that run concurrently with each other and exchange data to coordinate their execution. Upon installation, models register with the directory to make their presence known to the system. Models are likely to be implemented by different persons residing in different organizations and institutions. A model may also act as a wrapper for legacy code.

Observer: A component that is external to the computation and communicates with models is called an observer. Observers typically implement user interfaces for controlling model execution; they can also be software agents performing monitoring tasks or recording the execution of the computation for later inspection. An observer may communicate with several models. Different types of observers can dynamically connect to and disconnect from models, without requiring them to be re-programmed, re-compiled, or re-started. In fact, a model executes without knowledge of the specific observers linked to it. Observers locate models via the directory.

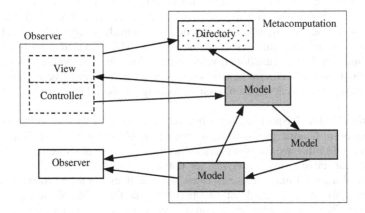

Fig. 1. ADIOS computations are structured according to a distributed MVC architecture and may include several models that communicate with each other. Component registration and lookup occurs via the directory. An arbitrary number of observers can monitor execution.

The interactions between these components are more formally captured as a set of protocols[1], supported via concrete interfaces and communication mechanisms. This provides developers with an accurate –and thus easy to use– model. An informal description of the ADIOS' protocols is briefly given in the following.

---

[1] Specifications of the interaction between components, rather than just a programming interface; this closely corresponds to the notion of a contract used in the literature.

2.2 Protocols

Directory Protocol: Defines how component address (and other) information is registered and retrieved using the directory. This request-response communication is introduced via a Java RMI interface, featuring the necessary registration and lookup routines. ADIOS provides a default implementation, which may be easily substituted with any other third-party directory service.

Computation Protocol: Describes the data exchange between models for the purpose of coordinating the execution of the computation. Inter-model communication is supported via type safe, asynchronous message passing. Messages were preferred over an RPC mechanism, such as Java RMI, because models typically interact with each other in an asynchronous peer-to-peer, rather than in a strict client-server, fashion. The underlying implementation is a version of the Hermes communication mechanism [20] adapted to the Java programming environment[2]. To achieve logically consistent communication between multiple models, causal domains can be defined according to which messages are ordered. Preserving causality in a group of cooperating processes can be important in a distributed system [21] and popular toolkits, e.g. the ISIS system [5], also provide corresponding communication support.

Control Protocol: Describes the means for initializing or modifying parameters of a model, and controlling its execution. A Java RMI interface includes the basic control methods of a model component. ADIOS does not introduce any multi-model control operations nor assumes any respective semantics. The provided primitives can be used to implement such functionality, if desired. Also, in case where different users should simultaneously control several models, their actions must be coordinated via distributed schemes, such as token passing, locking, or shared message boards.

Notification Protocol: Specifies how observers are being notified from the models. A subscription-notification mechanism, similar to the *Observer* pattern [10], is used for this purpose. In other words, observers subscribe to and unsubscribe from a model to start and respectively stop receiving its notifications. The number or type of the observers of a model may change dynamically and does not affect model execution. Notification events are broadcast to observers via the ADIOS' message passing mechanism. This de-couples model and observer execution, thereby eliminating potential performance bottlenecks and avoiding re-entrance problems that can be difficult to detect and handle in a distributed system. However, this allows only for asynchronous monitoring of models since their state may change before their notifications corresponding to older states reach an observer. This limitation is compensated by the fact that observers can receive notification events in causal order, thereby witnessing a logically consistent history of the entire computation. The latter is considered sufficient for typical observer tasks.

---

[2] For brevity, the message passing mechanism of ADIOS is not further discussed in this paper.

3 Programming in ADIOS

The elementary behavior of model components is captured via a base class, implementing the interfaces through which the main control, notification and computation actions occur. Programmers can inherit from this class as well as extend its interfaces to introduce application specific functionality. The next sections illustrate this process in more detail.

3.1 The Model Class

The *Model* class implements the basic functionality of models. It provides two interfaces that define primitives for the interaction with observers and other models respectively, corresponding to the aforementioned protocols:

```
interface ObserverDefs extends Remote {
  // control primitives
  void start(Object init_pars) ... ;
  void setBreakpoint(String label, long ticks) ... ;

    // notification primitives
  void subscribe(String name, String[] msg_types) ... ;
  void unsubscribe(String name, String[] msg_types) ... ;
  class ThreadStateMsg extends Msg {...}
}

interface ComputationDefs extends Remote {
  // empty
}
```

The *ObserverDefs* interface defines two control primitives. Method *start* initializes the model and begins its execution. Initialization data can be passed to the model as a serializable Java object; the actual object type is application dependent. Method *setBreakpoint* is used to suspend and resume execution. If n is positive, the model is suspended the nth time it crosses the corresponding breakpoint statement embedded in its code. Else, if n is zero or negative, model execution is resumed if it is indeed suspended within that breakpoint.

Methods *subscribe* and *unsubscribe* are used by observers to join and respectively leave a model's notification group. An observer must specify its name as well as the type of notification messages it wishes to receive. The base class defines a single notification message *ThreadStateMsg* carrying the state of the model's main execution thread; such a message is sent to observers for each thread state change. Additional messages may be defined to carry application specific state information.

The *ComputationDefs* interface is empty. This is because the actual messages exchanged between the models of a computation are a priori unknown. It is the application programmers who must define these messages when they design the each model interface as part of an entire computation. The empty interface nevertheless exists to underline that the communication between models should be defined via a separate interface, not as a part of the *ObserverDefs* interface.

The *Model* class also exports a few methods to be used by programmers to implement application specific behavior of model subclasses. The most important primitives are shown below:

```
abstract class Model implements ... {
  abstract void run();
  protected void breakpoint(String label);
  ...
  protected void notifyObservers() ... ;
  protected MsgCenter getMsgCenter() ... ;
}
```

Method *run* is an abstract method embodying the main execution thread of the model, and is invoked only once, when the model is started. This method must be implemented to perform the model's calculation. Method *breakpoint* is to be placed within run in locations where it is desirable to interrupt model execution via the corresponding control interface call. Several breakpoints with different labels can be placed within the main execution thread of a model.

Method *notifyObservers* is an up-call, invoked from within the base class code whenever the state of the main execution thread changes. The default implementation is to send a *ThreadStateMsg* notification to the observers of the model. This method can be overridden to send additional (state) information, if desired. Subclasses can send messages to a model's observer group via the messaging interface, which is obtained with a call to *getMsgCenter*.

3.2 Application Development – A Simple Example

Application development in ADIOS is a well-defined stepwise process. First, the application-specific interactions between the various components of the computation must be specified. Novel control, notification, and inter-model coordination aspects are introduced by augmenting the existing interfaces with new methods and messages, refining the corresponding protocols. This design task can be completed without lingering on the internals of each component; legacy code considerations could, however, pose some restrictions as to what is practically feasible. Then, each component can be implemented, as a subclass of the *Model* class, and tested in isolation by different teams. In a final phase, the components are connected to each other to form a distributed computation.

The development of user interface and visualization tools for a given metacomputation can commence as soon as the corresponding model definitions are complete. Due to the design of the system, an interface can be implemented even after the various models are developed. Also, several different analysis tools can be connected to a metacomputation at the same time without interfering with each other.

As an example, suppose we were to develop a simulation of a system with two 'planets' circling around a stationary 'sun', as depicted in Figure 2. This computation involves two models, calculating planet movement and exchanging positioning data with each other. For simplicity, we assume a common coordinate and time reference system between models. Also, suppose that users should be able to start the computation and continuously monitor the planets' trajectories. It should also be possible for the users to halt the simulation, modify the velocity of either planet, and continue with its execution.

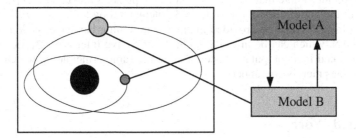

Fig. 2. Sketch of a metacomputation consisting of two loosely coupled models simulating the behavior of two planets in a closed-world gravitational system.

Designing this application in the ADIOS system translates into giving three definitions: a control method for setting a planet's velocity; a notification message that carries state information relevant to the observers of the simulation; a message with planet position data to be exchanged between models. These definitions can be expressed as extensions of the basic interfaces as follows:

```
interface PlanetObserverDefs extends ObserverDefs {
  // new control primitives
  void setVelocity(float vel_x, float vel_y, float vel_z);

  // new notification messages
  class PlanetStateMsg extends Msg {...}
}

interface PlanetComputationDefs extends ComputationDefs {
  // new data exchange messages
  class PlanetPosMsg extends Msg {...}
}
```

Each model must perform the actual calculation, complying with the agreed specification. A sketch of a possible implementation is given below:

```
class PlanetModel extends Model ... {
  ...
  void run() {
    ...
    MsgCenter mc=getMsgCenter();
    while (true) {
      mc.sendObservers(new PlanetStateMsg(...));
      mc.send(other_planet,new PlanetPosMsg(...));
      PlanetPosMsg m=(PlanetPosMsg)mc.receive(other_planet);
      // here comes the code for calculating the new position
      breakpoint("break");
    }
  }
```

It is important to note that the calculation of the planet's movement (appearing as a comment in the code) does not need to be implemented by the *PlanetModel* class or even using Java. It could be provided in any programming language, such as C, C++, or FORTRAN, which can be invoked via the Java Native Interface [23]. Legacy code can be integrated in a computation according to the same principle, in which case the model becomes merely a wrapper.

4   Related Work

Much work has been done in metacomputing and several infrastructures have been developed, e.g. Legion [15], Globus [9], and WebFlow/WebVM [4], to name a few.

A common objective of these systems is to allow collections of heterogeneous computing facilities to be used as a single, seamless virtual machine. As a consequence a lot of effort is invested to support resource discovery, binding, efficient resource allocation, object persistence, migration, fault tolerance, security, and language independence. ADIOS is a comparably lightweight system, intended for scientists who wish to swiftly interconnect local programs into a computational grid, using Java as a common 'software bus'. Since ADIOS does not make any restrictive assumptions about object installation and initialization, it could be augmented with interactive and automatic object placement mechanisms. In fact, ADIOS could be introduced as a structuring/communication layer on top of such all-encompassing infrastructures. For example, the so-called 'stationary agents' introduced in [24] as legacy program wrappers are essentially equivalent to ADIOS' model components. ADIOS could be ported on such a mobile agent platform with only a slight adaptation to its communication mechanisms.

While ADIOS lacks extensive programming and runtime support, it advocates a development methodology adhering to a concrete pattern. The aforementioned systems, which aim to serve a wide range of languages and applications, leave many design decisions to the programmer. Further, ADIOS structures the interaction between the components of a computation via Java RMI and typed messages. Developers are thus given guidance as to how to capture the interactions between the various parts of an application, directly in terms of the Java programming language. This is in contrast to other environments such as WebFlow [4] and JavaPorts [11] where the programmer must establish and communicate using TCP/IP channels. Similarly, the Nexus communication library [7] offers an array of message passing interfaces including MPI, which are quite 'low level' requiring language-specific adapters and preprocessors. To achieve interoperability at the message level, even pure Java MPI implementations, e.g. [2], must deal with buffers (i.e. arrays of bytes) rather than Java objects. Notably, ADIOS does not go so far as to provide full distribution transparency like other systems, e.g. Java// [8] and Do! [22]. Therefore the parts of a computation residing on different machines must be identified at the design stage. This is a minor drawback for coarse grain distributed computations where the various components are usually known in advance.

ADIOS enables programmers to instrument model code for the purpose of controlling its execution. Indeed, by combining breakpoints with notification messages it is possible to monitor a distributed computation in interactive step-by-step mode. Similar support is offered by debuggers and monitoring systems, e.g. DARP [1], which usually also come with advanced code instrumentation tools (ADIOS does not provide such tools). Further, the ADIOS system has similarities with groupware and collaborative simulation systems, such as CEV [6], Clock [14], TANGOsim [3]. Their design also heavily relies on the MVC architecture but focuses on centralized applications where state is maintained within a single entity. ADIOS can handle several asynchronously executing entities (models) and achieves fully distributed yet logically consistent monitoring of such a system. Only CAVERN [18], an architecture with focus on collaboration in large virtual spaces, supports an extensive range of distributed server topologies; the pattern proposed in this paper can be viewed as a combination of the "Replicated Homogeneous" and the "Client-server Subgrouping" scheme of CAVERN. Finally, ADIOS does not come with concrete implementations of monitoring and visualization software. Nevertheless, due to its design, any monitoring/visualization kit could be connected to an ADIOS metacomputation as an observer. For the time being, observers must be Java programs.

5 Conclusions and Future Work

Focusing on the main structuring and communication aspects of interactive distributed computations, ADIOS provides developers with both a design pattern and a programming framework. We believe that this dual approach simplifies the implementation of metacomputations considerably. Consisting merely of a few Java classes, ADIOS is a low-cost, portable system. No installation or maintenance of 'yet another' special-purpose runtime environment is required. Thus, ADIOS can serve as a rapid prototyping environment.

As mentioned above, there are quite a few extensions that could be introduced in ADIOS. Recently matured Java technology, e.g. Jini/JavaSpaces and Java Enterprise Java Beans could also be exploited to better integrate ADIOS in the Java development environment. Moreover, application development in ADIOS has many parallels with Aspect Oriented Programming [16]. The computation protocol but more importantly the control and notification protocols could be viewed as *aspects* of a particular application, which must be *interwoven* with existing component code. Thus an interesting endeavor would be to port ADIOS to an aspect-enabled development environment, and combine it with automated wrapper generation tools, e.g. [13]. At least in theory, it would then be possible to automatically produce metacomputation code simply by selecting the appropriate legacy programs and 'wiring' them together via a GUI editor. Scripting languages based on XML could also be used to describe the 'wiring diagrams' of metacomputations in text.

While considering these possibilities, we wish to employ the system in the development of complex applications in order to verify its advantages but also discover its limitations. For this reason, in collaboration with other scientists, we are now considering to use ADIOS in a distributed gas turbine engine simulation environment, described in [12]. We are confident that through this work we will be able to enhance our approach, making the system more attractive to scientists.

References

1. E. Akarsu, G. Fox, and T. Haupt. DAPR: Java-based Data Analysis and Rapid Prototyping Environment for Distributed High Performance Computations. ACM Workshop on Java for High Performance Network Computing, 1998.
2. M. Baker, B. Carpenter, G. Fox, S. Ko, and S. Lim. mpiJava: A Java MPI Interface, 1st UK Workshop on Java for High Performance Network Computing, 1998.
3. L. Beca, G. Cheng, G. Fox, T. Jurga, K. Oszewsk, M. Podgorny, and K. Walczak. Web Technologies for Collaborative Visualization and Simulation. Proceedings of the Eighth SIAM Conference on Parallel Processing for Scientific Computing, 1997. Also available as Technical Report SCCS-786, Syracuse University, NPAC, Syracuse NY, 1997.
4. D. Bhatia, V. Burzevski, M. Camuseva, G. Fox, W. Furmanski, and G. Premchandran. WebFlow – A Visual Programming Paradigm for Web/Java Based Coarse Grain Distributed Computing. Workshop on Java for Computational Science and Engineering, 1996. Also available as Technical Report SCCS-715, Syracuse University, NPAC, Syracuse, NY, June 1995.
5. K. Birman. Replication and Fault-tolerance in the ISIS System. Proceedings, 10th ACM Symposium on Operating System Principles (SOSP), ACM Operating System Review, 19(5) pp.79-86, 1985.
6. M. Boyles, R. Raje, and S. Fang. CEV: Collaborative Environment for Visualization Using Java RMI. ACM Workshop on Java for High Performance Network Computing, 1998.
7. J. Bresnahan, I. Foster, J. Insley, B. Toonen, and S. Tuecke. Communication Services for Advanced Network Applications. Proceedings of the International Conference on Parallel and Distributed Processing Techniques and Applications, Volume IV, pp. 1861-1867, 1999.
8. D. Caromel, W. Klauser and J. Vayssiere. Towards Seamless Computing and Metacomputing in Java. Concurrency Practice and Experience, 10(11--13) pp. 1043-1061, 1998.
9. I. Foster and C. Kesselman. Globus: A Metacomputing Infrastructure Toolkit. International Journal of Supercomputer Applications, 11(2) pp. 115-128, 1997.
10. E. Gamma, R. Helm, R. Johnson, and J. Vlissides. Design Patterns - Elements of Reusable Object-Oriented Software. Addison-Wesley, 1995.
11. D. Galatopoulos and E. Manolakos. Parallel Processing in Heterogeneous Cluster Architectures using JavaPorts. ACM Crossroads special issue on computer architecture, 5(3), 1999.
12. GasTurbnLab Overview. http://www.cs.purdue.edu/research/cse/gasturbn/overview.html
13. V. Getov, P. Gray, S. Mintchev, and V. Sunderam. Multi-Language Programming Environments for High Performance Java Computing. Workshop on Java for High Performance Network Computing, 1998.
14. N. Graham, T. Urnes, and R. Nejabi. Efficient Distributed Implementation of Semi-Replicated Synchronous Groupware. Proceedings of the ACM Symposium on User Interface Software and Technology (UIST'96), ACM Press, Seattle USA, pp. 1-10, 1996.
15. A. Grimshaw, M. Lewis, A. Ferrari, and J. Karpovich. Architectural Support for Extensibility and Autonomy in Wide Area Distributed Object Systems. Technical Report CS-98-12, University of Virginia, 1998.
16. G. Kiczales, J. Lamping, A. Mendhekar, C. Maeda, C. Lopes, J-M. Loingtier, and J. Irwin. Aspect-Oriented Programming. Proceedings of the European Conference on Object-Oriented Programming (ECOOP), Springer Verlag, 1997.
17. G. Krasner and S. Pope. A Cookbook for Using the Model-View-Controller Interface Paradigm. Journal of Object-oriented Programming, 1(3) pp. 26-49, 1988.
18. J. Leigh, A. Johnson, and T. DeFanti. CAVERN: A Distributed Architecture for Supporting Scalable Persistence and Interoperability in Collaborative Virtual Environments. Journal of Virtual Reality Research, Development and Applications, 2(2) pp. 217-237, 1997.

19. J. Leigh, A. Johnson, T. DeFanti, M. Brown, M. Ali, S. Bailey, A. Banerjee, P. Benerjee, J. Chen, K. Curry, J. Curtis, F. Dech, B. Dodds, I. Foster, S. Graser, K. Ganeshan, D. Glen, R. Grossman, R. Heiland, J. Hicks, A. Hudson, T. Imai, M. Khan, A. Kapoor, R. Kenyon, J. Kelso, R. Kriz, C. Lascara, X. Liu, Y. Lin, T. Mason, A. Millman, K. Nobuyuki, K. Park, B. Parod, P. Rajlich, M. Rasmussen, M. Rawlings, D. Robertson, S. Thongrong, R. Stein, K. Swartz, S. Tuecke, H. Wallach, H. Wong, and G. Wheless. A Review of Tele-Immersive Applications in the CAVE Research Network, Proceedings of the IEEE Virtual Reality 2000 International Conference (VR 2000), 1999.
20. S. Lalis. Hermes – Supporting Distributed Programming in a Network of Personal Workstations, Ph.D. Thesis Nr. 10736, Swiss Federal Institute of Technology, 1994.
21. L. Lamport. Time, Clocks and the Ordering of Events in a Distributed System, Communications of the ACM, 21(7) pp. 558-565, 1978.
22. P. Launay and J.-L. Pazat. The Do! Project: Distributed Programming using Java. Workshop on Java for High Performance Network Computing, 1998.
23. S. Liang. The Java Native Method Interface: Programming Guide and Reference. Addison-Wesley, 1998.
24. S. Markus, E. Houstis, A. Catlin, J. Rice, P. Tsompanopoulou, E. Vavalis, D. Gottfried, and K. Su. An Agent-based Netcentric Framework for Multidisciplinary Problem Solving Environments, Technical Report 99-025, Purdue University, 1999.

Mobile Agents Based on Concurrent Constraint Programming[1]

Marek Paralič

Department of Computers and Informatics, Faculty of Electrical Engineering and
Informatics, University of Technology in Kosice, Letna 9, 042 00 Kosice, Slovak Republic
Paralicm@tuke.sk

Abstract. This paper introduces an experimental framework for mobile agents.
It utilizes expressiveness and formal foundation of concurrent constraint
programming to solve the problem of system support for dynamic re-binding of
not transferable resources and inter-agent collaboration based on logic
variables. Proposed solutions make the agent-based programming easier and
more straightforward and on the other hand offer a basis for a more
sophisticated multi-agent system. The framework is implemented in the
Distributed Oz programming language that appears to the programmer as
concurrent, object-oriented language with data-flow synchronization. There are
two implementations of the system – one is based on freely mobile objects and
the other one is based on components (functors).

1 Introduction

The dynamically changeable, networked environment with distributed information
and computation resources is a permanent challenge for new techniques, languages
and paradigms supporting application design for such an environment in a
straightforward way. Perhaps the most promising among the new paradigms is the
mobile agent (MA) paradigm. The basic properties of mobile agents are autonomy
and mobility [18]. MAs are autonomous because of their capability to decide what
locations in a computer network they visit and what actions they take once being
there. This ability is given in the source code of MA (implicit behaviour) or by the
agent's itinerary set dynamically (explicit order). Mobile agents can move between
locations in a network. A location is the basic environment for execution of mobile
agents and therefore an abstraction of the underlying computer network and operating
system. MAs are agents because they are autonomous and they should be able to
cooperate.

Most of today's MA systems offer inter-agent communication. Only a couple of
them (e.g. Concordia[22], Gypsy[10], Mole[1]), however, offer means for agent
coordination too. Other interesting questions to which only little attention is paid in
the current frameworks for designing and running agent-based systems are [11]:
- application-level issues such as the ease of agent programming,

[1] The work described in this paper was supported by the grants Nr. 1/5086/98 and 1/6278/99 of
the Slovak Grant Agency.

J. Gutknecht and W. Weck (Eds.): JMLC 2000, LNCS 1897, pp. 62-75, 2000.

- control and management of agents, and
- dynamic discovery of resources.

In this paper, we present an experimental framework. It proposes a mechanism-level solution for some of the above-identified problems – especially simplifying of agent-based programming (by system support for re-binding of not-transferable resources) and agent coordination and collaboration support (using logic variables). To fulfil these goals the expressiveness and formal foundation of concurrent constraint programming offered by the Distributed Oz programming language is used.

The paper is structured as follows: In Chapter 2 we give an overview of Distributed Oz and Chapter 3 identifies its key properties for mobile computing. In Chapter 4 we introduce our experimental framework, while separately characterizing a mobile agent environment, a mobile agent abstraction and a mobile agent based application. Chapter 5 compares our proposed system to other state of the art MA systems and Chapter 6 concludes the paper.

2 Distributed Oz - Overview

Distributed Oz [8] is a distributed programming language proposed and implemented at DFKI (German Research Center for Artificial Intelligence), SICS (Swedish Institute of Computer Science) and Université catholique de Louvain. The current implementation of Oz is called Mozart and is publicly available at [4]. The foundation for distributed Oz is the language Oz 1, which was designed by Gert Smolka et al. at the Programming Systems Lab, DFKI [21] for fine-grained concurrency and implicit exploitation of parallelism.

The main characteristics of Oz are concurrency, first-class procedures with lexical scoping enabling powerful higher-order programming, logic variables, dynamic typing and constraint programming. The full Oz language is defined by transforming all its statements into a small kernel language – see Fig. 1.

```
S ::= S  S                                                        Sequence
  |  X = f(l₁:Y₁ ... lₙ:Yₙ)  |                                       Value
     X = <number>  |  X = <atom>  |  {NewName X}
  |  local X₁ ... Xₙ in S end  |  X = Y                           Variable
  |  proc {X Y₁ ... Yₙ} S end  |  {X Y₁ ... Yₙ}                  Procedure
  |  {NewCell Y X}  |  {Exchange X Y Z}  |  {Access X Y}            State
  |  if X then S else S end                                     Conditional
  |  thread S end  |  {GetThreadId X}                               Thread
  |  try S catch X then S end  |  raise X end                    Exception
```

Fig. 1. The Oz kernel language

The execution model of Oz consists of a shared store and a number of threads connected to it. Threads reduce their expressions concurrently. The store is partitioned into compartments for constraints, procedures and cells. As computation proceeds, the store accumulates constraints on variables in the constraint store [8].

Distributed Oz (DOz) preserves the language semantics of Oz and defines the distributed semantics for all Oz entities. Oz distinguishes:

- *stateless entities* – records, numbers, procedures and classes,
- *single assignment entities* – logic variables, futures (read-only capability of a logic variable), streams,
- *stateful entities* - cells (updateable mutual binding of a name and a variable), objects, reentrant locks, ports (asynchronous channel for many-to-one communication) and threads,
- *resource* – entities external to the shared store (their references can be passed at will, but the resource can be executed only on its home site).

The execution model of DOz differs from the execution model of Oz only by its partitioning on multiple sites. A site represents a part of a system, whereby each thread, variable, cell and port belongs exactly to one site. Each site is modeled as a number of threads connected to a store, but this store is accessible for any thread (which can be on a different site). Thus, DOz creates a so-called distributed store – the basic communication mechanism. An entity becomes accessible for others threads when it is exported. Exporting means sending out a message with an embedded reference to the entity. Symmetrically every thread imports an entity by receiving a message containing a reference. Distributed semantics defines what exactly happens by exporting and importing an entity for each type of entity. Briefly speaking, stateless entities are replicated and stateful entities can be either stationary or mobile. E.g. a *port* is stationary, so only the threads from the home site can put the message on the stream associated with the port itself. Other threads can only order this operation, which is then executed at the home site of the port. The port is identified by automatically generated references which are created by exporting the port. In contrast to it, mobile entities, such as objects, can move on remote invocation, so the operation is executed locally by the initiator of the operation. In distinction to simulated object mobility (by cloning and redirection) e.g. in Obliq [2], the DOz object do not consume the site resources after moving anymore and the eventual existing references on other sites to this object stay consistent.

The basic synchronization mechanism is data-flow synchronization using variables. Variables are logic variables and represent a reference whose value is initially unknown. There are two basic operations on logic variables: binding and waiting until they are bound. Lexical scoping preserves the unique meaning of each variable system-wide. Besides this, objects are concurrent with explicit re-entrant locking and ports are asynchronous channels for many-to-one communication ordered inside one thread and undeterministic between different threads.

An important feature of DOz is the support of persistent entities. Each stateless entity can be made persistent. That means each thread can save any rooted entity (entity itself and all entities reachable from it) to a file (operation *Pickle.save*) and creates in DOz terminology a *pickel*. Pickles are accessible through URLs. So an entity can outlive the lifetime of the program itself.

3   Distributed Oz Support for Mobile Code Paradigm

The Mozart implementation of the Oz programming language offers the following facilities to support of mobile code paradigm:

- *Freely mobile objects* – default kind of created object consisting of an object record, a class record containing procedures (the methods), a state pointer and a record containing the object's state. If the object is made available to other sites (by handing over a reference to it), distributed structure of proxies and one manager at the home site is transparently created. The only migrating part of the object is its state, because the class record is transferred to a site only once. The invocation of an object method at a site causes this migration if the state is not available locally [19]. The object record and the class record cannot be changed.
- *Conversion of Oz data and byte sequence by Pickles* – it is possible to save any stateless data structure to a file (identified by URL) that can be loaded later.
- *First-class modules* - functors (syntactic support of module specifications) can be dynamically linked and installed by module managers. There are two types of functors: compiled (obtained by executing a compilation of a functor definition) and computed (obtained by executing compiled functors whose definitions contain nested functor definitions) [3]. The advantage of computed functors is that they can have lexical bindings to all data structures supplied to their definitions by created compiled functors.
- *Heterogeneity* – the Mozart implementation of Oz offers compilers and emulators for different platforms (Linux, Solaris, Windows 9x/NT,...).
- *High-level communication* – applications can offer access to their entities by generating and passing a *ticket* (string reference to a data unit inside a running application) to any other Oz application and so establish a high-level communication connection between them.

4   System Description

The main goal of our experimental system for support of mobile agents is to combine the power of high-level distributed programming support with the mobile agent paradigm. As was shown in the previous sections, Mozart offers simultaneously the advantage of a *True Distributed System* and the means for building a *Mobile Code System* [17]. In the following subsections the experimental framework will be introduced: mobile agent environment built from servers and its services, key properties of mobile agent as programming entity and the methodology of building an agent-based application in our framework.

4.1   Mobile Agent Environment

The basic functions offered by a mobile agent environment are transport and management of agents. In today's agent systems like Aglets[14], Ara[16], Grasshopper[9], Gypsy[10]or Voyager[13], these services are offered by servers, which must be installed and running on every host computer that should be available for the mobile agents. Similarly our experimental framework in DOz contains two common modules: a *MAE* and *MaeAdmin*. Running the MAE functor on a host computer makes a basic environment for mobile agents available, whereby MaeAdmin is an optional administration tool. MAE offers the following functionality:

- Creation of a mobile agent with a unique identity,
- transport of an agent,
- sending a message to an agent (possibly on another host),
- getting the status information about an agent,
- system recovery after crash and
- foreign agents acceptance in case of running as docking server.

MAE in the current implementation of the system can be started only once per host computer. Therefore the unique identity of an agent can be achieved by combining the local name of an agent and the IP address of the host computer. Every agent created on a local MAE is a *home agent* for this MAE. On all other sites it will visit, it gains the status of a *foreign agent*. The MAE stores information about its entire home agents and currently available foreign agents in local database. The information about foreign agents is stored in the system only during time between the successful receiving from the previous host and successful sending an agent to the next one. The distributed architecture of MAE is shown in Fig. 2.

For the programmer of mobile agent based application, the mobile agent environment is represented by the MAE module, which must be imported. Importing a MAE module causes either the launching of a new environment, recovering with initialization values from persistent database for home and foreign agents and already connected other MAE servers after crash or getting a reference to an already started MAE local server. The last process is realized also by resuming every incoming mobile agent. Thus, an agent gets access to the key services of the mobile agent environment. The possibility of dynamic loading and installation of first-class modules is thereby very important. Beside the loading and connecting of the local MAE module the process of resuming of an MA includes:

- updating the agent's information about the current location,
- setting appropriate task for the current location,
- creating a new agent port for the high-level Oz communication and starting the service on it,
- adding information into the database of foreign agents,
- setting the appropriate application interface (see next subsection),
- sending a commitment to the previous site (if all steps were successful) and
- sending a log message to the owner of the agent (information about current location).

The agent migration in the first implementation of the proposed system was based on freely mobile objects, whereby an agent was implemented as an object derived from a special class (task-based agent). By giving over a reference to the agent (that is automatically generated when an agent is given on an Oz port), the underlying distributed object migration protocol [19], [20] causes the serialization and transportation of the object (i.e. agent) state. If the compiled code of the agent class is not available at the destination host (which is unique in the whole Oz space because of Oz internal names), this class is transferred too. This implementation was very straightforward and it fully utilized advanced Distributed Oz features, but supposed on-line connection with agent home server during the transport from one host to another.

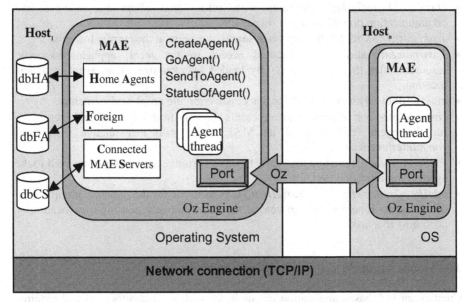

Fig. 2. Distributed mobile agent environment structure

In the current implementation (component based) the agent is an object too, but by each move the agent's class and current data state are separately saved and transported. This adopts the persistent procedure mechanism to enable independence from home server and system recovery after crash without the need for destroying all foreign and home agents present on the crashed location. The process of resuming an agent after move is in this solution extended for creating a new object of agent class and restoring the last data state from transported persistent data. In the next chapters we will consider the second implementation.

The communication between MAEs is realized in two layers: the first layer uses TCP sockets for exchanging of tickets for Oz ports. Oz ports then build a second, high-level communication layer, which can take advantage of Oz space data transparency. The Oz space offers the possibility to transparent copying of stateless entities and creating references for worldwide unique stateful entities. These possibilities can be fully utilized especially by the inter-agent communication.

4.2 Mobile Agents

Mobile agents in our framework are objects derived from a special class *MobileAgent* that offers the basic facilities expected by the MAE from agents. There are several features, attributes and methods of this class. The most important are:

- *Name*: attribute with the local unique name at the agent's home MAE,
- *Itinerary*: attribute with a list of *host/message* pairs with hosts that should be visited by the mobile agent and the first message, that it will receive there,
- *AgentTicket*: attribute with a ticket to an agent specific Oz port for incoming messages from other agents/applications,

- *Owner, OwnerTicket*: attributes with information about the address and communication port of the agent owner site,
- *Task*: attribute with the first message sent to the agent at the current location,
- *Environment*: attribute represented access to the local, application-specific resources after they are successfully loaded by resuming of an agent at a new location,
- *mae*: attribute with the current local accessible mobile agent environment,
- *commonInterface*: attribute that represents the path to dynamic loadable resources for the agent (consisting of an MAE home path and relative path from *commInterface* feature),
- *runServeStream*: a method that starts to serve current agent stream connected to the agent communication port,
- *addIItem, removeIItemL, removeIItemTask*: methods for the dynamic modification of the agents itinerary (add an item at the end, remove according to a location or according to a task).

4.3 Mobile Agent (MA) Based Applications

Creating an MA-based application in our framework is straightforward and requires only the following steps:

1• Identifying all fixed, not transferable resources needed by the application (i.e. their type) by means of abstract names and identifying parts of the transferable agent state.
2• Design and implementation of application-specific classes which are derived from the *MobileAgent* class and deal with agent state and other resources through their abstract names.
3• Designing and implementing an application that creates one or more instances of mobile agents, specifies their itinerary, sends them away, waits until they finish their jobs (or until the owner stops their work), and processes the results.
4• Design and installation of special environment modules (functors) in a compiled form which map the abstract sources of MA to the real local resources of the host computer, that should enable the execution of the MA based application.

Now let us see the process of designing and implementation an MA-based application in more detail on a simple example: information search agent. Suppose we are ice-hockey fans and we are interested in the current rating of NHL players – especially to find the player with the highest score rate.

In the first step, we identify the not transferable resources and what should be stored in agent state as the current result. In our case we will suppose that the visited host will own a database containing a table with information about NHL players. Furthermore we will suppose that one row of such a table contains at least columns with the player's name, the name of his club, his current score rate, assistance number and resulting point rate. So we will use abstract resource *data*, as a recordset the items of which will have the following fields: *player, team, score, assistance* and *points* corresponding to identified needed information. As a result we can store the whole record about the player with the current best score.

In the second step, we implement a class called *SearchNHL* (for source code See appendix A.1) which inherits from the *MobileAgent* class imported from the functor stored on the *mobileAgent.ozf* file. This class has an attribute *Result*, help attribute *maxScore* for storing the maximal current score rate in numerical form and three methods:

- *search()* searches in local database bounded to inherited attribute *environment* at field *data* and after simple comparison of current item with up to now highest score. If needed, the mobile agent updates the *Result* and *maxScore* attributes. After querying the whole database, the mobile agent will go to the next location according to its itinerary.
- *init()* sets itinerary and relative path to the functor responsible for loading not transferable resources.
- *getResult()* makes the result available to the outside of the agent,
- *setData(), getData()* application-specific methods for saving and restoring agent data state.

In the third step we write the code (See appendix A.2) that loads modules MAE and SearchNHL, creates an agent with name *myFirstAgent* and sends it to two host computers: *pent22.infosys.tuwien.ac.at* and *w5.infosys.tuwien.ac.at*. The mobile agent has the same job on both computers: searching the local database of NHL players and finding the player with the best score. After the agent returns, application presents the whole information about the best player together with the host's address where the result came from.

In the last step we should „install" our distributed application. There are only two conditions for correct functioning of the MA-based application. The first one is running and accessible mobile agent environment on the destination host computer. The second one is availability of module for loading of not transferable resources. Modules are specified by functors, which can import other modules and export any Oz entities. So we have to write a functor, that binds abstract resource identified by the name *data* on the real data source with information about NHL players. In our example, for simplicity, the information is saved as an Oz persistent entity – pickle. So our environment functors load pickled entity from specified and for every host unique URL and bind it to the exported entity data. Environment functors can load any available system resource (e.g. *Browser* module for displaying log information on every host) too. The source code for module specification available at *pent22* is listed in appendix A.3 and for *w5* host in appendix A.4.

5   Comparison to Other State-of-the-Art Solutions

Basic functions of mobile agent environments (in today's mobile agent systems represented by agent servers) are identified by the Mobile Agent System Interoperability Facility (MASIF) [12] and include:

- transferring an agent, which can include initiating an agent transfer, receiving an agent, and transferring classes,
- creating an agent,

- providing globally unique agent names,
- supporting the concept of a region,
- finding a mobile agent,
- ensuring a secure environment for agent operation.

Our experimental mobile agent environment in Distributed Oz offers all these basic functionalities except for the explicit support of regions (that could be added in a straightforward way). The security of agent execution is in the current implementation at basic level based on language mechanism of lexical scoping. Solving of this complex problem was not the main goal of our experimental framework and goes beyond the scope of this paper. On the other hand there are several facilities which overlap the functionality of current mobile agent systems. The most important two are: system support for dynamic re-binding of not transferable resources and utilization of logic variables to powerful data-synchronization and agent group communication.

5.1 System Support for Dynamic Re-binding of Not Transferable Resources

As it is pointed in [11] little attention is paid to application-level issues such as the ease of agent programming, control and management of agents and dynamic discovery of resources. The dynamic re-binding of not transferable resources at the MA system level is a small contribution that makes agent programming easier and represents a basis for dynamic discovery of system-specific resources. Simplification of agent programming resides on the following facts:

- The programmer has to identify the type of used resources in the design phase of an MA-based application and can debug the application on local available resources.
- An MA-based application does not require to be programmed in two separate parts: mobile agent and location like *context* in Aglets, *location services* in Ara, *place* in Gypsy or *service bridges* in Concordia.
- The installation of „server side" MA-based applications requires only to make the right connection between abstract date used in the interface and real data of the needed type.
- Data-based design of an MA application is more stable than if it would be tightly connected to services offered on needed data.

The combination of this mechanism and Distributed Oz feature that makes all stateful entities accessible through tickets and stateless entities through pickels builds a basis for dynamic discovery of system-specific resources. At the time of creating loadable server side modules the application one need not know which entity will be accessible after loading a pickel or taking a ticket.

5.2   Agent Group Communication and Data-Flow Synchronization Based on Logic Variables

In current MA systems the communication is usually supported at the level of synchronous or asynchronous message passing (e.g. Aglets, Concordia or Voyager). The agent coordination and collaboration is in today's system supported on a very low level or not at all. The exceptions are e.g. Concordia, Gypsy and Mole. Concordia offers the mechanisms of distributed events (selected and group-oriented) and strong or weak model of collaboration. By collaboration a group of *CollaboratorAgents* can share a reference to distributed *AgentGroup* object. AgentGroup collects results of a whole group and enables making a synchronous meeting for agents from its group where each agent can process the relevant part of the common results. Unlike the Concordia Gypsy offers *Supervisor-Worker* agents, implementing the master-slave pattern. The supervisor agent can be seen as a kind of container agent that carries and maintains the tasks. To coordinate more worker-agents, the supervisor uses a *Constraint Manager* to analyze the task constraints. System Mole supports sessions-oriented one-to-one communication by *RMI* and *Messaging* session objects and anonymous group communication based on events. Events are objects of a specific type containing some information. They are generated by the producers and transferred to the consumers which share common knowledge. Dependencies within agent groups are modeled using synchronization objects, which depending on input events, internal rules, state information and timeout intervals generate appropriate output events.

Our experimental framework utilizes the logic variables of DOz to enable control of the agent life cycle and inter-agent collaboration. By owner we mean the MA-based application that launches a mobile agent. In the current state the system owner can use the *StatusOfAgent* MAE procedure to check if the agent has already finished its job. Every thread applying this procedure to an agent object will be blocked until the agent finishes its job and binds the *endJob* feature (feature is object member like an attribute, but can be bound to a value only once) to the *unit* value.

Functionality of Concordia's distributed events can be reached in this way too. The programmer can define for any kind of event a special logic variable and store it in the agent's attribute. The value check of such a variable will block all checking thread (owner and all Oz sites, which received a reference from the owner). The computation will then continue immediately after the agent binds the variable at some location in the network to some value. Variables can be indirectly transported as stateless tickets and on the next location can be taken within the process of agent resuming. Dynamic grouping of agents or applications can be achieved by sharing the reference to a variable representing a specific event or result. At the system level for example one can add very easily another procedure *GetFinalResult()*, which can wait until the agent binds the final result (e.g. attribute *Result* of our example NHL MA on its last visited site) and save the last migration of the agent.

Unlike Concordia's *AgentGroup* the collaboration based on DOz logic variables does not need synchronous meet on the same location and unlike Gypsy Supervisor agent it does not bring the implementation overhead (heavy weight agents). Moreover by such group creation programmer can focus on the data to be exchanged and not on the structure that enables it (like e.g. in Mole).

6   Conclusions

In this paper we have presented an experimental framework for mobile agents implemented in a concurrent constraint based language (Distributed Oz). Distributed Oz offers several high level mechanisms for building a full featured mobile agent based system, especially freely mobile objects, dynamically loadable first-class modules and logic variables efficiently implemented by the on-line Distributed Unification algorithm[6]. These mechanisms are used to support dynamic re-binding of not transferable resources at the system level and for group communication/collaboration. This solution represents a good basis for designing more sophisticated MA-based application using a flexible agent hierarchy.

Acknowledgments

This papers was written during my research stay at the Distributed System Group (Technical University of Vienna) and I wish to thank all my colleagues at DSG, especially Mehdi Jazayeri, Wolfgang Lugmayr, Engin Kirda and Thomas Gschwind. The stay at the DSG was supported by the Aktion Österreich – Slowakei, founded by Austrian and Slovak Republics. I would like also to thank my supervisor, Prof. Milan Krokavec, for his help and encouragement during my PhD study.

References

1.   Baumann, J., Hohl, F., Rothermel, K., Straßer, M.: Mole - Concepts of a Mobile Agent System. WWW Journal, Special issue on Applications and Techniques of Web Agents (1998) Vol. 1(3) 123-137
2.   Cardelli, L.: A Language with Distributed Scope. Computing Systems. (1995) 8(1) 27-59
3.   Duchier, D., Kornstaedt, L., Schulte, Ch., Smolka, G.: A Higher-order Module discipline with separate Compilation, Dynamic Linking, and Pickling. Technical Report, Programming Systems Lab, DFKI and Universität des Saarlandes (1998)
4.   The Mozart Programming System, Deutsches Forschungszentrum für Künstliche Intelligenz GmbH, Universität des Saarlandes. Swedish Institute of Computer Science, Université catholique de Louvain, http://www.mozart-oz.org (1999)
5.   Haridi, S., Franzen, N.: Tutorial of Oz. Technical Report, in Mozart documentation, availale at http://www.mozart-oz.org (1999)
6.   Haridi, S., Roy, P.V., Brand, P., Mehl, M., Scheidhauer, R., Smolka, G.: Efficient Logic Variables for Distributed Computing. ACM Transactions on Programming Languages and Systems. To appear (2000)
7.   Haridi, S., Roy, P.V., Brand, P., Schulte, Ch.: Programming Languages for distributed Applications. New Generation Computing (1998) Vol. 16(3) 223-261
8.   Haridi, S., Roy, P.V., Smolka, G.: An Overview of the Design of Distributed Oz. In: Proceedings of the 2nd Intl. Symposium on Parallel Symbolic Computation (PASCO '97). Maui, Hawaii, USA, July 1997. ACM Press, New York (1997) 176-187
9.   IKV++ GmbH Informations- und Kommunikationssysteme: Grasshopper The Agent Platform – Technical Overview (1999)

10. Jazayeri, M., Lugmayr, W.: Gypsy: A Component-based Mobile Agent System. Accepted for 8th Euromicro Workshop on Parallel and Distributed Processing (PDP2000). Rhodos, Greece, 19. –21. January (2000)
11. Karnik, N.M., Tripathi, A.R.: Design Issues in Mobile-Agent Programming Systems. IEEE Concurrency (July-September 1998) 52-61
12. Milojcic, D., Breugst, M., Busse, I., Campbell, J., Covaci, S., Friedman, B., Kosaka, K., Lange, D., Ono, K., Oshima, M., Tham, C., Virdhagriswaran, S., White, J.: MASIF: The OMG Mobile Agent System Interoperability Facility. In: Proceedings of the Second International Workshop, Mobile Agents '98. Springer-Verlag (1998)
13. ObjectSpace, Inc.: ObjectSpace Voyager: ORB 3.0 Developer Guide (1999)
14. Oshima, M., Karjoth, G., Ono, K.: Aglets Specification (1.1). IBM Corporation (1998)
15. Paralic, M., Krokavec, M.: New Trends in Distributed Programming. In: Proceedins of IEEC'97, Oradea, Romania (1997)
16. Peine, H., Stolpmann, T.: The Architecture of Ara Platform for Mobile Agents. In: Proceedings of the First International Workshop on Mobile Agents, MA'97, Berlin. Lecture Notes in Computer Science, Vol. 1219. Springer Verlag (1997). Also published In: Mobility: Processes, Computers, and Agents. ed. by Milojicic, D., Douglis, F., Wheeler, R., Addison-Wesley and the ACM Press (1999) 474-483
17. Picco, G.P.: Understanding, Evaluating, Formalizing, and Exploiting Code Mobility. PhD thesis, Dipartimento di Automatica e Informatica, Politecnico di Torino, Italy (1998)
18. Rothermel, K., Hohl, F., Radouniklis, N.: Mobile Agent Systems: What is Missing? In: Proceedings of International Working Conference on Distributed Applications and Interoperable Systems DAIS'97 (1997)
19. Roy, P.V., Brand, P., Haridi, S., Collet, R.: A Lightweight Reliable Object Migration Protocol. Lecture Notes in Computer Science, Vol. 1686. Springer Verlag (1999)
20. Roy, P.V., Haridi, S., Brand, P., Smolka, G., Mehl, M., Scheidhauer, R.: Mobile Objects in Distributed Oz. ACM Transactions on Programming Languages and Systems, Vol. 19(5) (1997) 804-851
21. Smolka, G.: The Oz programming model. Computer Science Today. Lecture Notes in Computer Science, Vol. 1000. Springer Verlag, Berlin (1995) 324-343
22. Wong, D., Paciorek, N., Walsh, T., DiCelie, J., Young, M., Peet, B.(Mitsubishi Electric ITA): Concordia: An Infrastructure for Collaborating Mobile Agents. In: Proceedings of the First International Workshop on Mobile Agents, MA'97, Berlin. Lecture Notes in Computer Science, Vol. 1219 (1997)

Appendix:

A.1   nhl.oz

```
functor
 import
  Ma at '../../agent/mobileAgent.ozf'
 export
  SearchNHL
 define
  class SearchNHL from Ma.mobileAgent
     attr
          maxScore
          Result

     meth  init(Name Itinerary Owner OwnerTicket)
          Ma.mobileAgent,init(Name Itinerary Owner
OwnerTicket)
```

```
            Ma.mobileAgent.commInterface =
'/appMA/NHL/envir.ozf'
            maxScore <- 0
      end

      meth search()
          proc {FindMax X}
             if {String.toInt X.score} > @maxScore then
                Result <- f(player:X where:@location)
                maxScore <- {String.toInt
@Result.player.score}
             else  skip  end
          end
      in
          {ForAll @environment.data FindMax}
          {@mae.goAgent self}
      end

      meth getResult(?X)    X = @Result     end

      meth getData(?X)    X = f(@maxScore @Result)     end

      meth setData(X)
          maxScore <- X.1
          Result <- X.2
      end
   end
end
```

A.2   nhlApp.oz

```
  functor
   import
     Mae at '../../server/mae.ozf'
     SearchNHL at 'nhl2.ozf'
   define
     NA  Out  Admin
   in
     NA = {Mae.createAgent  SearchNHL.searchNHL
           myFirstAgent
           f(dest:"pent22.infosys.tuwien.ac.at" task:
  search)| f(dest:"w5.infosys.tuwien.ac.at" task:
  search)| nil}
     Admin = {Mae.mAE_server getAdminServerTool($)}
     {Admin message('Created agent: '#{NA getName($)})}
     {Mae.goAgent NA}
     Out = {Mae.returnAgent NA}
     if Out == 'a' then
        local R in
           R = {NA getResult($)}
           {Admin message("\nSearch results:\n\tteam:
  "#{VirtualString.toAtom R.player.team}#
  "\n\tplayer: "#{VirtualString.toAtom R.player.player}#
  "\n\tscore: "#{VirtualString.toAtom R.player.score}#
```

```
"\n\tassistance: "#{VirtualString.toAtom
R.player.assistance}#
"\n\tpoints: "#{VirtualString.toAtom R.player.points}#
"\n\twhere: "#{VirtualString.toAtom R.where}#"\n")}
      end
   else
      {Admin message("\nNo data found.")}
   end
end
```

A.3   envir.oz (at pent22.infosys.tuwien.ac.at)

```
functor
 import    Pickle
 export    Data
 define
   Data = {Pickle.load
'c:\\users\\paralicm\\mas\\appMA\\nhl\\Db2.src'}
end
```

A.4   envir.oz (at w5. infosys.tuwien.ac.at)

```
functor
 import    Pickle
 export    Data
 define
   Data = {Pickle.load
'/home/studs/paralicm/mas/appMA/NHL/Db1.src'}
end
```

Rethinking Our Trade and Science: From Developing Components to Component-Based Development

Clemens Szyperski

Microsoft Research, One Microsoft Way, Redmond WA 98052, USA
cszypers@microsoft.com

Almost all of traditional software engineering and applied computer science focuses on some kind of deliverable of supposedly closed nature. While traditional applications aren't really closed (they interact with other applications, middleware, and the operating system), the closed-world assumption is nevertheless a sufficiently useful approximation to enable the production of successful software. Shifting the emphasis from the production of the one deliverable to the production of systems that are composed out of components has an almost traumatic consequence. A lot of what we know about how to build software requires revision and sometimes radical departure from the established past. This talk spans much of the spectrum from why components are a good idea to why we need to rethink our trade and science to what approaches are now emerging to make all this possible.

J. Gutknecht and W. Weck (Eds.): JMLC 2000, LNCS 1897, p. 76, 2000.
© Springer-Verlag Berlin Heidelberg 2000

Franz Achermann and Oscar Nierstrasz

Software Composition Group, University of Berne[1]

Abstract. A namespace is a mapping from labels to values. Most programming languages support different forms of namespaces, such as records, dictionaries, objects, environments, packages and even keyword-based parameters. Typically only a few of these notions are first-class, leading to arbitrary restrictions and limited abstraction power in the host language. Piccola is a small language that unifies various notions of namespaces as first-class *forms*, or extensible, immutable records. By making namespaces explicit, Piccola is easily able to express various abstractions that would normally require more heavyweight techniques, such as language extensions or meta-programming.

1   Introduction

Virtually all programming languages support various notions of namespaces, or sets of bindings of labels to values. These include:

- **Interface**. Objects have a set of named methods.
- **Scopes**. Identifiers are bound in the enclosing static or dynamic scope.
- **Package**. A package provides a set of named services or components.
- **Keyword-based parameters**. Arguments to services are bound by keywords instead of position.

Typically, however, these notions are supported in different ways by a language, and each carries its own restrictions. This leads to a number of problems like *inflexible namespaces*, *frozen scoping rules*, and *limited abstraction*.

Inflexible Namespaces

An inflexible namespace can lead to name clashes. In open systems where components may be added or replaced at runtime, name clashes between components from different applications, domains, or vendors can cause system failures. The following lists symptoms that are due to inflexible namespaces:

- **Flat namespace**s. In older versions of Smalltalk, all classes must have unique names. To avoid name clashes, developers must follow naming conventions. Smalltalk Agent was one of the first Smalltalk implementations that provided namespaces. Now, most Smalltalk systems support namespaces. Similarly, classic C++ has one static namespace. Standard C++ [6] introduces namespaces as an additional language feature.

---

[1]   *Authors' address:* Institut für Informatik (IAM), Universität Bern, Neubrückstrasse 10, CH-3012 Berne, Switzerland. *Tel:* +41 (31) 631.4618. *Fax:* +41 (31) 631.3965. *E-mail:* {acherman, oscar}@iam.unibe.ch.

WWW: http://www.iam.unibe.ch/~scg.

J. Gutknecht and W. Weck (Eds.): JMLC 2000, LNCS 1897, pp. 77-89, 2000.

classes. Packages are nested, but inflexible. Two frameworks which — by chance — use the same package names, cannot be merged. The "solution" is to propose (internet wide) unique package naming conventions.

- **Restricted Scoping**. Python [14] has only three kinds of namespaces: one for global objects, one for class scope, and one for local block invocations. Although functions are first class values in Python, nested functions do not have closures. However, closures can be simulated by specifying values as default arguments.

- **Static Services**. Normally the run time environment (or the operating system) provides some static services. These services include printing to the console or accessing the local disk. These services normally operate within an implicit context. For example, the context defines where standard output should go (to the console or to a file), or the GUI context contains the look and feel of the user interface. It is in general notpossible to adjust this context only for certain parts of an application. For instance, a developer might wish to redirect output of some threads to the console, while other threads may output to the null device.

Frozen Scoping Rules

Most modern languages use static scoping. Identifiers are visible within the block where they are declared and may also be visible in blocks that are statically (i.e. textually) nested within that block. Identifiers in the scope of a module or package can be exported to be used in other modules.

In contrast to these statically scoped languages there exist languages with dynamic scoping, like Postscript. Identifiers are looked up following the call stack. Dynamic scoped language are often considered less safe to use and require more care to program in. However, there are also abstractions implemented in dynamically scoped languages that are hard or clumsy to implement in statically scoped languages. Such abstractions include properties that do not align with the functional structure and cannot be localized in modular units. Examples include failure handling, synchronization and coordination.

Limited Abstraction

The fact that namespaces are not available at runtime limits arbitrarily the expressive power of abstractions. A typical symptom of limited abstraction is programmers having to write a lot of boilerplate code. Examples of desirable abstractions include:

- A generic synchronization wrapper that wraps all the methods of an object to run in mutually exclusive mode. The inability to abstract over all methods of an object (in Java, for example) forces us to define a subclass that overrides each method to include the same synchronization code.

- An abstraction to generate proxies. A common use of proxies is to make distribution transparent. The proxy has the same interface as the original server object, but delegates all calls to the server object over the network. The proxy has similar code for all methods: it transfers arguments over the network, invokes the remote service, and waits for the result. For instance in Java RMI, the tool `rmic` automatically creates RMI proxies for remote objects out of their object code. But it is not possible to program the functionality of this tool directly in Java, without reading and writing Java bytecode. The reflection support in `java.lang.reflect` only allows one to inspect code, but not to change it.

present Piccola, a small language that introduces explicit namespaces as forms. We illustrate how forms overcome the problems we have listed. In section 3 we present two applications of dynamic namespaces that demonstrate how the uniform treatment of explicit namespaces allows simple abstractions to be implemented in Piccola that would require more heavyweight approaches such as metaprogramming or compiler extensions in other languages. Finally, the last two sections present related and future work.

2 Piccola

Piccola is designed to be a general purpose "composition language" [1][2]. That is, it is designed as a language for composing software components which may be written in a separate implementation language. Piccola's job is to express how components are configured, and to provide the connectors, coordination abstractions and glue abstractions needed to configure components. As such, the problems listed in the introduction are especially important for Piccola. We tackle these problems by unifying all related notions of namespaces as *forms* (immutable, extensible records):

Everything is a Form

Namespaces, contexts, interfaces, parameters, abstractions, scripts and objects are all modelled as forms. This unification leads to an extremely simple language, and allows us to abstract uniformly over all these related concepts.

Static and Dynamic Namespaces

Both client and server contexts are explicitly named, giving abstractions a fine degree of control over both static and dynamic scoping.

Explicit Namespaces

Namespaces can be explicitly manipulated and composed, making it quite a simple matter to combine, rename and compose packages or modules.

Keyword-Based Parameters

Abstractions are monadic, always taking a single form as a parameter, and returning a form (which possibly encapsulates an abstraction). First class arguments extend the expressiveness of abstractions.

2.1 Separation of Concerns

Structure in Piccola is modelled by *forms*. *State* is modelled by *channels*, which are used to store forms. *Behaviour* is modelled by *agents*, which communicate by sending and receiving forms through shared channels. *Abstraction* is provided by *services*, which are implemented by agents and channels.

Forms

Forms are finite mappings from labels (identifiers) to values. Forms are immutable. The primitive operators on forms are *extension*, *projection*, and *iteration* over the labels of a form. Form extension concatenates a form with either a single binding or another form, yielding a new form as a result. Projection looks up a value bound by a label in a form. Iteration over a form returns the set of defined labels in a form. (Sets are objects, which are encoded as forms.)

A form in Piccola is defined by a *script*, which is a sequence of bindings and form-expressions. Form-expressions are structured using parentheses or indentation, and separated using commas or newlines, in the style of Python. The comma or

```
aForm =
        aSubForm = ()              # a nested form
        aService(X): X             # service definition
        r(count = 3)               # form expression
```

The form `aForm` contains the labels `aSubForm`, `aService`, and all the labels that are returned by invoking the service `r`. If `r()` returns a form with label `aSubForm` or `aService`, these bindings will hide the bindings that precede the invocation. The service `r` is invoked with the argument form `count = 3`.

Channels

State is represented by *channels*. Channels have the semantics of locations in the asynchronous p-calculus [16]. Using channels, we can model blackboards, locks, reference cells etc. The semantics of Piccola is given in terms of the pL-calculus [13], a variant of the p-calculus in which agents communicate forms instead of tuples.

Agents

Agents implement the behaviour of a Piccola program. Agents communicate along channels and exchange forms. Unlike forms, agents and channels do not appear in the syntax of Piccola, but they can be directly instantiated, if necessary, by means of the predefined services `run` and `newChannel`.

Services

A service represents a function or procedure. It is represented by a replicated agent that reads from a channel (the service location) and evaluates a form as its result. The service-protocol specifies how the result channel gets passed from the caller to the callee [15][21]. Piccola has only four keywords, two of which are needed to define services. The value returned by a service may be denoted by **return**. A recursively-defined service must be declared with **def**, which constructs a fixpoint.

2.2   Static and Dynamic Namespaces

Piccola is statically scoped, and the static context of an agent is always explicitly accessible as a form called **root**. The dynamic namespace of a calling agent, however, is also available to the service invoked as a form called **dynamic**. (**root** and **dynamic** are the other two keywords of Piccola.)

Labels used in a script are normally looked up in the **root** form, and bindings will extend the **root** form. For example, this binding defines a service newDocument:

```
newDocument(X): wrap(newBasicDocument(X))
```

Agents evaluating form expressions textually below this binding have the identifier newDocument in their **root** form. More explicitly, we could also extend the **root** form to include the definition of the service newDocument:

```
(1) root =
(2)       root
(3)       newDocument(X): wrap(newBasicDocument(X))
```

This statement is read as follows: Replace the **root** form with a new form (Line 1). The new form is indented. It is the current **root** form (Line 2) extended with the service newDocument (Line 3).

Lookup of identifiers is done in the **root** form. Therefore, the body of the newDocument service is equivalent to:

```
root.wrap(root.newBasicDocument(root.X))
```

root namespace of the agent implementing the body of the service. Note that the argument label x is only defined in the **root** form of the service body.

The static scoping offered by these conventions is fine for most purposes, but some kinds of abstractions can only be conveniently implemented with the help of dynamic scoping. The **dynamic** namespace of an agent contains whatever is explicitly put there, and is passed automatically whenever the agent invokes a service. The following myPrintln service includes the current user in its output:

```
myPrintln(Text): println(dynamic.user + ":" + Text)
```

A caller of this service may change its dynamic namespace to include the current user:

```
dynamic = (user = "John")        # change dynamic
myPrintln("Hello")               # invoke service
```

Note that the dynamic namespace does not break encapsulation. Values that are not put into this form remain local. The dynamic namespace is useful for passing implicit information between agents, but it should not be misused as an alternative to explicit passing of parameters.

2.3 Explicit, First-Class Namespaces

The possibility to explicitly read and assign the **root** namespace enables us to directly support the various importing facilities found in other languages, like the *import package* statement of Java or the *from package import* facility of Python. The service load() locates a file containing a script, evaluates it, and returns the form defined by the script. Assume we have a script "hello.picl" with the contents:

```
# File: hello.picl
info: println("This is the hello script")
```

The script defines a form with a service bound by info. We can now:

- import all the bindings of the hello script and extend our **root** with them:
```
root = (root, load("hello"))
info()                           # invoke it
```

  This is equivalent to importing all names from a given module. If the service info is already defined, it will be overridden.

- import all the bindings but keep them in a separate nested form helloFile. This prevents our **root** namespace from getting cluttered up:
```
helloFile = load("hello")
helloFile.info()                 # and use it
```
  - import only the info service under a different name:
```
helloInfo = load("hello").info
helloInfo()                      # and use the service
```

The reader should note that these mechanisms can be combined. For example we can import a module, store it under a new name and rename selected services within. By using first-class forms to represent packages, language-specific import statements or namespace qualifiers become superfluous. We thereby overcome the problems related to rigid namespaces mentioned in the introduction.

Services in Piccola are monadic, taking a single form as a parameter. Keyword based arguments are transferred as nested forms. Since arguments are forms, form extension allows us to easily model *default arguments*. For instance, the following generic wrapper adds pre- and post- services to a given service:

```
myDefaults =          # a form with two (empty) services
    pre: ()
    post: ()
wrap(X)(Args):
    (myDefaults, X).pre()  invoke pre() in X or
Defaults
        res = X.service(Args)       # invoke main service
    (myDefaults, X).post()
    return res
```

The service wrap is curried. It first expects a form X with three labels: pre, service, and post. Invoking the service s = wrap(..) with a form Args calls pre(), then invokes the service with the passed Args form and finally calls post(). Observe how the pre and post service have a default. We prefix the argument form X with default bindings encapsulated in the form myDefaults. The projection (myDefaults, X).pre will extract the service bound to pre in X, if it exists. Otherwise the default service defined in myDefaults will be used.

3 Dynamic Abstractions

This section will outline two applications using dynamic namespaces that typically could not be implemented without either language extensions or meta-programming. The first example implements an exception handling mechanism as a library abstraction in Piccola, using dynamic namespaces to pass the exception handler to the context in which exceptions are raised.

The second example implements an ownership abstraction, realised as a wrapper for arbitrary forms and an evaluation context that may own certain objects. Only the owner can execute services of the wrapped objects. This is an example which is not commonly found as language construct. We conclude the section with some recommendations for disciplined use of the dynamic namespace.

3.1 Exceptions

An exception is raised during program execution as a reaction to some erroneous situation. The part of the program that detects the erroneous situation cannot handle it. Instead, it signals this situation and terminates execution. We say the program *raises an exception*. An exception handler, which was installed at an earlier point during program execution, catches the error and handles the exception, i.e. brings the system back to a consistent state.

The problem is how to transmit the flow of control from the place where the exception is detected to the appropriate handler. A simple approach would be to define some global exception-holding variables. After invocation of a service, the client is obliged to check this error state and handle it if appropriated. This solution is clumsy since each function call must be followed by an error check. It also does not work in a concurrent system, since all processes would share the same error slot. Another possibility is to extend the returned value to contain a flag that indicates whether the returned value is valid or an error occurred during its computation. This approach requires that we adapt all return values to reflect the change. Furthermore it assumes that all services have a reply, which, for example, may not be necessary for distributed notifications.

raising point to the appropriate handler. The exception handler is set as follows:

```
       try
          do: ...                    # use exception handler
          catch(E): ...              # handle an exception
```

The service try takes a form containing two services. The first is the do: service. Its body represents the scope of the exception handler. The handler itself is specified as a service catch(E) where E is the formal exception value. Whenever an exception occurs during the execution of the do: service, this handler is invoked instead of the normal continuation. Here is the implementation of the try and raise services:

```
(1) raise(E): dynamic.raise(E)       # delegate to dynamic raise
(2) try(block):
(3) exception = newChannel()
(4) return OrJoin                    # start agents left and right
(5)          left:
(6)              block.catch(exception.receive())
(7)          right:
(8)              raise(e):           # local raise abstraction
(9)                  exception.send(e)
(10)                 stop()
(11)             dynamic = (dynamic, raise = raise)
(12)             return block.do()
```

The OrJoin service (Line 4) takes two services (left and right) and executes them concurrently. It returns the result of whatever service first terminates. Consider first the scenario in which a block is executed that does not lead to an exception:

1. Two agents passed to OrJoin are started. The left agent has no impact as it is blocked on the local exception channel. This agent finally gets garbage collected, since no one ever will write to the exception channel.

2. The right agent runs block.do() (Line 12).

3. OrJoin receives the result of the right agent and returns this as the result of the try statement.

Next, consider the case where the block raises an exception:

1. The two agents are started. The left agent waits on the exception channel.

2. The right agent runs the block.do() (Line 12).

3. To raise the exception in the do() block, the global raise(..) (defined on Line 1) is invoked.

4. The global raise() delegates the exception to dynamic.raise() which is the local raise abstraction (Line 8).

5. The local raise sends the exception value along the exception channel (Line 9) and silently halts using the stop() service. This means that OrJoin will not see this service terminating.

6. The left agent is the only one to continue, fetching the exception value E, invoking catch(E) and returning (Line 6).

during invocation. This resembles the idiom used when programming with exceptions. The signature of a service that may raise an exception looks like aService(..., ExceptionHandler e). Compared to this approach, the explicit dynamic namespace has several advantages. First, it supports the separation of functional aspect from the error handling aspect. It seems more appropriate to directly relate the formal argument of a method to its functional aspect, instead of blurring it up with contextual arguments. It makes code more readable (thus maintainable) when unnecessary parameters are not visible. Imagine a function which does not raise an exception itself, but is required to pass the handler down to all services it uses. Finally, dynamic namespaces allow the programmer to introduce an exception handler later in the project development without rewriting code that neither handles exceptions nor detects erroneous situations.

Observe that the exception abstraction cannot be implemented as a simple wrapper that adds some pre- and post execution code. The reason is that raise must be accessible from anywhere *within* the executed block.

3.2 Ownership

In our second example we consider ownership of objects. An *ownable* object belongs to at most one owner. Only the owner can invoke services of the owned object. An ownable object can be *fetched* by an owner, which then has privileged access to it. The owner may release or transfer ownership. A notion of ownership can be used in various areas: for example synchronization for owned objects can be managed by the owner, or the owner can take over garbage collection issues on the owned object. Ownership can guarantee alias free references [17].

To translate an ordinary object into an ownable object, we do the following:

- Add an instance variable to store an owner.
- Add methods to fetch, remove, and transmit ownership. Of course, fetch will only work when the object is not owned for the moment. Remove and transmit are only possible, if the caller owns the object in question.
- Modify each method such that it expects an owner as additional argument. The precondition of the method is strengthened, as it is necessary that the passed owner be the owner of the object. Only when the passed owner owns the object can the method be performed, otherwise an exception is raised.
- All calls to the object methods must reflect the change and also include the owner.

Using explicit namespaces, it is possible to (1) build a generic abstraction wrap-Ownable(Form) that wraps all services of the form to check for ownership, and (2) to build an evaluator runAsOwner(Block) that runs a block of code with an owner. Assume we have object factories to create an owner, and an ownable:

```
          add(Ownable):  ...  # add the ownable
          remove(Ownable): .# remove the ownable
          loseAll: ...        # remove all ownables we have
      newOwnable:
          addTo(Owner):  ...
          release: ...
```

Given an instance o of ownable, then o.addTo(Owner) stores the owner, provided o is not already owned, and notifies the owner using Owner.add(o).

Evaluating a block within the context of an owner is now written as:

```
          runAsOwner(block):
              # create new Owner
              dynamic = (dynamic, currentOwner = newOwner())
                  block.do()                    # evaluate Block
              dynamic.currentOwner.loseAll() # drop all owned
```

This runs the block within a dynamic namespace with an associated (initially empty) owner. Finally, the generic wrapper that makes a form into an ownable form is:

```
(1) getCurrentOwner: dynamic.currentOwner
(2) wrapOwnable(Form):
(3)      ownable = newOwnable()       # delegate
(4)      newForm = wrapAllLambda      # adapt all services
(5)         form =
(6)              Form
(7)              releaseThisForm: ownable.release()
(8)         map(service)(Args):
(9)              if (getCurrentOwner().owns(ownable))
(10)                 then: service(Args)     # invoke service
(11)                 else: raise(NotOwnerException)
(12)     return
(13)         newForm
(14)         ownThisForm: ownable.addTo(getCurrentOwner())
```

The wrapper needs some explanation. Line 3 creates the ownable object as a delegate. Then all services of the wrapped form Form, extended with releaseThisForm are modified by a map function. The new function (Line 9 - 11) checks if the current (dynamic) owner owns this ownable object. If so it invokes the original service with the given arguments. Otherwise an exception is raised, signalling that the caller does not own the object. The library service wrapAllLambda uses form-iteration to get the set of defined labels (i.e. the exported services) of form.

Note that we include the additional service releaseThisForm (Line 7) into the map to ensure that only the current owner may release it. (Transfer of ownership is omitted in the code). We return the wrapped form (Line 13) extended with the service to acquire ownership (Line 14).

We can draw the following lessons from the two examples:

- Each feature requires a label in the dynamic namespace. Exceptions use raise, and ownership uses currentOwner to store the context sensitive information. We assume that these bindings do not conflict with other usages of the dynamic namespace.

- The users of the contextual abstractions do not need to access **dynamic** themselves. Instead it is better to provide static abstractions that access the context sensitive information, e.g. getCurrentOwner() in the second example.

- Contextual abstractions are used in pairs: Outside is an abstraction (e.g. try) that executes a piece of code (the do block) within a extended context. Within this block are clients of the contextual abstraction that invoke the service (e.g. raise) provided by the surrounding context. Using the contextual service not within the established context is a type error: it results in looking up a label in **dynamic** which is not bound.

4 Related and Future Work

Objects and many different variants of inheritance (e.g. Smalltalk-style vs. Beta-style inheritance [3]) can also be modelled as applications of forms as explicit namespaces [23]. In effect self is represented as a form containing the object's methods. Subclassing corresponds to extending the form representing self. A form is conceptually simpler than an object, since it lacks a notion of inheritance. For instance, in Self [25] objects have a parent link providing inheritance by means of delegation. Therefore, in Self delegation is built into the language, whereas we implement it using the forms.

Many scripting languages provide access to the environment by representing it as a dictionary. Python [14] has built-in functions to return its namespaces as dictionaries to enable introspection. Modification of these dictionaries, however, is undefined. A dictionary gives the programmer much more freedom than is presently possible with forms. In particular, labels of forms in Piccola are not first class values, whereas dictionaries for environments often use strings as keys.

Forms can also be compared to Odersky's variable functions [18]. Variable functions are mappings between sets of arbitrary values (not just from labels to forms), and can be updated to model state changes.

Namespaces play an emerging role in middleware: For instance the Corba naming service [19] uses nested namespaces to identify distributed objects.

Future work is required to clarify the relation between namespaces, and security and authentication issues. In an open system, mobile code runs in two modes: one mode gives unrestricted access to local resources, while restricted access employs a security manager to guard access and use of local resources. In the ambient calculus [4] an ambient corresponds to an administrative domain. An ambient can only access services within its domain. An interesting question to explore is whether we can unify ambients and namespaces.

Pict [20] is a language that takes the p-calculus as a core language and adds functions, assignment etc. as syntactic sugar. We used Pict for experiments in modelling software composition [22]. The pL-calculus is a result of these studies. It replaces tuple communication by form communication. Piccola is formally defined on the pL-calculus . It adopts the primitives of the pL-calculus (channels, and parallel overridden if necessary. The form-calculus [23] extends the set of core form operators. The additional operators are simple label restriction and form restriction to remove labels, and a matching operator to check for the existence of a label. Lumpe has developed a type system for the πL-calculus [13], but this system cannot be incorporated directly into Piccola, because it lacks parametric polymorphism and recursive types.

Common Lisp [24] allows the programmer to declare "special" variables to be dynamically scoped. Many languages now have features incorporated into their libraries that allow the programmer to create and use dynamic variables. For instance in Java2, the class java.lang.ThreadLocal contains a different value for each thread. Programmers use this class to store transaction identifiers or similar constructs.

Applications using dynamic namespaces have many similarities to programming with monads in functional languages. Monads are used to model state in a purely functional world [10][26]. The dynamic namespace builds on the notion of clients and providers of services. It therefore naturally extends to open, distributed systems, whereas monads are closely related to the lambda calculus.

In the area of object oriented languages, there exist several proposals to better support separation of concerns within a program. The proposal that seems the most attracting is aspect-oriented programming (AOP) [8]. In AOP, aspects are explicitly separated from normal classes. The *aspect weaver* merges the aspect into the source code. Using AOP can greatly reduce the complexity of code [11].

Many of the applications possible using dynamic namespaces can also be implemented using metaobjects and message passing control [5][7]. We consider the approach with explicit namespaces to be much more lightweight.

5 Conclusion

Piccola is a small language for composing software components. It is intended to be a general language suitable for expressing many different styles of components and composition abstractions. One way it achieves this is by unifying various notions of namespaces present in other languages, such as environments, interfaces, objects and packages, and making them explicitly manipulable as "forms."

Explicit namespaces make it possible in Piccola to have flexible static and dynamic scoping, to support various module concepts, and to implement generic wrappers that go beyond adding pre- and post methods to services. All this flexibility can be achieved with a minimal set of operators over forms and does not require the use of meta programming facilities.

A stable implementation of Piccola is available from the authors' web site. Work is ongoing in many areas, including experimental development of compositional styles for various application domains, reasoning about compositional properties, visualization, distribution, and flexible type systems.

Acknowledgements

We thank the members of the SCG for stimulating discussions and in particular Stéphane Ducasse and Matthias Rieger for helpful comments on a draft of this paper, and the anonymous referees for providing constructive and valuable suggestions.

[1]   Franz Achermann and Oscar Nierstrasz, **"Applications = Components + Scripts --
        A tour of Piccola,"** *Software Architectures and Component Technology*,
        Mehmet Aksit (Ed.), Kluwer, 2000, to appear.

[2]   Franz Achermann, Markus Lumpe, Jean-Guy Schneider and Oscar Nierstrasz, **"Piccola
        - a Small Composition Language,"** *Formal Methods for Distributed
        Processing, an Object Oriented Approach*, Howard Bowman and John
        Derrick. (Ed.), Cambridge University Press., 2000, to appear.

[3]   Gilad Bracha and William Cook, **"Mixin-based Inheritance,"** *Proceedings
        OOPSLA/ ECOOP'90*, ACM SIGPLAN Notices, vol. 25, no. 10, Oct.
        1990, pp. 303-311.

[4]   Luca Cardelli and Andrew D. Gordon, **"Mobile Ambients,"** *Foundations of
        Software Science and Computational Structures*, Maurice Nivat (Ed.),
        LNCS, vol. 1378, Springer Verlag, 1998, pp. 140-155.

[5]   Stéphane Ducasse, **"Evaluating Message Passing Control Techniques in
        Smalltalk,"** *Journal of Object-Oriented Programming (JOOP)*, vol. 12,
        no. 6, SIGS Press, June 1999, pp. 39-44.

[6]   D. Kalev, *Ansi/Iso C++ Professional Programmer's Handbook*, Que Professional
        Series, 1999

[7]   Gregor Kiczales, Jim des Rivières and Daniel G. Bobrow, *The Art of the Metaobject
        Protocol*, MIT Press, 1991.

[8]   Gregor Kiczales, John Lamping, Anurag Mendhekar, Chris Maeda, Cristina Lopes, Jean-
        Marc Loingtier and John Irwin, **"Aspect-Oriented Programming,"**
        Proceedings ECOOP'97, Mehmet Aksit and Satoshi Matsuoka (Ed.),
        LNCS 1241, Springer-Verlag, Jyvaskyla, Finland, June 1997, pp. 220-
        242.

[9]   Doug Lea, **"Design for Open Systems in Java,"** *Proceedings
        COORDINATION'97*, David Garlan & Daniel Le Mètayer (Ed.), LNCS
        1282, Springer-Verlag, Berlin, Germany, September 1997, pp. 32-45.

[10]   Sheng Liang, Paul Hudak and Mark P. Jones, **"Monad Transformers and
        Modular Interpreters",** *Conference Record of POPL'95*, San Francisco,
        California, 1995, pp. 333-343.

[11]   Martin Lippert and Cristina V. Lopes, **"A Study on Exception Detection and
        Handling Using Aspect-Oriented Programming,"** Technical Report
        P9910229 CSL-99-1, Xerox Parc Palo Alto, Dec. 1999.

[12]   Markus Lumpe, Franz Achermann and Oscar Nierstrasz, **"A Formal Language for
        Composition,"** *Foundations of Component Based Systems*, Gary Leavens
        and Murali Sitaraman (Ed.), Cambridge University Press., 2000, pp. 69-
        90.

[13]   Markus Lumpe, **"A Pi-Calculus Based Approach to Software Composition,"**
        Ph.D. thesis, University of Bern, Institute of Computer Science and
        Applied Mathematics, January 1999.

[14]   Mark Lutz, *Programming Python*, O'Reilly, 1996.

[15]   Robin Milner, **"Functions as Processes,"** Proceedings ICALP'90, M.S. Paterson
        (Ed.), LNCS 443, Springer-Verlag, Warwick U., July 1990, pp. 167-180.

[16]   Robin Milner, **"The Polyadic pi Calculus: a tutorial,"** ECS-LFCS-91-180,
        Computer Science Dept., University of Edinburgh, Oct. 1991.

[17]   James Noble, John Potter and Jan Vitek, **"Flexible alias protection,"** *Proceedings
        ECOOP'98*, Eric Jul (Ed.), LCNS 1445, Springer-Verlag, Brussels,
        Belgium, July 1998.

ference on Functional Programming, Baltimore, 1998.

[19]   Robert Orfali, Dan Harkey and Jeri Edwards, *Instant Corba*, Wiley, 1997.

[20]   Benjamin C. Pierce and David N. Turner, **"Pict: A Programming Language based on the Pi-Calculus,"** Technical Report, no. CSCI 476, Computer Science Department, Indiana University, March 1997.

[21]   D. Sangiorgi, **"Interpreting functions as Pi-calculus processes: a tutorial,"** RR 3470, INRIA Sophia-Antipolis, France, February 1999.

[22]   Jean-Guy Schneider and Markus Lumpe, **"Synchronizing Concurrent Objects in the Pi-Calculus,"** *Proceedings of Langages et Modèles à Objects'97*, Roland Ducournau and Serge Garlatti (Ed.), Hermes, Roscoff, October 1997, pp. 61-76.

[23]   Jean-Guy Schneider, **"Components, Scripts, and Glue: A conceptual framework for software composition,"** Ph.D. thesis, University of Bern, Institute of Computer Science and Applied Mathematics, October 1999.

[24]   Guy L. Steele, *Common Lisp The Language, Second Edition,* Digital Press, 1990.

[25]   David Ungar and Randall B. Smith, **"Self: The Power of Simplicity,"** *Proceedings OOPSLA'87, ACM SIGPLAN Notices*, December 1987, pp. 227-242.

[26]   Philip Wadler, **"Monads for functional programming,"** *Advanced Functional Programming*, J. Jeuring and E. Meijer (Ed.), LNCS 925.

Stand-Alone Messages

A Step Towards Component-Oriented Programming Languages

Peter H. Fröhlich and Michael Franz

Department of Information and Computer Science
University of California, Irvine
Irvine, CA 92697-3425, USA
`phf@acm.org, franz@uci.edu`

Abstract. We are concerned with the design of programming languages that support the paradigm of component-oriented programming.
Languages based on the accepted idea of combining modular and object-
oriented concepts fail to provide adequate support. We argue that messages should be separated from methods to address this shortcoming.
We introduce the concept of stand-alone messages, give examples for its
utility, and compare it to related approaches and language constructs.
Besides leading to interesting insights on the interaction of modular and
object-oriented concepts, we believe that stand-alone messages also provide a useful basis for further research on component-oriented programming languages.

1   Introduction

Component-oriented programming replaces monolithic software systems with
reusable *software components* and hierarchical *component frameworks* [30]. Components extend the capabilities of frameworks, while frameworks provide execution environments for components. Both are developed by independent and
mutually unaware vendors for late composition by third parties. Late composition requires that component-oriented software systems support *dynamic* and
independent extensibility. Dynamic extensibility enables the addition of new
components at run-time, while independent extensibility allows components and
frameworks from mutually unaware vendors to be composed.

While current approaches to component-oriented programming are largely
based on *component models* such as COM [16] and CORBA [23], recent research
has focused on programming language support [1,2,6,17,24,31]. Compared to the
implicit support provided by these models, supporting component-oriented programming *explicitly* in programming languages has two major advantages. First,
it enables a seamless development process since analysis, design, and implementation can use the same basic concepts to describe a software artifact. Second,
it allows compilers to perform extensive checking and to generate efficient code.
Direct support for component-oriented programming can thus be expected to
lead to more maintainable, reliable, and efficient systems.

J. Gutknecht and W. Weck (Eds.): JMLC 2000, LNCS 1897, pp. 90–103, 2000.

The minimal assumptions that frameworks and components make about each other are specified using *interfaces*. An interface is an abstraction of all possible *implementations* that can fill a certain role in the composed system [13]. We view interfaces as sets of *messages* (abstract operations) and implementations as sets of *methods* (concrete operations). Messages describe *what* effect is achieved by an operation, while methods describe *how* that effect is achieved. Multiple *instances* of an implementation can exist concurrently. We say that an implementation (or an instance) *conforms* to an interface if it provides methods for all messages in that interface. Interfaces are essential to component-oriented programming because they are the only form of coordination between component and framework vendors and the only means by which third parties can validate compositions.

A component-oriented programming language needs constructs to express interfaces and implementations and must also support dynamic and independent extensibility. In programming languages, interfaces and implementations should be modeled as *interface types* and *implementation types* respectively. In this manner, we can define the conformance of an implementation to an interface by the conformance of the corresponding types. Dynamic extensibility requires some form of polymorphism that allows different instances of implementation types to be bound to the same interface types at run-time. Inclusion polymorphism [5] in object-oriented languages such as Java [11] is one way to achieve this, although we prefer the term *implementation polymorphism* in this context. Independent extensibility requires some form of encapsulation that isolates components from their environment except for explicitly declared dependencies. Sealed encapsulation constructs [3] in modular languages such as Oberon [25] are one way to achieve this.[1] Therefore, combining concepts from modular and object-oriented languages should be a viable approach to the design of component-oriented programming languages [30].

However, simply *embedding* object-oriented concepts into a modular language unchanged is insufficient. If a component has to implement multiple interfaces defined by independent frameworks, syntactic and semantic interface conflicts can occur. These conflicts preclude framework combination and thus violate the principle of independent extensibility. To avoid these conflicts, messages must be given unique identities *independent* of the types in which they participate. This contradicts the object-oriented paradigm in which messages only have unique identities *within* a type. We propose the concept of *stand-alone messages* and discuss its ramifications for language design. In particular, we show that stand-alone messages simplify the integration of other desirable properties such as structural conformance. Separating the concepts of messages, methods, modules, and types opens a previously unexplored region of the design space for

---

[1] In analogy to Cardelli [3], we call an encapsulation construct *open* if neither visibility nor membership is restricted, *closed* if only visibility is restricted, and *sealed* if visibility and membership are restricted. Java's packages are closed in this sense, while modules in Oberon are sealed.

programming languages that seems well-suited for component-oriented programming.

In the next section we illustrate the problem of interface conflicts in a Java-like language. In Sect. 3 we develop the concept of stand-alone messages and show how it resolves interface conflicts. Section 4 discusses additional applications of stand-alone messages, and Sect. 5 surveys related work and compares it to our approach. Finally, in Sect. 6 we conclude with a summary of contributions and an outline for future work.

2   Interface Conflicts

Software components often need to conform to multiple interfaces for technical or marketing reasons. Consider a component that presents the results of a database query within a compound document. On the technical side, instances of this component might have to react to notifications from the database management *and* the compound document framework to keep their presentation current. On the marketing side, the component might increase its potential market if it could be composed with different database management and compound document frameworks. To support independent extensibility, it must be possible to develop components that conform to multiple interfaces even if those interfaces were defined by mutually unaware framework vendors.

As a simple example for the problems caused by framework combination, we attempt to develop a Stack component that is usable across four different frameworks. We assume a Java-like programming language in which (closed) packages have been replaced by (sealed) modules. Mapping interface types to interfaces and implementation types to classes is appropriate in such a language. The first framework defines the following interface:

```
module edu.uci.framework {
  public interface Stack {
    public void push (Object o);    // pre o ≠ null; post top = o
    public void pop ();             // pre ¬ empty
    public Object top ();           // pre ¬ empty; post result ≠ null
    public boolean empty ();        // "no elements?"
  }
}
```

The designer of this interface followed the textbook definition of the abstract data type Stack closely, and developing a class that implements this interface is straightforward. The second framework defines the following interface:

```
module gov.nsa.framework {
  public interface Stack {
    public void push (Object o);    // pre o ≠ null; post top = o
    public void pop ();             // pre size > 0
    public Object top ();           // pre size > 0; post result ≠ null
    public int size ();             // post result ≥ 0
  }
}
```

Instead of relying on an empty message, this vendor chose to work with the size of the Stack. To support this interface as well, we have to add a size method to our class which is again straightforward. We can even define the empty method in terms of the new size method to avoid some redundancy. Note that this relies on empty and size = 0 expressing identical semantics. The third framework defines the following interface:

```
module com.sun.framework {
  public interface Stack {
    public void push (Object o);    // pre o ≠ null; post top = o
    public Object pop ();           // pre ¬ empty; post result ≠ null
    public boolean empty ();        // "no elements?"
  }
}
```

Apart from simply removing the top element, the pop message in this interface also returns the top element. To support this interface as well, our class would have to implement two pop methods with *different* signatures.[2] However, since the signatures differ only in their return types, Java's overloading mechanism does not allow us to do this. We have just encountered an example of a *syntactic conflict* between two interfaces. In our Java-like language, it is not possible to express a class that implements this third interface in addition to the first two. The fourth and final framework defines the following interface:

```
module org.cthulhu.framework {
  public interface Stack {
    public void push (Object o);    // pre o ≠ null; post top = o
    public void pop ();             // pre ¬ empty
    public Object top ();           // pre ¬ empty; post result ≠ null
    public boolean empty ();        // "no elements?"
    public int size ();             // "how many pushes?"
  }
}
```

This interface is identical to the first interface, except for the additional size message. Unlike the size message in the second interface, this one returns the *number of remaining push operations* until some expensive internal restructuring occurs.[3] To support this interface as well, our class would have to implement two *different* size methods with *identical* signatures. However, since the signatures are identical, it is not possible to distinguish these messages. We have just encountered an example of a *semantic conflict* between two interfaces. In our Java-like language, it is not possible to express a class that implements this fourth interface in addition to the first two.

As our examples have shown, embedding object-oriented concepts unchanged into a modular language fails to address interface conflicts caused by framework

---

[2] Unlike the Java language specification [11], we distinguish the name of a message from its signature (the list of parameter types + the return type).

[3] This information might be necessary in a framework with real-time constraints. Implementations based on incrementally growing arrays can supply it quite naturally.

combination. Note that Component Pascal [22], Java [11], Modula-3 [4], and Oberon-2 [21], which are often regarded as "close approximations" of component-oriented programming languages [30], follow a similar design.

3   Stand-Alone Messages

In the Java-like language from Sect. 2, messages are declared within interfaces, while methods are declared within classes. Consequently, the identity of a message is *relative to* the interface in which it is declared, whereas the identity of a method is *relative to* the class in which it is declared. In the case of methods, this form of identity is needed to support polymorphism. Consider the following example:

```
...
edu.uci.framework.Stack stack = null;
...
stack = new edu.uci.components.ArrayedStack(16);
stack.push(new Integer(1));
...
stack = new edu.uci.components.LinkedStack();
stack.push(new Integer(1));
...
```

After we bind an instance of ArrayedStack to the reference stack, we expect the message push to invoke the *specific* push method declared for ArrayedStack. Similarly, after we rebind an instance of LinkedStack to the reference stack, we expect the *same* message push invoke a *different* push method declared for LinkedStack. Whenever the class of the instance bound to the stack reference changes, we want the identity of the methods invoked through that reference to change as well. In the case of messages, however, this form of identity is the reason for the interface conflicts described in Sect. 2. Since the identity of a message is only unique *within* an interface, combining two interfaces can result in two messages that are *not* unique within the combined interface anymore.

In order to avoid interface conflicts, we must break the symmetry between message and methods, both of which only have a unique identity within the *type* (interface, class) in which they are declared. Since methods must keep their relative identity to make polymorphism work, the only option is to decouple the identity of messages from interfaces. If messages should not have a relative identity to types anymore, the only reasonable scope in which they could be declared is that of the module. We call messages that have a unique identity relative to their declaring module *stand-alone messages*. The following example suggests a syntax for stand-alone messages in our Java-like language:

```
module edu.uci.framework {
    public message void push (Object o);    // pre o ≠ null; post top = o
    public message void pop ();             // pre ¬ empty
    public message Object top ();           // pre ¬ empty; post result ≠ null
    public message boolean empty ();        // "no elements?"
    public interface Stack { push, pop, top, empty }
}
```

This example shows how the first interface from Sect. 2 is declared using stand-alone messages. In particular, the last line of this example declares an interface *type* that consists of the four messages push, pop, top, and empty. However, note that this is very different from the original form of declaring an interface. In an external module that imports edu.uci.framework, the type edu.uci.framework.Stack would actually appear as follows:

```
interface edu.uci.framework.Stack {
    edu.uci.framework.push, edu.uci.framework.pop,
    edu.uci.framework.top, edu.uci.framework.empty
}
```

This implies that messages always have to be *fully* qualified in external modules:

```
...
edu.uci.framework.Stack stack = null;
...
stack = new edu.uci.components.ArrayedStack(16);
stack.edu.uci.framework.push(new Integer(1));
...
```

To avoid excessive qualifications, we introduce an aliasing construct for import declarations as found in Oberon [25]. A class that implements the interface edu.uci.framework.Stack is then expressed as follows:

```
module com.factorial.cool.extension {
    import f1 = edu.uci.framework;
    public class CoolStack implements f1.Stack {

        ...
        public void f1.push (Object o) { ... }
        public void f1.pop () { ... }
        public Object f1.top () { ... }
        public boolean f1.empty () { ... }
    }
}
```

To adapt this class to support all interfaces described in Sect. 2 we must import the relevant modules and declare a method for each message required. Since messages are always fully qualified, no interface conflicts can result. Note that we can also add a mechanism that allows component vendors to associate a single method with a number of messages to avoid some redundancy, especially a large number of forwarding methods.

Besides being useful in a pragmatic way, stand-alone messages also lead to an interesting insight regarding language design. Consider the design space for the identity of messages and methods in programming languages. As illustrated in Table 1, both can have identities relative to either modules or types. In object-oriented programming languages such as Java [11], the identities of messages and methods are relative to types. As we have seen, this design choice does not support independent extensibility because of interface conflicts. In modular programming languages such as Oberon [25], the identities of messages and methods (procedure headers and procedure bodies) are relative to modules. While

Table 1. Language design space for messages and methods.

	Message ∈ Type	Message ∈ Module
Method ∈ Type	Object-Oriented	*Component-Oriented*
Method ∈ Module	?	Modular

this design choice supports independent extensibility, it does not support dynamic extensibility because modules lack run-time polymorpism.[4] Using identities relative to types for messages and relative to modules for methods combines both of these drawbacks and also does not yield a practical design. Stand-alone messages, however, lead to language designs in which the identity of messages is relative to modules, while the identity of methods is relative to types. Thus, they support both dynamic and independent extensibility and open a previously unexplored region in the design space for programming languages. We believe that this region is well-suited for component-oriented programming, and that stand-alone messages clarify the relationship between component-oriented programming and modular and object-oriented concepts.

4   Additional Applications

We illustrate a number of additional applications for stand-alone messages, ranging from language properties to software engineering considerations.

Interface Combination. Since the identity of stand-alone messages is relative to modules instead of types, languages that support stand-alone messages have two useful properties regarding the *combination* of interface types. First, *any combination of interface types results in an interface type.* Second, *any combination of interface types preserves all constituent messages.* As shown in Sect. 2, these properties do not hold in Java [11], leading to syntactic and semantic interface conflicts respectively. C++ [28] and Eiffel [15] require additional language mechanisms to approximate both properties (see Sect. 5).

Structural Conformance. Conformance of an implementation type A to an interface type B can either be *declared* explicitly, as in Java [11], or *inferred* based on a *structural* property, such as A providing methods for all messages of B. Structural conformance has a number of advantages, especially for software evolution [12]. More importantly, a certain degree of structural conformance is *required* for component-oriented programming [1]. However, structural conformance is often seen as being "weaker" than declared conformance, because it can result in "accidental" conformance relations that the programmer did not anticipate. A typical

---

[4] Some modular programming languages *do* support polymorphism at compile-time or link-time. In Modula-3, for example, multiple modules can export the same interface [4]. The decision about which implementation to use is deferred until build-time. Standard ML provides similar capabilities [19].

example of this problem is an interface type Cowboy that includes a message draw and an interface type Shape that also includes a draw message, presumably with different semantics. In a language that supports stand-alone messages, accidental conformance of this kind is not possible. The draw messages would be defined in different modules and would therefore be distinguishable.

The use of structural conformance has been proposed before. In Modula-3 [4] structural conformance is used by default, but reference types can be *branded* to avoid accidental conformance. However, all brands in a composed system (a "program" in Modula-3) must be unique, which can restrict independent extensibility by mutually unaware vendors. The *compound types* proposal for Java [1] uses declared conformance for individual interfaces and structural conformance for combined interfaces. Although backward compatible with Java, compound types add additional rules to an already complex language and do not address the problem of interface conflicts at all. Another proposal for Java [12] requires that interfaces for which structural conformance should be used must extend an explicit marker interface Structural. In contrast to these approaches, structural conformance with stand-alone messages does not require any additional language constructs to avoid accidental conformance.

Minimal Signatures. An interesting application of structural conformance is that signatures of messages can be typed in a "minimal" way to express certain invariants. Consider a method that prints the top element of a Stack:

```
...
import f = edu.uci.framework;
...
// does not modify "s"
void printTop (f.Stack s) {
   if !s.f.empty() { print(s.f.top()); }
}
...
```

Instead of stating that printTop does not modify the Stack in a comment, we could add anonymous interfaces to our language and define its signature as follows:

```
void printTop (interface {f.empty,f.top} s)
```

Given this signature, only the empty and top messages could be sent to s, ensuring that printTop does not modify the stack.[5] While not providing a complete solution, this form of minimal signature specification can be used to address a subset of component re-entrance problems [18].

Design Guidelines. Stand-alone messages are also helpful as design guidelines during development. For example, consider designing an interface for bounded stacks based on the interface edu.uci.framework.Stack for unbounded stacks. The existing interface provides the messages push, pop, top, and empty. The only message not yet provided is full which indicates that no more elements can be pushed. This reasoning leads to the following interface:

---

[5] This only holds if printTop can not cast the parameter to another type that exposes more messages.

```
module edu.uci.framework.bounded {
  import f = edu.uci.framework;
  public message boolean full ();   // "no more pushes?"
  public interface Stack { full, f.push, f.pop, f.top, f.empty }
}
```

However, this interface does not capture the intended semantics accurately. Consider the precondition associated with the push message in Sect. 3. It states that push only fails if we pass **null** as a parameter, but for a bounded stack push should also fail if the stack is full. This insight leads to the following interface:

```
module edu.uci.framework.bounded {
  import f = edu.uci.framework;
  public message void push (Object o);   // pre ¬ full ∧ o ≠ null; post f.top = o
  public message boolean full ();         // "no more pushes?"
  public interface Stack { push, full, f.pop, f.top, f.empty }
}
```

Focusing on messages and their semantics thus helped us to uncover an inconsistency between the interfaces for bounded and unbounded stacks. While developers can not be forced to design semantically consistent interfaces, we believe that concentrating on messages facilitates this process.

Note how introducing a new push message enables us to express the semantic difference between bounded and unbounded stacks. The interfaces for bounded and unbounded stacks do not conform to each other, which is appropriate if we intend to model behavioral subtyping [14]. However, both interfaces *do* conform to the interface {f.pop, f.top, f.empty} and thanks to structural conformance we can avoid explicitly introducing this "virtual supertype."

5 Discussion

We survey component models, programming conventions, design patterns, and language constructs that could be used to resolve interface conflicts and compare them to stand-alone messages.

Component Models. Microsoft's COM is the component model that is most similar to our approach [16]. Instead of assigning unique identities to messages, COM assigns unique identities to interface types. Instead of relying on a transparent naming convention for modules, COM associates an automatically generated *globally unique identifier* (GUID) with each interface type. Contrary to most object-oriented programming languages, COM allows an implementation type to conform to multiple interface types *without* any conflicts. Combined interface types can also be expressed using COM's *category* mechanism.

While we emphasize explicit programming language support and the associated advantages, the two approaches are equivalent as far as interface conflicts are concerned. In particular, we could map stand-alone messages to singleton COM interfaces and interface types to COM categories.

Programming Conventions. A variety of programming conventions can be suggested to address interface conflicts. Defining naming conventions for messages is one of the simplest. The message push in the interface Stack in the module edu.uci.framework could by convention be named edu_uci_framework_Stack_push. While theoretically possible, we do not believe that such a convention is acceptable in practice. Additional mechanisms for introducing short local names for messages would be needed, complicating the resulting language. However, even if we accept this complication, we must define *new* conventions on how names should be abbreviated if we are concerned about readability. More complex programming conventions have been suggested as well [2].

A general problem with programming conventions is that they are not enforcable by the compiler. This applies to programming languages based on standalone messages as well, since we rely on module names that are unique by convention. However, no form of "globally unique identity" can be achieved without *some* convention, so our goal should be to make the conventions as unintrusive and transparent as possible. We believe that, in light of these considerations, conventions for module names are a good tradeoff.

Design Patterns. Certain design patterns can be used to resolve interface conflicts [10]. In a variation of the Command pattern, "messages" are modelled as a hierarchy of classes containing "parameter slots," while "message sends" are calls to a universal dispatch method. The dispatch method performs explicit run-time type-tests and calls the actual method corresponding to the dynamic type of the "message." This approach relies on the compiler to generate unique type descriptors for each class and thus prevents any conflicts between messages. However, static type-checking is not possible to the desirable extent.[6]

Variations of the Adapter, Bridge, and Proxy patterns can be used to map multiple conflicting interface types to a single implementation type. The idea is to insert additional forwarding classes between clients of an interface type and its implementation type. Messages sent to the forwarding class are routed to the corresponding method in the implementation. While this approach preserves static type-checking, it can be tedious to write the required forwarding classes without tool support.

Renaming Messages. In Eiffel, features inherited from ancestor classes can be *renamed* in a descendant class to avoid name clashes [15]. In our terminology, an implementation type conforming to multiple interface types can explicitly choose new local names for conflicting messages. Note that clients still use the messages declared in the original interface type, but the messages are "rerouted" in a way similar to the Adapter design pattern described above.

Although renaming can be used to resolve interface conflicts, the approach has two major drawbacks. First, renaming clutters up the name space of the

---

[6] Interestingly, stand-alone messages were originally inspired by this design pattern from the Oberon system [32]. Language constructs for messages appeared in Object Oberon [20], the protocols extension for Oberon [7], and finally Lagoona [8,9].

implementation type. We may have to invent a new name for a message that is less expressive than the original one, define naming conventions to keep readability up, and repeat this "renaming excercise" whenever we want to conform to an additional interface type. Second, renaming must be extended to combined interface types in addition to implementation types. This becomes particularly clumsy in terms of syntax if we also want to support anonymous interface types.

Explicit Qualification. C++ supports the explicit qualification of member functions by classes to avoid name clashes [28]. In our terminology, message sends can be qualified by the implementation type in which a method should be invoked. As defined in C++, this mechanism does not support implementation polymorphism as required for component-oriented programming.

However, we can generalize the idea of explicit qualification by allowing message sends to be qualified by interface types. Although this does not restrict polymorphism anymore, even a qualified message of the form Stack.pop is not necessarily unique, since multiple interface types with identical names could exist. Therefore, qualification must be extended to include module names as well, at which point the mechanism becomes equivalent to stand-alone messages, except for the redundant interface type.

Overloading Messages. Overloading is a form of ad-hoc polymorphism [5] supported by a number of programming languages such as Java [11] and C++ [28]. In our terminology, overloading essentially encodes parts of the signature of a message within its name and uses contextual information available when a message is sent to determine which *actual* message is being referred to.

Although overloading helps to avoid some interface conflicts, it has two major limitations. First, semantic conflicts can not be avoided by overloading since the semantics of a message can not be expressed by type systems in which type checking is decidable [26]. Second, avoiding *all* syntactic interface conflicts requires *all* combinations of parameter and return types to be distinct. This is not generally possible in the presence of subtyping and the coercions it implies.

6   Conclusions

In this paper, we were concerned with the design of programming languages that support the paradigm of component-oriented programming. The principles of dynamic and independent extensibility led to the idea that component-oriented languages can be designed by combining modular and object-oriented concepts. However, we found that even an idealized language designed according to this idea failed to support independent extensibility as soon as interface types were combined. The key insight to circumvent this problem was recognizing that messages can be separated from methods. While methods must have identities that are relative to implementation types, messages must have identities that are independent of interface types. We introduced the concept of stand-alone messages whose identities are relative to modules instead of types. We showed that stand-alone messages lead to language designs that support the combination of interface types as required. Additional examples also illustrated the utility of stand-alone messages for component-oriented programming. We compared stand-alone messages to related approaches and language constructs, observing that they generally lead to simpler solutions.

We believe that the main contribution of this work is an improved understanding of how modular and object-oriented concepts interact and how they can be combined to support component-oriented programming. Our insight that messages should be separated from methods can be viewed as another step towards the separation of concepts subsumed by classes in traditional object-oriented languages. Previous results in this direction include the separation of interface types from implementation types [27] and the separation of modules from types [29], both of which are now widely accepted. We believe that the concept of stand-alone messages will be useful as a basis for further research on component-oriented programming languages.

We plan to continue our work on language support for component-oriented programming. Our current focus is on formally defining the experimental programming language Lagoona [8,9] which is based on stand-alone messages and on improving its prototype compiler. Additional areas of interest include the integration of stand-alone messages with Java, the implementation of Lagoona on top of COM, techniques for efficient message dispatch, formal specifications in the presence of stand-alone messages, static guarantees on abstract aliasing and representation exposure, and declarative and constraint-based approaches to the consistent integration and configuration of components and frameworks.

Acknowledgements. We would like to thank Kimberly Haas, Ziemowit Laski, Jeffery von Ronne, Christian Stork, and the anonymous referees for valuable comments on earlier versions of this paper. We are also indebted to Wolfram Amme, Martin Büchi, Thomas Kistler, Riccardo Pucella, Clemens Szyperski, and Marcellus Wallace for many fruitful discussions. Special thanks to the Organizing Committee for being extraordinarily patient. This work was partially supported by the National Science Foundation under grant EIA-9975053.

References

1. Martin Büchi and Wolfgang Weck. Compound types for Java. In *Proceedings of the ACM SIGPLAN Conference on Object-Oriented Programming Systems, Languages, and Applications (OOPSLA)*, pages 362–373, Vancouver, Canada, October 1998. Published as ACM SIGPLAN Notices 33(10).

2. Martin Büchi and Wolfgang Weck. Generic wrappers. In *Proceedings of the European Conference on Object-Oriented Programming (ECOOP)*, pages 201–225, Cannes, France, June 2000. Published as Lecture Notes in Computer Science 1850, Springer-Verlag.

3. Luca Cardelli. Typeful programming. SRC Research Report 45, Digital Systems Research Center, 130 Lytton Avenue, Palo Alto, CA 94301, May 24, 1989.

4. Luca Cardelli, James Donahue, Lucille Glassman, Mick Jordan, Bill Kalsow, and Greg Nelson. (Modula-3) language definition. In Greg Nelson, editor, *Systems Programming in Modula-3*, chapter 2, pages 11–66. Prentice-Hall, Englewood Cliffs, NJ, 1991.
5. Luca Cardelli and Peter Wegner. On understanding types, data abstraction, and polymorphism. *ACM Computing Surveys*, 17(4):471–522, December 1985.
6. Matthew Flatt and Matthias Felleisen. Units: Cool modules for HOT languages. In *Proceedings of the ACM SIGPLAN Conference on Programming Language Design and Implementation (PLDI)*, pages 236–246, Montreal, Canada, June 1998.
7. Michael Franz. Protocol Extension: A technique for structuring large extensible software-systems. *Software: Concepts & Tools*, 16(2):14–26, July 1995.
8. Michael Franz. The programming language Lagoona: A fresh look at object-orientation. *Software: Concepts & Tools*, 18(1):14–26, March 1997.
9. Peter H. Fröhlich and Michael Franz. The programming language Lagoona. Technical report, Department of Information and Computer Science, University of California, Irvine, CA 92697-3425, 2000. Forthcoming.
10. Erich Gamma, Richard Helm, Ralph Johnson, and John Vlissides. *Design Patterns: Elements of Reusable Object-Oriented Software*. Addison-Wesley, Reading, MA, 1995.
11. James Gosling, Bill Joy, Guy Steele, and Gilad Bracha. *The Java Language Specification*. Addison-Wesley, Reading, MA, 2nd edition, 2000. To be published. Draft available at http://www.javasoft.com/.
12. Konstantin Läufer, Gerald Baumgartner, and Vincent F. Russo. Safe structural conformance for Java. Technical Report OSU-CISRC-6/98-TR20, Department of Computer and Information Science, The Ohio State University, Columbus, OH 43210-1277, June 1998.
13. Barbara Liskov and John Guttag. *Abstraction and Specification in Program Development*. MIT Press (McGraw-Hill), Cambridge, MA, 1986.
14. Barbara H. Liskov and Jeannette M. Wing. A behavioral notion of subtyping. *ACM Transactions on Programming Languages and Systems*, 16(6):1811–1841, November 1994.
15. Bertrand Meyer. *Object-Oriented Software Construction*. Prentice-Hall, Upper Saddle River, NJ, 2nd edition, 1997.
16. Microsoft Corporation. *The Component Object Model (Version 0.9)*, October 1995. Available at http://www.microsoft.com/COM/.
17. Leonid Mikhajlov and Emil Sekerinski. A study of the fragile base class problem. In *Proceedings of the European Conference on Object-Oriented Programming (ECOOP)*, pages 355–382, Brussels, Belgium, July 1998. Published as Lecture Notes in Computer Science 1445, Springer-Verlag.
18. Leonid Mikhajlov, Emil Sekerinski, and Linas Laibinis. Developing components in presence of re-entrance. In *Proceedings of the World Congress on Formal Methods in the Development of Computing Systems (FM)*, pages 1301–1320, Toulouse, France, September 1999. Published as Lecture Notes in Computer Science 1709, Springer-Verlag.
19. Robin Milner, Mads Tofte, Robert Harper, and David MacQueen. *The Definition of Standard ML*. MIT Press, Cambridge, MA, revised edition, 1997.
20. Hanspeter Mössenböck, Josef Templ, and Robert Griesemer. Object Oberon: An object-oriented extension of Oberon. Technical Report 109, Institute of Computer Systems, Eidgenössische Technische Hochschule, Zürich, Switzerland, June 1989.
21. Hanspeter Mössenböck and Niklaus Wirth. The programming language Oberon-2. *Structured Programming*, 12(4):179–195, 1991.

22. Oberon microsystems. *Component Pascal Language Definition*, September 1997. Available at `http://www.oberon.ch/`.

23. Object Management Group. The Common Object Request Broker: Architecture and Specification (Version 2.3.1), October 1999. Available at `http://www.omg.org/`.

24. Riccardo Pucella. The design of a COM-oriented module system. In *Proceedings of the Joint Modular Languages Conference (JMLC)*, Zürich, Switzerland, September 2000. To be published in Lecture Notes in Computer Science, Springer-Verlag.

25. Martin Reiser and Niklaus Wirth. *Programming in Oberon: Steps Beyond Pascal and Modula*. Addison-Wesley (ACM Press), Wokingham, England, 1992.

26. Michael I. Schwartzbach. Polymorphic type inference. Lecture Series LS-95-3, Basic Research in Computer Science, Department of Computer Science, University of Aarhus, Denmark, June 1995.

27. Alan Snyder. Encapsulation and inheritance in object-oriented programming languages. In *Proceedings of the ACM SIGPLAN Conference on Object-Oriented Programming Systems, Languages, and Applications (OOPSLA)*, pages 38–45, Portland, OR, November 1986. Published as ACM SIGPLAN Notices 21(11).

28. Bjarne Stroustrup. *The C++ Programming Language*. Addison-Wesley, Reading, MA, special edition, 2000.

29. Clemens Szyperski. Import is not inheritance—why we need both: Modules and classes. In *Proceedings of the European Conference on Object-Oriented Programming (ECOOP)*, pages 19–32, Utrecht, The Netherlands, June 1992. Published as Lecture Notes in Computer Science 615, Springer-Verlag.

30. Clemens Szyperski. *Component Software: Beyond Object-Oriented Programming*. Addison-Wesley (ACM Press), Harlow, England, 1998.

31. Wolfgang Weck. Inheritance using contracts and object composition. In Wolfgang Weck, Jan Bosch, and Clemens Szyperski, editors, *Proceedings of the Workshop on Component-Oriented Programming (WCOP)*, number 5 in TUCS General Publications, pages 105–112, Turku Center for Computer Science, Lemminkäisenkatu 14, FIN-20520 Turku, Finland, September 1997.

32. Niklaus Wirth and Jürg Gutknecht. *Project Oberon: The Design of an Operating System and Compiler*. Addison-Wesley (ACM Press), Wokingham, England, 1992.

The Design of a COM-Oriented Module System

Riccardo Pucella

Department of Computer Science
Cornell University
riccardo@cs.cornell.edu

Abstract. We present in this paper the preliminary design of a module system based on a notion of components such as they are found in COM. This module system is inspired from that of Standard ML, and features first-class instances of components, first-class interfaces, and interface-polymorphic functions, as well as allowing components to be both imported from the environment and exported to the environment using simple mechanisms. The module system automates the memory management of interfaces and hides the *IUnknown* interface and *QueryInterface* mechanisms from the programmer, favoring instead a higher-level approach to handling interfaces.

1 Introduction

Components are becoming the principal way of organizing software and distributing libraries on operating systems such as Windows NT. In fact, components offer a natural improvement over classical distribution mechanism, in the areas of versioning, licensing and overall robustness. Many languages are able to use such components directly and even dynamically. On the other hand, relatively few languages are able to directly create components usable from any language, aside from the major popular languages such as C, C++ or Java.

Interfacing components in standard programming languages has some drawbacks however. Since component models typically do not map directly to the large-scale programming mechanisms of a language, there is a paradigm shift between code using external components and code using internal modular units. Similarly, the creation of components in standard programming languages is not transparent to the programmer. Specifically, converting a modular unit of the programming language into a component often requires a reorganization of the code, especially when the large-scale programming mechanisms are wildly different from the component model targeted.

One direction currently pursued to handle the complexity and paradigm shift of using components in general languages is to avoid the problem altogether and focus on scripting languages to "glue" components together and sometimes even create components in a lightweight fashion, by simple composition. This approach is useful for small tasks and moderately simple programs, but does not scale well to large software projects where the full capabilities of a general language supporting large-scale programming structures is most useful.

A modern general language for programming in a component-based world should diminish the paradigm shift required to use components versus using the language native

J. Gutknecht and W. Weck (Eds.): JMLC 2000, LNCS 1897, pp. 104–118, 2000.

large-scale programming mechanisms. Moreover, it should be possible to reason about the code, by having a reasonable semantic description of the language that includes the interaction with components.

We explore in this paper the design of a language to address this issue. We tackle the problem by specifying a language that uses a notion of components as its sole large-scale programming mechanism, both external components imported from the environment and internal components written in the programming language. An internal component can be exported to the environment as is. The model of components on which the system is based is the COM model. Our reasons for this were both pragmatic and theoretical. Pragmatically, COM is widely used and easily accessible. Theoretically, it is less object-oriented than say CORBA [22], and one of our goals is to explore issues in component-based programming without worrying about object-oriented issues. Our proposed module system subsumes both the *IUnknown* interface and the *QueryInterface* mechanism through a higher-level mechanism based on signature matching.

We take as our starting point the language Standard ML (SML) [20]. SML is a formally-defined mostly-functional language. One advantage of working with SML is that there is a clear stratification between the module system and the core language. For our purposes, this means that we can replace the existing module system with minor rework of the semantics of the core language. Moreover, the SML module system will be used as a model in our own proposal for a component-based module system. Note that this is not simply a matter of implementing COM in SML, using the abstraction mechanisms of the language. We seek to add specific module-level capabilities that capture general COM-style abstractions.

This paper describes work in progress. The work is part of a general project whose goals are to understand components as a mean of structuring programs, at the level of our current understanding of module systems, and to provide appropriate support for components in modern programming languages.

2   Preliminaries

In this section, we review the details necessary to understand the module system we are proposing. We first describe the COM approach to component architectures, since our module system is intended to model it. The description is sketchy, but good introductions include [27,2] for COM-specific information, and [31] for general component-oriented information. We then describe the current module system of SML, since it provides the inspiration and model for our own module system.

2.1   Components à la COM

COM is Microsoft's component-based technology for code reuse and library distribution [27,19]. COM is a binary specification, and relies on a small number of principles. The underlying idea of COM is that of an *interface* to an object, where an object is just an instance of a component. An interface is a view of a component. Given a COM object, it is possible to query the object to see if it provides the given interface. If the object indeed provides the interface, it returns a pointer to the interface, and through this pointer it is possible to invoke the methods implemented by the interface. Specifically, an interface is simply a pointer to a table of function pointers (called a *vtable*), one for each method of the interface.

The identification of components and interfaces is done via globally unique identifiers: A component is identified by a class identifier (CLSID), and an interface by an interface identifier (IID). It is important to note that the CLSID of a component is part of its formal description. When an application registers a component with the system (so that other applications can use it), it adds the CLSID of the component to a system database. Similarly, an interface identifier is associated formally and permanently with a given interface. To use a COM component, one need the CLSID of the component, and the IID of an interface of the component. For example, the Win32 function *CoCreateInstance* expects a CLSID and an IID to create an instance of the component with that CLSID, and returns a pointer to the specified interface (it fails if no such interface is defined).

An interface can *inherit* from another interface. An interface A that inherits from interface B simply specifies that B's methods appear before the method specified by A in the vtable of the interface. It really is interface inheritance — not a word is said about implementation, which need not be shared by A and B.

A special interface is defined by the COM standard. This interface, *IUnknown*, is required to be inherited by every other interface. The interface (simplified for our purposes) is defined as follows in IDL[1]:

```
interface IUnknown {
  HRESULT QueryInterface ([in] const IID& iid,
                          [out] void **ppv);
  unsigned long AddRef ();
  unsigned long Release ();
}
```

Since *IUnknown* is inherited by every interface, every interface must defines those functions. They are the heart of the COM technology. The idea behind *QueryInterface* is that the programmer, having created an instance of a component and obtained a given interface A, can use the method *QueryInterface* of A to obtain another interface to the given instance. Various requirements are made of *QueryInterface*, summarized as follows:

1. Querying for *IUnknown* form any interface of a given component always returns the same pointer.
2. From any interface on a component, it is possible to query for any other interface provided by the component.

Point 1 is important because it defines the notion of *object identity*. The requirement is that no matter which interface to a given instance one is working with, querying that interface for the *IUnknown* interface is guaranteed to return a specific pointer, always the same no matter what interface was used to call *QueryInterface*. Therefore, if querying for *IUnknown* from two distinct interface yields the same pointer, one is sure that the

---

[1] IDL is an interface definition language, a notation used to describe interfaces. It essentially uses the C notation for types, augmented with attributes.

```
signature PEANO_SIG = sig
  type N
  val zero : N
  val succ : N -> N
end

structure Peano : PEANO_SIG = struct
  type N = int
  val zero = 0
  fun succ (n) = n+1
end
```

Fig. 1. Peano arithmetic

two interfaces are actually to the same instance. Point 2 ensures that all the interfaces of an instance are accessible from any interface of the instance.

The two final methods in *IUnknown*, *AddRef* and *Release*, are used for memory management of interfaces. COM implements a reference-counting scheme to manage components. *AddRef* is called whenever a new pointer to an interface is created, incrementing the reference count of the interface. *Release* is called when a pointer to an interface is not to be used anymore (for example, before the pointer variable goes out of scope), and simply decrements the reference count. When the count goes to 0, the memory associated with the interface can be freed by the system. Although greatly simplifying memory management, correctly using *AddRef* and *Release* to prevent memory leaks and dangling pointers to interfaces is not easy, and the burden of safety is put on the programmer.

Containment and aggregation are two ways of combining and reusing components. Containment is straightforward: a component C_1 (outer) is said to *contain* a component C_2 (inner) if C_1 uses C_2 in its implementation. In other words, C_1 is a client of C_2. The only requirement for containment is that upon initialization, the outer component should initialize the inner component. Aggregation is specific to COM, and can best be seen as an optimization of containment. Suppose the outer component C_1 wants to expose an interface actually implemented by the inner component C_2. Using containment, C_1 would need to define the interface and implement every method call by calling the inner component's interface. The inefficiency introduced by such indirection is slight, but if many such interface get redirected, the inefficiency accumulates. Aggregation is a mean of directly exposing the interfaces of inner components through to the outer component. An important property of aggregation concerns object identity: the inner component should not be recognizable as a distinct component. Therefore, both the inner and the outer component must return the same pointer when a query is made for *IUnknown*.

2.2   Modules à la SML

Having presented the COM framework, and delineated the target of our proposed module system, let us review the basics of the SML module system [16], our underlying model. It is not necessary for the reader to have a deep knowledge of SML to understand this presentation. It is sufficient to know that SML is a mostly-functional language, with first-class functions and a polymorphic type system which is statically checked: programs that do not type-check at compile-time are flagged as such and rejected. Excellent introductions to SML are available [23,32,8].

The basic elements of the SML module system are structures, signatures and functors. A structure is a package of possibly both types and values into a single unit. A signature is the "type" of a structure. Consider the example in Figure 1, a simple structure defining Peano arithmetic with its corresponding signature. The structure defines a type N of Peano integers, a value for *zero* and a function *succ*. The structure defines a Peano integer to simply be an integer, and the zero and successor to be simply 0 and +1. The signature *PEANO* explicitly specifies the types and values that are visible outside the structure. A signature *matches* a structure if the signature consistently denotes a subset of the types and values of the structure. Matching a structure with a signature declaring less information than the structure is called *signature ascription*. Suppose one wanted to define a structure like *Peano* but that did not have a successor function. One could use signature ascription to control the visibility, as in

```
structure Peano2 : sig
    type N
    val zero : N
end = Peano
```

This example also illustrate signature matching by inlining a signature description instead of using a named signature. In SML, signature matching is by default transparent: although signature ascription can weed out declarations, it does not hide the representation of the types. For example, the implementation of *Peano* uses integers to represent the type N. Although the signature does not specify the representation type, the system will still accept

```
3 + (Peano.zero)
```

as well-typed. In effect, the type N is viewed as an abbreviation for the type integer. In contrast, *opaque matching* (using the matching symbol :>) completely hides whatever information is not specified in the signature, including representation types. The above sample would then fail to type-check.

A functor is a parametrized structure. Suppose one wanted to write a structure defining elementary algebraic operations on the integers using Peano arithmetic. Since one may have multiple implementation of Peano arithmetic, the simplest way would be to parameterize the structure as follows:

```
functor AlgOpFun (structure P : PEANO_SIG) : sig
    . . .
end = struct
    . . .
end
```

which declares the functor *AlgOpFun* to take a structure P matching signature *PEANO_SIG* as parameter and creating a new structure using structure P in its body. Instantiating a functor is simple:

```
structure AlgOp = AlgOpFun (structure P = Peano)
```

3 Design of the Module System

After reading about the SML module system, one recognizes a strong similarity between the notion of a structure and the notion of the instance of a component[2]. A functor with no argument can be seen as a component, with the generated structure corresponding to an instance, and the notion of containment and aggregation bear a strong resemblance to functors with parameters. Of course, this preliminary intuition does not take into account interfaces and their behavior under the *QueryInterface* mechanism.

In this section, we introduce a module system based on the SML module system, and providing the notions of components and interfaces. We impose the following design criteria on our design of the system:

1. Component instances provide interfaces.
2. Interfaces provide both types and values.
3. Component instances and interfaces are first-class, that is they can be passed to and returned from functions, and stored in data structures.
4. Memory management of interfaces is hidden from the programmer.
5. The *QueryInterface* mechanism is subsumed by syntax.
6. Syntactically and operationally, there is no distinction between internal and imported components.
7. Exportable components are easily characterized and general mechanisms are used to make a component exportable.

Criteria 1–2 define the "architecture" of the module system, the relationship between components, interfaces and the core language. Criterion 3 is required if we want to emulate pointer-based interface manipulation. Criteria 4–5 are important to ease the use of the system: memory management under COM, although easier than it could be, is still fragile in that the user is responsible for managing reference counts explicitly (in practice, languages like C++ encourage the use of smart pointers to alleviate most of the burden). The *QueryInterface* mechanism is powerful, but very low-level. We can take advantage of patterns of use and provide a high-level mechanisms for accessing interfaces. Finally, criteria 6–7 are mandated by the fact that the module system will be used as the large-scale programming mechanism of the language. There should be no difference between code using an internal component versus an imported component. It is clear that not every Core SML type is exportable (since the interfaces must at the very least be expressible in IDL to be exportable), so restricting the notion of component to what can be meaningfully exported is too restrictive for components that we don't want to export, that are only used internally. A simple and elegant way to support exportable components and unrestricted internally-used components is a must for a truly usable system. We use signature ascription to achieve this.

3.1 Components and Interfaces

Let us give a quick overview of the basic elements of the module system. A component is defined as providing a set of interfaces. A component has a signature, which

---

[2] Especially if one adheres to the Edinburgh school, which advocates the creation of structures exclusively through the application of functors with no arguments.

```
interface_sig X_SIG = {
  val fooX : unit -> unit
}

interface_sig Y_SIG = {
  val fooY : unit -> unit
}

component_sig FOO_SIG = {
  interface X : X_SIG
  interface Y : Y_SIG
}

component FooComp () : FOO_SIG = {
  interface X = {
    fun fooX () = print "fooX"
  }
  interface Y = {
    fun fooY () = print "fooY"
  }
}
```

Fig. 2. Simple component example

assigns interface signatures to its interfaces. An interface defines types and values (including functions). An interface signature is simply the "type" of an interface. Signature ascription can be used to thin out interfaces from components or types or values from interfaces. At the present time, we require signatures to be named. Component definitions are generative: one needs to instantiate a component to use it.

Let us illustrate with a simple example, presented in Figure 2. To use component *FooComp*, one first instantiates it by

$$\text{val Foo = FooComp ()}$$

and accessing its elements is done using the dot notation, so that Foo.X.fooX () prints fooX. Interfaces are first-class, so it is possible to bind an interface, as in

$$\text{val FooX = Foo.X}$$

which corresponds to accessing the X interface of *Foo*. The type of an interface is simply the name of its signature, surrounded by $|| \cdots ||$, so that *Foo.X* has type $||X\_SIG||$. Similarly, component instances are first-class, and their type again is simply the name of their signature, surrounded by $| \cdots |$, so that *Foo* has type $|FOO\_SIG|$.

As a last remark, we mention that signature matching is opaque. If one wants to carry representation types through a signature, one needs to explicitly give the representation types in the signature, as in [9,12].

3.2   Parametrized Components

As the notation for component declarations suggests, every component is parametrized. In Figure 2, *FooComp* was a nullary component, a component with no parameters (hence the () in the declaration of *FooComp*). Here is a sample parametrized component:

```
component BarComp (val X :  ||X_SIG||
                   val Y :  ||Y_SIG||) : BAR_SIG = {
         . . .
         }
```

where *BarComp* is parametrized over interfaces matching *X_SIG* and *Y_SIG*. A simple instantiation would be

```
val Bar = BarComp (val X = Foo.X
                   val Y = Foo.Y)
```

passing in the corresponding interfaces from the *Foo* instance of *FooComp*.

3.3   Importing and Exporting Components

One key aspect of the COM framework is the possibility of accessing components written in different languages, and conversely, of providing components that can be accessed by different languages. Let us first see how to import a component in our system. We need a way to define an interface that is imported from the environment. This is done through an interface signature as in the previous cases, except that we need to specify the IID of every interface being imported.

```
interface_sig IMPORTED_IFC_SIG = {
     . . .
     } with_iid 00000000-0000-0000-0000-000000000000
```

The requirement being that the signature of an imported component must specify an IID for each interface.

Once all the interfaces that are part of the component to be imported are specified with their IID, we can import the component from the environment:

```
import ImportedFooComp : FOO_SIG = clsid
     00000000-0000-0000-0000-000000000000
```

where the component signature *FOO_SIG* specifies the interface signatures of the imported component. The component is imported through its class identifier (CLSID). The component so imported can be instantiated just like a native nullary component. Note that interface negotiation is done up-front: when a component is instantiated, it is checked that all the interface specified in the signature are present.

The converse of importing a component is to export a component. When exporting a component a program becomes a component server from which clients can create and instantiate components. Given a component BarComp, one exports it using the declaration:

```
export BarComp : BAR_SIG with_clsid
     00000000-0000-0000-0000-000000000000
```

The class identifier specified must be a new GUID, as is the rule in COM programming[3]. The component to be exported must be a nullary component. The component signature must again specify interface signatures with interface identifiers.

In order for the exported component to be a valid COM component, its interface must at least be expressible in IDL. As we are using Core SML as our core language, we characterize the SML types that can be naturally represented in IDL via a suitable mapping. One possible definition follows: we say that a type τ is *IDL-expressible* if either of the following holds: τ is *int, bool* or *real*; τ is a record type with all field types IDL-expressible; τ is an algebraic datatype with the alternative types all IDL-expressible; τ is a list with an IDL-expressible element type; τ is a component signature; or τ is an interface signature. An interface signature I is *IDL-expressible* if every type it defines is IDL-expressible and if for every value v of type τ, either of the following holds: τ is *int,bool* or *string*; or τ is a function type of the form $\tau_1 \to \tau_2$ with τ_1 and τ_2 either *unit*, IDL-expressible or tuples of IDL-expressible types.

A key feature of the design is that at export time, one can use signature ascription to keep only the portions of a component which are IDL-expressible. The component itself is fully usable from within the language, while the restricted version is usable from without. This still requires the programmer to possibly partition the interfaces into those that are intended to be exported and those that do not, but at least the underlying framework is the same, and moreover the implementation can be shared across the interfaces.

3.4   Dynamic Interface Negotiation

The mechanism of section 3.3 for importing components assumes that the interface negotiation is done up-front, when the component is instantiated. Clearly, this cannot cover all cases of interest: one may want to use a component that can be either of two versions, both containing an interface A, but one containing an "optimized" version of the interface, called A'. Clearly, one should try to use interface A' if it is available, otherwise downgrade to using A. To do this, we introduce a notion of dynamic interface negotiation to handle components in a way compatible with other languages.

We provide an interface case construct to dynamically query a component instance for a given interface:

```
ifc_case x
   of FOO => ...
    | BAR => ...
   else => ...
```

This form evaluates to the appropriate expression if instance x supports any of *FOO* or *BAR*, or if none of the cases apply. To fully benefit from this construct, it is useful to introduce a primitive operation **instanceOf**. Given any interface A, **instanceOf** A returns the underlying component instance of the interface.

---

[3] We do not specify how such GUIDs are created. Presumably through the programming environment.

4   Discussion

The main question with respect to the preliminary design of our module system, as described in the previous section, is the appropriateness of the model to capture COM-style component-based programming as it exists.

First, note that the system subsumes, at least at this point, a module system like SML's, modulo an extra level of indirection. A structure can be seen as an instance with a single interface, and functors are just components. Although the design forces us to write all structures as functor applications, and we need to access the code indirectly through the interface, one could imagine syntactic sugar that would give modules an SML flavor.

Having first-class component instances and interface provide most of the flexibility needed to handle common COM-style programming in a type-safe manner. For example, first-class interfaces allow the definition of *interface-polymorphic functions*, functions which are polymorphic over a given interface type. One can for example define a function of type

```
val foo : ||FOO_INTERFACE|| -> int
```

that can be applied to any interface matching the *FOO_INTERFACE* interface signature. Any instance of a component with such an interface can be used with that function (by passing in the interface). Since it is always possible to extract the underlying instance of an interface, one can also return interfaces while keeping a handle on the underlying instance. One could imagine a more advanced type system that would record not only the type of interface required by such a function, but also the set of interfaces that are accessed from that interface. We leave this investigation for the future. We can similarly define component-polymorphic functions, where one can moreover use the subtyping relation on components induced by signature ascription to define say functions to act on any component providing interface *FOO* and *BAR*.

Regarding the suitability to interact with the COM framework through imported and exported component, the basic notions are by design compatible. The hiding of *IUnknown* and of *QueryInterface* greatly simplifies both the design and the code. Memory management is hidden from the user, using a combination of automatically generated underlying calls to *AddRef* and *Release*. and reliance on garbage collection and finalization, in the style of the Direct-to-COM compiler [7].

We have not yet carefully investigated the issues of containment and aggregation. As we mentionned earlier, those composition mechanisms have a flavor of functor application, but the match is not exact. One can write a parametrized component, but the parameterization cannot be over another component (component instances are first-class, but not components themselves). A component can be parametrized over an instance, but this then implies that a component has to be instantiated before being used as a parameter to another component. One could solve this problem by making components higher-order, allowing them to be used as arguments to parametrized components, or returned from such. Higher-order components correspond to higher-order functors in a SML-style module system, which greatly complicate the module system theory, especially in regard to the interaction with types [17,9,13]. With higher-order components, one could provide syntactic sugar for convenient aggregation and containment mechanisms.

However, when such components are exported, the issues raised by Sullivan *et al* [30, 29] with regard to the rules required to ensure the legality of COM components arise, and need to be addressed. This is another area of future work.

A word about implementation is in order. We use two different implementation mechanisms, one for internal components, one for imported components, along with specific handling for exported components. Internal components are handled in more or less the same way modules are handled in current SML implementation, modulo first-class interfaces and component instances. Imported components rely on the underlying *CoCreateInstance* for creation, and *QueryInterface* for access to interfaces. Instances of imported components are represented by their *IUnknown* interface pointers, allowing for equality checking. For exported components, the generation of the appropriate layout of the vtables can be done on the fly, at export time.

5   Related Work

A lot of work has been done independently on both module systems and component systems, but none quite taking our approach. Most work in programming language support for components consists of providing access to components from within a language's abstraction mechanism. For example, Java [6] and C++ [28] both map components onto classes. Similarly, functional approaches pioneered by Haskell [24,25,3,4] and then used in OCaml [15,14] and SML [26] rely on a combination of abstract types and functions to interface to components. One can write classes implementing components in Java and C++, and using the functional approach in Haskell, but the notions do not match exactly. Our approach to studying the problem is to express components with a language *explicitely* geared towards talking about components and interfaces.

The closest language in spirit to our effort is Component Pascal [21], a language providing extensible records that has been used to implement COM components. However, the problem is again that there is a paradigm mismatch between the structuring mechanisms of the language and components. Component Pascal is a modular language for writing components, but components themselves are not the modularity mechanism of the language.

COMEL [10,11] was our original inspiration for this work. The mechanism of hiding *IUnknown* and *QueryInterface* are similar, but the difference is that COMEL is a small language meant for a study of the formal properties of the COM framework, while our proposal is for an extension of an existing language to support component-based code structuring mechanisms.

6   Conclusion

We have presented in this paper a preliminary design for a module system that directly incorporates the notions of components and interfaces as defined in COM. The design is rough, but the basic idea is clear. The system can subsume a powerful module system such as SML's, and is directly compatible with COM's model of the world. Work is now needed to complete and evaluate the design. Aside from the issues raised in the text concerning aggregation and higher-order components, we are working on a formal semantics for the module system, both a static semantics (types and their propagation) and a dynamic semantics (the execution model and interaction with the COM runtime system). The implementation has to be completed and systems built using it.

Finally, and this is once again future work, it is of great interest to investigate the relationship between our approach and the approach supported by structuring mechanisms such as units [5] and mixins à la Jigsaw [1].

Acknowledgments . Thanks to Greg Morrisett for many discussions on module systems and COM. Thanks to Peter Fröhlich for a thorough reading of the paper and many comments that helped shape the presentation. Thanks to Dino Oliva, Erik Meijer and Daan Leijen for early discussions about various aspects of COM. Thanks as well to John Reppy for general inspiration.

References

1. G. Bracha. *The Programming Language Jigsaw: Mixins, Modularity and Multiple Inheritance.* PhD thesis, Department of Computer Science, University of Utah, 1992.
2. D. Chappell. *Understanding ActiveX and OLE.* Microsoft Press, 1996.
3. S. Finne, D. Leijen, E. Meijer, and S. Peyton Jones. H/Direct: A binary foreign language interface for Haskell. In *Proceedings of the 1998 ACM SIGPLAN International Conference on Functional Programming*, pages 153–162. ACM Press, 1998.
4. S. Finne, D. Leijen, E. Meijer, and S. Peyton Jones. Calling hell from heaven and heaven from hell. In *Proceedings of the 1999 ACM SIGPLAN International Conference on Functional Programming*, pages 114–125. ACM Press, 1999.
5. M. Flatt. *Programming Languages for Reusable Software Components.* PhD thesis, Rice University, 1999.
6. J. Gosling, B. Joy, and G. Steele. *The Java Language Specification.* Addison Wesley, 1996.
7. D. Gruntz and B. Heeb. Direct-To-COM compiler provides garbage collection for COM objects. In *Proceedings of the 2nd Component User's Conference (CUC)*, July 1997.
8. R. Harper. Programming in Standard ML. Online tutorial notes available from `http://www.cs.cmu.edu/~rwh/introsml/% linebreak[2]index.html`, 1998.
9. R. Harper and M. Lillibridge. A type-theoretic approach to higher-order modules and sharing. In *Conference Record of the Twenty-First Annual ACM Symposium on Principles of Programming Languages.* ACM Press, 1994.
10. R. Ibrahim and C. Szyperski. The COMEL language. Technical Report FIT-TR-97-06, Faculty of Information Technology, Queensland University of Technology, Brisbane, Australia, 1997.
11. R. Ibrahim and C. Szyperski. Can Component Object Model (COM) be formalized? — the formal semantics of the COMEL language. Work-In-Progress, IRW/FMP'98. Also appears as Technical Report TR-CS-98-09, The Australian National University, 1998.
12. X. Leroy. Manifest types, modules, and separate compilation. In *Conference Record of the Twenty-First Annual ACM Symposium on Principles of Programming Languages*, pages 109–122. ACM Press, 1994.
13. X. Leroy. Applicative functors and fully transparent higher-order modules. In *Conference Record of the Twenty-Second Annual ACM Symposium on Principles of Programming Languages*, pages 142–153. ACM Press, 1995.
14. X. Leroy. Camlidl user's manual. Online manual available from `http://caml.inria.fr/camlidl/`, 1999.
15. X. Leroy, J. Vouillon, and D. Doligez. The Objective Caml system. Software and documentation available from `http://pauillac.inria.fr/ocaml/`, 1996.

16. D. MacQueen. Modules for Standard ML. In *Conference Record of the 1984 ACM Symposium on Lisp and Functional Programming*, pages 198–207. ACM Press, 1984.

17. D. B. MacQueen and M. Tofte. A semantics for higher-order functors. In *Fifth European Symposium on Programming*, volume 788 of *Lecture Notes in Computer Science*, pages 409–423. Springer, 1994.

18. Microsoft Corporation. *Developing for Microsoft Agent*. Microsoft Press, 1997.

19. Microsoft Corporation and Digital Equipment Corporation. The Component Object Model Specification. Draft version 0.9, available from http://www.microsoft.com/com, 1995.

20. R. Milner, M. Tofte, R. Harper, and D. MacQueen. *The Definition of Standard ML (Revised)*. The MIT Press, Cambridge, Mass., 1997.

21. Oberon Microsystems Inc. Component Pascal language report. Available from http://www.oberon.ch, 1997.

22. Object Management Group. The Common Object Request Broker: Architecture and Specifications (revision 1.2). OMG document 93.12.43, Object Management Group, 1993.

23. L. C. Paulson. *ML for the Working Programmer*. Cambridge University Press, second edition, 1996.

24. J. Peterson and K. Hammond (Eds). Report on the programming language Haskell, version 1.4. Technical report, Department of Computer Science, Yale University, 1997. Available from http://www.haskell.org.

25. S. Peyton Jones, E. Meijer, and D. Leijen. Scripting COM components from Haskell. In *Proceedings of the Fifth International Conference on Software Reuse*. IEEE Computer Society Press, 1998.

26. R. Pucella, E. Meijer, and D. Oliva. Aspects de la programmation d'applications Win32 avec un langage fonctionnel. In *Actes des Journées Francophones des Languages Applicatifs*, pages 267–291. INRIA, 1999.

27. D. Rogerson. *Inside COM*. Microsoft Press, 1997.

28. B. Stroustrup. *The C++ Programming Language*. Addison Wesley, Reading, MA, third edition, 1997.

29. K. J. Sullivan and M. Marchukov. Interface negotiation and efficient reuse: A relaxed theory of the component object model. Technical Report 97-11, Department of Computer Science, University of Virginia, 1997.

30. K. J. Sullivan, J. Socha, and M. Marchukov. Using formal methods to reason about architectural standards. In *Proceedings of the International Conference on Software Engineering*, pages 503–513. ACM Press, 1997.

31. C. Szyperski. *Component Software*. Addison Wesley, 1997.

32. J. D. Ullman. *Elements of ML Programming*. Prentice-Hall, ML97 edition, 1998.

A   Microsoft Agent

A popular example in the literature concerned with interacting with COM is Microsoft Agent [18]. It is an interesting example because it is simple yet non-trivial, and allows for nice demonstrations. Microsoft Agent provides a server in charge of loading little animated characters that can interact on the screen. The Agent Server is a component with a single interface, *IAgent*. Here is first the Agent Server component signature, and import from the environment.

```
component_sig AGENT_SERVER = {
  interface IAgent : I_AGENT
}

import AgentServer () : AGENT_SERVER = clsid
  A7B93C92-7B81-11D0-AC5F-00C04FD97575
```

Here is an extract of the *I_AGENT* interface signature. Note that the method *getCha-racter* returns an *AGENT_CHARACTER* which is as we shall see a component instance that represent a character that can be animated.

```
interface_sig I_AGENT = {
  val load : string -> (int,int)
  val unload : int -> unit
  val register : |AGENT_NOTIFY_SINK| -> sinkID
  val unregister : sinkID -> unit
  val getCharacter : int -> |AGENT_CHARACTER|
  ...
} with_iid A7B93C91-7B81-11D0-AC5F-00C04FD97575
```

A character is implemented by its own component, with the following signature. We concentrate on the *IAgentCharacter* interface. Other interfaces are available to intercept and process commands to the characters, but we will not be considering those in this example.

```
component_sig AGENT_CHARACTER = {
  interface IAgentCharacter : I_AGENT_CHARACTER
}
```

We do not need to import the corresponding component from the environment, since the creation of characters is restricted to the *getCharacter* function of the Agent Server component. Indeed, the *AgentCharacter* component does not explicitly exist in Microsoft Agent.

The *IAgentCharacter* interface is used to control a character, to make it appear, move about the screen, speak and animate.

```
interface_sig I_AGENT_CHARACTER = {
  val setPosition : int * int -> unit
  val getPosition : unit -> (int * int)
  val play : string -> int
  val stop : int -> unit
  val show : bool -> int
  val speak : string * string -> int
  ....
} with_iid A7B93C8F-7B81-11D0-AC5F-00C04FD97575
```

The simplest example of code using such an interface is the following, which simply displays an agent for 10 seconds.

```
fun test () = let
  val AS = AgentServer ()
  val val (charId,_) = AS.IAgent.load ("merlin")
  val val Char = AS.IAgent.getCharacter (charId)
in
  Char.IAgentCharacter.show (0);
  Char.IAgentCharacter.speak ("Hello world","");
  sleep (10000);  (* wait for 10000 milliseconds *)
  AS.IAgent.unload (charId)
end
```

We leave the task of defining abstraction and combinators to help dealing with characters in a sane way, in the style of [25], as an exercise to the reader.

Oberon as an Implementation Language for COM Components:
A Case Study in Language Interoperability

Jürg Gutknecht

ETH Zentrum
CH-8092 Zürich
gutknecht@inf.ethz.ch

Abstract. This is a short report on a short project, carried out during a 3-month sabbatical stay at Microsoft Research in the fall of 1998. The motivation for this endeavor was double-faced: On one hand, verify the degree of language independence promised by the COM component technology and, on the other hand, explore COM as a potential commercial environment and framework for Oberon applications. The project finally converged towards a simple case study, an electronic bank implemented in Oberon as a COM server under Windows NT and illustratively used by a Visual Basic client.

Keywords: Components, COM, Language Interoperability, Oberon.

1   Oberon as an Autonomous Platform

Project Oberon [1] was started in 1986 by Niklaus Wirth and the author of this report. Oberon as a *language* [2] extends the line of Pascal and Modula-2, Oberon as a *system* is a compact and fully modular operating system for personal computers. The first Oberon implementation was targeted to Ceres, a proprietary National Semiconductor 32000 based hardware platform. From this original version, several evolutions and numerous implementation variants have emerged. For example, one native implementation (for Intel PCs) and four embedded implementations (for Windows, Macintosh, Linux, and Unix on Intel, PowerPC and SPARC hardware) of Oberon System 3 [3] exist today.

Even though Oberon is an attractive software development language and platform, it is hardly used in commercial projects because of its incompatibility with "the standards". In essence, neither the Oberon system nor products developed with it are able to communicate with any non-Oberon host environment in any nontrivial way. It is therefore desirable to adapt Oberon to a universal component framework like COM (Common Object Model) [4, 5] that enables components (sometimes called *controls*) from different programming cultures to collaborate orderly on an appropriate level of abstraction.

J. Gutknecht and W. Weck (Eds.): JMLC 2000, LNCS 1897, pp. 119-133, 2000.

2   Oberon as a COM Participant

In order to explain the essential steps towards Oberon (or any other programming language) as a COM participant, we first recall that COM uses an elaborate concept of *interface* with the aim of decoupling clients from component implementations. The two main aspects of the COM interface technology correspond directly to the two main aspects of adapting Oberon to COM. They are

- the "1 object implements n (immutable) interfaces" relation in combination with a runtime interface querying mechanism

- the IDL (Interface Description Language) formalism used to specify individual interfaces

IDL is a notation that is used in slightly different variations in high-level object-oriented frameworks like CORBA [6] and COM to describe interfaces formally but independent of the implementation language and thus to serve as a common denominator for language interoperability. However, in practice, IDL explicitly or (worse) implicitly dictates a variety of technical details "behind the scenes" like memory mapping of data types and procedure calling conventions that implementation languages have to comply with. As IDL is close in style and spirit to the C/C++/Java language family, members of this family are in favor compared to, for example, Oberon. Concretely, the following problems occurred in the course of our project:

- the need for data types not supported by Oberon (for example, unsigned integers and bit arrays of different sizes)

- the need for tag-free structured types (structured types in Oberon carry a tag to support run-time typing and garbage collection)

- the need for a "standard" procedure calling protocol requiring, for example, callers to pop parameters from the stack (in Oberon, parameter popping can be done by callees because parameter omitting is not allowed)

We solved these problems more or less ad hoc by

- mapping unsupported IDL data types to closest possible Oberon data types

- introducing a "no tag" compiler directive for record types and array type

- introducing a "standard call" compiler directive for procedures and functions

Examples

```
TYPE
  UINT = LONGINT;
  WORD = INTEGER;
  DWORD = LONGINT; HRESULT = LONGINT;
```

```
GUID = RECORD [notag]
  p1: LONGINT;
  p2, p3: INTEGER;
  p4: ARRAY 8 OF CHAR
END;
```

```
PROCEDURE QueryInterface [stdcall] (this: Interface;
  iid: GUID; VAR ifc: Interface): HRESULT;
```

The other major aspect to be dealt with is the "1 object implements n interfaces" relation, where every implemented interface is immutable and corresponds to a certain "facette" of the implementing object. Although this looks similar to Java's interface concept at first sight, it is important in our context to zoom-in to the nuances. In the case of Java, interfaces implemented by a class are "inherited" and are thereby an aspect of the class definition. Strong typing, i. e. compile-time polymorphism and compile-time consistency checks apply in this case. In contrast, interface implementation in COM is a pure implementation issue on an instance basis. In its utmost generality, individual COM objects could "develop" during their life time and change the set of interfaces they implement without destroying the system's integrity, i. e. without invalidating any client's compiled code. The price to pay for such added flexibility is a separate interface management for each object at runtime.

Mainly for the sake of transparency, we have chosen an explicit approach in our case study and have resisted the temptation to hide the interface mechanism behind additional language constructs and compiler support. However, we should mention that we were aiming at a prototype rather than at a commercial product like, for example, *Component Pascal Blackbox* by *Oberon Microsystems* [4]. Our implementation is based on the following type *Interface*:

```
TYPE
  Interface = POINTER TO RECORD
    vtbl: IUnknownVT;
    obj: Object;
    next: Interface;
    iid: GUID
  END;
```

We cannot understand the details of the *Interface* type without recapitulating some very basic COM terminology and technical notions. First, a *v-table* is a table of virtual methods describing the functionality of an interface. Second, *IUnknown* is the most basic of all COM interfaces. It contains the *Query*-method and two methods for reference counting. All other interfaces must be extensions of *IUnknown*, i. e. they must contain *IUnknown's* methods as a subset. Finally, a *GUID* is a globally unique identifier that typically denotes a certain published interface or another reusable entity.

vtbl is now a pointer to the *v-table* of this interface (*IUnknown* or any extension thereof), *obj* refers to the underlying object implementing this interface, *next* serves as a link connecting the set of interfaces implemented by the underlying object, and *iid* is the GUID of this interface.

The following is an exemplary declaration of two v-tables in COM Oberon, belonging to the interfaces *IUnknown* and *IPersist* respectively. Note that v-tables are record structures consisting of function pointers and that type extension is used to denote interface extensions. Also notice that the result of an interface query is a pointer to an instance of type *Interface*. *HRESULT* is COM's universal type for return codes.

```
TYPE
 IUnknownVT = POINTER TO RECORD
  QueryInterface: PROCEDURE [stdcall] (this: Interface;
   iid: GUID; VAR ifc: Interface): HRESULT;
  AddRef: PROCEDURE [stdcall] (this: Interface): LONGINT;
  Release: PROCEDURE [stdcall] (this: Interface): LONGINT
 END;

 IPersistVT = POINTER TO RECORD (IUnknownVT)
  GetClassID: PROCEDURE [stdcall] (this: Interface;
   VAR clsid: GUID): HRESULT
 END;
```

COM Oberon objects are again instances of a pointer based structured type:

```
TYPE
 Object = POINTER TO RECORD
  prev, next: Object;
  mcref: LONGINT;
  ifc: Interface
 END;
```

mcref subsumes the COM reference count. The entirety of objects currently in use by COM (i.e. with mcref > 0) are linked to a ring via *prev/next* in order to prevent the Oberon garbage collector from reclaiming objects used by COM but not by Oberon. Finally, the *ifc* field in type *Object* refers to the list of interfaces implemented by this object.

The following COM Oberon program excerpt may serve as an illustrative example. It implements the *Query*-method of the *IUnknown* interface.

```
PROCEDURE [stdcall] QueryInterfaceImpl (this: Interface;
  iid: GUID;
  VAR ifc: Interface): HRESULT;
  VAR str: ARRAY 40 OF CHAR;
BEGIN
  DecodeGUID(iid, str); ifc := this.obj.ifc;
  WHILE (ifc # NIL) & ~EQUGUID(iid, ifc.iid) DO
   ifc := ifc.next
  END;
  IF ifc # NIL THEN INC(this.obj.mcref); RETURN Sok
   ELSE RETURN EnoInterface
  END
END QueryInterfaceImpl;
```

Remarks

- The pointer links between v-table entries and implementations and between objects and interfaces are created at object creation time.

- The *IUnknown* interface is an implicit part of every member in the list of interfaces supported by an object. Additionally, *IUnknown* is included in this list as an explicit member, in order to guarantee a consistent answer on querying the object for *IUnknown*.

- The reference counting mechanism could easily be refined, i.e. the reference count that is now stored centrally in an object could easily be distributed to the different interfaces that it supports.

- Our run-time model easily allows objects to implement multiple instances of the same interface. This in contrast to models based on a mapping of "implements" to inheritance of virtual classes that need the help of additional (and complex) constructions like nested classes. Multiple instances of an interface are useful, for example, in the case of multiple connection points provided by a server object, where each of them is represented by an individual *IConnectionPoint* interface. As a fine point note that connection point interfaces are not included in the list of interfaces implemented by an object, because they are retrieved directly via the *FindConnectionPoint* method rather than via their GUID and *Query*.

One interesting point about COM is its universality not only in terms of language independence but also in terms of operating system independence. Nevertheless, *Windows* is the natural platform for COM, so that we decided to use Windows (NT, to be more precise) as target platform for COM Oberon, both as a development system and as a runtime system. Consequently, we had to provide

- an Oberon interface layer connecting Oberon with the basic Windows API

- a tool to generate a Windows compatible executable format from Oberon binaries

The Oberon interface definition of the Windows API consists of two modules *Kernel32* and *ADVAPI*. They are used by some low-level Oberon modules, notably by the modules *Kernel*, *Registry* and *Console*. *Kernel* is Oberon's native kernel implementing garbage collection, object finalization etc., *Registry* supports registration of *(keyword, value)* pairs in the Windows registry, and *Console* allows simple trace output from Oberon to the Windows console. The executable format generator in its current form is called *PELinker*. It simply links (compiled) Oberon module hierarchies to portable Windows executables (i.e. DLL and exe-files in PE format).

3   Case Study: An Electronic Bank as a COM Oberon Control

The choice of an application, i.e. of an exemplary implementation of a COM control in Oberon was guided by the following list of checkpoints:

- The application code should be compact. The COM-related code should dominate the implementation.

- The application code should not be trivial. It should include dynamic data structures beyond the list type and fast algorithms that are not typically available in higher-level client languages like Visual Basic.

- The control should produce special events resulting from its entire history rather than just from individual calls or uses.

We finally decided for an *electronic bank* that is able to efficiently manage a potentially huge number of accounts and that provides the following functionality:

- Open (new) account with given *identification* (name), *initial balance* (positive or negative) and *lower limit* (negative).

- Query balance of specified account.

- Add/withdraw specified amount to/from specified account.

With that, our checkpoints were easily met: We simply implemented the bank as an ordered binary tree and defined *bankrupcy* as a special event.

The "multicultural" character of COM and its benefits can perhaps best be demonstrated in the case of a *controller* using a somewhat abstract language to manipulate components on a somewhat abstract level. From the perspective of the controller, components are then encapsulated "small worlds" whose internals do not have to be fully understood. Obviously, the benefits of such a component approach are particularly impressive, if the "small worlds" have a complex infrastructure and are implemented in a "foreign" language.

As illustrated in Figure 1, we chose Visual Basic as a controller environment and container for our COM Oberon electronic banking control. The following Visual Basic project depicts a possible implementation of a client.

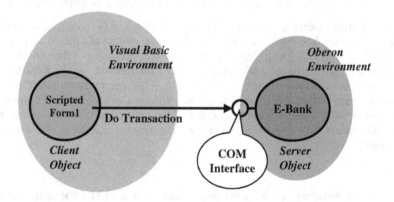

Figure 1. Structural Overview of the Electronic Banking Case Study

Form1

```
Private Sub Command1_Click()

 Dim x As Object
 Dim e As New Class1 'smart agent
 Dim f As New Class2 'standard agent

 Set x = CreateObject("COMOberon")
 MsgBox x 'write default VALUE property

 x = "My E-Bank" 'customize VALUE property
 MsgBox x

 MsgBox "OWN " & x.Open("OWN")
  Rem open bank's own acc
 MsgBox "X " & x.Open("X", 500, -1000)
  Rem open account "X", balance 500, lower limit -1000
 MsgBox "Y " & x.Open("Y", 2000, -2000)
  Rem open account Y, balance 2000, lower limit -2000
 MsgBox "X " & x.Trans("X", 200)
  Rem add 200 to "X", balance 700
 MsgBox "Y " & x.Trans("Y", 100)
  Rem add 100 to "Y", balance 2100
 MsgBox "X " & x.Trans("X", 400)
  Rem add 400 to "X", balance 1100
 MsgBox "Y " & x.Query("Y")
  Rem get balance of "Y", balance 2100
 MsgBox "Y " & x.Trans("Y", -3300, f)
  Rem Bank throws Bankrupt Exception
  Rem Standard agent f catches and reports "Bankrupt"
  Rem Transaction fails, bal 2100
 MsgBox "Y " & x.Trans("Y", -3300, e)
  Rem Bank throws Bankrupt Exception
  Rem Smart agent e catches and adds 100 from reserve
  Rem Transaction succeeds, balance -1200
 MsgBox "A " & x.Open("A", 10000, -1000)
  Rem open acc "A", balance 10000
 MsgBox "B " & x.Open("B", -800, -2000, e)
  Rem open acc "B", balance -800
 MsgBox "X " & x.Trans("X", -2500, e)
  Rem Bank respects lower limit of "X", balance -1000
 MsgBox "C " & x.Trans("C", 800)
  Rem Bank refuses transaction on unexisting account

End Sub
```

Class1

```
Implements IeventHandling
Dim reserve As Integer

Public Sub IEventHandling_HandleBankrupcy(x As Variant,
  ByVal ub As Long)
  If reserve \ 10 >= -ub Then amt = -ub
   Else amt = reserve\10
  MsgBox x.Trans("OWN", amt) & " added"
  reserve = reserve - amt
End Sub

Private Sub Class_Initialize()
  reserve = 8000
End Sub
```

Class2

```
Public Sub HandleBankrupcy()
  MsgBox "Bankrupt"
End Sub
```

Apart from some standard COM interfaces like *IUnknown* and *IPersistPropertyBag*, Visual Basic communicates with its servers via the *IDispatch* interface. *IDispatch* is a generic interface that is based on *runtime message dispatching* (in contrast to compile-time dispatching used by "ordinary" object-oriented languages). Runtime dispatching obviously refines to method identification and parameter checking/decoding at message arrival time. The *IDispatch* interface provided by our electronic banking control is implemented as procedure *InvokeImpl* (see source listing in the Appendix). The different kinds of messages are distinguished by parameter *dispid*. *dispid = 0* signalizes access to the canonical *property* VALUE that, in our case, is the bank's name. *wflags* in this case specifies the type of access (GET or PUT). The further cases *dispid = 1, 2, 3* correspond to the methods *Open*, *Query*, and *Trans(action)* respectively. All method parameters are of the standard type *VARIANT*. The variants currently supported by COM Oberon are *VARIANT* (again), *BSTR* (Basic string), integers, long integers, and *IDispatch* interfaces. Notice that our dispatcher allows omitted parameters at the end of a parameter list.

The *IDispatch* parameter variant is used by our banking control to pass an *event agent* who is supposed to handle the *bankrupcy* event. It is noteworthy that this mechanism allows objects like *agents*, implemented in the client's own language, to be passed to the server. In fact, delegating the routine-details of a task to a server (or possibly to multiple servers) while still keeping control over the handling of special events is an interesting software design pattern that has been successfully propagated under the title of "event-oriented programming" by Visual Basic and other environments. It always emphasizes a controller's role of "glue logic".

For the purpose of illustration, we have implemented two different kinds of event agents corresponding to two different Visual Basic classes and to two different calling techniques. The essential point in both cases is the fact that the COM Oberon object now acts as a client calling a *source interface* (or "outgoing interface") that is implemented elsewhere, in this case on the side of the event agent. Our COM Oberon control defines its source interface explicitly and formally by means of a *type library* and by corresponding entries in the Windows registry. The following *odl* description (to be compiled into the type library by the *midl* compiler) reveals that the source interface is an *IDispatch* interface called *IEventHandling*:

```
[uuid (51238A13-75D2-11D2-9303-00A0C99334B2),
 helpstring("COM Oberon type library"), lcid(0),
 version(1.0)]

library COMOberon {
importlib("STDOLE32.TLB");

[uuid (51238A14-75D2-11D2-9303-00A0C99334B2),
 version(1.0), oleautomation]

dispinterface IEventHandling {
properties:
methods: [id(1)] void HandleBankrupcy (VARIANT* x,
 int ub); };

[uuid(8C74F345-6A54-11D2-9302-00A0C99334B2),
 helpstring("COM Oberon control"), version(1.0)]

coclass COMOberon {
 [default, source] dispinterface IEventHandling; }; };
```

IEventHandling features just one method *HandleBankrupcy* that takes one variant parameter and one integer parameter. The variant parameter refers to the *IDispatch* interface of the COM Oberon control that generated the event, and it thereby enables the event agent to communicate back.

Note now that *Class1* (see the Visual Basic client code above) *implements* the *IEventHandling* interface, thereby making beneficial use of the callback possibility by transferring the lacking amount to the *OWN* account of the event-causing control (up to a certain percentage of the global reserves). *Class1* event agents (like *e*) therefore guarantee the availability of the outgoing interface, so that our COM Oberon control can proceed as planned.

The situation is different for event agents like *f* of a class that does not (explicitly) implement *IEventHandling*. In this case, the COM control needs to find a different way of calling the agent. An obvious solution is to use the *IDispatch* interface that is generated implicitly by the Visual Basic compiler and that, by definition, comprises the set of public subroutines of the class. Note that in this case the calling COM Oberon control has to carry the full burden of checking consistency between call and called implementation. This in contrast to the previous case, where the check is done by the Visual Basic compiler using the type library.

The strategy used by the COM Oberon control is this: If the class of the event handling object implements the interface defined by the type library, use it, otherwise assume that a simple, variant of *HandleBankrupcy* without parameters is implemented. In terms of run-time COM, this strategy is expressed as follows (for details see the source listing of procedure *Bankrupt* in the Appendix):

```
{ Get event agent's IDispatch interface I from parameter;
  Query I for interface IEventHandling as defined
   by the type library;
  If answer is positive, use IeventHandling
  Else try to get dispid of HandleBankrupcy from I;
   If answer is positive, use I
   Else apply default event handling
}
```

Figure 2 summarizes the presented case study. In particular, it depicts the different COM objects involved, their role and their mutual relations.

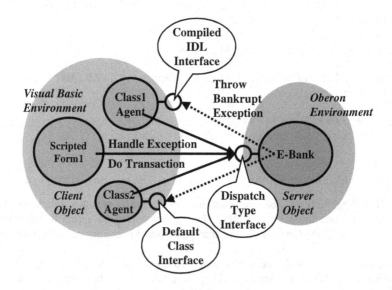

Figure 2. Refined Structure of the Electronic Banking Case Study

Remarks

1. The inclusion of an explicit event agent in the interface between client and server is not an optimal solution. If our COM Oberon control would qualify as an *ActiveX* control (i.e. if it would support all the necessary interfaces), the Visual Basic container would by its own establish an event connection with our control via the *IConnectionPointContainer* mechanism. Our COM Oberon implementation is prepared for this.

2. Our electronic banking control uses the *IPersistPropertyBag* mechanism to save its only property (its name) persistently. However, no provision is made yet for the actual contents of our control (i.e. the collection of accounts) to be persistent. This would be easy with the direct use of Oberon's file system. However, we would prefer an implementation that consequently uses *IPropertyBag*.

3. Our COM Oberon control is currently embedded into a DLL, and it therefore appears as an "in process" server. Thanks to COM's transparency along the process distance axis, we do not anticipate problems with porting it to an "out of process" server, but this would be a worthwhile, separate experiment.

4   Conclusion and Outlook

We have designed and implemented a prototype of a fully-grown COM control in Oberon that is ready to be used by any COM client and in particular by Visual Basic and HTML. The implementation is based on an underlying compiler/linker/run-time framework connecting Oberon with Windows. Our experience has shown that COM can in fact serve as a technology for a seamless integration of a "foreign" language like Oberon (not necessarily belonging to the C-"family") into a widespread operating system like Windows or, in other words, that it can provide a viable environment for "small worlds", implemented in foreign languages.

However, we consider our COM Oberon control a prototype mainly because Oberon is still lacking any institutionalized framework that supports the COM interface mechanism. For example, Oberon's arsenal of types is not rich enough to provide a full image of the IDL data types. Also, the compiler directive mechanism allowing standard calls and tag-free structures is tentative. What is actually needed is comprehensive support by both the language and the compiler for

- Interface querying and management on a per-object basis

- Compiling and generating interfaces in IDL

We plan to design and develop such support in the near future. However, we do not plan to map the "implements" relation to multiple interface inheritance along the C++/Java lines.

We further plan to combine the development just mentioned with our "active object" concept. Active objects are *self-controlling* (in contrast with remote-controlled) by one or multiple in-scope light-weight processes and are therefore fully self-contained. We believe that the "active object" model is particularly appropriate in the case of dynamic controls like *movies* that are self-active by nature.

Acknowledgement

My foremost thanks go to Tony Williams for providing a most interesting and effective but no less enjoyable environment for my 3-month stay at Microsoft Research. I am very impressed of the high standards set and maintained by Tony and his team. My warmest thanks also go to the other members of Tony's group and in particular to Crispin Goswell and Dennis Canady for their valuable and competent help with COM and Visual Basic, without it I would not have been able to successfully complete my prototype. I also won't forget many inspiring discussions with Tony, Walt Hill and Charles Frankston.

I also gratefully acknowledge the valuable comments of the referees on an earlier version of this article and, last but certainly not least, the truly "fundamental" contribution of my collaborator Emil Zeller. His "Windows Oberon" implementation at the moment includes the compiler adjustments, the linker and the API-kernel mentioned in the text. Thanks to his profound knowledge of both the Windows culture and the Oberon culture and to his super-efficient way of working, remote control from Redmond to Zurich worked well in this case.

References

[1] Wirth, N., Gutknecht, J., Project Oberon - The Design of an Operating System and Compiler , Addison-Wesley, 1992, ISBN 0-201-54428-8.

[2] Reiser, M., Wirth, N., Programming in Oberon - Steps Beyond Pascal and Modula, Addison-Wesley, 1992, ISBN 0-201-56543-9.

[3] Fischer, A., Marais, H., The Oberon Companion: A Guide to Using and Programming Oberon System 3, vdf Hochschulverlag AG, ETH Zurich, 1998, ISBN 3-7281-2493-1.

[4] C. Szyperski, Component Software - Beyond Object-Oriented Programming, Addison-Wesley, 1998, ISBN 0-201-17888-5.

[5] Box, D., Essential COM, Addison-Wesley, 1998, ISBN 0-201-63446-5.

[6] Object Management Group, The Common Object Request Broker: Architecture and Specification, Revision 1.1., 1992.

Appendix

A.) Source Code of the COM Oberon *IDispatch*-Implementation

```
PROCEDURE [stdcall] InvokeImpl (this: Interface;
 dispid: DISPID;
 iid: GUID; lcid: LCID; wFlags: WORD;
 VAR par: DISPPARAMS; VAR res: VARIANT;
 excpInfo: EXCEPINFO;
 VAR pArgErr: UINT): HRESULT;

 VAR i: INTEGER; a: Account; amt, min: LONGINT;
  id: String; eventIfc: Interface;

BEGIN
 CASE dispid OF
  0: (*property VALUE*)
    IF ODD(wFlags DIV 2) THEN (*DISPATCHPROPERTYGET*)
     STRtoVARIANT(this.obj.val, res); RETURN Sok
    ELSIF ODD(wFlags DIV 4) THEN (*DISPLAYPROPERTYPUT*)
     VARIANTtoSTR(par.rgvarg.arg[0], this.obj.val);
     RETURN Sok
    ELSE RETURN Efail
    END |
  1: (*Open*)
    IF ODD(wFlags) THEN (*DISPATCHMETHOD*) i := 0;
     WHILE par.cArgs > 4 DO DEC(par.cArgs); INC(i) END;
     IF par.cArgs = 4 THEN
      VARIANTtoDIFC(par.rgvarg.arg[i], eventIfc);
      DEC(par.cArgs); INC(i)
     ELSE eventIfc := NIL
     END;
     IF par.cArgs = 3 THEN
      VARIANTtoLONG(par.rgvarg.arg[i], min);
      DEC(par.cArgs); INC(i)
     ELSE min := 0
     END;
     IF par.cArgs = 2 THEN
      VARIANTtoLONG(par.rgvarg.arg[i], amt);
      DEC(par.cArgs); INC(i)
     ELSE amt := 0
     END;
     IF par.cArgs = 1 THEN
      VARIANTtoSTR(par.rgvarg.arg[i], id);
      DEC(par.cArgs); INC(i)
     ELSE id := "OWN"
     END;
     Open(this, eventIfc, id, amt, min, a);
     LONGtoVARIANT(a.bal, res);
```

```
        RETURN Sok
      ELSE RETURN Efail
      END |
  2: (*Query*)
      IF ODD(wFlags) THEN (*DISPATCHMETHOD*) i := 0;
       WHILE par.cArgs > 1 DO DEC(par.cArgs); INC(i) END;
       IF par.cArgs = 1 THEN
        VARIANTtoSTR(par.rgvarg.arg[i], id);
        DEC(par.cArgs); INC(i)
       ELSE id := "OWN"
       END;
       a := Search(this.obj.AB, id);
       IF a # NIL THEN LONGtoVARIANT(a.bal, res)
        ELSE STRtoVARIANT("unknown", res)
       END;
       RETURN Sok
      ELSE RETURN Efail
      END |
  3: (*Transaction*);
      IF ODD(wFlags) THEN (*DISPATCHMETHOD*) i := 0;
       WHILE par.cArgs > 3 DO DEC(par.cArgs); INC(i) END;
       IF par.cArgs = 3 THEN
        VARIANTtoDIFC(par.rgvarg.arg[i], eventIfc);
        DEC(par.cArgs); INC(i)
       ELSE eventIfc := NIL
       END;
       IF par.cArgs = 2 THEN
        VARIANTtoLONG(par.rgvarg.arg[i], amt);
        DEC(par.cArgs); INC(i)
       ELSE amt := 0
       END;
       IF par.cArgs = 1 THEN
        VARIANTtoSTR(par.rgvarg.arg[i], id);
        DEC(par.cArgs); INC(i)
       ELSE id := "OWN"
       END;
       Trans(this, eventIfc, id, amt, a);
       IF a # NIL THEN LONGtoVARIANT(a.bal, res)
        ELSE STRtoVARIANT("unknown", res)
       END;
       RETURN Sok
      ELSE RETURN Efail
      END
   ELSE RETURN Efail
   END

END InvokeImpl;
```

B.) Source Code of the *Bankrupt* Callback Mechanism

```
PROCEDURE Bankrupt (this: Interface; dispIfc: Interface;
  unbal: LONGINT);


  VAR hr: HRESULT; vtbl: IDispatchVT; newIfc: Interface;
    dispid: DISPID; b: BSTR;
    name: LONGINT; h: HANDLE; par: DISPPARAMS;
    res: VARIANT;
    pArgErr: UINT;

BEGIN
  IF dispIfc # NIL THEN (*try type library interface*)
    hr := dispIfc.vtbl.QueryInterface(dispIfc,
      oiidCOMOberon, newIfc);
    IF HRESULTOK(hr) THEN
      par.cArgs := 2; par.cnamedArgs := 0;
      NEW(par.rgvarg); par.rgvarg.arg[0].vt := VTI4;
      par.rgvarg.arg[0].v1 := unbal;
      NEW(h); h.ref := SYSTEM.VAL(REFANY, this);
      par.rgvarg.arg[1].vt := VTDISPATCH;
      par.rgvarg.arg[1].v1 := SYSTEM.VAL(LONGINT, h);
      vtbl := SYSTEM.VAL(IDispatchVT, newIfc.vtbl);
      Log("Call Invoke");
      hr := vtbl.Invoke(newIfc, 1, NULLGUID, 0, 1, par,
        res, NIL, pArgErr)
    ELSE (*try class interface*) NEW(b);
      STRtoBSTR("HandleBankrupcy", b);
      name := SYSTEM.VAL(LONGINT, b) + 4;
      vtbl := SYSTEM.VAL(IDispatchVT, dispIfc.vtbl);
      hr := vtbl.GetIDsOfNames(dispIfc, NULLGUID, name,
        1, 0, dispid);
      IF HRESULTOK(hr) THEN
        par.cArgs := 0; par.cnamedArgs := 0;
        Log("Call Invoke");
        hr := vtbl.Invoke(dispIfc, dispid, NULLGUID,
          0, 1, par, res, NIL, pArgErr)
      END
    END
  END

END Bankrupt;
```

Modularisation of Software Configuration Management

Henrik Bærbak Christensen

Centre for Experimental Computer Science
University of Aarhus
DK-8200 Århus N, Denmark
Tel.: +45 89 42 31 88
Email: hbc@daimi.au.dk

Abstract. The principle of modularisation is one of the main techniques that software designers use to tame the complexity of programming. A software project, however, is complex in many other areas than just programming. In this paper, we focus on one of these complex areas, namely software configuration management, and outline how modularisation is natural and powerful also in this context. The analysis is partly based on experiences from case studies where small- to medium-sized development projects are using a prototype tool that supports modular software configuration management.

1 Introduction

The importance of software configuration management is widely accepted as evident from the prominent role it plays in the Capability Maturity Model [18]. It can also quickly lead to complexity and confusion as developers have to overview not only a high number of software entities but also a high number of *versions* of them. When software entities becomes versioned the *configuration* problem arises: Which versions of which entities must I combine in order to get a consistent and meaningful system?

Tichy termed this the *selection problem* [23], and thereby hinted at the solution adopted by most configuration management tools: Every software entity version has attributes like author, creation time stamp, status, etc. A query can then be run over all versions of all software entities and a subset of versions is selected where the attributes of each version meet the criteria of the query. To uniquely specify a certain bound configuration, e.g. a customer release, the adopted solution is to use *labels* or *tags*; symbolic names that are associated a specific entity version. Thus entity versions that are part of, say, customer release "5.4.1" are labelled with an appropriately named label like "Release5.4.1". Examples of tools based on this approach are ClearCase [13] and CVS [4].

Seen from the viewpoint of modular programming languages, the relation between a configuration and the entity versions that it is composed of, is an odd relation. In modular programming languages like Java [1], Oberon [19], BETA [16], etc., the relation between the client and the provider of functionality

J. Gutknecht and W. Weck (Eds.): JMLC 2000, LNCS 1897, pp. 134–146, 2000.

is stated in the client as a *use* statement: Module A *uses* module B, because A requires the functionality of B to be functionally complete. In label-based software configuration management, the inverse relation exists: Entity versions state that they *are-used-in* a specific configuration.

The drawback of this approach is that the configuration itself is not explicitly represented. There is no manifest object in the database of versions (the repository) that represents the configuration and therefore we cannot easily identify, query, or manipulate it nor reuse it in a new context—it is not modular. This is in contrast to the perception of the developers (and certainly the customers) who have a strong notion of what, say "Release 5.4.1", is and represents.

In this paper, we describe the *Ragnarok architectural software configuration management model* that allows software configuration management to be handled in a modular way. The model has been presented elsewhere (see [8,9,2]); the main focus of this paper is to discuss the modularisation aspect of this model in greater detail and highlight how the concept of modules brings many of the benefits known from programming language modules into the configuration management domain. It does so primarily through examples, some taken from case studies of using "Ragnarok", a prototype tool that handles software configuration management in a modular way.

2 Ragnarok Software Configuration Management Model

The Ragnarok software configuration management model is characterised by:

- A *component* concept that allows source code fragments and related data of an abstraction to be treated as a cohesive whole under version control. [1]
- *Relations* that state relationships between specific states (versions) of components.
- *Transitive* check-in and check-out algorithms that ensures that the repository stores rooted configurations of component versions.

The logical design of a software system can be viewed as a directed graph: Nodes are software entities like e.g. classes or modules and edges are relations between entities like e.g. 'part/whole', or 'depends-on'. In the Ragnarok model, nodes are termed *components* and model software abstractions at any granularity: Class, module, subsystem, system. Components contain the underlying data defining the abstraction such as source code files, documentation, etc. As an example, a component representing class foo in a C++ project will typically contain the source files foo.h and foo.c++.

Relations between components model the underlying logical relations: Composition, functional dependency, inheritance, etc. Like relations between programming language modules they are uni-directional "use"-relations: Stated in the client component, specifying the supplier.

---

[1] Note that a Ragnarok component does not form a unit of separate deployment and should not be confused with 'component' as defined in e.g. COM or CORBA.

Components are defined within a named *project*, i.e. a namespace. Components are *named* and are uniquely identified through their hierarchical position in the project as defined by the composition relations, similar to naming in hierarchical file systems. A client component in one project may state a relation to a supplier component in another project, as the (project name, hierarchical component name) pair uniquely identifies the supplier component[2].

Components are versioned. A *component version* is a "snapshot" of a component at a specific point in time. Relations are always between *specific* component versions: In Fig. 1 component City version 5 depends specifically on component Unit version 9, not on Unit in general (the figure is explained in detail below in section 2.1).

Like traditional configuration management tools, Ragnarok maintains a single version database (the repository) and many, local, workspaces where developers modify the software components. A check-in operation copies components from a workspace to the repository thereby publishing new versions of the components. The opposite operation is a check-out that copies component versions to a local workspace for viewing and editing.

To ensure consistency of the specific relations between component versions, both check-in and check-out operate in the *transitive closure of relations*. This is similar to object graph persistence offered by some programming languages, like for instance Java object serialisation [1] and persistent store in BETA [5]: When an object is copied to a persistent storage not only the object itself but also all objects in the transitive closure of object references are stored. In Ragnarok a check-in of a component not only creates a new component version, but new versions of changed components in the transitive closure of component relations. New component versions are only made if necessary, that is, if the component contents has changed (source code and/or relations).

The Ragnarok model does presently not allow two different versions of the same component to coexist in a single configuration.

2.1   An Example

Consider a fictitious software team that is developing a strategy game. In the game, a player controls a region of land, comprising various cities, by means of military units. The game domain is implemented in a module, Model, that is composed of classes Terrain, City, and Unit, modelling fundamental game concepts. Figure 1a) shows a milestone, Model version 11. In the figure, the version group for a component is depicted as a box with rounded corners containing the component versions (small squares with the version numbers inside) organised in a version graph. Solid line arrows going out of a component version represent composition relations, dashed line arrows represent functional dependencies. So, Model version 11 is composed of Terrain version 7, City version 5, and Unit version 9—and City version 5 depends on (Unit, 9) and (Terrain, 7), and so on.

---

[2] However, the present Ragnarok tool does not support relations across project boundaries for technical reasons.

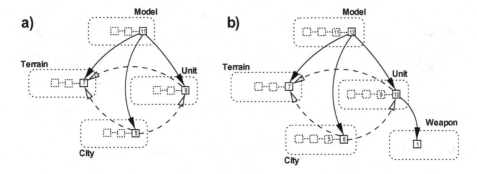

Fig. 1. The evolution of a game domain module. Component versions are numbered squares, organised as a version history. The rounded box is the version group containing all versions of a given component. Relations between component versions are shown as arrows.

To illustrate a check-in, consider a situation where an inner class, Weapon, is added to class Unit. After implementation and testing, a new version of Model is created, see Fig. 1b), as follows: The transitive check-in is propagated to component Weapon, its contents stored and a new version identity, 1, established. A relation to (Weapon, 1) is added to Unit, and a new version 10 created. City lies on a path to a modified component and is thus checked-in with a relation to (Unit, 10) and finally Model is checked-in. A new version of Terrain is not necessary, as it does not lie on a path to Weapon.

The check-out trivially reverses the check-in process: The root component version is checked out, then the check-out is propagated transitively to all related component versions. Thus, checking out (Model, 11) will reestablish the old configuration without the Weapon component.

2.2 Modular Configuration Management

In our example, the Model component represents the game domain. Let us assume that another team is involved in developing the graphical user interface for the game, represented by a GUI component.

The user interface developers can work independently of the game domain changes as they can use a stable version, (Model, 11), as illustrated in Fig. 2a). Later the game domain developers announce a new internal release to be integrated with the user interface: (Model, 13). This identity, (Model, 13) in Fig. 2b), is all the interface developers need to retrieve the full game domain configuration to their workspaces (classes City, Unit, etc.); they do not have to worry about what classes it contains or depends on, in which versions, and how they are related.

This is an essential modular benefit of the Ragnarok model: The complex, internal, structure of the game domain module is abstracted away; what remains is a very simple "interface" namely the version- and component identity—enough to correctly recreate the module in that particular configuration.

a)

Model   **GUI**

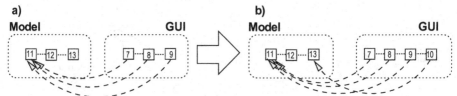

b)

Model   **GUI**

Fig. 2. An integration scenario. The sub-structure of the two components is not shown.

2.3   Unification of Version and Bound Configuration

One consequence of the Ragnarok model is that the concepts of "version" and "bound configuration" are unified. E.g. (Model, 11) is a version of the game domain module, but it also defines the bound configuration of all (versions of) classes embodied in it.

How does this compare to labelling/tagging in CVS, ClearCase, or similar tools? A label is simply an attribute of a given file version. Though it is possible to label all file versions of the internal release of the game domain module with some appropriate label, there is still no identifiable object in the repository that embodies "Model version 11". As it is at this level developers discuss and understand their system, this is an unfortunate *impedance mismatch* between the design domain and the configuration management domain. In the Ragnarok model, (Model, 11) is a manifest object in the repository that can be queried and manipulated.

2.4   Dynamic Relations

Relations stated between components in the configuration domain are not restricted to mirror the static relations between logical design entities in the design domain. A user may also state e.g. dynamic dependencies between entities. An example is an entity that calls another using socket communication instead of using procedure calls—in the former case the relation may not be inferred from the import clauses in the source code. The Ragnarok transitive check-in will traverse any relation stated in a project and ensure that a configuration is version controlled as a unit. We acknowledge that it is difficult to make a comprehensive check of the correspondence between the actual dynamic dependencies and the relations in the corresponding Ragnarok project. In practice, however, missing relations are quickly found by "debugging"; releases are built in a special workspace and if a relation is missing, the checked out configuration behaves differently from the configuration the developer (thought he) checked in.

3   Case Study Scenarios

The Ragnarok prototype tool is presently used in three small- to medium-sized projects with the following main characteristics:

	ConSys	BETA Compiler	Ragnarok
Used since	Mar. 96	Feb. 97	Feb. 96
Data	C++, SQL, binary	BETA, C, html	BETA
Platform	NT	Unix, NT	Unix, NT
No. developers	3	4	1
No. components	160	40	33
No. files	1340	290	160
No. lines (KLOC)	240 + binary	120	45

General experiences have been reported in [7,2]. Here we will outline some scenarios that have arisen in the case studies. The scenarios will be contrasted with CVS as representative of label-based models.

3.1 Application Version Identification

The Mjølner BETA compiler is a compiler for the object-oriented, statically typed programming language BETA [16]. The source code and technical documentation are managed by Ragnarok. One feature of Ragnarok is the ability to associate script-invocations on actions like check-in and check-out. In the compiler group, the scripts associated with the root component (that is, the component that represent the compiler as a whole) generate a small BETA source code fragment containing a string identifier that is assigned a value equal to the Ragnarok generated version identity of the component. This source fragment is compiled into the compiler executable and the string is printed when the compiler is called:

`Mjølner BETA Compiler version 5.4.5 (711) for WinNT/Win95 (i386) (MS)`

where "(711)" is the version identity assigned by Ragnarok.

Thus developers who use compiler pre-releases can report the exact version identity of the compiler in an error description to the development team. As this identity is automatically generated it is trustworthy compared to the manually maintained "5.4.5" identity.

The main point is not that such a script is a "nice feature" but that there indeed exists a single component version, here with identity "711", that uniquely embodies the exact configuration of the versions of all 290+ source files of the compiler.

In CVS the only way to uniquely define such a bound configuration is to label all file versions with some symbolic name. This is a manual and, for large systems, time-consuming process and therefore often not done in practice. For instance, Asklund reports that the labelling process in a large industrial case study takes more than 90 minutes [3]. In contrast, a Ragnarok check-in is proportional to the size of the change, not to the size of the system.

A more severe problem is that the set of labels is unstructured; it is simply a set of text strings. The underlying configurations that the labels identify, however, are structured in the time dimension; thus developers are forced to track the evolution of configurations *manually* (contrary to the idea of tool support). Ragnarok tracks the evolution of versions in a version tree, and as a component version also identify the configuration rooted in it, the evolution of configurations is naturally organised. Below the version graph command (vg) has been run on the BETA compiler component to display its versions, thus outlining the evolution of compiler configurations. The command automatically contracts less interesting versions (symbolised as [...]). The Ragnarok tool allows a version identity to be associated with a symbolic name, for instance the name "r5_0a" can be used as synonym for (compiler, 700) in the tool.

```
1:compiler/(v608#)% vg
Version graph of component compiler
[...]
(v603'r4_2_before_COM')
[...]
(v700'r5_0a')
[...]
(v708'r5_0b')
[...]
(v711'r5_0cde')
```

3.2   Subsystem Identification

A mail received from an inexperienced developer on the BETA compiler project is an example of another often seen request: *How do I find out which version of the SYNTHESIZER module was used in release 695 of the compiler?* As Ragnarok maintains the versioned relations between components, the answer is found using a list version command (vr) of version 695 of the compiler. The list version command enumerates all component versions in the transitive closure of relations rooted in a given component version:

```
1:compiler/(v608#)% vr 695
List version (v695) of component compiler
1:compiler (v695)
  2:CHECKER (v133)
  3:SYNTHESIZER (v234)
  4:CONTROL (v102)
  5:GENERATOR (v391)
    8:COFF (v16)
      39:TEST (v3)
    9:ELF (v37)
      35:TEST (v12)
    (and so on...)
```

Ragnarok outputs the component versions transitively related to version 695 of the compiler component; all component names are prefixed with an integer component ID, and the version is listed in parentheses. So the answer to the posed question is SYNTHESIZER version 234.

In CVS the only way to identify a configuration and thereby a sub-configuration is through the labelling technique. As all files bear the same label it is generally difficult to estimate the exact set of files that goes into a given *sub*configuration; the CVS repository has only information about the full set of files, not how they are related.

3.3 Evolving Architectures

Modern software development methods favour *iterative development* where designs and code are refined and expanded gradually. One of the case studies, the ConSys project, more than tripled its size in terms of lines of code and number of modules over a two year period. Ragnarok allows modules to be added and removed, their contents changed, and relations between modules to be altered.

As any check-in will snapshot the transitive closure of modules and the specific relations interrelating them, all such architectural changes are stored and reproducible. Ragnarok essentially version controls *architectural evolution* just as much as the underlying source code evolution. The next section shows an example of this.

If a given file version does not have a specific label, $\mathcal{L}$, in CVS, there is no simple way to interpret it: Is it because the file was deleted before configuration $\mathcal{L}$ was created? Is it because it was added after? Or, did the developers forget to label the file version? Likewise, if the dependency structure between classes changes during the evolution of a module, there is no way to tell this in CVS. You have to check-out the various configurations and inspect the import-relations in the source code to guess at these changes.

3.4 Architectural Difference

Often it is convenient to view the differences between two configurations, say two releases of a system, in terms of changed, added or deleted modules; i.e. at the *logical, architectural* level. These are easily missed if provision is only given for calculating 'diffs' on the level of file contents as e.g. in CVS diff.

Below is shown the output of an architectural difference calculation command (dr) between version 9 and 30 of component GeoSpace from the Ragnarok project:

```
15:Ragnarok/DataModel/GeoSpace/(v71#)% dr 9 30
Difference between version 9 vrs 30
15:GeoSpace (v9) <--> (v30)
    Name change: PhysicalBackbone -> GeoSpace
    Parts:
        AbstractionLayer: Deleted
        ALRegister: Deleted
        Landscape(v21) : Added
16:Landmark (v12) <--> (v32)
25:Utility (v3) <--> (v5)
31:Decoration (v2) <--> (v5)
```

Ragnarok lists component IDs and names, version identities for the two configurations being compared, and architectural changes. We note that the GeoSpace component has changed name. Its sub-architecture has changed as two components have been deleted, AbstractionLayer and ALRegister, while component Landscape has been added. We also note that Utility and Decoration have remained relatively stable, while the Landmark component has been modified a lot (few/many versions of the components). The corresponding normal 'diff' that lists file contents differences is 532 lines long.

It should be noted that architectural difference calculations can also be used to minimise deployment packages. Consider a software system targeted for upgrading; if the version identity of the configuration presently installed is known, an architectural difference calculation between the installed and the new configuration will list exactly what modules need to be upgraded and what modules have remained stable. This list can be used to produce a minimal upgrading package that only contains changed modules.

CVS can only report file contents changes as it does not keep track of relations between modules.

3.5   Branching and Merging

Check-in and check-out of a component affect all components in the transitive closure. This transitive behaviour also applies when a *branch* is created during development. A branch is often used to handle parallel work, for instance to keep control of bug-fixes for a released system while development of new features is going on at the same time. Then bug-fixes are made in a maintenance branch while new features are added on the development branch.

The Ragnarok model makes branching sub-configurations easy as there is no problem of finding out what components to branch: Through their relations the components themselves already know. The branching operation simply propagates throughout the transitive closure. The same applies when merging a branch back again.

This is a relief at the technical level but even more so at the conceptual level. Conceptually, the Ragnarok model allows you to express the obvious: "I need to branch this version of this module", as there is a manifest component version to perform this action on. Ragnarok will then take care of the tedious details of doing the actual branching of relevant source code files, components, and update their relations.

Buffenbager et al. describe three different branching strategies for label-based systems [6]. It is interesting to note that Buffenbager et al. describe their recommended "merge-at-a-label" strategy as "a low-level integration mechanism, but well-suited to today's SCM systems" and argue in favour of a tool layer to implement their strategy. Though Ragnarok does not implement their recommended strategy presently, its understanding of software as interrelated abstractions and its track-keeping of changed components provide a strong basis for such a future extension.

3.6   Software Reuse

Software reuse is perhaps the most important technique to reduce the production cost of software. While systematic software reuse is a complex matter both organisationally and technically, a prerequisite for a systematic approach is proper identification of the assets that are reused in order to track dependencies, updates, etc. Again, the modular approach of the Ragnarok model guarantees unique identification of assets. Moreover, because any component version maintains relations to all other component versions depended upon, getting access to a reusable asset is eased as only the asset itself needs to be known: Other assets depended upon will automatically be copied to a workspace upon check-out.

4   Discussion

The Ragnarok model guarantees consistency in a technical sense: It will reproduce configurations at check-out exactly as they were at check-in. However, to what extent checked-in configurations are also *logically* consistent in the sense that they will compile, link, and represent "sound" designs, must be defined by team policies. Both the Consys- and BETA compiler teams have adopted an "integrate early" development process that force them to be rather strict concerning when components can be checked in: The underlying source code must be "well-behaved" before a check-in is acceptable. Other policies are possible if teams work independently and announce explicit version identities for integration as exemplified in section 2.2. With such a "integrate late" policy, versions can be made more often; as convenient code snapshots during experimentation, etc.

Ragnarok treats any change as having impact on all components that directly or indirectly are related to the changed component. This is a pessimistic view: Standard wisdom is that it should be possible to change a module's implementation without affecting other modules as they only rely on its interface. However, a main objective of configuration management is *traceability*—we need to track all changes. Often developers inadvertently break the contract of a module even though they only change its implementation. Such an erroneous change will cause problems for depending modules and here Ragnarok's conservative approach may help in tracing the source of the problem.

On first sight, one may be concerned about the amount of component versions created during manipulations like check-in, branching, etc., and fear that the model leads to a combinatorial explosion of versions in the repository. Our case studies show that this is not the case: An analysis of the component versions in the repositories of the case study projects shows that the number of component versions is proportional to the number of check-ins and to the number of changes; thus combinatorial explosion does not occur. Detailed data is provided in [2].

5   Related Work

A number of other software configuration management models, tools, and languages also support or can simulate a modular view of software configuration management to some extent, notably systems like Adele [11], PCL [25], NUCM [26]
COOP/Orm [17], and POEM [14,15]. Adele, PCL, and NUCM are systems that
define broader versioning models than that of Ragnarok and they can simulate
the Ragnarok model more or less naturally. Adele is commercially available and
NUCM is available in the public domain. However, no data has been published
on actual usage of these models from the viewpoint of modular configuration
management as presented here. COOP/Orm and POEM have versioning models
very similar to Ragnarok but both are research prototypes that have not yet
been tried in a realistic setting.

Modern component technologies must also address the configuration problem.
CORBA/OMA involves a *change management service* to handle compatibility of
interface versions, but this area has not yet been standardised [22, §13.3.2]. The
Microsoft COM technology prescribes a convention where a globally unique integer value, a GUID, must be assigned every published component interface [20],
thus providing a simple but strict version control. The Ragnarok model similarly assigns a unique identity to a component version, and the ID is unique in
a *deep* sense: The ID uniquely identifies the specific versions of *all* components
depended upon. As classes in COM must only depend on COM interfaces and
as a new GUID must be assigned if a COM interface changes (even if only semantically), a GUID is theoretically also unique in the deep sense. In practice,
however, programmers often fail to follow the conventions, leading to broken
configurations. In Ragnarok the creation of the ID is a by-product of a check-in,
not a prescribed action that must rely on developer discipline or support from
available tools. Thus we find the credibility of Ragnarok's IDs stronger. We of
course acknowledge that the scope of Ragnarok is much more limited: A Ragnarok ID can only be understood in the context of the relevant project, not as an
entity with its own global semantics as is the case with a COM GUID.

6   Conclusion

Software development is a complex task in every way. The principles of abstraction and modularisation are vital techniques to tame complexity in the domain of
software design and implementation. In this paper, we have discussed how these
principles can also bring benefits in another important and complex domain, namely software configuration management. Our presentation has motivated these
benefits by outlining examples from our case studies, representative of problems
encountered in practical software development and configuration management.

We have outlined important characteristics of the Ragnarok software configuration management model and described how this model is well suited to handle
configuration management in a modular way. It is not the intent, however, to
emphasise the Ragnarok model as the only feasible model. The main message is
that modular configuration management is indeed viable and beneficial and we

encourage configuration management tool producers to provide more and better support for a modular approach in commercially available systems.

The Ragnarok prototype tool is provided free of charge and can be downloaded from the Ragnarok home page:

http://www.daimi.au.dk/~hbc/Ragnarok/

References

1. K. Arnold and J. Gosling. *The Java Programming Language, Second Edition.* Addison-Wesley, 1998.
2. U. Asklund, L. Bendix, H. B. Christensen, and B. Magnusson. The Unified Extensional Versioning Model. In *System Configuration Management* [21], pages 100–122.
3. U. Asklund and B. Magnusson. A Case-Study of Configuration Management with ClearCase in an Industrial Environment. In R. Conradi, editor, *Software Configuration Management*, Lecture Notes in Computer Science 1235, pages 201–221. ICSE'97 SCM-7 Workshop, Springer Verlag, 1997.
4. B. Berliner. CVS II: Parallelizing Software Development. In *USENIX*, Washington D.C., 1990.
5. S. Brandt. *Towards Orthogonal Persistence as a Basic Technology.* PhD thesis, Department of Computer Science, University of Aarhus, Feb. 1997.
6. J. Buffenbarger and K. Gruell. A Branching/Merging Strategy for Parallel Software Development. In *System Configuration Management* [21], pages 86–99.
7. H. B. Christensen. Experiences with Architectural Software Configuration Management in Ragnarok. In B. Magnusson, editor, *System Configuration Management*, Lecture Notes in Computer Science 1439, pages 67–74. SCM-8 Symposium, Springer Verlag, 1998.
8. H. B. Christensen. RAGNAROK: *An Architecture Based Software Development Environment.* PhD thesis, Department of Computer Science, University of Aarhus, June 1999.
9. H. B. Christensen. The Ragnarok Architectural Software Configuration Management Model. In R. H. Sprague, Jr., editor, *Proceedings of the 32nd Annual Hawaii International Conference on System Sciences*, Maui, Hawaii, Jan. 1999. IEEE Computer Society.
10. J. Estublier, editor. *Software Configuration Management*, Lecture Notes in Computer Science 1005. ICSE SCM-4 and SCM-5 Workshops, Springer Verlag, 1995.
11. J. Estublier and R. Casallas. The Adele Configuration Management. In Tichy [24], chapter 4.
12. IEEE Computer Society Press. *Proceedings of the 18th International Conference on Software Engineering*, 1996.
13. D. B. Leblang. The CM Challenge: Configuration Management that Works. In Tichy [24], chapter 1.
14. Y.-J. Lin and S. P. Reiss. Configuration Management in Terms of Modules. In Estublier [10].
15. Y.-J. Lin and S. P. Reiss. Configuration Management with Logical Structures. In *Proceedings of the 18th International Conference on Software Engineering* [12], pages 298–307.

16. O. L. Madsen, B. Møller-Pedersen, and K. Nygaard. *Object-Oriented Programming in the BETA Programming Language.* Addison Wesley, 1993.
17. B. Magnusson and U. Asklund. Fine Grained Version Control of Configurations in COOP/Orm. In I. Sommerville, editor, *Software Configuration Management,* Lecture Notes in Computer Science 1167, pages 31–48. ICSE'96 SCM-6 Workshop, Springer Verlag, 1996.
18. M. C. Paulk, C. V. Weber, B. Curtis, and M. B. Chrissis. *The Capability Maturity Model—Guidelines for Improving the Software Process.* Addison-Wesley, 1997.
19. M. Reiser and N. Wirth. *Programming in Oberon.* Addison Wesley, 1992.
20. D. Rogerson. *Inside COM.* Microsoft Press, 1997.
21. SCM-9 Symposium. *System Configuration Management,* Lecture Notes in Computer Science 1675. Springer Verlag, 1999.
22. C. Szyperski. *Component Software.* Addison Wesley Longman Higher Education, 1998.
23. W. F. Tichy. Tools for Software Configuration Management. In Jurgen F. H. Winkler, editor, *Proceedings of the International Workshop on Software Version and Configuration Control,* Grassau, West Germany, Jan. 1988. B. G. Teubner, Stuttgart.
24. W. F. Tichy, editor. *Trends in Software: Configuration Management.* John Wiley & Sons, 1994.
25. E. Tryggeseth, B. Gulla, and R. Conradi. Modelling Systems with Variability using the PROTEUS Configuration Language. In Estublier [10].
26. A. van der Hoek, D. Heimbigner, and A. L. Wolf. A Generic, Peer-to-peer Repository for Distributed Configuration Management. In *Proceedings of the 18th International Conference on Software Engineering* [12], pages 308–317.

Leonardo: A Framework for Modeling and Editing Graphical Components

Erich Oswald

Institut für Computersysteme
ETH Zürich
oswald@acm.org

Abstract. Leonardo is an interactive graphics editor that we developed for the ETH Oberon system. We describe the object-oriented framework that it provides for modeling, viewing, and editing graphical objects, and we address the question of how its visual components can adapt when new kinds of objects are integrated in its model. Our goal is to provide a graphical component architecture where extensions can be added at run-time, i. e. without requiring existing parts to be recompiled or reloaded. To prove the feasibility of our design, we present a non-trivial extension which integrates objects that are specified in a graphical description language within Leonardo.

1 Introduction

Modern graphical user interfaces (GUI) are increasingly often based on a *compound document* model; examples include COM [13], JavaBeans [7], or Gadgets [9]. One of the crucial properties of such a compound document model is that any provider can develop *components* that everybody else can then integrate within arbitrary documents because components and documents adhere to an abstract protocol that defines how they interact with each other.

In principle, the same should be possible with *structured 2D graphics* [14]. A generic container (which we call a *figure*) should be able to integrate arbitrary graphical objects (which we call *shapes*), even if they are delivered in separate packages, possibly by different providers. It would then be possible to develop a generic graphics editor that can deal with arbitrary kinds of shapes as long as they conform to an abstract protocol.

Nevertheless, there is a difference between compound documents and such a shape framework. Traditional components are part of a GUI, which means that users can control them interactively and that the GUI defines much of their look and feel. In terms of the model-view-controller (MVC) paradigm [8], such components thus deal with view and controller aspects. To add new kinds of components means to extend the framework's set of views and controllers. Whether they refer to a model object or not is irrelevant as far as the framework is concerned. Compare this to structured graphics. There the representation of an abstract figure serves as the model of a document. This model is displayed

J. Gutknecht and W. Weck (Eds.): JMLC 2000, LNCS 1897, pp. 147–160, 2000.
© Springer-Verlag Berlin Heidelberg 2000

and edited in a visual component. To add new kinds of shapes to a graphics editor thus means to extend its model.

If it is our intention that the model of a document is able to integrate independently developed objects, we need to resolve several issues that are not always taken into account in compound document architectures. These issues are discussed in the following paragraphs.

Duplicate type and object hierarchies. The GUI of an MVC-based application must be able to deal with extensions to its model. In the general case, each model object is accompanied by a matching visual object. Thus, the complete type and object hierarchies exist twice: once in the model and once in the GUI. Moreover, non-visual and visual object structures must be kept consistent whenever there is a change in the document. An example of an architecture that follows this principle is Unidraw, a framework for building domain-specific graphical editors [15]. Unidraw splits graphical components into *subjects*, which are abstract representations of domain-specific objects, and *views*, which display subjects within a GUI. For each subject type there must be at least one view type, and for each subject in a figure there must be a view in every editor window that displays the figure.

Compound document architectures often avoid the problem of duplicate hierarchies by allowing document models to recursively contain visual components. This for example allows users to embed illustrations, tables, and GUI controls within text models. However, such a document model becomes tightly bound to its user interface because visual components can be part of both the model and the GUI domain. Reusing the document model within another component framework is likely to be difficult or even impossible.

Editing tools. New kinds of components in the model must be made accessible to users. For compound documents and graphical user interfaces, this is usually not a problem since components tend to be rectangular. Users merely select the kind of object that they wish to integrate and click with the mouse at the location where the new object should be inserted. However, this simple approach may not be appropriate for integrating components that have detailed geometry, for example a spline curve whose shape is defined by a series of control points. In general, it should be possible to extend the application that manages the document by new editing tools – without having to recompile existing program code.

Separation of views and controllers. Several component frameworks soften the distinction between views and controllers and assign both functions to a single type or class. In a system that loads code on demand, however, it may be beneficial to avoid loading controller code for merely displaying an embedded component (e. g. a graphical illustration within a text document), in order to minimize the required amounts of disk transfer and memory consumption. Editing functionality should only be loaded when a user actually requests to change an embedded document.

Generic object inspection. Editing functionality sometimes applies to generic objects. For example, users may want to view and manipulate non-geometric properties of a selected object. The Gadgets framework [9] therefore provides a generic inspector panel with which users can view and edit the public properties of any Oberon object. A property's type (e.g. boolean, string, or numeric) defines the kind of visual component that is used to display its value. Similarly, the JavaBeans framework [7] solves the problem of inspecting arbitrary components ("beans") with a specific naming scheme. For a class Abc, class AbcBeanInfo (if it exists) is expected to contain additional information about the properties of Abc objects. Similarly, a class AbcPropertyEditor may provide a custom user interface for editing a bean of class Abc.

Existing research on graphics editors, exemplified by Juno [10] or Briar [4], is usually focused on how geometrical constraints can be specified and solved. With Leonardo, however, the main goal has been to investigate how extensibility in a graphical model affects documents that display and edit such a model. Hence, Leonardo can serve as a case study for other developers of complex applications requiring extensibility in the model area of a MVC-guided document architecture.

2   Shape Framework

The Leonardo shape framework offers a highly extensible, persistent model for representing 2D graphics. It does so by providing four distinct type hierarchies: one for structuring a graphical scene into a hierarchy of objects, a second for defining the behavior these objects assume, a third for modeling undoable actions, and a fourth for abstracting from the properties of the underlying graphics interface.

2.1   Oberon Objects

Many objects in Leonardo are derived from ETH Oberon's standard object type Objects.Object [5]. A special procedure, called *handler*, is bound to each object. The handler dynamically dispatches any message record derived from Objects.ObjMsg, resulting in an *open message interface* [9]. This means that any message can be sent to every object without changing the object's interface. If a handler does not know a message, it can choose to ignore the message or forward it to the handler of its base type, inheriting the latter's default behavior. It is also common for Oberon messages to be broadcast within an entire object graph, especially within the set of visible components. Parent nodes in such a graph forward unknown messages to their successors to guarantee that they reach their destination.

Another important property of Objects.Object and its extensions is that they can be bound to *object libraries*. Oberon's library mechanism provides an efficient and simple solution for storing complex object graphs in a file. Hence, any object is easily made persistent by properly handling the corresponding object messages in its handler.

2.2   Figures and Shapes

The Leonardo object framework offers two extensions of `Objects.Object`, called `Shape` and `Figure` (see Fig. 1). Shapes are abstract graphical objects. Each shape

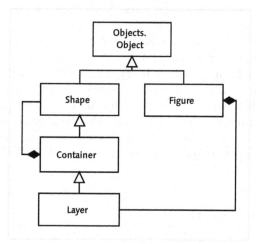

Fig. 1. The shape type hierarchy (in UML style notation)

contains fields that link it to its neighbors and to the shape that contains it, a description of its bounding box, and a small amount of state information, such as whether it is currently selected. Examples of shapes are rectangles, captions, lines, splines, and images.

Figures on the other hand are model objects that represent entire shape trees. They keep track of a current shape selection and notify attached views when a figure's contents have changed. Besides, they maintain a list of undoable commands. Instead of applying any changes directly upon receiving a message, shapes add actions to a figure's current command. Because actions are also derived from an abstract base type, the set of available actions can be extended whenever necessary.

Shapes that contain other shapes are called *containers*. Containers not only add structure to a graphical scene, they can also change the behavior of their component shapes. This is possible because messages are often not directly sent to the shape that should handle them; instead, they are *broadcast* to all shapes in the figure. Hence, containers can choose to adjust or not forward messages that are addressed to one of their components (a scheme named *parental control* in [9]). Examples of containers exercising parental control are *layers*, which are special containers at the top of the shape tree. Layers can be instructed to not display, print, or locate their components. They then ignore the corresponding messages and do not forward them to their components.

2.3   Message Hierarchy

Clients normally access and modify the shapes in a figure by initializing the fields
of a specific message type and broadcasting the message within the figure. The
abstract message types that are relevant to Leonardo are illustrated in Fig. 2.
As can be seen, Leonardo provides a common base type ShapeMsg. This allows

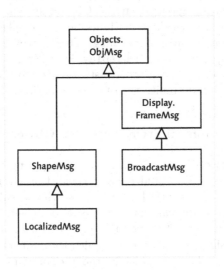

Fig. 2. Abstract message type hierarchy

handler procedures to quickly decide if a message is a shape message or not.
Moreover, containers by default forward all unknown messages that are derived
from ShapeMsg to their components, thus guaranteeing that future message extensions reach their destination. Examples of messages that are derived directly
from ShapeMsg include messages that deal with the current selection, with integration and deletion of shapes, and with rearranging the order in which shapes
are painted.

Localized messages are shape messages that operate within a local coordinate system. They contain an affine transformation matrix which maps points
(x, y) from a shape's local coordinate system to global figure coordinates. Local
coordinates are at first identical to global coordinates. A container can modify
the local coordinates of its components by exercising parental control, i.e. by
adjusting the transformation matrix of a localized message before forwarding
it. Because containers also adjust unknown extensions of LocalizedMsg in that
manner, they automatically handle future localized messages properly. Examples of localized messages include messages for drawing shapes, for determining
which shapes are within a rectangular area or overlap it, and for transforming
shapes. For rendering shapes, Leonardo uses Gfx, a high-level graphics library

for Oberon [12]. Gfx can output general paths, raster images, and text on various devices, which are represented by abstract context objects. These contexts implement an abstract rendering interface on a specific device, e. g. a screen or printer.

Broadcast messages are required because some events may affect shapes from more than one figure, for example when a shared pen object (cf. Sect. 2.4) that they rely on is updated. Messages that correspond to these events must be sent to all visual components in the Oberon system. However, extensions of `ShapeMsg` cannot be broadcast within Oberon's display space because they are not derived from `Display.FrameMsg`. This is why another abstract base type `BroadcastMsg`, derived from `Display.FrameMsg`, is required. Containers by default forward all unknown broadcast messages to their components, once again guaranteeing compatibility with future extensions.

2.4   Modeling Graphical Styles with Pen Objects

Many graphical objects can be drawn by decomposing them into paths, i. e. connected sequences of lines and curves. To abstract from the capabilities of the underlying graphics library, Leonardo uses what it calls *pens* for rendering path-like objects. A shape can connect a pen to an output device, position it somewhere, and then move it along lines, arcs, and cubic Bézier curves [11].

Examples of basic pens are *strokers*, which leave a trail of a given color, pattern, and thickness, and *fillers*, which fill the interior of a path with a given color and pattern. More advanced pens do not render anything themselves; instead, they modify the traversed path and delegate this modified path to another pen, which may in turn modify and forward it again. The resulting pen cascades offer a very flexible method for creating various special effects, as can be seen in Fig. 3, where a *dasher* converts the visited path (topmost curve) into a series of dashes (second curve) and sends them to an *arrow pen*. The latter converts the dashes into outlines and shapes their end points as arrow heads (third curve). Finally, the resulting outlines are processed with a filler pen (bottom curve).

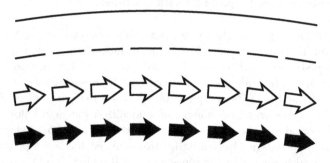

Fig. 3. Increasingly complex pen hierarchies applied to a simple curve

Pen objects represent what are often called *stroke* or *fill styles* in other graphics packages. However, unlike most of these styles, pens are not limited to a fixed set of choices. They are extensible and hierarchically structured. New effects can either be created by introducing new type extensions that implement the abstract pen interface or by aggregating instances of existing pen types to form new combinations. Java 2D [6] uses a similar scheme for abstract stroke and fill attributes, but keeps `Stroke` and `Paint` objects in separate type hierarchies. Besides, there is no notion of combining several `Stroke` and `Paint` objects into cascades, thus not taking full advantage of the power that the abstract interfaces of these types offer.

3   Editor Framework

Based on the figure model, the Leonardo architecture provides a small viewing and editing core, as illustrated in Fig. 4. This viewing and editing core is complemented by a potentially unlimited number of extensions.

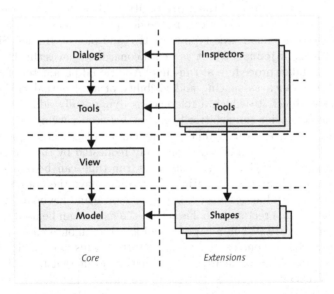

Fig. 4. Overview of Leonardo's architecture

3.1   Basic Viewing

Shapes have the intrinsic capability of rendering themselves on abstract Gfx context objects. It thus appears justified to use a single type of view which can display any figure by letting individual shapes handle redraw requests themselves. While this softens the barrier between model and view and makes the model depend on the underlying interface for rendering graphics, it avoids the duplicate hierarchy problem that was mentioned in Sect. 1. Besides, the model is still independent of any concrete output device and GUI since the Gfx context interface only describes abstract output devices.

A Leonardo view is an extension of a *frame*, which is the basic GUI component in the Oberon system. It maps requests to display or print itself into render messages, which it in turn forwards to its figure model. These basic views, albeit simple, can be integrated within any Oberon document that accepts frames as components, including text documents and dialog panels. To integrate Leonardo figures in a different component framework, only a new Gfx context extension and a basic visual component would have to be implemented.

3.2   Controller Functionality

The difference between *passive* components, which only display a model, and *active* components, which allow manipulating it, is that the latter process mouse and keyboard input and map them to operations that change the displayed model. To let users edit figures directly in the document where they are embedded, Leonardo uses the same frame type for active and passive frames. Since frames are derived from `Objects.Object` as well, Leonardo achieves this by exchanging the frame's handler procedure at run-time. Additional parameters for the active rôle of a frame, such as spacing and visibility of an eventual grid, are placed in a separate object, to which a reference is dynamically added to the frame. Hence, frame behavior can arbitrarily change between viewing only and editing at run-time. Moreover, editing functionality can be placed in a separate module, which is only loaded when editing is actually requested by the user.

This method of exchanging behavior at run-time can be generalized even further. Most applications for editing 2D graphics have the notion of a current tool, which defines what actions are bound to mouse and keyboard input events. For example, when a rectangle tool is active, the mouse can be used to insert new rectangles in a figure. When a caption tool is active, mouse clicks place a caret marker where subsequent keystrokes are inserted. This and similar behavior is easily incorporated into Leonardo by associating a different frame handler with each tool. Whenever a tool is activated, the current handlers of all Leonardo editor frames are replaced by the new tool handler. Because code for different tools can reside in different modules, tool code only needs to be loaded when the tool is first activated.

3.3   Object Inspection

Some editing operations, for example assigning a different font to a caption, cannot effectively be performed by directly manipulating an object with the mouse. Dialog windows where new values for an object's properties can be entered in the fields of a form and where actions can be invoked by clicking on buttons are preferable for such indirect manipulations. Since Leonardo is supposed to deal with extensible models, we are mainly interested in generic object inspection.

We mentioned in Sect. 1 that the Gadgets framework provides generic inspector dialogs which list exported attributes of a selected object. However, the set of available attribute types is limited and conveys little semantic information. For example, while color values are modeled as integer attributes, the standard inspector displays their value in an integer text field instead of providing a more meaningful GUI element, such as a color chooser. Furthermore, standard inspectors do not support Leonardo's undoable commands. The JavaBeans approach with its customized property editor classes looks more promising. However, as an Oberon module (from whose name the resulting object file name is derived) may host more than one type, the relationship between class names and file names is less direct in Oberon than in Java. Instead of extending Java's naming scheme to deal with combined module and type names, Leonardo uses the central registry of ETH Oberon to map from object type names to object inspector names. More precisely, an object's generator attribute, which uniquely identifies its type and handler, is interpreted as a key into a dictionary that associates this key with the name of a command procedure. When Leonardo asks the operating system to execute this command, the system automatically loads the corresponding module if necessary. The command procedure is free to build an arbitrary user interface for manipulating the object from which the key was derived. (On a side note, most inspectors in Leonardo copy a prefabricated dialog panel from a public library and fill in its form fields with attributes of the inspected object.) Finally, the called command procedure places the new inspector panel in a public variable to make it accessible to Leonardo. Neither the modules that implement shape types nor those of the Leonardo core need to be recompiled to add or exchange dialog panels.

3.4   Adapting the Existing Application GUI

When new functionality is added to an application, new controls in the form of menu commands and buttons must be incorporated in the application's existing GUI to make them accessible to users. One approach to automate this process would be to again use a central registry for maintaining a list of known tools and build the Leonardo GUI dynamically. On the other hand, Oberon applications tend to strictly separate user interface from program code. Their dialog panels are regular documents that can be edited like any other kind of document. Oberon users are thus able (and even accustomed) to tailor dialog panels to their needs and tastes. To nevertheless encourage a common look and provide some level of consistency in its GUI, Leonardo uses the LayLa layout language [3] for specifying all its panel documents. By copying relevant parts of LayLa descriptions that specify existing Leonardo panels, new GUI parts attain a similar look and feel as existing ones. Still, we feel that this is an ad-hoc solution and that the problem of retaining a consistent look and feel in the GUI of an extensible application needs to be further explored.

4   Sample Extension: Vinci Shapes

As a non-trivial example that displays Leonardo's potential for extensibility, we present an extension for integrating shapes whose appearance is specified in a dedicated graphical description language. Our rationale is that textual descriptions are superior to interactive editing when creating a figure involves instancing structures repeatedly and positioning shapes at exact, possibly calculated, coordinates. Our goal is to combine the power of a graphical description language with that of interactive editing, striving for a package that is more powerful than either of its components.

4.1   The Vinci Graphical Description Language

We developed Vinci, a graphical description language, as another application of our Gfx library. Used on its own, Vinci lets users and applications describe arbitrary graphics in textual form, comparable to Postscript page descriptions [1]. In the remainder of this section, however, we focus on how Vinci descriptions can be seamlessly integrated within Leonardo figures and vice versa.

The Vinci interpreter consists of a custom parser that converts Vinci source code into a corresponding Scheme program [2]. The latter is then executed by a Scheme interpreter that has been adapted to support Oberon objects. Scheme has been chosen because it is easy to implement and has well-defined semantics. It also features a standard library whose procedures can be used by Vinci descriptions. Vinci is a full programming language, supporting constant and procedure definitions, conditional execution, and loops. In addition, it supports the specification of graphical paths, the placement of text labels, and localized changes to graphical attributes.

Packages are additional Vinci source files that extend the set of known definitions. Moreover, importing a package may result in additional Oberon modules being loaded; these can extend the set of built-in operators. For example, by importing the **images** package, Vinci descriptions gain access to additional library functions that let them load and draw raster images.

Shape integration. Because Vinci expressions can evaluate to Oberon objects, Leonardo shapes can be accessed from within Vinci descriptions by calling standard functions to instantiate shape objects through their generator procedures or to import them from a public library. Since shapes also use Gfx contexts to render themselves, a Vinci program can render a shape by calling a corresponding library function. This library function sends a Leonardo render message to the shape in question, passing it the Gfx context on which the Vinci description is supposed to render itself.

4.2   Vinci Shapes

As Leonardo shapes can be integrated in Vinci, Vinci descriptions can be embedded in Leonardo figures with a Vinci-specific shape extension. Vinci shape descriptions consist of a series of constant and function definitions. When a Vinci shape is requested to render itself, it searches a function that is called `render` in the corresponding description. If it finds one, it lets the Vinci interpreter evaluate this `render` function within the Gfx context that it received in the render message. Similar functions serve to compute the shape's bounding box or to perform hit-tests.

By importing a special `shapes` package, a Vinci description can declare global shape values to be components of the corresponding shape. Interactive users can individually select and transform these component shapes, thus manipulating position and orientation of the corresponding Vinci shape. In its simplest form, a Vinci shape contains a rectangular frame. This frame defines the shape's coordinate system and bounding box. Users can drag this frame around and resize it at will. However, there is no fine-grained control over any aspect of the shape other than its local coordinate system. Other Vinci shapes therefore declare multiple component shapes, each of which can be moved around individually, permitting users to change the geometry of a Vinci shape in a fine-grained manner.

To further customize Vinci shapes, global values in their descriptions can be exported as parameters. These parameters become properties of the shape and can be accessed and modified with the standard Oberon object messages.

4.3   Vinci Tool and Inspector

The Vinci tool simply lets users select a Vinci source file and integrate corresponding shapes in a figure. When a Vinci shape is inspected, the associated command iterates over the shape's exported parameters and appends appropriate dialog elements to a panel document. Because the specific type of each parameter is declared in the shape's description, the correct kind of GUI element is easily determined.

4.4   Vinci Example

To illustrate the power of Vinci descriptions, Fig. 5 shows a screenshot of a Leonardo session. The bottom right window displays the source code of the regular polygon shape that can be seen in the top left window. It reveals that polygon descriptions base their coordinate system on a rectangular `frame` component and that they export parameters which define the number of corners they have and which pen they use to paint themselves. The corresponding inspector panel is displayed in the top right window. The second shape in the figure window is a line that automatically calculates and displays its own length. Its inspector panel is shown in the bottom left window. The parameters in that inspector allow users to choose color, font name and size, and a unit for the displayed length. Furthermore, the line's end points are components of the shape which users can interactively drag around.

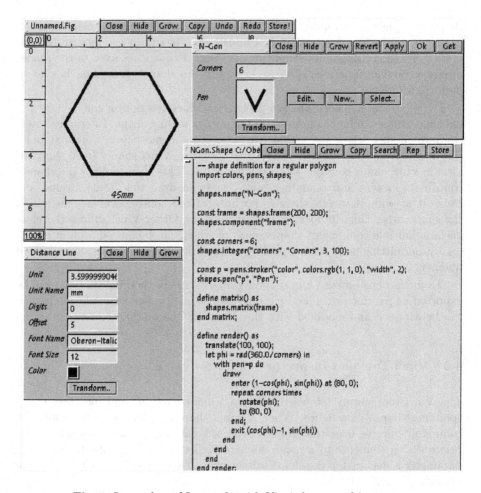

Fig. 5. Screenshot of Leonardo with Vinci shapes and inspectors

5   Code Size

To give an impression of how much code is used for which parts of Leonardo, Table 1 lists the number of modules and the number of statements (as given by Oberon's Analyzer tool) of the May 2000 release of Leonardo, including Vinci shapes. As expected, the viewer component is remarkably small compared to the other parts. The number of modules and statements for the model part and for the editor part are roughly the same, but model extensions tend to involve more code than the corresponding tool and inspector code. If there seems to be a mismatch between essential and extension code for pens, this is because the basic pen module already implements several concrete pens in addition to defining the abstract pen interface.

Table 1. Number of modules and statements in Leonardo

	Essential		Extensions	
	Modules	Statements	Modules	Statements
Shapes	1	1322	6	5072
Viewer	1	339	–	
Pens	1	908	1	584
Editor	3	3264	7	2734

6 Conclusions

We have presented an overview of a powerful framework for representing, viewing, and editing graphical components. Extensibility has been an essential design factor and has been validated in the case of a non-trivial example integrating a graphical description language within the framework.

In the model domain, a small framework defines structure and behavior of an extensible shape hierarchy, including persistent storage and undoable commands. A persistent hierarchy of pen objects abstracts from the capabilities of an underlying graphics interface. Not only can the set of shapes be extended without changing existing interfaces; the same applies to shape functionality (due to the use of an open message interface and abstract undoable actions) and the set of pens, leading to an architecture which is extensible in three dimensions.

In the view domain, a single module suffices to integrate any figure as a component within any document. No shape-specific viewing functionality is required, avoiding the problem of duplicate hierarchies. Although basic view components provide no editing functionality, in-place editing is easily achieved by exchanging frame behavior at runtime. A generic view component can be used because rendering can be delegated to individual shapes, yet without binding shapes to a specific component architecture.

In the controller domain, Leonardo relies on a generic scheme which uses exchangeable tools for direct manipulation and custom inspector panels for generic inspection. With only minimal changes to existing GUI components, new functionality can be added without requiring existing modules to be recompiled.

As an example of Leonardo's extensibility, we have presented Vinci, a graphical description language, and a shape extension integrating Vinci descriptions within Leonardo. Mutual integration of Leonardo shapes in Vinci and Vinci descriptions in Leonardo is straightforward because both rely on the abstract context interface of the underlying Gfx library to draw graphics, which in our case is essential for embedding graphical models within another and within various component frameworks.

References

1. Adobe Systems, Inc., *PostScript Language Reference Manual*, second edition, Addison–Wesley, 1990.
2. W. Clinger and J. Rees (ed.), "The Revised[4] Report on the Algorithmic Language Scheme," *ACM Lisp Pointers*, 4(3), 1991, 1–55.
3. J. Derungs, "LayLa: Layout Language – eine Beschreibungssprache für Gadgets," Diploma Thesis, Institut für Computersysteme, ETH Zürich, 1996.
4. M. L. Gleicher and A. Witkin, "Drawing with Constraints," *The Visual Computer*, 11(1), 1994, 39–51.
5. J. Gutknecht, "Oberon System 3: Vision of a Future Software Technology," *Software – Concepts and Tools*, 15, 1994, 26–33.
6. Sun Microsystems, Inc., "Java 2D[TM] API home page," http://java.sun.com/products/java-media/2D/.
7. Sun Microsystems, Inc., "JavaBeans: The Only Component Architecture for Java Technology," http://java.sun.com/beans/
8. G. E. Krasner and S. T. Pope, "A Cookbook for Using the Model-Viewer-Controller User Interface Paradigm in Smalltalk-80," *Journal of Object-Oriented Programming*, 1(3), August 1988, 26–49.
9. J. L. Marais, *Design and Implementation of a Component Architecture for Oberon*, Ph. D. Thesis, Diss. ETH No 11697, ETH Zürich, 1996.
10. G. Nelson, "Juno, a Constraint Based Graphics System," *Computer Graphics*, 19(3), 1985, 235–243.
11. E. Oswald, "Drawing Pens: An Extensible Approach to Rendering Vector Graphics," short presentation at *Joint Modular Languages Conference*, Linz, Austria, 1997.
12. E. Oswald, "Gfx – High-Level 2D Graphics for Oberon," ftp://ftp.inf.ethz.ch/pub/ETHOberon/Contrib/Gfx/
13. D. Rogerson, *Inside COM*, Microsoft Press, 1997.
14. J. M. Vlissides and M. A. Linton, "Applying Object-Oriented Design to Structured Graphics," *Proceedings of the 1988 USENIX C++ Conference*, USENIX Association, October 1988, 81–94.
15. J. M. Vlissides and M. A. Linton, "Unidraw: A Framework for Building Domain-Specific Graphical Editors," *ACM Transactions on Information Systems*, 8(3), July 1990, 237–268.

OMX-FS: An Extended File System Architecture Based on a Generic Object Model

G. Rivera and M. Norrie

rivera@inf.ethz.ch, norrie@inf.ethz.ch

Institute for Information Systems
Swiss Federal Institute of Technology (ETH)
ETH-Zentrum, CH-8092 Zurich, Switzerland.

Abstract. The exponential growth in hardware performance has reduced to a minimum the distinction on the software side between basic functionality, provided by the operating system, and extended functionality, provided by applications. Nowadays, a lot of advanced features such as multimedia handling are already integrated into the system itself. Given this trend, it is surprising that the current vision of the file management system still remains so close to the level of the physical storage structure of a file, following the basic equivalence of *file = pathname*. In this paper, we present OMX-FS, a multi-user distributed object-oriented file system, based on the generic object model OM. OMX-FS considers files as objects and introduces concepts typical of object-oriented database systems, enabling both application developers and users to interact with the file system at a higher-level of logical abstraction. We describe the implementation of OMX-FS in the Oberon environment.

Keywords: File System Architecture, Multi-user Distributed Persistent Object-Oriented File System, Object Data Model, Oberon.

1 Introduction

While, in the past, the design of an operating system was influenced by constraints such as computer performance and the limited functionality of resources, now such hardware limitations have in practice disappeared and the focus has moved to the correctness, functionality and flexibility of the software.

As Szyperski noted in [19], it is difficult to make a clear distinction as to whether a program is an application or just a part of the operating system. The tasks of *early* operating systems were to boot the computer, run a few applications (e.g. word processor, drawing tool, spreadsheet) and manage a few peripherals (printer, storage drives etc.). Nowadays, extended functionalities such as multimedia and network handling are considered as indispensable features of an operating system.

Given this development, it is strange to note that, in existing versions of commercial operating systems, the file system architecture still remains close to the level of the physical storage structure of a file, following the equivalence of

J. Gutknecht and W. Weck (Eds.): JMLC 2000, LNCS 1897, pp. 161–174, 2000.

file = pathname. This simple equivalence between a file and its physical location in terms of a hierarchical directory structure is severely limited, if one considers the complex way in which users interact with applications and the operating system.

A file system can be considered as a special case of a database in terms of managing persistent data. The basic, simple approach is to consider a file system as just a table (directory) containing the name of the file and the address of its header (where all information on the sectors allocated for the file is stored). The obvious question to then ask is why do we not integrate the powerful features of an object-oriented database system such as high-level object abstraction, binding between data and code, role modelling for classification, and support for managing relationships between objects into the file system functionality.

We have taken exactly this approach in developing OMX-FS, a multi-user distributed object-oriented file system, based on the generic object data model OM. OMX-FS makes a step forward in terms of logical abstraction by considering files as objects and introducing typical concepts of object-oriented database systems. This functionality and flexibility allows both application developers and users to interact with the file system at a higher logical level.

To illustrate the potential benefits of such an approach, we consider a simple example of current technologies for managing a web site. Basically, a web page contains text, links and images. Usually, commercial tools are available to organise the whole construction process. If a web designer moves or renames files, inserts images and creates links, the tool provides the necessary changes within the HTML code, managing possible dangling references, missing files or other similar errors. This means that such a web design tool provides a transparent database where all the information on the constructed web site is managed. For example, there is information on which images are contained in an HTML page or which links are set to local files. Such a tool supports the web designer in the development and maintenance of web pages. However, the information (metadata) about the whole web site structure is stored within the database of the HTML design tool and cannot be accessed by other applications or from the operating system itself.

One reason for this style of *information hiding* is that many applications are actually *black boxes*, having minimal or no interface at all to other applications. There are many reasons why software developers wish to provide only a minimal interface to their tools. The most important one is to limit the scope of other developers or users. In fact, a completely open interface (for example for a graphical user interface or for metadata information) means that an application developer would have the possibility to control the application itself from other tools. Vendors do not always consider this desirable.

We take the view that it would be better if an application could *declare* to the file system, how it wants to organise and structure the files. In OMX-FS, a user or application notifies the system of the logical organisation structure of their files, specifying features such as which associations exist between files and how they are classified. By introducing into the file management system concepts familiar in database systems, we are able to attain a higher level of structural and operational abstraction. Since this is done at a *low level* within the operating system, all applications have the potential to share this knowledge and optimise performance, use of resources (such as disks) and information redundancy.

In this paper, we present OMX-FS and its implementation in the Oberon environment. We begin in section 2, with a review of existing file systems, presenting their main strengths and weaknesses. In section 3, we present our vision of a file system and in section 4 we describe the core model behind our architecture, motivating why such an object model is good for the design of a multi-user distributed object-oriented file system. In section 5, we then explain the concepts, functionalities and implementation details of our file system OMX-FS. To show the generality of our model, we describe briefly in section 6, how we used the model to develop a document management system, IDEOMS, showing the strengths of combining database and file system technologies. In section 7, we give concluding remarks and outline future work.

2   State of the Art

In [3] and [4], Borghoff provides an exhaustive review of distributed file and operating systems. From the side of file systems, he considers in his work 13 traditional and 3 object-oriented distributed file systems. He classifies them under different criteria, according to their transparency level and heterogeneity, to the changes made on the kernel level, to their communication protocols, connections and Remote Procedure Call (RPC) facilities, to their security issues and failure handling, and to their availability.

In addition to the well known traditional file systems such as the Network File System (NFS), the Andrew File System (AFS), the Remote File Sharing (RFS) or the Xerox Distributed File System (XDFS), we studied various other architectures focussing especially on the object-oriented ones since they are closer to our approach. Of the object-oriented distributed file systems presented in [3], DOMAIN and Helix seem to be very network oriented, investigating the performance aspects of distribution, while SWALLOW, dated 1980-81, focusses more on the data storage aspects and also introduces object modelling concepts.

Comparing all of the significant features of these distributed file systems, we note that, in many cases, the focus of the project is set only to some specific performance aspects. In our opinion, a *global vision* of the whole design and architecture is missing. As a result, there is a lack of basic general concepts supported by a powerful core abstract model. Rather, we find good file systems with extremely valid but limited features, which perform particular tasks in a very efficient way. We think that a file system should be as general and flexible as possible in its conception, and only then should it be extended and specialised for specific needs in a further step, following the object-oriented paradigms of programming, as stressed in [19].

If we consider the industry standards in terms of the file systems in commercial operating systems such as Windows [7] or MacOS [8], we note that such an approach of a *higher* functionality level file system is in practice not considered at all. The concept and its implementation is left to the applications on the top of the system. BeOS [2] does introduce a file system implemented over a database system. However, the Application Programming Interface (API) of its file system unfortunately offers only a limited part of all of the features of a database system. BeOS supports two different APIs (POSIX and C++) and its file system interface is in practice similar to other *usual* file system APIs. In addition, it supports an efficient indexing system for advanced queries and a journaling system for system integrity. However, typical database notions of role and association modelling for semantic file classification and for managing relationships between files are not supported. In other words, BeOS has many unused potentialities.

A flexible approach is taken by the JavaOS [18]. This operating system actually contains a database system, but it just stores system specific information such as configuration information for Java components and its use is not intended for other applications. The file system in JavaOS is actually provided as *system service*. At the moment, there is no version of a file system with integrated database functionalities, but the open architecture of JavaOS does not a priori exclude future variants from realising this possibility.

A possible explanation of this disinterest in developing a database-oriented view of a file system could be the underlying database technologies, which are often too restrictive with limitations in terms of support for associations, constraints, classification structures and object evolution. For example, both relational and object-relational database management systems proved to be too restrictive in terms of their semantic modelling capability. While object-oriented database management systems are better suited to manage complex structures and multimedia data, current commercial systems tend to have no or very limited support for constraints and rather restrictive classification structures. Research projects on object-oriented database systems which support all of those notions (as for example OMS, described in [14]) can open new directions for applications development. The lack of this *global vision* for a database-oriented view of the file system motivated us to embark on the OMX-FS project.

3   OMX-FS Vision

Before presenting the details of the OMX-FS system, we first present our vision of next generation file systems. In our vision, a file system should allow persistent and distributed objects to be worked with in a multi-user environment. Persistence has to be transparent, i.e. an application developer can handle objects without needing to know if they are local or remote. When an object is created, per default it should be transient and then, in a second step, it can be made persistent at any time. When an object becomes persistent, and it is stored on a machine connected to a network, it could be distributed too. The whole process should be reversible, i.e. a persistent distributed object could become transient as it was after its creation.

Each object has a type and the level of abstraction should support the possibility to specialise the behaviour of the objects through type inheritance. The file system should provide a unique type definition *File* (as an object storing a sequence of bytes), and each application could extend existing types, defining new ones. For instance, returning to the example in the introduction, a web design tool could provide a new type *HTMLFile*, with more attributes (i.e. the preferred browser to show the source file) and more (possibly overridden) methods (i.e. print the HTML source and print the HTML page contents).

The system should provide a rich classification of objects. It should be possible to define classifications (called *collections*) where objects can be inserted and removed. These provide a logical means of organising objects (role modelling), independent of the objects' types. This means, that the system should be able to provide a distinction between typing and classification. Just as there exists a subtype constraint between types, it should be possible to define a subcollection constraint between collections to represent more specialised classifications of objects. Furthermore the file system should support a mechanism to associate objects. An association structure is very similar to a collection. The basic difference is that while a collection contains objects, an association contains pairs of associated objects. An association is therefore referred to as a binary collection. As a direct consequence of having all of these functionalities provided through types, collections and association hierarchies, the file system is able to provide not only extended management functionalities, but also extended querying possibilities to perform operations over the entire file structure.

Last but not least, from conception, the whole architecture should be thought of as a multi-user environment, where users can share objects and define access rights over them. A distributed multi-user system is the precondition for support of user working activities.

Figure 1 serves to illustrate our vision — even though we leave the detailed explanations of the concepts and notations until later sections in the paper. On the left side, there is a directories (folders) hierarchy as exists in *usual* file systems. Aliases are used to classify the same file in different ways. Note that an alias is actually an entry in the system itself, as a file. Files do not have any knowledge about their aliases. This means that when a file is deleted, all of its aliases remain as dangling references.

On the right side, files are logically organised into collections. A file can be inserted into more than one collection since collections actually contain references to objects rather than object instances. If a file is deleted, no dangling references will remain in the system. Further, to find out, for example, all the private mails, a user simply needs to intersect the two collections `Private` and `Mails`. Note that the collection structure can support both direct and hierarchical access to files.

In this section, we presented the overall conceptional structure of our file system. OMX-FS introduces a higher logical file classification and association scheme for both application developers as well as *normal* users, focussing more on the work organisation itself rather than on the physical aspects such as the

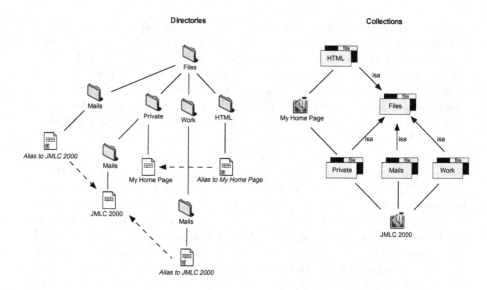

Fig. 1. Directories and Collections

distributed storage location. OMX-FS ensures a *backward compatibility* in the users working habits: They can still work with files and organise them in the same manner as they do with other file systems. In the next section, we detail a generic object model supporting such concepts and how they can be easily mapped into the architecture.

4   OMX-FS Generic Object Model

Which object model best suits our requirements? One of the best known general object-oriented modelling techniques is the Unified Modeling Language (UML), described in [6] and [17]. UML is intended to support all stages of application development from initial design to implementation. On the other hand, the object data model OM, described in [12], [13] and [11], is a generic object data model with influences from extended entity relationship models and semantic data models, as well as from object-oriented paradigms. OM can be considered as providing a data abstraction layer above the UML object model specific for database applications: OM models objects, classifications and associations, whereas UML models objects, their properties and interactions. OM combines ideas from conceptual modelling with object-oriented concepts and is a good framework on which to build a data management system while retaining independence of a particular implementation platform. Note however, that OM is not only a structural model, but also an operational model with operations over both object roles and associations.

The OM data model draws a clear distinction between the notions of *typing* and *classification*, and this clear distinction between the type model and the data model yields several advantages. The characteristics of objects in terms of interface and implementation are specified by the underlying type model. OM is then used to specify object roles and associations and thus deals with issues of classification and relationships between objects of the same abstraction level. One of the main advantages of this approach is that the data model is independent of a particular type model and can therefore be supported in many programming environments and implementation platforms. In fact, the generic model has been instantiated in a number of environments including ones based on C++, Java, Oberon and Prolog. Additionally, a major advantage for application support is that the separation of typing from classification allows us to distinguish between issues of representation and data semantics.

OM specifies various constructs, such as types, subtypes, collections, subcollections, constraints over these collections (partition, disjoint, cover and intersect), associations between collections and constraints over these associations (cardinality). Unary collections have atomic values as elements and, generally, represent entity roles of the application domain. Associations are binary collections with pair values as elements and represent relationships between entities of particular roles. In the operational model of OM, all operations which can be applied to unary collections can also be applied to binary collections. However, there are some operations which can only be applied to binary collections since they assume that the elements are pair values.

Fig. 2. OM Graphical Notation

Figure 2 shows the essential constructs of the OM data model and its graphical notation. Types are defined by shaded boxes, unary collections by unshaded boxes with the type of the member values (membertype) specified in the shaded region and associations between collections (source and target) by oval-shaped boxes.

To clarify, we explain the OM constructs with two examples. The first one in figure 3 shows the advantages of the distinction between typing and classification. We model a simple hierarchy of figures such as *rectangles* and *squares*. This can be modelled by defining a set **Figures**, a subset **Rectangles** of the set **Figures**, and a subset **Squares** of the set **Rectangles**. This is the *semantic* way to classify these figures. On the other side, we have to focus on their representation. The type **rectangle** has four attributes: An origin (**x,y**), a width **w** and a height **h**. The type **square** has actually only three attributes, because a square is a special case of a rectangle where $w = h$. For this reason, from the point of view of the implementation, it would be better to have the type **rectangle** as a subtype of **square**, thereby eliminating redundancy. OM allows this distinction, thereby introducing more flexibility into the application design.

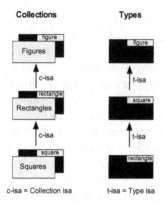

Fig. 3. Distinction between Type and Classification

The second example explains how to model in OM. Relationships between entities of the application domain are represented by associations over collections. For example, in figure 4, we have an association **Accesses** which relates elements of the collection **Users** to elements of the collection **Files**.

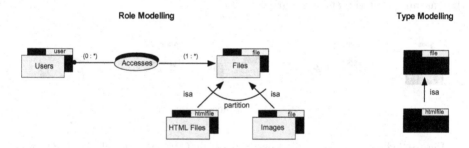

Fig. 4. Modelling in OM

In order that we can perform operations over such associations, it is necessary to specify a direction. The association **Accesses** is actually represented by a collection of pairs of values such that the first elements of the pairs belong to **Users** and the second elements belong to **Files**. We refer to **Users** as the *source collection* and to **Files** as the *target collection* of **Accesses**.

An association has cardinality constraints which specify the possible levels of participation of associated objects. In figure 4, the cardinality constraints specify that an element of **Users** can be associated with 0 up to an unlimited number of elements of **Files** and an element of **Files** must be associated with at least one element of **Users**.

Furthermore, as stated previously, a collection is a logical way to organise objects, independently of their type. For instance, note that the collection **Files** has the membertype **file**, while **HTMLFiles** the membertype **htmlfile**. This membertype defines the context in which objects are accessed in the collection. Generalising, the membertype can be considered as a *view* on the objects. This view is not unique: Potentially the object could be *viewed* through different collections (for instance `Files` and `HTMLFiles`) and hence through different types as determined by the membertypes of these collections. A different view means a different type which in turn means different attributes and functionality. This allows us to model role-dependent behaviour of objects. OM also supports role modelling in terms of object evolution. In OM, with a *dress* operation, an object can dynamically gain a new type (new attributes and new functionalities). Analogously, a *strip* operation is the inverse one of losing a type.

Figure 4 shows an example of a subcollection with constraints. The collection `Files` has two subcollections `HTMLFiles` and `Images`. An *is-a* relation between subcollections means that every object contained in a subcollection has also to be an element of the supercollection. Further, the *partition* constraint in this example demands that every object of `Files` must also be an element of exactly one of `HTMLFiles` or `Images`.

The OM data model introduces the necessary flexibility for application design. In our case for file system design, it allows files to be simultaneously classified in different ways, for operations to have context dependent behaviour and for dependencies to be represented through associations. OMX-FS is an extended file system which enables application developers and users to organise their *file space* in terms of OM constructs. Thus they can dynamically create new file types, collections and associations and freely move files within the overall file structure. Access to files can be provided directly, by navigation through the structure or by means of queries over the file structure. In the next section, we describe how OMX-FS has been implemented in the Oberon environment.

5   OMX-FS Implementation

OMX-FS is implemented in Oberon-2. The programming language Oberon [15] is a high-level, strongly-typed language, which allows rapid prototyping with strict formality. Another advantage of Oberon, besides the high level of the language, is the concept of modularity which allows separate compilation. The decomposition of code into different modules enables a good level of abstraction in the implementation of programs with a complex structure.

Before starting to describe the current state of the work, we would like to stress that the aim of this project is not to investigate the low level aspects of a file system, such as disk layout and cache management strategies. All of these problems are, in our case, left to the Oberon System: OMX-FS uses the same low-level disk management structure as the Oberon System, which is described in detail in the complete reference to the Oberon System [21]. Our primary goal is to provide a prototype which can show the advantages of having OM concepts embedded into a file system. The physical aspects of storing bytes and system performance optimisations should come in a second step, when the concepts of OMX-FS are proven. Given that the underlying storage structure of OMX-FS is the same as that of the Oberon System, exhaustive performance results and evaluation can be found in [21].

We chose to integrate our file system as part of the Oberon System 3, described in [5], because of the many advantages it offers. First of all, sources are public domain and for this reason we can make modifications within the operating system directly. Further, the Oberon System is programmed in Oberon itself, and the strict formality of the programming language is mirrored in the operating system. From the technical side, the Oberon System provides dynamic loading and unloading of modules (load on demand) – a very important feature especially during application development. It also supports an interface check of modules at compilation time and even at execution time. This implies that, at run time, the system is able to check if a module interface was previously changed and then, in that case, not to load and link the invalidated module. Finally, the Oberon System provides efficient automatic garbage collection, a critical factor for an object-oriented environment.

OMX-FS is a hierarchy of (modules) layers. At the bottom, we have the *Operating System Interface (OSI) Layer*. All the low-level operations are defined in this layer. The idea is to provide portability. A change of the platform implies only a change and a recompilation of the OSI modules, leaving the rest of the hierarchy untouched.

On top of the *OSI Layer*, we have both the *Storage Management System (SMS) Layer* as well as the *Network Management System (NMS) Layer*. The first one provides object persistence. In [1], the authors describe the important features for a persistent system. First of all, the system should be orthogonal and the persistence should be a property of any arbitrary value and not only limited to certain types. All values should have the same rights to persistence and, if a value persists, so will its type descriptor (metadata). Finally, the system should provide transparency between persistent and transient objects.

In OMX-FS, each persistent object has a unique global identifier. This identifier is composed of three values: a computer IP address, a storage unit number and a reference number. A persistent object is identified by a unique reference number because it is stored in a specified storage unit (identified by a unique number), which was created on a specified computer (identified by its unique IP address). With these three values, we are able to uniquely identify each persistent (and potentially distributed) object of the system. Our concept of *global unique identifier* allows a straightforward and flexible handling of distributed objects. We compared OMX-FS with DOMAIN, another file system which stresses the distribution aspect. In DOMAIN, each object has a unique identifier generated by the concatenation of a system value (node-id) and a time-stamp. Objects are then located through a searching algorithm. With our approach, there is no need for any searching algorithm.

The *SMS Layer* defines the storage units responsible for the physical storage of the data onto disk. As illustrated in figure 5, a storage unit has a references part which contains pairs of values, specifying, for each object in the storage unit, its reference number and its position in the physical location. The data

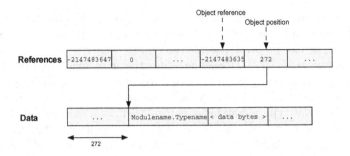

Fig. 5. Storage Units Structure

part is the physical place where objects are stored. An object is saved in the following format: First of all, the metadata information is stored; this means the type of the object (in the Oberon System a type is uniquely identified as `Modulename.Typename`). Then the attributes of the object are externalised and written as a raw stream of bytes into the physical location. Note that during the internalisation process, the metadata information first allows the object to be generated and then the call of its load method gives the appropriate semantics to the raw stream of bytes read. The same approach is taken by *Oberon-D*, a project described in [9] and [10] where the aim is to add database functionality to the Oberon System.

A storage unit is supposed to be local. For this reason, it contains only the object references and not the object global identifier, because the IP address and storage unit number would always be the same. Storage units load objects only on demand. This means, when a storage unit is opened, only its references are internalised into the main memory (RAM). In a second step, when a reference is requested, the storage unit loads the object into RAM too (if not previously *demanded* and already loaded). Obviously, storage units recognise cyclic structures of objects to prevent an infinite loop. Furthermore, they optimise the saving process. A flag bit is used to avoid the save operation of an unchanged object. Storage units also provide garbage collection if objects are deleted. This garbage collection is one of the performed actions during a commit phase of the file system. The commit operation is the final step in the successful completion of a work activity.

The *NMS Layer* provides object distribution in the system, which is reached with a peer to peer mechanism. Thus, each OMX-FS system running on a machine is at the same time server and client. If it needs a remote object, it requests that object from another remote OMX-FS server (the global identifier provides all the necessary information), and itself is always ready to send objects locally (physically) saved to other remote OMX-FS clients.

The communication between machines is implemented using a Remote Procedure Call (RPC) mechanism combined with XML coding over a well established Internet protocol, HTTP. XML-RPC has now become a standard and it is defined in [20]. The process to send an RPC is divided into the following steps: The requester generates an XML file, which is sent to the remote machine where an

HTTP server waits for XML requests. The receiver parses the file, executes the code and sends back another XML file containing the result of the operation if it succeeded, or else an error report.

The *Object Model (OM) Layer* provides the implementation of all the OM constructs (such as types, collections and associations) and their operations. It defines the concept of *workspace*, which contains data (such as new types) and metadata (such as type hierarchy structure), defines a storage unit to store the information, and contains object access rights for the users. The *OM Layer* also provides both the definition of the type File and its access (read/write) mechanism. A *file object* contains information such as the creation and modification date, a label and the address of the (Oberon System) sector allocation table, which specifies the physical storage structure of the file content (bytes stream).

The sharing structure of objects in OMX-FS is kept very flexible. First of all, the owner of an object has to set the permission rights for other users. Three permission rights are possible: *read-write* (attributes can be changed and methods executed), *read-only* (attributes can only be read and no method can be executed) and *no sharing*. At run-time, there are four different modes to access an object (if a user has the required permission rights). The first possibility is to set a *read-write* lock on the object. It is an exclusive lock, because no other user could access the same object, either in read-write or in read-only mode. The second possibility is to set a *read-only* lock on the object. This allows multiple concurrent access of the object from different users. The third mode is the *glimpse* mode, where a user works only with the reference to the object and does not need to lock it. Such a mode is useful especially if users perform operations like inserting an object into a collection, where actually the only data required is the reference of the object to be inserted, and not the whole object itself. Finally, for the case that access is forbidden, the system provides a *no access* mode.

At the top of the module hierarchy, the layer *OMX-FS Interface* presents the complete API for application developers. The file system is based on the OM model and applies its definitions and constructs. There is a one to one relationship between a file system and a workspace. In this way, it would be possible to have more than one file system on a machine. Furthermore, well known concepts such as that of directory disappear and are replaced by new ones such as collections. Collections allow files to be organised in a similar way to directories but, as shown in figure 1, they allow different classification schemes, are more flexible (collections contain only references to objects and not the objects themselves) and also efficient. Moreover, other OM structures and operations such as, for example, associations between objects, or queries over objects are easily introduced into the file system.

6   IDEOMS

The Integrated Document Environment based on the OMS system (IDEOMS) [16] was our first approach to an object-oriented file management system. It is actually an application on top of an object-oriented database system (OMS) [14], modelled using the OM object data model. It allowed us to determine the necessary requirements for a high-level file management system – later realised as OMX-FS. The objective was to build a *wish list* of *high-level* functionalities of the file system (in the form of an API), in order to be able to integrate them into the file system itself and to efficiently provide them to all other overlying applications.

The underlying idea of IDEOMS is to support typical database operations on documents, such as queries and the specification of dependencies between documents. Furthermore, given that an important aspect of document management is the classification and retrieval of documents, IDEOMS allows documents to be dynamically classified in several different ways independent of the document format. Rich classification schemes, combined with powerful querying facilities, support document retrieval. In IDEOMS, this is achieved through the classification structures and the full algebraic query language of the underlying OM data model. Finally, support for cooperative working among users wishing to collaborate on and share documents requires also a multi-user system with distributed access, supporting access and concurrency control mechanisms to ensure the integrity of the document database. In IDEOMS, this sharing mechanism is on a higher-level of abstraction, thereby simplifying the work of users.

7   Conclusions and Future Work

In this paper, we presented our concept of a multi-user distributed object-oriented file system modelled through the object model OM and implemented under Oberon System 3.

The current state of OMX-FS is that all features described, along with a graphical user interface, have been implemented. Future work consists primarily of tuning the system for performance improvements and also providing the necessary applications for operational validation of the system.

Performance improvements will focus first of all on the XML-RPC mechanism. In fact, an RPC mechanism assumes that all the code is executed remotely. This is optimal if you consider a Wide Area Network (WAN) such as the Internet, where the data exchange is very expensive in terms of performance. In a Local Area Network (LAN) such as an Intranet, this performance aspect related to the bandwidth is reduced. In the case that the server is overloaded, the client could actually lock an object, copy it locally, work with a *local wrapper* of that object (changing attributes, executing code) and then when the client releases it, send all the local object data back to the server. We plan to investigate various heuristics to determine under which conditions such a variant would be optimal.

To validate all the new concepts introduced by OMX-FS, we plan to write applications on the top of this file system. For example, we intend to implement a simple one, such as a *light* version of a text editor or web browser, or possibly both integrated together. Such an application could directly work with objects instead of pathnames. Further, it could allow users to dynamically create new ways to classify documents or to relate files with each other using associations. In this way, a user could focus more on which files have to be managed rather then on where they are physically located.

References

1. M. P. Atkinson and O. P. Buneman. Type and Persistence in Database Programming Languages. *ACM Computing Surveys*, 19(2):105–190, 1987.
2. Be Inc., California, USA. *The Be Book*, 1999.
3. U. M. Borghoff. *Catalogue of Distributed File/Operating Systems*. Springer-Verlag, 1992.
4. U. M. Borghoff and K. Nast-Kolb. *Distributed Systems: A Comprehensive Survey*. Technische Universitaet Muenchen, 1989.
5. A. Fischer and H. Marais. *The Oberon Companion. A Guide to Using and Programming Oberon System 3*. VDF, 1998.
6. Booch G., Jacobson I., and J. Rumbaugh. *The Unified Modeling Language User Guide*. Addison-Wesley, 1998.
7. Custer H. *Inside the Windows NT File System*. Microsoft Press, 1994.
8. Apple Technical Library. *Inside Macintosh: Files*. Addison-Wesley, California, USA, 1996.
9. Knasmüller M. Adding Persistence to the Oberon-System. Technical report, Institute for Computer Science, Johannes Kepler University, A-4040 Linz, Austria.
10. Knasmüller M. Oberon-D: Adding Database Functionality to an Object-Oriented Development Environment. Technical report, Institute for Practical Computer Science System Software), Johannes Kepler University, A-4040 Linz, Austria.
11. M. C. Norrie. *A Collection Model for Data Management in Object-Oriented Systems*. PhD thesis, University of Glasgow, Dept. of Computing Science, Glasgow G12 8QQ, Scotland, December 1992.
12. M. C. Norrie. An Extended Entity-Relationship Approach to Data Management in Object-Oriented Systems. In *12th Intl. Conf. on Entity-Relationship Approach*, Dallas, Texas, December 1993.
13. M. C. Norrie. Distinguishing Typing and Classification in Object Data Models. In *Information Modelling and Knowledge Bases*, volume VI, chapter 25. IOS, 1995. (originally appeared in Proc. European-Japanese Seminar on Information and Knowledge Modelling, Stockholm, Sweden, June 1994).
14. M. C. Norrie and A. Würgler. OMS Object-Oriented Data Management System: Introductory Tutorial. Technical report, Institute for Information Systems, ETH Zurich, CH-8092 Zurich, Switzerland, 1998.
15. M. Reiser and N. Wirth. *Programming in Oberon*. Addison-Wesley, 1992.
16. G. Rivera, M. C. Norrie, and A. Steiner. IDEOMS: An Integrated Document Environment based on OMS Object-Oriented Database System. In *4th Doctoral Consortium CAiSE'97*, Barcelona, Spain, June 1997.
17. J. Rumbaugh, Jacobson I., and Booch G. *The Unified Modeling Language Reference Manual*. Addison-Wesley, 1998.
18. T. Saulpaugh and C. Mirho. *Inside the JavaOS Operating System*. Addison-Wesley, 1999.
19. C. A. Szyperski. *Insight ETHOS: On Object-Orientation in Operating Systems*. VDF, 1992.
20. UserLand Software, Inc., Dave Winer. $http://www.xmlrpc.com/$.
21. N. Wirth and J. Gutknecht. *Project Oberon*. Addison-Wesley, 1992.

On Adding a Query Language to a Persistent Object System

Markus Knasmüller[1]

BMD Steyr, Sierninger Straße 190, A-4400 Steyr, Austria
knasmueller@bmd.at

Abstract. Object oriented programming languages as well as persistent object systems are usually accessed by explicit navigation along the relations (i.e. the pointers) between the objects. End users of a "database", however, prefer to have a query language, which allows them to specify database queries regardless of the mechanism that is used to navigate through the database. In this paper we show a simple technique for adding a query language to an object-oriented programming language. We translate the query, in our case an OQL query, into a program and execute this resulting program. So an ordinary program offers the results of the queries. The compilation and execution is done "on the fly", which means that the user is not aware of the translation. In this paper we present how the translator works, how to write such a translator, and the advantages of our chosen method.

1 Introduction

Object-orientation was invented twice: once by the programming languages people and once by the database people. The two camps are usually separated, in spite of the many commonalities in their goals and approaches. Programming languages deal with transient objects in main memory. They are concerned with data abstraction, inheritance and polymorphic operations, while persistent storage of objects is often ignored or poorly supported. Databases, on the other hand, deal with persistent objects on a disk. They are mainly concerned with modelling complex relations between objects as well as with efficient access methods and query languages. The separation is also evident in the use of different languages: Smalltalk, C++ or Java on the one hand, and mostly OQL on the other hand. Although it is usually possible to access a database from a program, the notations and access mechanisms differ from the techniques used for transient objects.

Persistent object systems aim at unifying the two worlds. A database is viewed as a set of objects that happen to be persistent but are otherwise accessed and manipulated just like any other object in main memory. The idea is to view the database as a virtual extension of the computer's memory. All objects - transient or persistent - are referenced via pointers. The run time system makes sure that persistent objects are loaded from disk when they are needed and stored to disk when they are not used any

---

[1] Markus Knasmüller is on leave from Johannes Kepler University Linz, Department of Practical Computer Science (Systemsoftware).

J. Gutknecht and W. Weck (Eds.): JMLC 2000, LNCS 1897, pp. 175-185, 2000.
© Springer-Verlag Berlin Heidelberg 2000

more. For the programmer, there is no difference between transient and persistent objects. They are declared, generated and used in exactly the same way. In a radical view, there seems to be no database at all because it is maintained automatically behind the scenes.

However most persistent object systems have one disadvantage. They are usually accessed by explicit navigation along the relations (i.e. the pointers) between the objects. End users of a database, however, prefer to have a query language, which allows them to specify database queries regardless of the mechanism that is used to navigate through the database. A common standard for object-oriented query languages is the Object Query Language (OQL) defined by the Object Database Management Group (ODMG) [1]. This language is similar to SQL, which is used in relational database systems. However there are just a few implementations of OQL. Most systems support either none query language or they define their own query language.

In this paper we show a simple way how to add OQL to a persistent object system. This technique can even used without any change of the persistent object system and therefore a query language could be added to an existing system. We used this technique when implementing the Oberon-D project [2]. Oberon-D introduces database functionality in the Oberon System, which was originally developed by Niklaus Wirth (the father of Pascal) and Jürg Gutknecht at ETH Zurich [3]. However instead of Oberon each other programming language could be used and by using this method a query language could be added to each persistent object system. Afterwards the user is able to access the persistent heap via OQL queries. These queries can either be specified using a graphical user interface or in the form of embedded OQL from within a program.

2 Motivation and Aims

Various object-oriented database systems or persistent development environments have defined query languages (for example: ODE: CQL++ [4], O2: O2SQL [5], and Iris: OSQL [6]). Since we did not want to define yet another query language we decided to implement an existing one. In spite of some disadvantages (see, e.g., [7]) the query language OQL, which was defined by the Object Database Management Group (ODMG) as a standard for object-oriented databases [1], was chosen. The standard includes an object model; using the OMG Object model as the basis, an object definition language (ODL), an object query language (OQL), and the definition of a C++ and a Java binding.

Before we started with the implementation of our ODMG binding we defined the following design goals:

☐ It should be as simple as possible
☐ There should be no changes to the used programming language and the used persistent object system.
☐ The full OQL language should be supported.
☐ If ODL/OQL is translated to programming code, the code should be short and readable.

☐ In the case of an error in the ODL/OQL code the user should get an error message referring to the ODL/OQL code and not to the object-oriented code into which ODL/OQL is translated.

☐ The query language should smoothly fit into the persistent object system, i.e., it should be possible to make OQL queries from within object-oriented programs.

3 The ODMG Object Model

The basic modelling primitive of the ODMG object model is the object. Objects can be categorized into types. The behaviour of objects is defined by a set of operations that can be executed on an object of the type. The state of objects is defined by the values they carry for a set of attributes. In this section only the parts of the object model, which are relevant for the implementation of a query interface, are mentioned. For detailed information see [1, Chapter 2].

For defining interfaces to object types that conform to the Object Model the specification language ODL (Object Definition Language) is used. The primary objective of the ODL is to facilitate portability of database schemas across conforming ODBMSs.

Each type is defined in one interface. It defines the external interface supported by instances of the type - that is, their attributes and the operations that can be invoked on them. The following source code shows an example for an object type definition:

```
interface Module : SEObject
{
    attribute String name;
    attribute Long codesize;
    Set<Proc> procs;
    Set<Var> vars;
};
```

This example defines a type *Module*, which is a subtype of *SEObject*. *Module* has two attributes (*name* and *codesize*) and two operations (*procs* which returns a set of *Procs* and *vars* which returns a set of *Vars*).

An enumeration defines a type that has the instances named in the enumeration declaration. Structures have a fixed number of named slots each of which contains an object or a literal. Examples for these types can be seen in the following source fragment:

```
enum color {red, black, white, green, grey};
struct address {attribute String name, attribute String nr} adr;
```

Collections contain an arbitrary number of elements that are all instances of the same type. Within collections, the model supports both ordered and unordered collections, where the order is defined either by the sequence in which objects are inserted or by the value of one of the attributes of the objects that are the members of the collection. Collections may allow or disallow the same object to be present in the collection more than once. Each collection has an immutable identity; two collections may have the same elements without being the same collection. Similarly, inserting, removing, or modifying an element of a collection does not create a new collection.

The type *Collection* is an abstract type, with the subtypes *Set*, *Bag*, *List* and *Array*. It is possible to iterate over the elements of a collection. Iteration is done by defining an *Iterator* that maintains a current position within the collection to be traversed.

4 Using the Query Language

This section describes the object query language named OQL [1, Chapter 4], which supports the ODMG object model. OQL is a superset of standard SQL. Thus, any select SQL statement, which runs on relational tables, works with the same syntax and semantics on collections of ODMG objects. Extensions concern object-oriented notions, like complex objects, object identity, path expressions, polymorphism, operation invocation, late binding and so on.

OQL can either be used as a stand-alone language or as an embedded language. If it is used as a stand-alone language the user can write the query in any window or in any file. It is possible to execute the query with the command *OQL.Run (name | ^ | *)*. Within the query he can access all visible names, that means all persistent roots and all exported global module variables. The results of the query are shown in the output viewer.

If OQL is used as an embedded language there are two ways to call OQL commands from Oberon programs: one can call a method of a collection object, i.e., *col.Select (cmd)*, *col.Exists (cmd)*, or *col.ForAll (cmd)*; alternatively, one can call the procedure *OQL.Query (cmd, res)*. The parameter *cmd* is a string containing an OQL command in which all visible variables can be used (i.e., local variables, global variables or persistent roots).

The *ForAll* method is a universal quantification, which returns TRUE if all the elements of the collection satisfy the query or otherwise FALSE. The *Exists* method is an existential quantification, which returns TRUE if one of the elements of the collection satisfies the query or otherwise FALSE. With the *Select* method, all objects of the collection, which satisfy the query, can be fetched. That means *col.Select (age = 15)* returns the same result as the OQL statement *select * from col where col.age = 15*.

The procedure *OQL.Query (cmd, res)* executes the OQL command *cmd*, and returns the result in the parameter *res*, which is a structure of type *OML.Value*. *Value* has an attribute *class* indicating the type of the result as well as attributes for each possible type of result. A very simple example of such a call is *OQL.Query ("3 < 4", res)* which retrieves a value *res* with *res.class = OML.Bool* and the boolean attribute *res.b = TRUE*.

The following example shows an Oberon-2 application that accesses an ODMG software database containing information about modules (type *Module*), procedures (type *Proc*) and variables (type *Var*). Each module has a *name*, a *codesize*, a set of procedures *procs*, and a set of variables *vars*. A global variable *mods* holds the set of all modules. The procedure *Query* in the following source code shows how to perform OQL queries from within the source code (an asterisk after a declared name means that the name is exported).

```
MODULE SWDatabase;

IMPORT OML;

TYPE
    Module* = POINTER TO ModuleDesc;
    ModuleDesc* = RECORD
        name*: ARRAY 32 OF CHAR;
        codesize*: LONGINT;
        procs*: OML.Set;
        vars*: OML.Set;
    END;

    Proc* = POINTER TO ProcDesc;
    ProcDesc* = RECORD
        name*: ARRAY 32 OF CHAR;
        vars*: OML.Set;
    END;

    Var* = POINTER TO VarDesc;
    VarDesc* = RECORD
        name*: ARRAY 32 OF CHAR;
        type*: SHORTINT; (* unique number ident. type *)
    END;

VAR mods: OML.Set; (* set of all modules *)

PROCEDURE Query*;
    VAR c: OML.Collection; res: OML.Value;
BEGIN
    (* -- e.g. all modules with codesize > 500 *)
    c := mods.Select ("codesize > 500");
    (* -- e.g. all local variables with name "i" *)
    OQL.Query ("select var from mods, mods.vars as var where var.name = 'i' ", res);
        (* => the value of res.class = OML.Pointer and res.o is a reference to the result set *)
    (* -- e.g. all procedures of module "Types" *)
    OQL.Query ("select m.procs from mods as m where m.name = 'Types' ", res);
        (* => the value of res.class = OML.Pointer and res.o is a reference to the result set *)
    (* ... *)
END Query;

END SWDatabase.
```

As it can be seen, the relevant procedures and commands are offered by the special module *OQL*, which is the programming interface to the world of the query language.

5 Implementation

We translate the ODL/OQL code into an object-oriented program, compile the generated program on the fly and execute it afterwards. The user gets the result values from the program, although he is not aware of the translation. This process can be seen in Figure 1. The advantage of using this approach was the ease of executing procedures. So it is not necessary to rebuild the parameter calling, e.g., we had no problems with building or rebuilding the stack. This is very important, because procedures, especially type bound procedures, are often called in OQL code. Using an interpreter would be a little bit faster, but when accessing a database this extra compilation time does not really matter, because most of the time is consumed for file accessing.

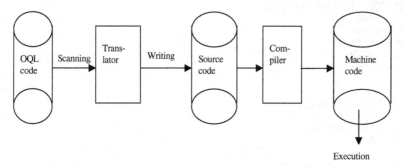

Fig. 1. Translating ODL/OQL code into object-oriented programming language code

Using this strategy the main task was to implement a translator from ODL/OQL to Oberon-2. This was done with the help of the compiler generator Coco [8]. Coco translates an attributed LL(1) grammar, into an recursive descent parser and scanner. Using this technique it is very simple to change the language. If we would like to use another language than Oberon-2, the main changes can be done in the attributed grammar. There is no necessity for big changes in the source code.

Depending on the structure of the automatically generated module (see the listing below), the translator has four main jobs.

```
MODULE OQLSrc;
    IMPORT OML, ....
    CONST ....
    TYPE .....
    VAR res*: OML.Value;
    ......
    PROCEDURE Do*;
    BEGIN res := ....
    END Do;
END OQLSrc.
```

These four main jobs are:

☐ Writing the import list: If the ODL/OQL code uses an Oberon module, this module has to be appended to the import list, if it is not already a member of the list.
☐ Writing the constants: The constants are defined in the ODL part of the code.
☐ Writing the type definitions: Most type definitions are generated from the ODL part. But sometimes a new type also has to be generated because of an OQL statement (e.g., a projection).
☐ Writing the statements: The statements are produced as a result of translating the OQL code.

For each job we are using one global text. At the end of the translation process, we append these four texts and get the generated module as a result. In the following some generated pieces of source code are shown as examples for the functionality of the translator.

5.1 Translating ODL Code

ODL code consists of constants and type definitions. It is rather simple to translate these ODL definitions into program code, because the structure is similar. You have an identifier, a type, and in the case of constants, a value. In Oberon-2, as well as in other programming languages, you also have an identifier, a type, and a value, so the job is just to change the order of these things and set semicolons etc. Furthermore, the ODL type must be translated to the respective type of the used programming language.

5.2 Translating Simple OQL Queries

The basic construct of the OQL grammar is a *Query*. A *Query* can be a literal (e.g., *nil*), a simple operation (e.g., "+"), but also a *Select* statement. Queries are translated to ordinary procedures. However, the resulting code will usually contain less procedures than there are queries, because whenever possible two or more procedures are combined into one.

Each procedure consists of four (optional) parts: Variable declarations, statements, a return value and the type of the return value. The following code fragment shows a template of an automatic generated procedure.

```
PROCEDURE Do*;
    VAR declarations
BEGIN
    statements
    res.x := return value; res.class := return type
END Do;
```

Therefore, three texts and a variable determining the result type are needed. We show this with the help of the simple query: 4 (the integer literal). Translating this query we have empty variable and statement texts. The result text is equal to "4" and the result type describes the type SHORTINT. Table 1 shows the automatic generated procedures for some simple OQL queries.

Table 1. Automatic generated procedures for some example queries

Query	Generated procedure

4	PROCEDURE **Do***;
	BEGIN
	  res.x := 4; res.class := OML.Sint
	END Do;

4 + 4711	PROCEDURE **Do***;
	BEGIN
	  res.x := 4 + 4711; res.class := OML.Int
	END Do;

4 + 4711 < 50	PROCEDURE **Do***;
	BEGIN
	  res.x := 4 + 4711 < 50; res.class :=
	OML.Bool
	END Do;

Of course the variable and statement texts are not always empty. For example, the simple query

```
root
```

(accessing the persistent root with name *"root"*, which is of type *SoftDBTypes.Module*), uses these texts, too. In this case some source code must be produced to get the root into memory, and so the statement text consists of *Persistent.GetRoot (o, "root")*. The used variable *o* has to be declared in the variable part, with *"o: SoftDBTypes.Module"*, whereby, in fact, we do not use *o* as a variable name, but we append a unique number, so for example *o1*. The result text would be *"o"* and the result type is *SoftDBTypes.Module*.

Most queries can also be translated in this simple way, it is often enough to append the type bound procedures of module *OML*. The query

```
count (root)
```

for example, would use the texts described above, but would change the result type to LONGINT and would append *.Cardinality ()* to the result text (= *"o.Cardinality ()"*). The generated source code can be seen below.

```
MODULE OQLSrc;

IMPORT OML, Persistent;

TYPE
    OMLBagPtr = POINTER TO OML.BagDesc;

VAR res*: OML.Value;
```

```
PROCEDURE Do*;
    VAR o1: OMLBagPtr;
BEGIN
    Persistent.GetRoot (o1, "root");
    res.x := o1.Cardinality (); res.class := OML.LInt
END Do;

END OQLSrc.
```

5.3 Translating Larger Queries

Queries, such as *avg*, *sum*, *for all* and *exists* are a little bit more complicated. They require an iteration over a collection. An iterator has to be initalizied and in each step of the iteration an action is necessary. For example, when translating the query,

$$\texttt{exists x in Students: x.matnr > 9000000}$$

the condition *x.matnr > 9000000* must be checked for every object *x* of the collection *Students*. This leads to some extra code in the statement part or in the computation of the result value. The translation of the above query is shown below.

```
MODULE OQLSrc;

IMPORT OML, Persistent, ODLExample;

TYPE
    ODLExampleStudentPtr = POINTER TO ODLExample.StudentDesc;
    OMLSetPtr = POINTER TO OML.SetDesc;

VAR res*: OML.Value;

PROCEDURE Query0 (VAR par0: ODLExampleStudentPtr): BOOLEAN;
BEGIN
    RETURN (par0.matnr > 9000000)
END Query0;

PROCEDURE Query1 (): BOOLEAN;
    VAR o1: OMLSetPtr; it2: OML.Iterator; o3: ODLExampleStudentPtr;
BEGIN
    Persistent.GetRoot (o1, "Students");
    it2 := o1.CreateIterator (); it2.Next (o3);
    WHILE it2.Stable () DO
        IF Query0 (o3) THEN RETURN TRUE END;
        it2.Next (o3)
    END;
    RETURN FALSE
END Query1;

PROCEDURE Do*;
BEGIN
    res.b := Query1 (); res.class := OML.Bool
END Do;

END OQLSrc.
```

5.4 Translating Select Queries

Of course the most complicated query is the *select* query. This is not only because a *select* query can have *where*, *group by*, *having* and *order* clauses. There are also some special problems: for example, the projection clause can only be translated after some subsequent clauses of the select query have been processed.

Starting with an ordinary *select * from Students*, the translator has to generate code for allocating and initializing a new collection with the same element type as the collection *Students*. Furthermore, an iteration over *Students* is necessary. In each step the element is inserted into the new collection.

When we add a *where* clause to the query, e.g., *select * from Students where matnr > 9000000*, it is necessary to check the condition in each iteration step. Other possible additions are a projection and an *order by* clause.

Using a projection the translator has to generate a new type for the projection result and another iteration over the resulting query. In each iteration step the collection elements are transformed to the new type.

Using an *order by* clause the translator has to generate a comparison procedure *wp* and has to append *.Sort (wp)* at the resulting collection. The *OML* method *Sort* will sort the collection and return a *List*. A full example can be seen in [9, chapter 3.5.5]

6 Conclusions

This paper showed how a query language could be added to a persistent object system. We decided to use OQL based on the ODMG object model. We translate OQL queries into object-oriented programs, which we compile and execute on the fly. The resulting source code is short and readable. The user is not aware of this translation and has the impression that the OQL query is interpreted. Even in the case of an error in the ODL/OQL code the user gets an error message referring to the ODL/OQL code, whenever possible. Also errors like accessing a NIL-reference causes an error message instead of a run-time error. The query language fits smoothly into the persistent object system, i.e., it is possible to make OQL queries from within object-oriented programs.

Future work will concentrate on the improvement of the graphical user interface and on porting this concept to other programming languages.

Acknowledgments

I wish to thank Prof. Hanspeter Mössenböck and Prof. Gerti Kappel for their support of this project. Furthermore I want to thank Prof. Markku Sakkinen for his careful reading of an earlier version of this paper and for his numerous suggested improvements.

References

1. Catell, R.G.G. (ed.): The Object Database Standard: ODMG-93. Addision Wesley (1996)
2. Knasmüller, M.: Adding Persistence to the Oberon System. Proc. of the JMLC 1997, Linz, Lectures Notes in Computer Science, Springer-Verlag, Berlin Heidelberg New York (1997)
3. Wirth, N., Gutknecht, J.: The Oberon System, Software – Practise and Experiences, 19, 9 (1989)
4. Agrawal, R., Gehani, N.H.: Ode: The Language and the Data Model, Proc. ACM SIGMOD 1989 Int'l Conf. Management of Data, Portland, Oregon (1989) 36-45
5. Deux, O.: The Story of O_2, IEEE Trans. on Knowledge and Data Enginnering, 2, 1 (1990) 91-108
6. Fishman, D., et. al.: Overview of the Iris DBMS, In: Kim, W., Lochovsky, F. (ed.) Object-Oriented Concepts, Databases, and Applications, Reading MA: Addision Wesley (1989) 219-250
7. Sakkinen, M.: More about ODMG-93 standard, and a bit about manifestos, Technical Report, Johannes Kepler University of Linz (1996)
8. Mössenböck, H.: A Generator for Production Quality Compilers, Proc. of 3rd Int. Compiler-Compiler Workshop, Schwerin, Lecture Notes in Computer Science, Springer-Verlag, Berlin Heidelberg New York (1991)
9. Knasmüller, M.: Oberon-D On Adding Database Functionality to an Object-Oriented Development Environment, Trauner-Verlag, Linz (1997)

Project C2 - A Survey of an Industrial Embedded Application with Native Oberon for PC

Josef Sedlacek[1] and Jürg Gutknecht[2]

[1]Radiar, Dr. J Sedlacek, CH-7554 Sent, Switzerl

[2]Department of Computer Science, ETH Zürich

Abstract. By order of the Colortronic company a successful industrial project was realized which serves to highly accurate feeding of material. Design goals included a modern graphical user interface for the control of the feeding process and a versatile system architecture able to support different hosts. The software was implemented using the Native Oberon system for PC developed by ETH Zürich. This brief survey reports about a perspective from the point of view of industrial software and hardware development.

1   Introduction to Project C2

The presented project was born due to the need of a new industrial system driving material feeders. Such feeders are mainly used for plastic extrusion and injection, however, they may be used for other purposes too. The feeding occurs continuously with a selectable feeding rate measured in mass per time. The crucial point is the ability to continuously feed a proper blend of materials according to a recipe of up to eight components.

2   System Architecture

Figure 1 shows a particular configuration of feeding equipment by the example of plastic extrusion [1]. A hopper is hung up on a scale (schematically shown as an old fashion scale). A rotating screw at the bottom transports the material outside of the hopper into a blender. There are up to eight such hoppers positioned together in order to feed a blend of the desired recipe. The scale measures weight loss of the material per time. The speed of the feeding screw controls the feeder to the desired feeding rate. When the weight of the material falls below a certain limit, the material is refilled by opening the refill valve. From the blender the material goes into the extruder, where it is heated up and pressed together to achieve the right reactions. The material then comes out through a jet of the desired shape, for example a tube, a profile etc., and then goes for further treatment. The length of the whole configuration

J. Gutknecht and W. Weck (Eds.): JMLC 2000, LNCS 1897, pp. 186-196, 2000.

can be up to 40m. The mechanical feeding system is connected to the I/O port of a CPU via motor box.

The C2 box is the main node of the configuration. It contains the CPU whose main task is process control. It can communicate with a host system by using one of the following protocols: Colortronic, Siemens S3964R, Modbus, Profibus and Allan Bradley which are all industry standards, or with TCP/IP. As a physical layer RS485 and Ethernet can be used.

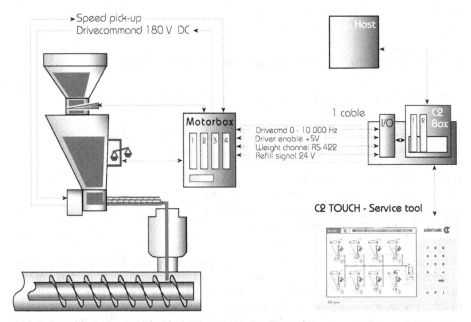

Fig. 1. System C2 Configuration

The visual user interface node C2 Touch is equipped with a touch screen and a small keypad. It is not mandatory in the case of a host featuring a customer-implemented user interface.

3   System Requirements

The C2 project was guided by different requirements. Generally speaking, flexibility is needed in order to be able to adjust to different customers' needs. Such needs may not be known completely at the time of implementation, and they may evolve in unexpected directions. They may concern functional aspects, mechanic dimensions, costs, long-term availability of system parts etc.

For example, one requirement was the mechanical dimension of the board to meet the EURO standard for long boards (100 x 220 mm) in order to be compatible with an existing system.

For the feeding part the following points were important:

1. Highly accurate dosage control
2. Multi protocol communicability with other system components
3. Suitable and effective user interface

To achieve 1 the system has to act in real time. A minimum system has to meet points 1 and 2. A simple system satisfying 1, 2 and 3 is economically interesting.

It now follows a short recapitulation of the system selection procedure and the implementation of the system.

4   Choosing the Operating System and Hardware

In the selection process the following needs have been followed up:

(a)	Real time capability
(b)	Lean and resource-efficient base system not relying on disk
(c)	Good communication support
(d)	Low cost
(e)	Hardware with long lifetime (minimum 15 years)
(f)	Operating system as complete as possible
(g)	Open source, optimal system transparency
(h)	Experiences from previous projects
(i)	Modern system architecture

Points (a) to (c) were mandatory, (d) and (e) important. Today's hardware technology evolves very fast. This stands in contradiction to the demanded life-time of an industrial system, where spare parts have to be available for at least 15 years as stated in (e). This led to the decision to use the most widely spread and thus the most stable PC hardware with some custom adjustments satisfying (a) to (c). With this, point (d) is obviously met as well. For industrial compatibility the PC104 bus was chosen. The custom C2 board was designed according to the mentioned 100 x 220 mm EURO board specification. Figure 2 shows the complete computer with 4MB RAM and 8MB Flash PROM as a secondary memory that runs the feeding application.

The selection of an operating system was a more or less straightforward procedure. Due to previous experience with industrial projects using Modula-2 [2] and PC Native Oberon [3] from ETH Zürich, the PC Native Oberon system made it immediately to the final round of our choice. However, other systems were also examined. Windows CE would satisfy most of the points but has disadvantages regarding costs and openness of the system. Also, Oberon's novel component oriented architecture is much leaner. The overall performance of systems based on a C or C++ run time kernel is much worse, especially regarding the graphic user interface. One further possibility would have been the use of a commercial visualization system like Fix from the Intellution company. However, the Oberon system outperforms such a solution with a more stable and reliable operation. Thus, our final choice was Native Oberon for PC.

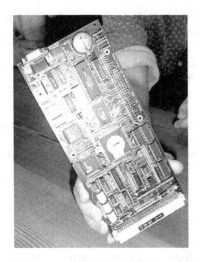 

Fig. 2. The minimum system: C2 board with a 386 PC104 CPU

5   A Quick Conceptual Overview of Native Oberon

We first recapitulate that Oberon is both a language (in the Pascal-Modula-line) and a general purpose, modular operating system for personal workstations [4]. Its API is a static hierarchy of interfaces, where each interface consists of a logically connected collection of data types and procedure signatures. Implementations can be adapted or customized to specific needs without destroying the system's integrity. In this respect, Oberon is a generic operating framework much rather than a classical operating system.

Oberon System 3 [5] is an evolution of the original Oberon system ported to Native PC platforms and is therefore also called Native Oberon for PC. It comes with an integrated generic object framework and with a graphical user interface (GUI) toolkit called *Gadgets* that is based on the object framework. Objects are by concept hierarchically composable, and they feature built-in functionality for a persistent representation. Therefore, they are often called *components*. The Gadgets GUI toolkit offers both a highly interactive visual component builder and a scripting language interpreter.

Some preprogrammed components (also called controls) come with the system, for example, checkboxes, text fields, sliders, lists, panels, and document frames. The latter two are of type *container*. Note that the notion of component in Oberon comprises a large spectrum of granularity. For example, character glyphs and the whole display screen are components of extreme granularities.

There are two ways to extend the arsenal of existing components: Programming or constructing. Programming a new component essentially amounts to implementing a well-specified message protocol of type "parental control". New components can alternatively be constructed interactively by using the component builder or descriptively by using the scripting language interpreter. In both cases, the resulting construct (however complex it may be) can be persistently registered under some name in an object library. Both programmed and constructed components can later be reused for further constructions. Programmed components are instantiated in some generic form via a so-called generator procedure *Module.Generator*. Constructed components are simply recalled from their library in their current state via their qualified name *Library.Component*.

It should be added that non-visual components are supported by the Gadgets system as well. They typically serve as models of some instance of the Model-View-Controller (MVC) design pattern. However, visual objects may act as models as well. Views of visual objects are called *camera-views*.

6   Implementation of the C2 Project

In spite of the fact that Native Oberon was developed as a general purpose operating system for a personal workstation rather than for special purpose embedded systems, the implementation of the C2 System based on Native Oberon was surprisingly straightforward. Especially the built-in component framework mentioned above and excellently described in [7] made it possible to quickly achieve commercially successful solutions. Thanks to Oberon's resource efficiency, low cost hardware could be used.

The implementation can be divided into parts emphasizing different aspects. We shall first discuss low-level aspects such as process management and device drivers and then high-level aspects mainly oriented towards the user interface.

6.1   Process Oriented Aspects

The main task of our application is the precise control of the feeding process. In order to achieve this a system with true real-time capability was needed.

Perhaps surprisingly, we implemented the desired real time behavior based on two simple and existing system facilities:

1. The hardware interrupt system
2. The Oberon task loop

The Oberon task loop is a task scheduler operating on procedure granularity. It requires the programmer to decompose tasks into a sequence of "instantaneous" actions, i. e. into non-preemptive procedure calls of short duration. Based on the interrupt system and the cyclic task scheduler we were able to implement all needed functionality in a clear way without any problems regarding the garbage collector.

In detail the system has to read in real time:

- up to twelve weight scales in a precise time grid
- a level sensor for detection of the extruder speed
- the speed of up to twelve motors

- bit input for feeder enable, start, stop etc.
- custom external sensors
- input of variables over two host and a service channel
- the touch screen interface and the keyboard
- network

respectively to control in real time:

- up to twelve motor speed drive commands also in a precise time grid
- bit output for motor enable, alarm relais etc.
- output to hosts and service channel
- the display

6.2   Device Oriented Aspects

The low level parts of the Native Oberon operating system for PC are implemented in a general manner and required few changes only. They are summarized in the following sections.

6.2.1   Boot Loader

In the basic application no floppy or hard disks are present. For this reason it was necessary to adapt the boot process. The C2 custom hardware supports an 8 MB flash memory. A DIP switch allows to select between two different modes of booting. The first mode is the usual boot mode that loads the boot file from floppy or hard disk in the standard Oberon manner. In the second mode, the boot loader code located in flash memory is mapped as a system-accessible ROM module which is detected during the BIOS Power-On-Self-Test. In this case, interrupt vector 19 is changed to point to the start of the boot loader within the flash memory, which is then executed instead of the default boot procedure. The adapted code is essentially the standard Native Oberon loader with very minor modifications.

6.2.2   Touch Screen Driver

In a more advanced C2 application, a graphic user interface was implemented. Thereby, the mouse was replaced by a touch screen that reports the position of each touch via a serial channel. Only a single statement had to be added in the implementation of module *Input* to achieve a proper connection with higher levels of the application:

```
PROCEDURE Mouse*(VAR keys: SET; VAR x, y: INTEGER);
VAR dx, dy: INTEGER;   ok: BOOLEAN;
   rawkeys, state: SET;
BEGIN
 IF Kernel.break THEN
    Kernel.break := FALSE; CoreHalt(13)
 END;
```

```
IF C2TControl.GetTouch(keys, x, y) THEN
   (* C2 project *) RETURN
END;
IF ScrollLock IN flags THEN
    . . .
END
END Mouse;
```

6.2.3   V24

On the C2 board four serial channels are implemented using two SC26C92 DUARTs. Together with the COM1 and COM2 ports, six serial channels are available in total. With a minor change in module V24 it is possible to use all serial channels in all applications based on V24 like, for example, in the GUI component V24.Panel. This is the *Receive* procedure:

```
PROCEDURE Receive*(port: LONGINT;
   VAR x: SYSTEM.BYTE;  VAR res: LONGINT);
   VAR p: Port;
BEGIN
   IF C2duaConn.PortValid(port) THEN (* C2 project *)
     IF C2duaConn.PortInited(port) THEN
       C2duaConn.ReadBytes(port, x, 1)
     END
   ELSE (* end C2 project *)
     p := ports[port];
     REPEAT UNTIL p.tail # p.head;
     x := p.buf[p.head];
     p.head := (p.head+1) MOD BufSize
   END;
   res := 0
END Receive;
```

6.3   User Interface Oriented Aspects

The project drew substantial profit from the built in support for components, and in particular from the object persistence scheme and from the interactive Gadgets GUI toolkit. The possibility to see the results immediately while developing components was very valuable. However, human desires are manifold, and the look of the different controls had to be customized to industrial habits. The redesign was done by an artist with the obvious consequence that the visualization method of practically every GUI control had to be reprogrammed. The final outcome is shown in Figure 3. Thanks to the "open source" situation and the clean separation of looks-methods and functionality-methods, this was a relatively harmless task. In the following, we briefly touch some selected not-yet-supported requirements concerning the Gadgets GUI framework that came up in the course of our project.

6.3.1   Non-rectangular Shapes

The redesigning artist suggested GUI controls of a non-rectangular shape. This implied a generalized rendering model whose implementation we approached via transparent frames and rendering masks. Concretely, module *BasicFigures* was replaced by module *C2Picts*, where the type *Figure* was extended to act as a drawing mask for pictures of type *Pictures.Picture*.

6.3.2   TextFields

A new type of transparent and read-only text fields were also suggested for the representation of process variables. For this purpose, a new module *C2TextFields* was derived from the original module *TextFields*. For ordinary text fields, the input method had to be adjusted to a touch screen scenery. We decided in favor of the following solution: When a text field on the touch screen is selected for input, it changes its look, and a companion field appears in the menu bar. The new value can then be "typed" on a virtual keyboard.

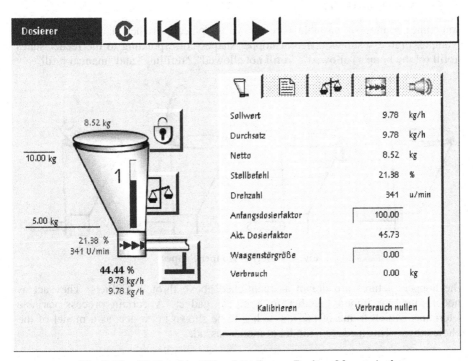

Fig. 3. The C2 Graphical User Interface as Designed by an Artist

6.3.3   Non-movable Gadgets

A change had to be made in module *Gadgets* in order to prevent users from accidentally moving GUI controls with a touch.

6.3.4   Parameterized Generators

Our process control application uses a large amount of variables which are instantiated as components, i. e. as extensions of the basic object type *Objects.Object*. Currently, up to eight feeders are supported, each of them described by some 80 real-time variables. In addition, a line-type object acting as a "parent" of the feeders is used for purposes like recipe specification, alarm handling, display etc. In total, there are almost 700 real-time variables, each of them acting as a model control that can be visualized textually and graphically. After startup, each of these controls needs to be generated via an Oberon generator procedure. In the original Native Oberon system, generator procedures cannot have parameters. As a consequence, a special generator with some unique name would have to be used for every single control, which would quickly lead to a proliferation of generator procedures. Instead, we would prefer generic generator procedures that accept textual parameters. As a consequence, we propose to enhance the *lib.GetObj* method to allow a construct like:

GeneratorModule.GeneratorProc <textual parameter> ~

6.3.5   Models of Models

Sometimes values of variables are shown graphically rather than textually. For example, Figure 4 shows different hopper shapes corresponding to the feeder states "refill (of the hopper) allowed", "refill not allowed", "refilling" and "manual refill".

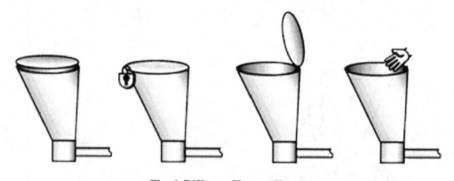

Fig. 4. Different Hopper Shapes

The hopper pictures are drawn as mentioned above through C2Picts. They act as models and are joined together to a movie gadget. A certain process variable determines which frame of the movie has to be shown i.e. it acts as a model of the whole movie. This leads to a model of model cascade.

How Components Pay Out in Practice

Is "component-oriented" just a buzzword? What does it mean in the practice of a real industrial project and how do they pay out for an industrial customer?

The C2 project was and still is the result of team collaboration. This team comprises people with different experience and views of topics like product strategy, specific user knowledge, feeding process, graphic design, software engineering, physics etc. Especially the aspects of the visual user interface were discussed in every detail in order to achieve an optimal result.

From the point of view of software development the results of numerous brain storming meetings had to be checked for feasibility. Sometimes seemingly good proposals required changes that would have lowered the structural quality of the software. Often, "fast prototypes" had to be constructed. We learned that the availability of a rich variety of visual components was paramount for the ability of customizing the industrial product according to the final user's preferences and to achieve the desired corporate identity.

7   Conclusion or "What Was Achieved and What Is Still to Be Done"

Using Native Oberon for PC as an open-source system it was surprisingly easy to realize an economically successful industrial embedded system. In the meantime, some hundred systems in different versions have been delivered. An economically important point was the efficiency of the development, made possible by the simplicity and clarity of the system and by the excellent and super-fast programming environment. Among the many beneficial aspects let us emphasize just two. First, the strong typing strategy of the Oberon language helped immensely with producing software with very few errors. Faulty or unsound thoughts in the programmer's mind are often corrected immediately by an uncompromised typing system, thereby truly educating the programmer to produce better software. Second, Oberon's consequent modular structure optimally decouples different concerns and allows a far-reaching reuse of implemented topics. It also supports a high degree of integration that we made use of, for example, in the case of the component framework. All in all, the chosen approach led to a very resource-efficient and stable system, typically running in the field 24 hours a day and seven days a week without break-down.

The C2 project will evolve in next years. Thanks to the extensibility of the system and to its compact and sound basis, our product easily allows new features to be added to its robust kernel without compromising the overall reliability. The desired variety of the visual representation in terms of graphical user interface will necessitate further work in this area.

Acknowledgements

The C2 product is the result of the work of a team whose members all have been very important. Special thanks go to Marcel O. Rohr, the initiator and leader of the C2 project, to Rainer Wolf for his end user oriented knowledge and his deep experience in feeding technology, to Carsten Holzapfel for his overall support, and to Joachim Ernst for the graphical design.

Without the excellent support from ETH Zürich, this project could not be finished. For this, we would like to express our thanks to the entire Oberon System 3 team and in particular to Pieter Muller who responded swiftly to all simple and complicated questions arising.

Finally, we would also like to thank the referees for their valuable suggestions.

References

[1] T. Kaupel, P. Müller, R. Wolf, Quo Vadis Dosiertechnik am Extruder, "Wägen, Dosieren + Mischen", Vol. 31, No 2, p. 21, Verlagsgesellschaft Keppler-Kirchheim mbH, Mainz, 2000

[2] J. Sedlacek, Zeitgemässe Entwicklung, EC Woche Nr. 36, AT Zeitschriftenverlag, 1990

[3] J. Sedlacek, OMEGA - Ein industrielles Projekt mit Oberon, SGA - Bulletin der ETH Nr. 15, 1996

[4] N. Wirth, J. Gutknecht, Project Oberon, Addison-Wesley, 1992

[5] J. Gutknecht, Oberon System 3: Vision of a Future Software Technology, Software - Concepts & Tools, Springer, February 1994

[6] J. Gutknecht and M. Franz, Oberon with Gadgets: A Simple Component Framework, Implementing Application Frameworks: Object-Oriented Frameworks at Work - Wiley 1999

[7] J. L. Marais, Design and Implementation of a Component Architecture for Oberon, Diss. ETH No 11697, 1996

System Architecture and Design Using Co-operating Groups of Real and Abstract Components

B. Kirk *

Robinson Associates, Red Lion House,
St Mary's Street, Painswick, Glos., GL6 6QG, United Kingdom
b.kirk@robinsons.co.uk

Abstract. Many techniques long used for the partitioning and packaging of hardware are gradually being adopted for software with the move to using co-operating self-contained software components.

There has been a trend over the last decade towards implementations based on multiprocessor distributed concurrent systems with software components allocated to processors.

Designing the system-wide operation, synchronisation and exception handling for such a complex system becomes impossible at the level of traditional process synchronisation primitives, as it becomes intellectually unmanageable to grasp the system-wide behaviour when tackled piecemeal and 'bottom up'.

An alternative top down approach to structuring and designing the overall behaviour of highly concurrent systems implemented using components is presented. It is based on using one or more simple abstract state machines to define the system-wide synchronisation required in terms of the desired system-level behaviour rather than in terms of the low-level synchronisation primitives chosen for the fine grain of the implementation solution.

A practical example involving the creation of a high availability processing system made up of several commercial quality computers is used to illustrate the concept.

Keywords: Software components, abstract components, abstract state machines, system architecture, partitioning, subsystems, patterns, concurrency and synchronisation

1 Introduction

„There is a character in natural things which is created by the fact that they are reconciled, exactly, to their inner forces."

We are living in exciting times. There are several trends that present us with challenges ... low cost connectivity (wired and wireless), low cost multiprocessing and ever more ambitious application projects being attempted but still with inadequate conceptual and implementation tools. The initial hype of OO (object orientation) has only been vaguely fulfilled. In many cases rather than bringing clarity to design and

J. Gutknecht and W. Weck (Eds.): JMLC 2000, LNCS 1897, pp. 197–210, 2000.
© Springer-Verlag Berlin Heidelberg 2000

implementation it has brought unfathomable complexity and obscurity hidden in incompatible forests of classes. Whilst inheritance and program frameworks can be a boon when they are well designed and used sympathetically in the right context, many implementors have learned to their chagrin that they also inherit all the bugs and poor design decisions in the underlying model behind the classes that they adopt and try to adapt. It is sadly but rightly true that the perceived quality of the finished product is equated with the quality of its poorest part, which is often in a class library outside our control.

The evolution towards using components looks promising as the basic concepts have been in use for hundreds, if not thousands, of years. At least more issues are separated and the hegemony of class hierarchy can be replaced and complemented by separation of component definitions and the possibility of assigning them to processes for runtime flexibility. There is also the prospect of standard software components becoming used in a similar way to hardware (mechanical, electrial and electronic components) with their flexibility and economic benefits too. Even so the subject of how to organise these components in simple, generic and useful ways is not obvious. This applies to structures of organisation as well as patterns of system behaviour at different levels of abstraction. A simple systematic approach to handling the four principle kinds of control structures is also needed to complete the conceptual framework.

This Paper introduces a technique that has been used to help structure very large concurrent systems (50+ processors, many 100s of components) where it is important to explicitly define the overall system behaviour in order to orchestrate the individual behaviour of the components that make up the system. For example the behaviour of a whole shoal of fish (a system) is quite distinctive, but it is made up of the contributions of behaviour of the components from which is made i.e. many very similar fish and the water, predators and the food context in which they exist. Interestingly at the system level this abstract concept is not executable, but it is a design-time artefact which determines the overall system behaviour at runtime. Back in our technical world the term abstract state machine has been coined to describe the way in which the concept can be very simply implemented and system behaviour easily understood by the teams of implementors designing and building the components.

Although the architectural and design concepts in this paper make extensive use of state machines it should not be thought that it is about low level concepts. The state machine model can be applied through the spectrum of abstractions from highest to lowest, from modelling the lifecycle of a black hole to the orbital energy states of an electron.

2 System Architecture Evolves

„If the patterns out of which a thing is made are alive,
then we shall see them over and over again, just because they make sense."

The development of system architecture has been slow to evolve in the computing domain, often being spurred on by the gradual refinement of programming languages making it possible to express solutions more clearly and tackle larger and larger systems, as well as the cost of computers plummeting over the last 50 years by about an order of magnitude per decade.

In other fields system architecture has been explored and analysed by architects [2] eager to understand the way the world works and to design buildings and networks of roads which suit the needs, behaviour and dynamics of their inhabitants. It was recognised very early by architects that the identification of patterns (of behaviour and of construction) is fundamental to building effective and economical solutions, in this case for people living [2, 3].

On the computing side, even in the early days, telephone systems (using relays) were partitioned into subsystems (exchanges) and used formal diagramming techniques as design and documentation aids, particularly finite state machines to define the complete (normal and exceptional) behaviour of the subsystems and components. This 'pile of co-operating machines' concept was soon absorbed into software design, the classic example being Dijkstra's elegant partitioning of the THE operating system into a set of abstractions, implemented as distinct machines in layers of software [4]. This led to the idea of separating software into components and having organised subsystems of components acting together to provide a service [6], which was then formalised into a more general concept based on the notion of co-operating actors performing collectively [1].

In a similar way the humble state machine was being refined, firstly in the direction of Petri nets (which have one or more control tokens whereas a state machine only has one). Large state machines became unwieldy and the popularity of modularisation [12] provided a practical solution in the form of Statecharts [8] which could also be nested to partition the complexity.

A further advance, again from the telephone industry, was the concept of the state event machine [11] which provided a natural way for separate state machines, based on logical partitioning, to naturally interact with each other on a co-operating basis by communicating events from one to another. In turn this led to the idea of software components being internally structured as one or more state event machines [9] in order to completely define the behaviour. These concepts and techniques were combined to provide practical approaches for designing and implementing large real-time multiprocessor systems [9], execution time itself was now introduced as a criteria for modularisation [10]. By this time processing and communications hardware components had become low cost commodities [7] throwing more emphasis on the need to have simple, clear design techniques.

Component based system design has now started to come of age and the software industry is embracing the concept. Recent books on Component Software [13] and

UML (Unified Modelling Language) design [5] give a good insight into component concepts and design approaches.

Presently the architectural techniques needed to structure and organise very large systems of components are in their infancy. This paper introduces a pragmatic approach to defining an architecture which is flexible, simple and practical for analysing, designing and implementing a system as a set of co-operating logical subsystems, each comprising a set of co-operating components.

Our quest here is to find a simple and elegant way to model the *physical structure*, the *logical structure* and the *behavioural structure* of the system. This is achieved by analysing the problem to clearly understand its intrinsic patterns of usage and then expressing exactly that in the design for the solution [3]. Once this is understood and achieved then the actual implementation in terms of component oriented software becomes trivial, and testable.

3 A System Design Model

> *„It is only because a person has a pattern language in their mind
> that they can be creative when they build.“*

Design is the fulcrum between the problem and its solution and it achieves its purpose by offering a conceptual model (or set of abstractions) which can be used to map the problem, via the model, into a solution which implements the model. So what conceptual model (generic set of practical patterns) can we use to form the design of component based software ?

First of all we need to ask what properties this model should have, for example it needs to …

1.　be intrinsically simple
2.　be expressed in a language (preferably visual) that can be understood by both technical and non-technical people
3.　make overall system behaviour clear, from the 'top down', like the shoal of fish
4.　make component behaviour clear from the 'bottom up', like individual fish
5.　make modularisation by logical cohesion clear e.g. accounting, transport, packing, feeding in a machine
6.　be capable of defining the complete behaviour of the system at all levels i.e. both normal behaviour and the responses to abnormal and unexpectedly delayed events
7.　offer a direct (1:1) traceable mapping between the problem and its component based solution
8.　enable the solution to be easily mapped onto a single or multiprocessor platform in an extensible way
9.　be easily testable, in parts and as a whole

Previous papers [7, 9] have described the model shown in Figure 1.

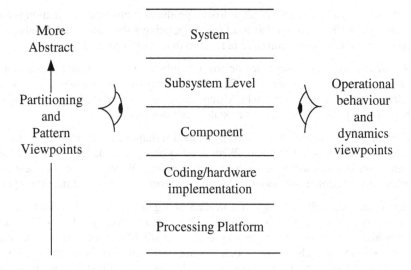

Fig. 1. Abstraction levels for component based system architecture and design

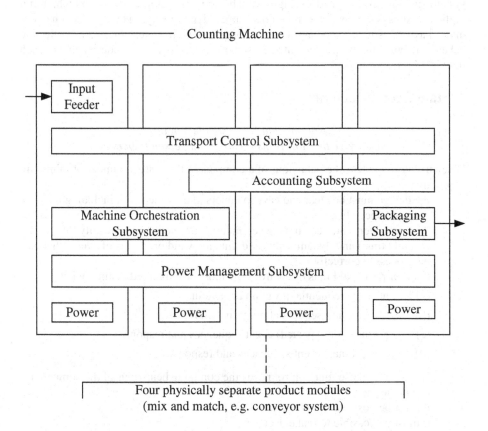

Fig. 2. Partitioning into Physical and Logically Cohesive Parts

An example shown in Figure 2 is taken from a production machine automation project where the system is represented as a set of co-operating subsystems. Each subsystem encapsulates some logically cohesive behaviour in the application domain..

A subsystem may span processors or run on only a single processor, this can be achieved simply and transparently [7]. Each subsystem comprises a set of co-operating software components which may each be implemented using traditional Wirthian structured programming or as state event machines.

The dynamics of the model are defined by sequence diagrams defining the interaction between subsystems, see Figure 3. Within subsystems they define the interactions between components (software or hardware based). Within the components the dynamics *and* functional behaviour are defined in terms of state event machines [11].

This approach meets all the properties needed in a general framework model except one. It has been used to design and implement very large industrial control systems (whole production lines) using up to 50 processors with 10's of subsystems and many 100's of components. The property that has not been fully met is mapping a system onto multiple processors where the system behaviour is defined by an *abstraction which is not implemented on any of the processors individually*. An example is a system specifically designed for high availability with multiple processors which run replicated subsystems which can be hotswapped dynamically. The system behaviour must have a single 'availability' abstraction which determines the collective behaviour, but must be implemented in some practical way in a subsystem on each individual processor.

4 State Event Machines

„Nothing that is not simple and direct
can survive the slow transmission from person to person"

When trying to express the behaviour of a component there are a number of minimum requirements ...

1   the design must be clear and easy to understand by the team, including non software specialists
2   the component interface must be completely defined, both statically (at compile time) and dynamically (to define the valid orderings of events that can be processed correctly)
3   the four principal kinds of control flow must be expressed distinctly i.e.

   (a)   'normal' sequential program behaviour

   (b)   'exceptional' sequential program behaviour

   (c)   'normal' (or expected) event sequences and responses

   (d)   'exceptional' event sequences and responses

   By defining these four control needs the complete behaviour of the component can be defined.
4   it must be possible to invoke actions
5   it must be possible to make decisions

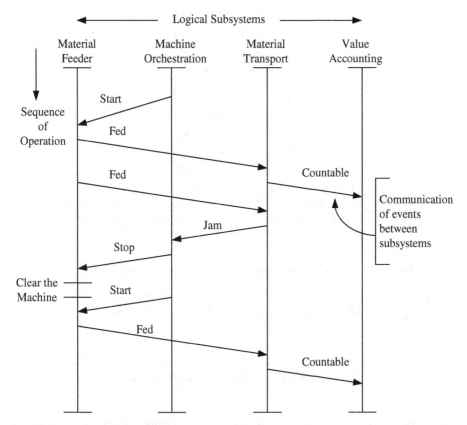

Note: Each subsystem evolves through the sequencing of its own
states as the system operation flows down the page

Fig. 3. Sequence Diagram defining the intended interaction between the parts
(it can be used at either subsystem or component level or both)

Programming languages such as Pascal, Modula and Oberon are not well adapted to expressing such needs explicitly and clearly. Other languages such as Java and Ada attempt to provide additional constructs, for example exception handling, but these are often misunderstood and misused.

As a design notation the humble state event machine is specifically geared to satisfying the above requirements. The symbols used are shown in Figure 4, its basic element are

(a)   the state
(b)   the action
(c)   the decision
(d)   internal events (between components in the same subsystem)
(e)   external events (between components in separate subsystems)

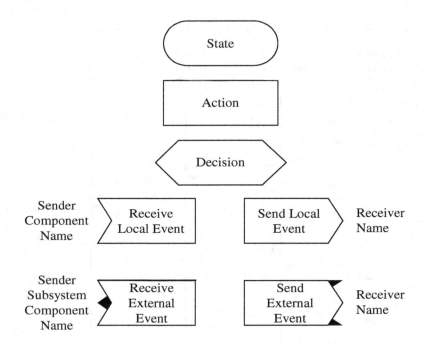

Fig. 4. Notation Symbols for State Event Machines

The general form is to first of all decide what distinct states exist within the component as it sojourns through its lifecycle. This also provides a nice overview of the scope and context of its behaviour. Then after each new state define the set of events that are valid in the new context (and also implicitly define all the events which are not valid in that context). Some sequence of actions, decisions, sending message or receiving message follows each of the events - ultimately leading to a change of state.

So this simple design notation makes it easy to specify the complete behaviour of a component, it is also very easy to mechanically translate the design diagram into program code, using any language, but preferably a strongly typed one.

In the implementation the coding of the 'event catcher' after each new state can provide great flexibility. For example a debug version of it can log all invalid messages for future analysis (they should not exist!). Alternatively in a safety critical application receiving such an event message might gracefully and safely shut down the system. These strategies can be altered by just changing the event handler, the rest of the program is unchanged.

In real time systems where 'life must go on', the sets of messages can be classified as normal operations, abnormal but acceptable operations and, say, damaging operations; each can be handled in an appropriate way given the current context.

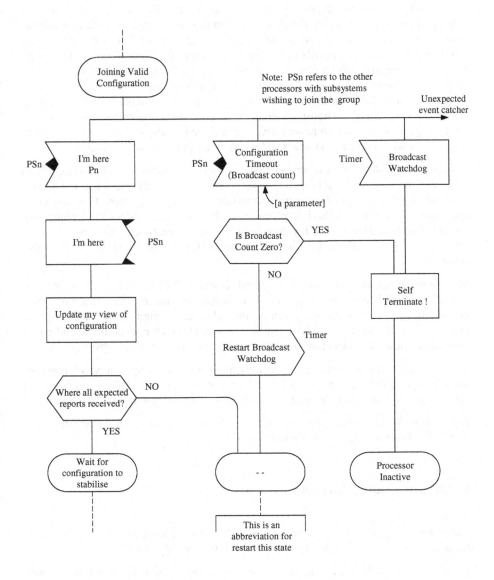

Fig. 5. Fragment of a State Event Machine

5 Orchestration

So an approach to naturally grouping sets of logically cohesive components into a subsystem emerges as a basic design concept. There is interaction between the components within a subsystem and interaction between components of one subsystem with those of another. Often it makes sense to use anthropomorphic metaphors such as having an administrator [6] to manage the subsystem level interface and to hide the details of the implementation inside it. Similarly there may be an error manager which detects possibly many faults from components within a particular subsystem and collates them into a single fault which is reported in 'system' terms rather than internal subsystem jargon. For example in a note counting machine a note jam in the transport might cause error reports from 50 or more sensors which expect the note which never arrives. But there is really only one report needed: this defines which note has jammed and where it has jammed in the machine.

Somehow subsystems must be orchestrated. Imagine the subsystems as sections of an orchestra, the violins, the cellos, the timpani, the woodwind, the brass and the basses. Each section has players (orchestral components!). Typically there is a conductor who guides and channels the interpretation of the score (the system level objective), controls the dynamics of speed, volume and feeling. Sometimes there can be two or more conductors working together if the orchestra is huge and a choir is also involved.

In most machines this conductor is a central 'controller' which ultimately defines the overall machine behaviour e.g. power on, initialisation, run up, operation, run down, power off, safety cut out, etc. Even so the subsystems often still provide copious amounts of real concurrency, for example a machine which counts, binds and packs sorted bank notes at 40 locations simultaneously, each with its own subsystem locally.

Typically this 'conductor' is just another component in the subsystem which manages the lifecycle of the machines operation. Hence it runs on one of the processors and can be designed, implemented and tested like any other subsystem of components.

But what if there is no explicit processor available to run on, or if the nature of the system level control algorithm is purely abstract ?

6 Abstract State Machines

„What makes a flower whole, even though all its cells are more or less autonomous,is the genetic code,which guides the process of the individual parts. "

In some cases orchestration is needed at the overall system level but the control algorithm is abstract, it therefore cannot reside on any one subsystem on one or more processors. In other words the lifecycle of the system can be defined by a state machine which is purely abstract, it contains only states and normal and exceptional transitions but no actions. Hence the adoption of the term Abstract State Machine.

This is in contrast to real state-event machines which also receive and send messages (to their own subsystem components or other subsystems) and do actions.

The concept is best explained using a practical example. A high availability computer is needed, made from several ordinary industrial PCs. There must be no 'master' computer which can act as the 'conductor', so there is no fixed locus for orchestrating the lifecycle of the system. The scheme involves having a set of computers running the application in tandem, with the prospect of additional computers dynamically applying to join the set and also faulty computers being ejected from the operational set by the others, or by self terminating. The objective is to provide the application service on a continuous basis by using redundancy and hot-swapping. An abstract state machine which describes the required system lifecycle behaviour is shown in Figure 6, the lifecycle flows from top to bottom of the diagram, the notation is defined in Figure 7.

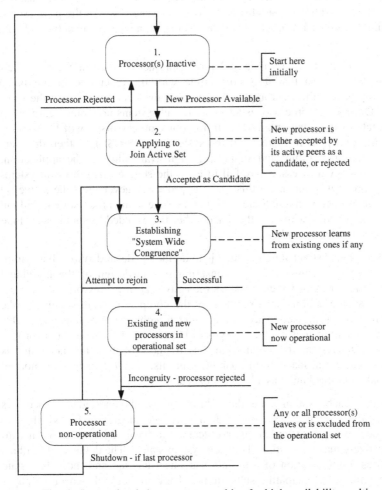

Fig. 6. System-level abstract state machine for high availability multiprocessor

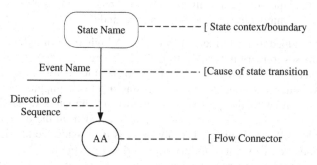

Fig. 7. State Machine Notation

State 1 is where it all starts, initially there are no processors active. When at least one becomes active the system (in the abstract) moves to State 2 where the processor(s) interact seeking to join an active set, or if there is none then creating an active set with one member.

Assume for a moment there are already 2 processors active, then in State 2 a new processor has to establish that it is compatible with the other two before being accepted (it may have a different application or even the wrong version of the same application). Once a new processor is accepted its subsystems now must learn about the detailed state of the other subsystems in the other processors it will be working with, this is what happens in State 3. If the system achieves State 4 then there are now 3 processors co-operating and supporting high availability of the application. When in State 3 a new processor may fail to learn the state of the other subsystems and be able to prove it to them. In this case the processor never joins the active set and never becomes operational in State 5. When in State 4 any processor can fall out of operational congruency with the others and either be excluded by them or exclude itself from the active set (or both!).

So the purpose of the abstract state machine is to define the desired *system* behaviour. It effectively forms a dominant design constraint on the design of the individual subsystem in each processor which manages the active set of processors. In abstract state machines all the actions are executed by the co-operating subsystems, at the system level they are abstracted away and are hidden within each system state. This is why the ASM notation does not have a symbol for actions. Of course the algorithm in each of these subsystems is contained in one or more of its components and is expressed as a state event machine to guarantee that its complete behaviour (normal and exceptional) is defined and has a locus of execution.

Note that within each system state the subsystems in the individual processors exchange message sequences (documented in sequence diagrams) by which they conclusively decide when *system events* are deemed to have happened and when to agree to collectively make transitions between system states. The detailed algorithms are expressed as a combination of a system sequence diagram and individual state event machines for the participating subsystems. They are not included in the paper as they are particular to the application domain and proprietary in nature.

7 Conclusions

„The cure of the part should not be attempted
without the treatment of the whole. "

A simple generic architecture for component based systems has been described. It partitions the system into logically cohesive (but possibly distributed) subsystems. In turn these subsystems are comprised of components which are defined in terms of state event machines for clarity and completeness. At a system level one or more abstract state machines may define the behaviour of the overall system, particularly if there is no fixed locus of control in the system.

The interaction between subsystems provides the means for them to co-operate and synchronise their operation. This can be done either by one or more 'conductors' which run within subsystems and explicitly orchestrate the system behaviour or by one or more abstract state machines which implicitly orchestrate it.

Systems have been successfully built using both models, the appropriate design choice or a combination of them, depends on the nature of the application. Although it is conceivable to nest subsystems, components and even state machines no practical problem has yet been encountered that required this. In the interests of simplicity nesting should be used with diffidence and then only to reflect nesting implicit in the original problem or to break the solution down into intellectually manageable and testable pieces. In general the architecture of the solution should be derived directly from the architecture of the problem and the pattern of structure and behaviour that are intrinsic to it.

8 Acknowledgements

The author would like to acknowledge helpful discussions on clarifying these concepts with Jim and Niall Cooling, Dean Gifford, Bernhard Leisch, Libero Nigro and Jon Teague.

The paper is dedicated to Charles Alexander for revealing simple yet profound insights in his book, The Timeless Way of Building [3]. All the quotations in the paragraph headings are from this book, except the last one which is from an ancient Greek philosopher.

References

[1]   Agha G and Hewitt C:
        Actors: a conceptual foundation for concurrent OO programming.
        In Research Directions in OO Programming, pp 49-74, MIT Press, Cambridge,
        MA (1987)

[2]   Alexander C: Notes on the Synthesis of Form
       Harvard University Press, Cambridge 38, Massachusetts (1964)

[3]   Alexander C: The Timeless Way of Building
       Oxford University Press, New York. ISBN 0-19-502402-8 (1979)

[4]   Dijkstra E: The Structure of the 'THE' Multiprogramming System
       Communications of ACM, Vol 11, No 3, pp 341-346, May (1968)

[5]   Douglas B P: Real Time Systems/UML
       Addison Wesley, ISBN 0-201-65784-8

[6]   Gentleman W M: Message passing between sequential processes: the reply
       primitive and the Administrator Concept.
       Software Practice and Experience, Vol 11, pp 435-466 (1981)

[7]   Gifford D, Kirk B, Leisch B: A Component Based Architecture for CAN
       Systems
       5th International CAN Conference, San José, CA (1998)
       ICC 98 Proceedings, published by CAN in Automation

[8]   Harel D: Statecharts: a visual formalism for complex systems.
       Science of Computer Programming, 8, pp 231-274 (1987)

[9]   Kirk B, Nigro L: DART, Distributed Architecture for Real Time
       Advances in Programming Languages P Shulthess (ed.)
       Universitatsverlag Ulm GmbH, pp 325-366
       Proceedings of Joint Modular Languages Conference (1994)

[10]   Kirk B, Nigro L and Pupo F: Using real time constraints for modularisation
       Lecture Notes in Computer Science, 1204, Springer Verlag pp 236-251 (1997)

[11]   Jacobson I: Object Oriented Software Engineering
       Addison Wesley, Reading, MA (1993)

[12]   Parnas D L: On the criteria to be used in decomposing systems into modules
       Communications of the ACM, December (1972)

[13]   Szyperski C: Component Software – Beyond OO Programming
       ACM/Addison Wesley, ISBN 0-201-17888-5 (1999)

Abstraction and Modularization in
the BETA Programming Language

Ole Lehrmann Madsen

Computer Science Department, Aarhus University,
Åbogade 34, DK-8200 Århus N, Denmark
Ole.L.Madsen@daimi.au.dk

Abstract. One of the characteristics of BETA is the unification of *abstraction* mechanisms such as class, procedure, process type, generic class, interface, etc. into one abstraction mechanism: the *pattern*. In addition to keeping the language small, the unification has given a systematic treatment of all abstraction mechanisms and lead to a number of new possibilities. Patterns and their instances are intended for modeling concepts and phenomena in the application domain and provide the *logical structure* of a given system. *Modularization* is viewed as a means for describing the *physical structure* of a program. Modules are units of program text that may be edited, stored in libraries, exist in different variants, be separately compiled, etc. Modularization is provided by a language-independent mechanism based on the context-free grammar of the language. In principle, any correct sequence of terminal and nonterminal symbols of the grammar can be a module.

1 Introduction

Abstraction is a fundamental means for dealing with complexity. As Hoare describes it, "In the development of our understanding of complex phenomena, the most powerful tool available to the human intellect is abstraction." [10]. In programming languages, abstraction mechanisms are important constructs for organizing complex programs. By abstraction mechanism, we mean a language construct that defines a template or pattern for creating instances. A class is a pattern for creating objects, a procedure is a pattern for creating procedure activations, a process type is a pattern for creating processes, etc. Abstraction lead to formation of concepts for understanding and organizing knowledge about the real world. In order to support this process, we make use of conceptual means such as composition and classification. Composition has been supported by programming languages in many different ways: procedures may be defined by other procedures, and data types may be defined by other data types, etc. One of the benefits of object-orientation is the support for classification by means of the subclass mechanism.

One of the unique characteristics of BETA is the unification of abstraction mechanisms such as class, procedure, function, process type, generic class, interface, excep-

J. Gutknecht and W. Weck (Eds.): JMLC 2000, LNCS 1897, pp. 211-237, 2000.
© Springer-Verlag Berlin Heidelberg 2000

tion type, etc. into one abstraction mechanism: the *pattern*. Besides keeping the language small, the unification has given a systematic treatment of all abstraction mechanisms and lead to a number of new possibilities. Examples are that constructs like subclassing, virtuality, nesting, and variability are available for classes, procedures, and other abstraction mechanisms as well.

Like abstraction, it is also important that a programming language has powerful means for supporting *modularization*. A module is a physical entity that may be manipulated in various ways – a set of modules may e.g. be composed to form larger entities or modules.

Patterns and their instances are intended for modeling concepts and phenomena in the application domain and provide the *logical structure* of a given system. In BETA, *modularization* is viewed as a means for describing the *physical structure* of a program in terms of modules, interface modules, implementation modules, etc. Modules are units of program text that may be stored in files, placed in libraries, exist in different versions and variants, be separately compiled, etc. For BETA, modularization is provided by a language-independent mechanism based on the context-free grammar of the language. In principle, any correct sequence of terminal and nonterminal symbols (a so-called *sentential form*) of the grammar can be a module. The module system provides means for combining sentential forms into complete programs.

In this paper, we will briefly summarize abstraction mechanisms in BETA and refer to other references for a more elaborate description. We will then give a more detailed description of the principles for handling modularization.

In BETA, most abstraction mechanisms have been unified into the pattern concept. One might then wonder why the notion of a module has not been covered by pattern as well. In many other languages, the concept of class and module are considered identical. This is the case in Eiffel [28], although Eiffel also makes use of the concept of cluster, which is a group of related classes. The concept of abstract data type might be traced to the class construct of Simula [5,27,11] and has later been supported by different constructs. In Concurrent Pascal [4], the class-construct has been used to support abstract data types, as well as processes and monitors. In the Modula-like languages [38,39], the concept of module/package is used and in CLU [17], some hybrid form is used. This might indicate that constructs like class, module and abstract data type in CLU are just different variations of the same construct.

In the Modula-like languages, there is a separation between module and type. It seems that the concept of type is closer to the concept of class than that of module. In the design of BETA, we have found it useful to distinguish between class and type (patterns) on the one hand and that of a module on the other hand. Szyperski [31] also supports this viewpoint, and is one of the few examples of a detailed discussion of the need for class as well as module. We do not think that such matters can be decided in an objective matter. Like most other languages, BETA is an experiment that is supposed to test the validation of some ideas/theories. The idea of distinguishing between abstraction mechanisms and modularization mechanisms are examples of such ideas to be tested. In the conclusion, we will return to an evaluation of these issues.

2 Abstraction Mechanisms

For the design of BETA, an important observation was that most programming languages provide a number of abstraction mechanisms that all have certain common properties. Examples of such abstractions are: procedures as in Algol, classes as in Simula, types as in Pascal, functions as in Lisp, and task types as in Ada. A common characteristic of these abstraction mechanisms is that they describe entities with a common structure and that they may be used as generators for instances of these entities:

- The instances of a procedure are procedure-activations.
- The instances of a class are objects.
- The instances of a function are function-activations.
- The instances of types are values.
- The instances of task types are tasks.

In addition to the above mentioned abstraction mechanisms, there are several other examples, such as generic classes, and exception types.

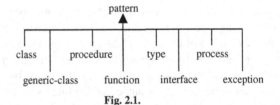

Fig. 2.1.

The first goal of BETA was to develop a language construct that could be viewed as a generalization of all known abstraction mechanisms. Concrete abstraction mechanisms could then be viewed as specializations as shown in figure 2.1. Here class, procedure, type, etc. are shown as specializations of the more general abstraction mechanisms: the pattern. The pattern construct is the only abstraction mechanism in BETA. A pattern may be used as a class, procedure, type, etc. A pattern used as a class is often referred to as a class pattern; a pattern used as a procedure (method) is often referred to as a procedure pattern, etc.

In this paper, we will not give a detailed account of BETA. Please consider [14,18,23]. We will, however, attempt to describe some of the abstraction mechanisms of BETA. Before introducing BETA syntax, we will start by an example using a syntax in the style of C++ and Java. Consider the example in figure 2.2. It contains the following elements:

```
class Person: { … };
class Set:
  { proc insert(e: ref object): { do … };
    virtual proc display(): { do … };
    …
  };
proc main():
  { Joe: obj Person;
    S: ref Set
  do S = new Set;
    S.insert(Joe);
    S.display()
  };
```

Fig. 2.2.

- The classes Person and Set.
- The procedure main.
- A declaration like Joe: **obj** Person describes a part-object. A Person-object is generated when main is called and Joe denotes this object during the lifetime of the main-activation.
- A declaration like S: **ref** Set describes a reference variable, which may refer instances of class Set.

Class and procedure are examples of abstraction mechanisms. By abstraction mechanism, we mean a named template for generating instances of some kind. A class generates objects and a procedure generates procedure-activations. Instances are generated by the following constructs:

- **new** Set creates an instance on the class Set.
- R.display() creates an instance of the procedure-attribute display of R.

There are a number of similarities between objects and procedure activations: In Algol-like languages, a procedure-activation consists of a procedure-activation-record and an execution of the code of the procedure. The structure of a procedure-activation-record is very similar to the structure of an object. An object consists of a number of data-items and some local procedures that may be virtual. A procedure-activation record also consists of a number of data-items in the form of parameters and local variables. In addition there may be local procedures, if the language supports block-structure. In addition, a procedure-activation-record may have a reference pointing to the calling procedure-activation-record (often called the dynamic link). In block-structured languages, a procedure-activation-record may have a pointer to the statically enclosing procedure-activation-record (often called the static link). In Simula, classes may be nested, so Simula-objects also have a static link.

In Simula, a class may have parameters similar to procedure parameters. The class-parameters are used for generation of a class-instance. A Simula-class may also have a do-part like a procedure. The do-part is executed when a class-instance is generated. The parameters and do-part of a class play the role of constructors in mainstream languages like C++ and Java. In Simula, the do-part has a further role, since an object may also be a coroutine. The do-part describes the head-activation of the do-part.

In Simula, at least, the structure of objects and procedure-activations are thus very similar and there is a basis for identical treatment. A procedure-activation may be considered to consist of creation of the procedure-activation followed by an execution of its do-part as shown in figure 2.3.

```
m: ref main;
m = new main;
m.execute
```

Fig. 2.3.

It is then also possible to execute m several times by reapplying m.execute. The object m may then be considered similar to a static procedure instance similar to a Fortran subroutine. For people familiar with the Simula coroutine mechanism, it should be well known that it is meaningful to re-activate a coroutine-object.

It is of course also meaningful to access the attributes of m as in m.Joe.

In BETA, there is no distinction between class and procedure, i.e. the keywords **class** and **proc** in the example may be removed. The resulting patterns may then be instantiated in different ways. Either in an object-like way where a reference is kept to the object or a procedure-like manner where an object is created and its do-part immediately executed.

In addition to the attributes declared by the pattern, the objects may have a static link in cases of textual nesting and a dynamic link in case there is a do-part.

The example in figure 2.2 is shown using BETA syntax in figure 2.4.The following changes have been made:

```
Person: (# ... #);
Set:
    (# insert:
          (# e: ^object
          enter e[]
          do ...
          #);
       display:< (# ... #);
       ...
    #);
main:
    (# Joe: @Person;
       S: ^Set
    do &Set[] -> S[];
       Joe[] -> S.insert;
       S.display
    #);
```

Fig. 2.4.

- The keywords **class** and **proc** are eliminated.
- { and } are replaced by (# and #).
- **ref** has been replaced by ^.
- **obj** is replaced by @.
- **virtual** is replaced by <.
- **new** is replaced by &.
- Assignment has the form exp -> v, where the value of exp is assigned to v.
- The symbol [] as in Joe[] signals that a reference to Joe is the value of Joe[]. This is in contrast to Joe that describes a copy of Joe (almost) is the value.
- The parameter part (e: **ref** Object) is replaced by e: ^object **enter** e[].
- Instances of a pattern may be created in two ways:
  - o The constructs &Set[]. The value of &Set[] is a reference to the new Point-instance and corresponds to the new-operator in most object-oriented languages.
  - o S.display. Here a new display-instance is generated and executed (by executing its **do**-part). This corresponds to procedure-activation.
    It is also possible to create an instance of S.display and then subsequently execute it corresponding to figure 2.3.

2.1 Benefits of the Unification

The unification of abstraction mechanisms has the following benefits:
- All abstraction mechanisms are treated in a systematic way, and there is focus on the abstraction-instance relationship.
- Syntactically and conceptually, the language has become simpler.

- There are a number of new technical possibilities. A good unification of concepts/constructs should result in a mechanism that covers the original mechanisms and gives some new possibilities as well.

There may of course also be disadvantages. Abstractions such as class, procedure and exception are still useful concepts. The unification implies that there is no syntactical difference between class patterns, and procedure patterns, etc. In the original design for BETA, the main goal of the 'pattern-exercise' was to obtain a systematical structure for all abstraction mechanisms. The final language might still have special constructs for common abstractions like class and procedure. However, the experience from practice seems to be that there is no demand for such special constructs.

In the rest of this section we will briefly summarize some of the benefits of the unification. We will mainly discuss the class- and procedure constructs. As mentioned, patterns may also be used to describe abstraction mechanisms such as functions, coroutines, concurrent processes, and exceptions, so most of the remarks made below are also valid for these abstraction mechanisms. For examples of this, see [18].

Subpattern
The subpattern mechanism covers subclasses as in most other languages. That is it is possible to organize class patterns in a usual classification/inheritance hierarchy. In addition, procedure patterns may be organized in a subprocedure hierarchy in the same way as classes may be organized in a subclass hierarchy. This was the subject of an early paper on BETA called *Classification of actions or inheritance also for methods* [16]. Inheritance for procedures is based on the **inner**-mechanism known from Simula. By means of **inner** it is possible to combine the **do**-parts of patterns.

In general, procedure inheritance is a powerful mechanism that gives additional possibilities for defining general patterns. Examples of patterns defined by using procedure inheritance are concurrency abstractions such as monitor and Ada-like rendezvous and control abstractions such as iterators.

Virtual Pattern
Display in figure 2.4 is an example of a virtual procedure. One of the main contributions of BETA is perhaps the notion of virtual class (or type). The virtual class concept is a mechanism for defining generic classes and provides an alternative to generic classes as in Eiffel or templates as in C++.

Since there is no difference between class and procedure in BETA, a virtual class is a virtual pattern used as a class. Consider the example in figure 2.5. Here we have added classes Student and Employee, which are subclasses of Person. The class Set has a new attribute element:< Object, which is an example of a virtual class pattern. A virtual pattern may be used as other patterns to specify the type of a reference variable. An example of this is the parameter e of insert, which is declared to be of type element. Since Object is the super pattern of all patterns, e may refer to any object of the program execution.

Since e may refer any object, it is possible to insert instances of all classes in the set S. If for some reasons we want to restrict a set to include only instances of the pattern `Person`, we may declare a subclass of `Set` as shown in figure 2.6.

The virtual pattern element has been bound to `Person`. This means that all variables of type `element` in `PersonSet` are now of type `Person`. The type of the argument of insert is `Person`, which means that only `Person`-objects may be inserted into the `Set`.

```
Person:
  (# name : @text; age: @integer #);
Student: Person(# id: @integer #);
Employee: Person(# ... #);
Set:
  (# element:< Object;
     insert:
       (# e: ^element
       enter e[] do ...
       #);
     display:< (# ... #)
  #);
main:
  (# Joe: @Person;
     Lisa: @Student
     S: ^Set
  do &Set[] -> S[];
     Joe[] -> S.insert;
     Lisa[] -> S.insert;
     S.display
  #);
```

Fig. 2.5.

We have also added an operation add to illustrate that a reference like e may be used as of type `Person`. The expression e.age is legal since e is of type `Person` and `Person` is known to have an age-attribute.

It is possible to make further subclasses of `PersonSet`. In `StudentSet`, element is further bound to `Student`. This means that the elements of `StudentSet` are restricted to be instances of `Student`.

```
StudentSet: PersonSet(# element::< Student #)
```

The unification of abstraction mechanisms into patterns has resulted in a simple extension of the concept of virtual procedures to virtual classes. The concept of virtual classes has been discussed in several papers, and we refer to [19,21,25] for further details of virtual patterns. The concept of virtual class may be applied to other OO languages than BETA [33], and may be seen as an object-oriented version of genericity. Further unifications and refinements of the virtual pattern mechanism are discussed in [7,8,12,35,36].

```
PersonSet: Set
  (# element::< Person;
     add:
       (# e: ^element
       enter e[]
       do (if e.age < 18 then
               young + 1 -> young
             else elder + 1 -> elder
           if)
       #);
     young,elder: @integer
  #);
P: ^PersonSet
```

Fig. 2.6.

Nested Pattern

Algol 60 introduced the notion of block structure, which in Algol 60 means that proce-dures may arbitrarily nested. Simula extended this to allow nesting of classes and procedures. Block structure has been adapted by many languages since Algol, mainly imperative languages such as Pascal, but is also available in the Lisp-dialect Scheme. It was included in Java 1.1.

In BETA patterns may be nested, which means that procedure patterns as well as class patterns, etc. may be nested.

In an OO setting, nesting of classes is an interesting aspect and several examples of this have been documented in the literature [20,22,24,26,40].

The class construct makes it possible to *encapsulate* data-items and operations that together constitute a logically related whole. Block structure makes it possible to in-clude classes among items being encapsulated. This makes it possible to place a class in a proper context, just as data-items and procedures may be placed in the context of an object. From a modeling, point-of-view OO languages without block structure can model properties of phenomena in terms of objects with data-items and procedures. With nesting, it is possible to include classes in the properties available for modeling a given phenomenon. In addition to the references mentioned above, see [7] for a good discussion of block structure from a modeling point-of-view.

Nested class patterns make it possible to define a class pattern as an attribute of an object. Often other classes define the structure of an object. Nested patterns make it possible to define such classes where they logically belong.

Nested classes may be used to define objects with several interfaces [26]. An inter-face is an abstract pattern with only virtual patterns. Consider an interface `Print-able`. A class, `Person` that implements the `Printable` interface may do this by defining an internal subclass of `Printable`. The `Printable`-interface of a `Person`-object may then be accessed via instances of the subclass of `Printable`. This style of programming is used to support the Microsoft Component Model in BETA [30].

In Objective C [34] and Java, a class may implement several interfaces. Since all operations are implemented as a flat list of operations, it is necessary to have rules for handling possible name conflicts between operations in the interfaces. By implement-ing interfaces by means of nested classes, the interfaces are properly encapsulated and isolated from each other. The disadvantage in BETA is, of course, that each interface implementation has to be named.

In [20,40] it is shown that nested classes in many cases may be an alternative to multiple inheritance, although it may not in general replace multiple inheritance.

Pattern Variable

BETA includes the notion of pattern variable. This implies that patterns are first class values that may be passed around as parameters to other patterns. By using pattern variables instead of virtual patterns, it is possible dynamically to change the behavior of an object after its generation. Pattern variables cover procedure variables (i.e. a variable that may be assigned different procedures). Since patterns may be used as classes, it is also possible to have variables that may be assigned different classes, etc.

Singular Objects

In BETA, it is possible to describe objects that are not instances of patterns. An object may be described directly as in prototype-based languages like Self [37].

Singular objects are inspired by similar constructs in other languages:

- Algol 60 has the concept of an *inner block*, which may be viewed as a singular procedure call.
- Simula has the notion of *prefixed block*, which may be viewed as a singular object.
- Pascal has the notion of *anonymous type*, which makes it possible to describe the type of a variable as part of the variable declaration.
- Finally, Java 1.1 has also introduced the notion of *anonymous class* corresponding to BETA's singular objects.

The combination of block-structure and singular objects makes it convenient to express inheritance from part objects. For examples of this, see [20]. Although BETA has singular objects, it does not support delegation.

Concurrency

Patterns may also describe active objects. In BETA, an active object is an object that has its own thread of execution. An active object may execute as a Simula-style coroutine or in concurrency with other active objects. We shall not give technical details here, but just mention that the **do**-part of an object is the head of the thread.

Semaphores are used as the primitives for synchronization. A semaphore is a low-level mechanism and it should only be used to define higher-level synchronization abstractions. The pattern mechanism together with inner is well suited for defining abstractions like monitor and Ada-like rendezvous.

3   Modularization

In previous section, we have briefly introduced language mechanisms for describing objects and patterns of a BETA program execution. In this section, language mechanisms for describing the physical organization of BETA programs will be introduced. A non-trivial BETA program will usually consist of several pages, so it is desirable to be able to split such a description into smaller, more manageable units. Such units are in general called *modules*. A module is a convenient part of a program typically kept in a file (or in a database), manipulated by an editor, and translated by a compiler.

As mentioned, patterns and objects are intended for representing concepts and phenomena from the application domain. The modularization mechanisms on the other hand are motivated by the following reasons:

- Most reasonably sized programs can be conveniently split into modules of logically related elements, since it is cumbersome to handle large programs. Large programs are easier to understand if split into a number of smaller units.
- When editing it is easier to manage a number of small modules instead of one large program.

- When several people are working on a project, each person can work on his own set of modules.
- Modules can be saved in a library and shared by several programs. Good modularization mechanisms will thus improve reusability of code as well as designs.
- It is good practice to split a module into interface modules (often referred to as specification modules) and implementation modules. An interface module defines how a module can be used, and an implementation module describes how a module is implemented. This makes it possible to prevent users of a module from seeing details about data representation and implementation of algorithms.
- Certain modules may exist in several variants. One example of this is different implementations of the same (interface) module. Another example is variants of a module corresponding to different computers. If a module has several variants, it is important that the common part of two or more variants exists in only one copy. It should only be necessary to separate out the code that differs between variants; otherwise, maintenance becomes more complicated, since the same change may have to be made for several variants.
- A module may be used as a unit to be separately compiled. When changing parts of a large program, it is not acceptable to be forced to recompile the whole program, since this may take several hours. With separate compilation of modules, only the modules that have been changed and those that are affected by these changes have to be recompiled. Below we explain how one module may be affected by changes in another.

In the following section, language constructs for describing modularization are introduced. Thereafter, we discuss how to apply these language constructs and why they are useful and necessary.

Fragments

The language constructs for describing program modularization are **not** considered part of the BETA language. The reason is that BETA is a language for describing objects and patterns of a BETA *program execution*, while the modularization language is for describing the physical organization of just the *program*. The structuring of the program execution in terms of objects and patterns will of course also be reflected in the program, but in addition, the program itself may be organized in modules that do have to follow the structuring in terms of objects and patterns. The two languages are thus intended for quite different purposes. The modularization language is called the fragment language, since it describes the organization of BETA programs in terms of *fragments*. (The notion of a fragment will be introduced below.) The fragment language is used for communicating with *The Fragment System*, which is the component of the Mjølner System [29] that handles storing and manipulation of fragments. The terms fragment language and fragment system are used interchangeably when this causes no confusion.

The fragment language is independent of BETA. The principles behind the fragment language can in fact be used to describe modularization of most programming languages, and a proposal has been worked out for Pascal.

The fragment language is grammar-based. The idea is that any correct sequence of terminal and nonterminal symbols defined by the grammar is a legal module. The fragment language describes how such strings may be combined into larger strings.

Forms

As mentioned, the principle of modularization in BETA is grammar-based and may be applied to any language with a well-defined grammar. To emphasize this, we will use a small toy language with a syntax that differs from BETA, but similar to the one used in figure 2.2. Part of the grammar of the language is shown in figure 3.1. In figure 3.2 examples of strings derived from the nonterminals of our example grammar are shown.

```
<Decl> ::= <Class>
         | <Proc>
         | <Object>
         | <Reference>
<Class> ::= class <name> ':' <ObjectBody>
<Proc> ::= <Type> proc <name> <Args> ':' <ObjectBody>
<ObjectBody> ::= <Super> '{' <Decls> <DoPart> '}'
<Super> ::= <name> | <empty>
<Decls> ::= <Decl> | <Decls> ';' <Decl>
<DoPart> ::= <empty> | 'do' <Stmts>
<Stmts> ::= <Stmt> | <Stmts> ';' <Stmt>
<ObjectSpec> ::= <name> | <ObjectBody>
<Object> ::= <names> ':' obj <ClassName>
<Reference> ::= <names> ':' ref <ClassName>
<names> ::= <name> | <names> ';' <name>
<Stmt> ::= <Assignment> | <ProcCall> | <Return> | <IfStmt> |
...
<IfStmt> ::= (if <exp> then <Stmts> <ElsePart> if)
```

Fig. 3.1.

	Nonterminal	Examples of derived form
1.	<ObjectBody>	{ T: obj text do 'hello' -> T }
2.	<ObjectBody>	{ P: <ObjectBody>; R: ref P do ... }
3.	<Decl>	X: obj int
4.	<Proc>	int proc Foo(a,b: obj int): { <DoPart> }
5.	<DoPart>	do return a*b
6.	<Stmt>	(if B then <Stmt> if)
7.	<IfStmt>	(if B then <Stmt> if)

Fig. 3.2.

Rows 1 and 2 show examples of strings generated form the nonterminal <ObjectBody>. The string in row 1 consists only of terminal symbols, whereas the string in row 2 contains an unexpanded nonterminal, <ObjectBody>.

A string of terminal and nonterminal symbols derived from a nonterminal A is called an *A-form*, or sometimes just a *form*[1]. The derived strings in figure 3.2 are all examples of forms. Forms are the basic elements used to define modules in the Mjølner System. The fragment language has language constructs for combining forms into complete programs. Consider, for example, the forms 4 and 5 in figure 3.2. By substituting the DoPart nonterminal of form 4 by form 5, we get the form in figure 3.3.

```
int   proc   Foo(a,b:   obj
int):
      { do return a*b }
```

Fig. 3.3.

The fragment language is a notation for describing how nonterminals in one form may be replaced by other forms.

Slots

A form may contain several nonterminals having the same syntactic category. This is the case with the form in figure 3.4, which has two DoPart nonterminals. In the fragment language, it is necessary to be able to refer separately to each nonterminal. Each nonterminal must therefore have a name that uniquely identifies it.

```
class Counter:
    { int proc Up(n: obj int):
          { <DoPart> };
      int proc Down(n: obj int):
          { <DoPart> }
    }
```

Fig. 3.4.

In the Mjølner System, several tools manipulate forms, thus not all nonterminals are necessarily to be used by the fragment system. The nonterminals used by the fragment language are called *slots* since they define openings where other forms may be inserted. They are marked by the keyword SLOT. A nonterminal defining a slot has the syntax:

    <<SLOT T:A>>

where T is the name of the slot and A is the syntactic category. Also note that slots are enclosed by << and >> instead of < and >. This is done purely for technical reasons. A nonterminal must begin with a symbol (here <<), which is not in the vocabulary of the language. Since < is used as less_than in BETA, it cannot be used to begin a nonterminal. The form in figure 3.4 may instead be described as in figure 3.5.

```
class Counter:
    { int proc Up(n: obj int):
          { <<SLOT Up:DoPart>> };
      int proc Down(n: obj int):
          { <<SLOT  Down:DoPart>>
    }
    }
```

Fig. 3.5.

Slot names and BETA names belong to different languages, thus

---

[1] In formal language theory, this is called a *sentential form*.

there is no possibility of confusing BETA names and slot names. In the above example, there is a pattern called Up and a slot called Up. In practice, users of the Mjølner System often use the same name for a pattern and a corresponding slot.

Fragment-Form

In the fragment language, each form must be given a name and its syntactic category specified. A fragment-form is a form associated with a name and a syntactic category. In figure 3.6, a name and syntactic category has been added to the form of figure 3.5. The construct ---Counter:Class--- specifies that the name of the form is Counter and that it is derived from the syntactic category (nonterminal) <Class>.

```
---Counter:Class---
class Counter:
{ int proc Up(n: obj int):
        { <<SLOT Up:DoPart>> };
  int proc Down(n: obj int):
        { <<SLOT Down:DoPart>> }
}
```

Fig. 3.6.

Fragment-Group

Often it is convenient to define a set of logically related fragment-forms together. For this purpose, it is possible to define a group of fragments, called a *fragment-group*, which consist of one or more fragment-forms. In figure 3.7 is shown an example of a fragment-group consisting of the forms Up and Down. In the following, the term *fragment* refers to either a fragment-form or a fragment-group.

```
---Up:DoPart---
    do n+1 -> n; return n
---Down:DoPart
    do n-1 -> n; return n
```

Fig. 3.7.

Fragment Library

The fragment system handles the storing of fragment-groups in a library, called the fragment library. In the Mjølner System, the fragment library is implemented on top of the computer's file system. The fragment language refers to fragment-groups stored in the fragment library by means of a *fragment name* (or just *name*). The

```
name /home/smith/Counter;
---Counter:Class---
class Counter:
{ int proc Up(n: obj int)
        { <<SLOT Up:DoPart>> }
  int proc Down(n: obj int):
        { <<SLOT Down:DoPart>> }
}
```

Fig. 3.8.

Mjølner System assumes a hierarchical name structure in the style of UNIX directories. In figure 3.8, the fragment of figure 3.6 has been given a **name** that specifies that the Counter-fragment is placed in the file /home/smith/Counter[2].

---

[2] In the Mjølner System, the **name**-directive is not written explicitly in the fragment group. The reason is that a fragment-group is stored in a file, which defines its name. In this paper, we use the **name**-directive to ease the presentation of the fragment system.

Note that `Counter` is used for three different purposes: the name (file) of the fragment group, the name of a form (`---Counter:Class---`) and the name of a class. As these names belong to different domains there are no problems with ambiguities.

Origin of a Fragment-Group

The *origin part* of a fragment-group specifies a fragment-group that is used when binding fragment-forms to slots. In figure 3.9, the fragment-group from figure 3.7 has been given an **origin**. The origin of `CounterBody` is the fragment-group `/home/smith/Counter`.

```
name /home/smith/CounterBody;
origin /home/smith/Counter;
---Up:DoPart---
    do n+1 -> n; return n
---Down:DoPart---
    do n-1 -> n; return n
```

Fig. 3.9.

The origin must have free slots corresponding to `Up` and `Down`. The origin construct specifies that the fragment-forms `Up` and `Down` be substituted for the corresponding slots in `Counter`. The result of this substitution is a form, called the extent of the fragment.

A fragment defines a unique form, called the *extent* of the fragment. The extent of the above fragment is a combination of `CounterBody` and `Counter`. The combination is obtained by filling in the slots in the origin with the corresponding fragment-forms. In the above example, this gives the form in figure 3.10.

```
class Counter:
    { int proc Up(n: obj int):
            { do n+1 -> n; return n }
        int proc Down(n: obj int)
            { do n-1 -> n; return n }
    }
```

Fig. 3.10.

```
name betaenv;
---betaenv:ObjectBody---
{ proc PutText{T: obj Text): { ... };
    class Stream: { ... };
    class Text: Stream{ ... };
    class File: Stream{ ... };
    class Object: { ... };
    class int: { ... };
    class char: { ... };
    ...
    <<SLOT LIB: Attributes>>;
    Program(): <<SLOT Program:ObjectBody>>;
do Program();
}
```

Fig. 3.11. The basic BETA environment

The Basic Environment

The Mjølner System provides a basic environment that defines the most important standard patterns and objects. In addition, this environment initiates and terminates the execution of any BETA program. The basic BETA environment is the fragment betaenv[3] shown in figure 3.11. As can be seen, this fragment defines a number of standard patterns. In addition, the fragment has two slots: Program and LIB.

A complete BETA program that makes use of betaenv may be defined by defining the Program slot. The fragment-form in figure 3.12 is an example of a very simple BETA program. The extent of the fragment mini1 is the form in figure 3.13.

```
name mini1;
origin betaenv;
---Program:ObjectBody---
  {
  do PutText('Hello world!')
  }
```
Fig. 3.12.

As can be seen, the Program fragment has been substituted for the Program slot in betaenv. In the Program fragment, it is therefore possible to use any name, which is visible at the point of the Program slot in betaenv. PutText is visible at the Program slot and is therefore visible in the Program fragment. It would also have been possible to

```
{ proc PutText(T: obj Text):...
  ...;
  Program():
    {
    do PutText('Hello world!')
    }
  do Program();
}
```
Fig. 3.13.

make use of patterns like int, char, Text, etc. Later in this section, we shall return to the question of visibility.

Defining Libraries

The LIB slot in betaenv is intended for making a set of general declarations to be used by other programs. The difference between such a library and a program is that the library is a list of declarations whereas the program is a single object-body. Figure 3.14 is an example of a library consisting of two procedures. By substituting the LIB slot in betaenv with

```
name mylib;
origin betaenv        ;
---LIB:Decls ---
proc Hello():
  { do PutText('Hello') }
proc World():
  { do PutText('World') }
```
Fig. 3.14.

the LIB fragment-form, we obtain the form in figure 3.15.

---

[3] In the rest of this paper, simple names without directory paths are used for specifying the names of fragment-groups.

As can be seen, the library procedures are inserted at the point of the LIB slot. This means that in the LIB fragment-form it is possible to see all names visible at the point of the LIB slot in betaenv.

Note that the extent of mylib is not an executable program, since the Program slot has not

```
{  ...
   proc Hello():
      { do PutText('Hello') };
   proc World():
      { do PutText('World') };
   Program():
      <<SLOT Program: ObjectBody>>;
do Program();
}
```

Fig. 3.15.

been defined. In the next section, we shall show how to make use of a library in a program.

Include

When making libraries like mylib, we need a mechanism for combining several fragments into one fragment. The **include**-construct makes this possible. In figure 3.16, we have a program that makes use of the mylib library.

The effect of the **include** mylib is that the procedures defined in mylib can be used in the Program fragment-form. Formally, the fragment-forms of mylib become part of the

```
name mini2;
origin betaenv;
include mylib;
---Program:ObjectBody---
{
do Hello(); World();
}
```

Fig. 3.16.

fragment mini2. In the above example, mini2 may be understood as a fragment-group consisting of the fragment-forms in mylib and the Program fragment-form. This implies that the extent of mini2 is obtained by substituting the LIB slot in betaenv by the LIB fragment-form in mylib and by substituting the Program slot in betaenv by the Program slot in betaenv by the Pro-

```
{  ...
   proc Hello(): { do 'PutText('Hello) };
   proc World(): { do PutText('World') };
   Program():
      {
      do Hello(); World();
      }
do Program();
}
```

Fig. 3.17.

gram fragment-form in mini2. The result is the form in figure 3.17.

Since the patterns in mylib are inserted at the point of the LIB slot, they are visible at the point of the Program slot. This is where the Program fragment-form in mini2 is inserted, i.e. the procedures Hello and World are visible inside the Program fragment-form. A fragment-form may have more than one **include**. This makes it possible to use several library fragments in the same fragment.

Body

When defining a fragment it is often desirable to be able to specify one or more fragments that must always be included when using the fragment. This is often the case when a fragment is separated into an interface fragment and one or more implementation fragments. The **body** construct specifies a fragment that is always part of the extent. In figure 3.18, a **body** has been added to the Counter fragment-group of figure 3.8. The body-directive specifies that the CounterBody fragment is always to be used whenever the Counter fragment is used. CounterBody is shown in figure 3.9.

```
name Counter;
origin betaenv;
body CounterBody;
---LIB:Attributes---
class Counter:
  { int proc Up(n: obj int):
      { <<SLOT Up:DoPart>> };
    int proc Down(n: obj int):
      { <<SLOT Down:DoPart>> };
  }
```

Fig. 3.18.

Separation of Interface Implementation

Organizing a program as a collection of fragments (modules) is one way of dealing with the complexity of large programs. A large system, however, consists of a large number of fragments. A fragment may use a number of other fragments (via origin, include or body), and be itself used by a number of other fragments. The result may in fact be a fairly complicated structure. For this reason it is necessary to limit the interconnections between fragments. Furthermore, knowledge about the details of a fragment should be limited whenever possible. A fundamental technique in the design of software systems is to distinguish between the *interface* and *implementation* of a module. The *interface* of a module describes the part of the module, which is visible from modules that use it. This includes a description of how to use the module and is sometimes called the *outside view* of the module. The implementation of a module is the part of the module, which is necessary to realize it on a computer. This is sometimes called the *inside view* of the module.

An important issue is the notion of *encapsulation* or *information hiding*. Encapsulation means that access to the implementation part of a module is not possible from outside the module, i.e. the implementation of a module is hidden. This means that the usage of a module cannot depend upon internal details of its implementation, and thus it is possible to change the implementation of a module without affecting its usage.

Encapsulation and separation of interface and implementation may also save compilation time. In the Mjølner System, as in most other systems, fragments (modules) can be separately compiled. A change in an implementation module can then be made without recompilation of the interface module and modules using the interface module. This can yield significant savings in compilation time. On the other hand, a change in an interface module implies that all modules using it must be recompiled. This can be extremely time consuming, therefore we recommend carefully designing critical interfaces to reduce the need for future changes. It is, however, not possible to avoid such changes since the requirements for an interface usually change over time.

Programming takes place at different abstraction levels. The interface part of a module describes a view of objects and patterns meaningful at the abstraction level where the module is used. The implementation level describes how objects and patterns at the interface level are realized using other objects and patterns. To sum up, encapsulation and separation of interface and implementation have the following advantages:

- The user of a module can only access its interface and thus cannot make use of implementation details.
- It is possible to change the implementation without affecting the usage of a module.
- A change in an implementation module can be made without recompilation of the interface module and modules using the interface module

```
name Counter;
origin betaenv;
body CounterBody;
---LIB:Decls---
class Counter:
  { int proc Up(n: obj int):
        { <<SLOT Up:DoPart>> };
    int proc Down(n: obj int)
        {   <<SLOT   Down:DoPart>>
};
    <<SLOT rep: Decls>>
  }
```

Fig. 3.19.

```
name CounterBody;
origin Counter;
---Up:DoPart---
    do V+n -> V; return V
---Down:DoPart---
    do V-n -> V; return V
---rep:Decls---
    V: obj int
```

Fig. 3.20.

The fragment language supports encapsulation and separation of interface and implementation. One fragment defines the interface while others define the implementation.

The counter-fragment in figure 3.8 may be considered an example of an interface-fragment and the corresponding fragment in figure 3.9 may be considered an example of an implementation-fragment. This example is very simple in the sense that there is no state associated with a Counter-object.

In principle, we might define state in the form of variables in the implementation-fragment as shown in figures 3.19 and 3.20. The Counter-form has been added a SLOT rep, where new declarations may be inserted. In CounterBody a form ---rep:Decls--- has been added. The rep-form contains a declaration of a variable V, which represents the state of the Counter object. In the DoPart-forms Up and Down, the variable V is being used. By substituting the

```
class Counter:
  { int proc Up(n: obj int)
        { do V+n -> V; return V };
    int proc Down(n: obj int)
        { do V-n -> V; return V };
    V: obj int
  }
```

Fig. 3.21.

forms in counterbody with the slots in Counter the form in figure 3.21 is obtained.

```
name Counter;
origin betaenv;
body CounterBody;
---LIB:Attributes---
class Counter:
 { int proc Up(n: obj int)
      { <<SLOT Up:DoPart>> };
   int proc Down(n: obj int)
      { <<SLOT Down:DoPart>> };
   rep:    obj    <<SLOT
rep:ObjectBody>>
 }
```

Fig. 3.22.

```
name CounterBody;
origin Counter;
---Up:DoPart---
   do rep.V+n -> rep.V;
   return V
---Down:DoPart---
   do rep.V-n -> rep.V;
   return rep.V
---rep:ObjectBody---
   { V: obj int }
```

Fig. 3.23.

Due to some implementation restrictions in the Mjølner system, variables will have to be encapsulated in objects. The fragments 3.18-3.19 will then have to be written as shown in figures 3.22 and 3.23.

Visibility
The fragment system also controls visibility of names. Consider the fragment CounterUser in figure 3.24. In CounterBody, the fragments betaenv and Counter are visible.

```
name CounterUser;
origin betaenv;
include Counter;
---Program:ObjectBody ---
 { C: obj Counter;
   N: obj int
 do C.up(8);
    C.down(4) -> N;
 }
```

Fig. 3.24.

The fragment CounterBody is part of the extent of CounterUser, since it can be reached from CounterUser via include Counter and from Counter via **body** CounterBody. CounterBody is, however, not visible from CounterUser, since only fragments reachable via **origin** and **include** are visible.

If **body** CounterBody in figure 3.22 is replaced by **include** CounterBody, then CounterBody will be visible in CounterUser.

For a given fragment there is a dependency graph that has a node for each fragment referred to via **origin**, **include** and **body**. The dependency graph for CounterUser is shown in figure 3.25.

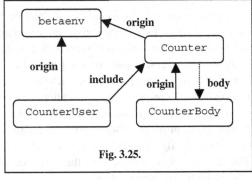

Fig. 3.25.

The *extent* of a fragment F is the form obtained by combining all fragments in the dependency graph for F. The extent for CounterUser is obtained by combining the fragments CounterUser, betaenv, Counter, and CounterBody.

The *domain* of a fragment F is the form obtained by combining the fragments from the part of the graph obtained by following only **origin** and **include** from F. I.e. **body** links are excluded from the domain. The domain for CounterUser is obtained by combining the fragments CounterUser, betaenv, and Counter.

Visibility is defined by means of the domain of a fragment. Inside a fragment F, only the fragments in the domain of F are visible. For CounterUser, only the fragments betaenv, and Counter are visible whereas CounterBody is not visible. This means that it is not possible to write the following statement within CounterUser:

```
C.rep.V + 1 -> C.rep.V
```

If we in CounterUser add a directive: **include** CounterBody, then CounterBody will be visible and the above statement will be legal.

Alternative Implementations

It is possible to have several implementations of a given interface module. In general, this means that different fragments may define different bindings for slots in a given fragment. In figure 3.26, the interface of a Stack-class is shown. A corresponding implementation using an array is sketched in figure 3.27.

```
name stack;
origin betaenv;
---LIB: Attributes ---
class Stack:
  { rep: obj <<SLOT rep: ObjectBody>>;
    proc Push(e: ref Object):
      { <<SLOT Push: DoPart>> };
    ref object proc Pop():
      { <<SLOT Pop: DoPart>> };
    proc New(): {<<SLOT New: DoPart>> };
    bool proc isEmpty():
      { <<SLOT isEmpty: DoPart>> }
  }
```

Fig. 3.26. Stack interface

Suppose that we want to define an alternate implementation of the stack from the previous section. In the alternative implementation, stack objects are represented as a linked list. The list implementation is sketched in figure 3.28.

A stack fragment may be used as shown in figure 3.29. Note that stackUser does not define a complete program, since no implementation of the stack has been selected. This can be done by adding a specification like **body** arrayStack to stackUser. This will include the array implementation of the stack.

However, in many cases it will be desirable to delay the selection of the implementation. In figures 3.30a and 3.30b are shown two fragments using stackUser. The arrayStackUser selects the array implementation and the listStackUser selects the list implementation.

Program Variants

Often, several variants of a given program are needed, usually if variants of a given program have to exist for several computers. The main part of the program is often the same for each computer. For maintenance purposes, it is highly desirable to have only

```
name arrayStack
origin stack
---rep: ObjectBody ---
   { A: [100] ref object;
     Top : obj int
---Push: DoPart ---
   do rep.top+1 -> rep.top;
      e -> rep.A[rep.top]
---Pop: DoPart---
   do rep.top-1 -> rep.top;
      return
rep.A[rep.top+1]
---new: DoPart---
   do 0 -> rep.top
---isEmpty: DoPart ---
   do return (0 = rep.Top)
```

Fig. 3.27.

```
name listStack
origin stack
---rep: ObjectBody---
   { head: ref elm;
     elm: class
        { T:ref Object;
          next: ref elm }
   }
---Push: DoPart---
   do …
---Pop: DoPart ---
   do …
---new: DoPart---
   do …
---isEmpty: DoPart---
   do …
```

Fig. 3.28.

```
name stackUser;
origin betaenv;
include stack;
---program:ObjectBody-
--
{ Joe,Lisa: obj Per-
son;
  S: obj Stack;
  X: ref Person
do S.new;
   Joe -> S.Push;
   Lisa -> S.push;
   S.pop -> X
}
```

Fig. 3.29.

```
name arrysStackUser;
origin stackUser;
body arrayStack;
```

Fig. 3.30a.

```
name listStackUser;
origin stackUser;
body listStack;
```

Fig. 3.30b.

one version of the common part. In the Mjølner System program variants are handled in the same way as alternative implementations of a module, i.e. different variants of a module bind some of the slots differently. To support this, an **mdbody**-directive may be used to define different bindings of slots for different platforms.

In figure 3.31, is shown a simplified version of the fragment defining the BETA compiler. The BetaCompiler fragment includes various platform independent fragments. In addition it has a **mdbdoy**-directive that selects between three different fragments for code generation.

When the fragment `BetaCompiler` is compiled, the compiler selects one of `SparcGenerator`, `IntelGene-rator` or `PowerPcGenerator` depending on the platform selected when calling the compiler. The compiler has a switch that decides which **mdbody** to select. By default this switch is the target-platform.

The **mdbody**-directive can be generalized by adding user-defined variables to be used for selection of body-parts. This generalization has, however, not been made in the Mjølner System.

```
name BetaCompiler;
origin betaenv;
include SyntaxHandler;
include SemanticChecker;
include SemanticAnalyzer;
mdbody sparc    SparcGenerator
       intel    IntelGenerator
       powerpc PowerPcGenerator
---Program:ObjectBody---
...
```

Fig. 3.31.

Visibility and Binding Rules

We now summarize the rules for binding slots, and give a precise definition of the extent and domain of a fragment. A general skeleton of a fragment is shown in figure 3.32. The origin G is optional. There may be m (m >= 0) **include**-directive and k (k >= 0) **body**-directives.

The *origin-chain* of F is a list of fragments:

G, G1, G2, ... Gn

where G is the origin of F, G1 is the origin of G, etc. The fragment Gn has no origin. Usually, Gn will be the basic environment betaenv. The origin-chain must be finite without duplicates. The fragment-forms in F are bound by searching for free slots in the origin chain, starting with G. The *fragment-dependency graph* of F has a node for each fragment referred to via origin, include and body. The dependency graph is constructed as follows:

```
name F;
origin G;
include A1;
include A2;
...
include Am;
body B1;
body B2;
...
body Bk;
---F1: S1---
    ff1
---F2: S2---
    ff2
...
---Fn: Sn ---
    ffn
```

Fig. 3.32.

- A directed edge is made **from** F **to** its origin.
- A directed edge is made **from** F **to** each fragment it includes.
- Construct the dependency graph for each body fragment F.
- Steps 1-3 are repeated for each fragment referred by **origin**, **include** and **body**.

The dependency graph must be acyclic, i.e. there should be no loops. This means that a fragment cannot include itself directly or indirectly via other fragments. An example of a dependency graph is given in figure 3.25.

The extent of F is the extent of its origin, the extent of all fragments included, plus the extent of all bodies, and finally F itself. This may be described using the following equation, where we rely on the reader's intuition for the definition of the operator ⊕:

```
extent(F)   =   extent(G)
                ⊕ extent(A1) ⊕ extent(A2) … ⊕ extent(Am)
                ⊕ extent(B1) ⊕ extent(B2) … ⊕ extent(Bk)
                ⊕ ff1 ⊕ ff2 ⊕ … ⊕ ffn
```

Note the recursive nature of extent. Anything in the extent of the **origin** is part of the extent of F, and similarly for **include** and **body**. The recursion is finite since the dependency graph is acyclic. Eventually, there will be a fragment without an origin and fragments without include and body parts.

The domain of F has a similar recursive definition. The domain of F includes the domain of the origin, the domain of all included fragments and the fragment itself. The body fragments are not included in the domain. The following equation describes the domain:

```
domain(F)   =   domain(G)
                ⊕ domain(A1) ⊕ domain(A) ⊕ … ⊕ domain(Am)
                ⊕ ff1 ⊕ ff2 ⊕ … ⊕ ffn
```

4 Discussion and Conclusion

In [6] the term *programming in the large* was introduced to characterize the construction of large and complex systems. The main point made by DeRemer and Krohn is that structuring a large collection of modules to form a system (programming in the large) is essentially a different activity from that of constructing the individual modules (programming in the small). They propose the use of different languages for the two activities: a *module interconnection language* should be used for describing the modular structure, and a conventional programming language should be used for describing the contents of modules. They also propose a module interconnection language called MIL~75. The BETA Fragment System is an example of such a module interconnection language.

In the introduction there is a short discussion of the handling of modularization in various programming languages, including a discussion of whether or not we need both class and module. As should be evident from this paper, BETA does distinguish between the two mechanisms. For a more detailed discussion these issues, please see the paper by Szyperski [31].

The pattern mechanism was designed to be the ultimate abstraction mechanism that covers all most other abstraction mechanisms in programming languages. To a large extent this goal seems to have been satisfied. There are as in all other languages, parts of the language that will benefit from changes. It is more than 20 years ago that the basic ideas of BETA were devised. Today there are new requirements for programming languages that calls for improved abstraction/language mechanisms. These include better support for unification of programming paradigms such as object-oriented, functional, constraint, concurrent and prototype-based programming [26]. In addition support for various forms of architectural- and design patterns [9] is needed.

For the fragment system, the conclusions are less clear. One the one hand we still find a need for a separate module-interconnection language for the reasons mentioned in the beginning of section 3. We also think that the grammar-based principles of the Mjølner System are simple and clean. The users of the Mjølner System complain about various elements of the fragment system. These are mainly related to implementation restrictions. One example of this is that it is not allowed to declare variables in a `Decls`-slot as used in figure 3.19. Another perhaps more important problem is the borderline between patterns and fragments, which is not always clear. Before going further into that we will compare the fragment system with the conclusions of Szyperski. Szyperski lists the following requirements of a module concept:

1. Compile-time abstraction
2. Syntactical structure in a large system
3. Orderly scoping of names and interrelations using the import graph.
4. Natural units of information hiding, separate compilation and dynamic loading.
5. Orderly use of global variables and procedures (comparable to class variables and class methods)

The following are Szyperski's non-requirements for modules:

6. Modules need not be nested.
7. Modules should definitely not be nested within other structures like classes
8. Modules have no special run-time semantics

We think that the Mjølner Fragment System satisfies 1, 2, 3, 4 and 8. There is a borderline between scoping in the fragment system and scoping in the language (BETA). The fragment system handles import and visibility of fragments from other fragments. The fragment system determines the extent of a given fragment. The extent is a BETA form and within this extent the scoping rules of BETA apply.

The Fragment System does not handle 5. BETA patterns can be arbitrarily nested and nested patterns/classes provides a clean alternative to global variables and class methods [22]. It is not clear from the paper how Szyperski views the relationship between nested classes and modules.

The Fragment System does allow 6 and 7. It is possible to declare slots within an arbitrary class or procedure. This makes it possible to factor out certain parts of a class and only include it in programs that need this functionality.

There is a borderline between variants and alternative implementations. The selection of variants/alternative implementations is made at compile-time by the fragment system. This prevents more than one implementation of a fragment in a given program. One module might need an array implementation and another might want a list implementation. An `arrayStack` and a `listStack` are both stacks. Similarly the current compiler can only handle one platform. It might be desirable to have the same compiler generate code for several platforms. This will require that different implementations can coexist and language mechanisms for selecting between an implementation must be available. The implication of this is that the fragment language is no longer just a compile-time mechanism. It will be necessary to be able to handle fragments at run-time. In case of reflection/meta programming, we will also need to be able to manipulate fragments as run-time entities. Some of these issues are discussed in [3].

It is well known that variants and alternative implementations can also be implemented using subclasses. If we extend fragments to handle the above requirements, then the borderline between class and fragment may be even fuzzier.

Szyperski deliberately does not discuss generic modules as found in Ada. For BETA patterns and objects represent the logical part of a system in the sense that patterns represent concepts and objects phenomena. Fragments are physical entities in the form of program forms. Generic fragments will then be fragments that are parameterized by syntactic entities consisting of other forms. Such generic fragments may be useful, but has not been investigated.

Acknowledgements. BETA was designed by Bent Bruun Kristensen, Birger Møller-Pedersen, Kristen Nygaard and the author. The grammar-based principle used to define the Mjølner Fragment System was originally proposed in [15] and later refined through the Mjølner Project through discussions with Jørgen Lindskov Knudsen, Peter Andersen, Bent Bruun Kristensen, Kim Jensen Møller, Claus Nørgaard, and Elmer Sandvad. Section 3 of this paper is based on Chapter 17 in [18]. Part of this work has been supported by the *Danish National Centre for IT-research* through the project *Centre for Object Technology*.

References

1. Ada: Reference Manual for the Ada Programming Language – Proposed Standard Document, United States Dep. of Defense, July 1980.
2. Arnold, K., Gosling, J.: The Java Programming Language. Addison Wesley, 1996.
3. Astrup, A.L., Rasmussen, L.-L. H.: Thuesen: P.: Draupner – a way of programming. Master Thesis, Computer Science Department, Aarhus University, 1989.
4. Brinch-Hansen, P.: The Programming Language Concurrent Pascal. IEEE Trans Software Engineering, 1(2), (1975), 149-207.
5. Dahl, O.-J., Nygaard, K., Myrhaug, B.: Simula 67 Common Base Language. Technical Report Publ. no. S-2, Norwegian Computing Center, Oslo, 1968.
6. DeRemer, F.L., Krohn, H.: Programming-in-the-Large versus Programming-in-the-Small. IEE Transactions on Software Engineering, 2(2), 80-86, 1976.
7. Ernst, E.: **gbeta** – a Language with Virtual Attributes, Block Structure, and Propagating, Dynamic Inheritance. Ph.D. Thesis, Computer Science Department, Aarhus University, 1999.

8. Ernst. E.: Propagating Class and Method Combination. In: Guerraoui, R. (ed.): 13th European Conference on Object-Oriented Programming, Lisbon, June 1999. Lecture Notes in Computer Science, Vol. 1628. Springer-Verlag, Berlin Heidelberg New York, 1999.

9. Gamma, E., Helm, R., Johnson, R.E., Vlissides, J.: Design Patterns: Elements of Object-Oriented Software Architecture. Addison-Wesley, 1994.

10. Hoare, C.A.R.: Notes on Data Structuring. In: Dahl, O.-J., Dijkstra, E., Hoare, C.A.R.: Structured Programming. Academic Press, 1972.

11. Hoare, C.A.R.: Proof of Correctness of Data Representation. Acta Informatica, 4, 271-281, 1972.

12. Igarashi, A., Pierce, B.C.: Foundations for Virtual Types. In: Guerraoui, R. (ed.): 13th European Conference on Object-Oriented Programming, Lisbon, June 1999. Lecture Notes in Computer Science, Vol. 1628. Springer-Verlag, Berlin Heidelberg New York, 1999.

13. Knudsen, J.L., Löfgren, M., Madsen, O.L., Magnusson, B.: Object-Oriented Environments – The Mjølner Approach. Prentice Hall, 1994.

14. Kristensen, B.B., Madsen, O.L., Møller-Pedersen, B. Nygaard, K.: Abstraction Mechanisms in the BETA Programming Language. In Conference Record of the Tenth Annual ACM Symposium on Principles of Programming Languages. Austin, Texas, January 1983.

15. Kristensen, B.B., Madsen, O.L., Møller-Pedersen, B. Nygaard, K.: Syntax-Directed Program Modularization. In: Degano, P., Sandewall, E. (eds.): Interactive Computing Systems. Amsterdam: North-Holland, 1983.

16. Kristensen, B.B., Madsen, O.L., Møller-Pedersen, B. Nygaard, K.: Classification of Actions or Inheritance also for Methods. In: 1st European Conference Object-oriented programming, Paris, France, June 1987. Lecture Notes in Computer Science, Vol. 276. Springer-Verlag, Berlin Heidelberg New York, 1987.

17. Liskov, B., Snyder, A., Atkinson, R., Schaeffert, C.: Abstraction mechanisms in CLU. Comm. ACM, 20(8), 564-576, 1977.

18. Madsen, O.L., Møller-Pedersen, B., Nygaard, K.: Object-Oriented Programming in the BETA Programming Language. Addison Wesley/ACM Press, Wokingham, England, 1993.

19. Madsen, O.L., Møller-Pedersen, B.: Virtual Classes, a Powerful Mechanism in Object-Oriented Languages. In: Proc. OOPSLA'89, New Orleans, 1989.

20. Madsen, O.L., Møller-Pedersen, B.: Part Objects and their Locations. In: (Magnusson, B., Meyer, B., Perrot, J.F. (eds.): Proc. Technology of Object-Oriented Languages and Systems – TOOLS10. Prentice-Hall, 1993, pp. 283-297.

21. Madsen, O.L., Magnusson, B., Møller-Pedersen, B.: Strong Typing of Object-Oriented Languages Revisited. In: Proc. OOPSLA'90, Ottawa, Canada, 1990.

22. Madsen, O.L.: Block Structure and Object-Oriented Languages. In: Shriver, B.D., Wegner, P. (eds.): Research Directions in Object-Oriented Programming. Cambridge MA: MIT Press, 1987.

23. Madsen, O.L.: An Overview of BETA. In [13].

24. Madsen, O.L.: Open Issues in Object-Oriented Programming - A Scandinavian Perspective. Software Practice and Experience, Vol. 25, No. S4, Dec. 1995.

25. Madsen, O.L.: Semantic Analysis of Virtual Classes and Nested Classes. In: Proc. OOPSLA'99, Denver, Colorado, 1999.

26. Madsen, O.L: Towards a Unified Programming Language. In: Bertino, E. (ed.): 14th European Conference on Object-Oriented Programming. Lecture Notes in Computer Science, Vol. 1850. Springer-Verlag, Berlin Heidelberg New York, 2000.

27. Magnusson, B.: An Overview of Simula. In [13].

28. Meyer, B.: Object-Oriented Software Construction. Prentice-Hall, 1988.

29. The Mjølner System, http://www.mjolner.com.

30. Rogerson, D.: Inside COM - Microsoft's Component Object Model, Microsoft Press, 1997.
31. Szyperski, C.A.: Import is Not Inheritance – Why We Need Both: Modules and Classes. In: Madsen, O.L. (ed.): 6th European Conference on Object-Oriented Programming, Lisbon, June/July 1992. Lecture Notes in Computer Science, Vol. 615. Springer-Verlag, Berlin Heidelberg New York, 1992.
32. Stroustrup, B.: The C++ Programming Language. Addison-Wesley, 1986.
33. Thorup, K.K.: Genericity in Java with Virtual Types. In: Aksit, M., Matsouka, S. (eds.): 11th European Conference on Object-Oriented Programming. Lecture Notes in Computer Science, Vol. 1241. Springer-Verlag, Berlin Heidelberg New York, 1997.
34. Thorup, K.K.: Objective-C. In: Zamir, S. (ed.): Handbook of Object Technology. CRC Press, 1999.
35. Thorup, K.K., Torgersen, M.: Unifying Genericity - Combining the Benefits of Virtual Types and parameterized Types. In: Guerraoui, R. (ed.): 13th European Conference on Object-Oriented Programming, Lisbon, June 1999. Lecture Notes in Computer Science, Vol. 1628. Springer-Verlag, Berlin Heidelberg New York, 1999.
36. Torgersen, M.: Virtual Types are Statically Safe. In: Bruce, K. (ed.) 5th Workshop on Foundations of Object-Oriented Languages, (San Diego, CA, January 16-17, 1998).
37. Ungar, D., Smith, R.B.: SELF – The Power of Simplicity. In: Proc. OOPSLA'87, Orlando, FL, 1987.
38. Wirth, N.: Programming in Modula-2 (fourth edition). Texts and Monographs in Computer Science. Springer-Verlag, Berlin, 1988. First edition: 1982.
39. Wirth: N.: The programming Language Oberon. Software – Practice and Experience, 18:7, 671-690. July 1998.
40. Østerbye, K.: Parts, Wholes and Sub-Classes. In Proc. European Simulation Multiconference, ISBN 0-911801-1, 1990.

Design of Multilingual Retargetable Compilers: Experience of the XDS Framework Evolution

Vitaly V. Mikheev

Excelsior, LLC, Novosibirsk, Russia
vmikheev@excelsior-usa.com

Abstract. The XDS framework has been developed since 1993. During this time, it has been serving as a production compiler construction framework as well as a base for research projects. Completely written in Oberon-2, XDS uses a *mixed design* technique amalgamating modular and object-oriented approaches. It combines advantages of both approaches, at the same time avoiding drawbacks inherent to each of them if used separately. In this paper we set out how the mixed design approach contributes to extensibility of the framework with respect to including support for new input languages and target architectures and implementing new optimizations. In the first part of the paper we give an overview of the XDS framework architecture emphasizing which parts are worth applying the object-oriented design. In the second part, we describe our experience of extending XDS with support for the Java language and implementing interprocedural and object-oriented optimizations.

Keywords: object-oriented design, front-end, back-end, Java, performance, native code

1 Introduction

Most modern compilers have a multi-layer hierarchical architecture with many replaceable components. They also usually have many forms of intermediate representation (IR) of a program being compiled. However, the advantages that can be obtained from the system organization justify such a complexity. First, the architecture allows implematation of compiler for new input languages at a lower cost that is a good example of software reuse. In fact, a compiler designed in this way may be considered as a *compiler construction framework* rather than a solid application. This is the mainstream approach to compiler construction today and many production compilers have a similar architecture, for instance the IBM's XL compilers for FORTRAN, C/C++, and Java [5]. Another advantage of a multi-layer compiler design is the ability to produce code for different platforms (target architectures) that contributes to portable software development. The widespread virtual machine technology with portable byte-code is not the only way to achieve portability. It also may be supported in a multi-layer compiler construction framework by providing a component responsible

J. Gutknecht and W. Weck (Eds.): JMLC 2000, LNCS 1897, pp. 238–249, 2000.
© Springer-Verlag Berlin Heidelberg 2000

for target-specific code generation for each platform[1] just like it is supported by providing a virtual machine for each of them. However, the multi-language and multi-platform support may lead to sacrificing performance of generated code that is unacceptable for production compilers. In the next sections we describe our solutions of that problem applied to the translation of Java to native compiled code. Finally, the multi-layer architecture allows adding new optimizations to the compiler. It is a very important point because code optimization is the subject of active investigations today. Using new optimizing techniques obtained from the latest research results is essential to construct "state-of-the-art" optimizing compilers.

The rest of the paper is organized as follows: Section 2 describes the XDS framework architecture, Section 3 focuses on the role of object-oriented design in compiler construction. Our experience of extending the XDS framework is described in Section 4. Finally, Section 5 summarizes the paper.

2 The XDS Framework Overview

XDS (eXtensible Development System) is a framework on which base several compilers have been developed. Among input programming languages supported by XDS are Modula-2, Oberon-2 [15], JVM bytecode, Java and two Nortel Networks' proprietary languages intended for telecommunication software development. Native code generation is implemented for the following target architectures: Intel x86, m68k, SPARC, PowerPC and VAX. As many other compilers, XDS also supports "via C" cross-compilation in order to be available for a wide variety of platforms. Furthermore, having the multi-component architecture, the XDS framework may be used for other purposes than compiler construction. The *XDS family tools* reusing particular framework components are built on top of XDS. A *converter from Modula-2 to C++* text has been developed for code migration purposes. The *static analyzer* [14] allows one to reveal run-time errors in large programs written in Modula-2, Oberon-2 or Java without execution. The *InterView source code browser*[18] is aimed at maintenance and reengineering of large-scale software systems. With its help, developers are able to find and visualize any program entity properties and non-trivial data-flow dependencies across the whole project. InterView supports a project database and a comprehensive query language. The database generation component is built into the XDS compilers for Modula-2, Oberon-2 and Java.

The XDS framework architecture is shown in Fig. 1. A common part of all tools built on XDS is the *project system* which is a supervisor responsible for system component management. In general, it takes a *system configuration file* and a *user project file* and invokes the respective framework components, for instance, compiling source files to object code. In particular, the project system is responsible for smart recompilation of out-of-date modules. After compilation,

---

[1] Strictly speaking, a portable run-time support is also required, but this problem is much simpler than retargetable code generation so it is left out of the scope of this paper.

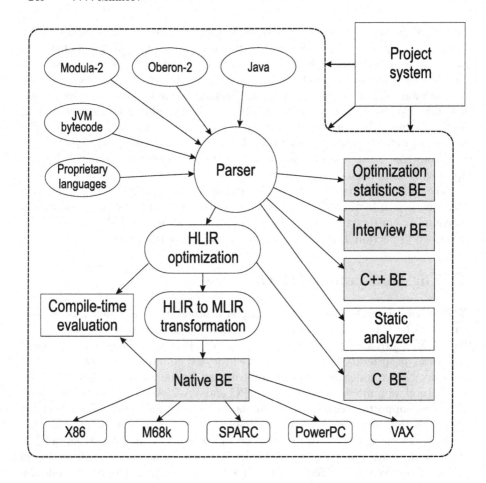

Fig. 1. XDS framework architecture

it produces a *response file* containing a list of files generated. The project system may also use a template provided as part of system configuration to generate such a response file that allows XDS compilers to use any linker or maker to create executable file or perform other types of further processing, if required. Some points are worth noting here. The configuration of working system, including source languages, target platforms, code generation settings (e.g. optimization control, alignment etc.), is constructed on-the-fly. In other words, given configuration and project settings the project system composes the actual tool deciding on which components should be invoked. Note that such compiler organization allows generating object code for two "platforms" at the same time that makes sense, for instance, if the either platform is the InterView database.

In XDS, as in most modern compilers, there are separate front-end (FE) and back-end (BE) components. In general, FE parses source files to produce some kind of IR, and BE, in turn, takes the resulting IR and generates object code. However, strict meaning of the concepts usually varies from system to system. The following questions can help to make it clear:

1. What kind of intermediate representation does FE produce?
2. Is FE target independent?
3. Is BE language independent?

The answer to question 1 for XDS is the attributed syntax tree denoted in Fig. 1 as the high-level intermediate representation (HLIR). Other alternatives used in compiler construction research projects are either a stack-oriented bytecode of some virtual machine [10] or a low-level instruction representation [7]. Nowadays, it is widely acknowledged that the syntax tree keeps all information required for further optimizations which is usually lost in the other forms of IR [8,9]. Different approaches have been proposed to solve the problem. One of them is to provide low-level representation with extra information, which can be used, then for some specific optimizations. In our opinion, this approach suffers from inability to incorporate new optimizations into the compiler without reimplementing the IR construction component. Another good reason to have IR as the syntax tree is that XDS back-ends are not limited to object code generation. For instance, the InterView data base generator and the static analyzer that we consider as XDS back-ends, demand IR to preserve as much information about source text as possible. In some cases, we had to carry out a large amount of work to meet that requirement. For example, our JVM bytecode FE uses a special technique based on symbolic computations to reconstruct the original syntax tree from JVM instructions and type information residing in JVM class files [1]. Some of related works [8,11] do not follow this way and reconstruct syntax tree only partially. However, our experience shows that it results in less optimized code and decreases reusability of the FE component. Finally, the tree is the most appropriate IR for converter to C++. Thus, we strongly believe that the attributed syntax tree is the best choice for IR, which compiler's FE should produce.

The same reasoning may be taken into account when answering question 2. XDS FE is completely target-independent but in some of related works [10] FE performs target-depended jobs, e.g. field offset computation, constant evaluations depending on memory layout, etc. We deem the profits that can be obtained from such a decision do not outweigh the disadvantages that come with the lack of portability.

Another part of the XDS framework architecture is the HLIR optimizer. Its mission is to perform optimizations on the tree. Procedure inlining, constant propagation, object-oriented optimizations are implemented in the HLIR optimizer. After optimization, HLIR is converted to the middle-level intermediate representation (MLIR). This is implemented as an extra tree traversal and serves as a preliminary phase for native code generation. At this stage, the initial tree

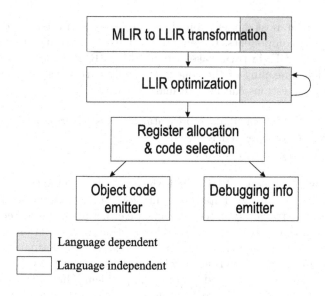

Fig. 2. XDS native BE organization

representation is simplified, for example, *synchronized block* in Java is transformed to *try-finally* block [2], thus reducing the number of different operators in
MLIR. In particular, it allows BEs to be language-independent to the maximum
extent because the conversion unifies operators from different languages to some
common representation. MLIR, in turn, can be thought of as input language for
native BE.

An ideal compiler architecture should have language-independent BE component. Theoretically, this goal may be achieved through appropriate BE design
and it would be a good solution in case of supporting only one input language.
Certainly, it is possible to implement a unified BE that takes MLIR generated
by any language-specific FE and produces code but at cost of worse code performance. Several significant examples are given in Section 4. Thus, question 3
has the following answer: XDS native BEs contain language-dependent parts.

Fig. 2 shows a common structure of XDS native BE. At first stage, MLIR is
converted to the triad form [12] called the low-level intermediate representation
(LLIR). In fact, LLIR can be considered as an abstract (target-independent) low-
level instruction set. First, BE performs some simple optimizations just on the
representation, after that it is transformed to SSA (Static Single Assignment)
form to make the majority of optimizations such as common subexpression elimination, dead code removal, etc. At the next phase LLIR is converted into the
DAG (Direct Acyclic Graph) form (set of trees) to accomplish an optimal code
selection with the bottom up tree rewriting technique [6]. We use the BURG tool
that produces rewriters in Oberon-2 from description of the rewriting grammars
representing the target architecture (instruction set and addressing modes). Each

grammar rule is attributed with a "rule cost" that depends on target architecture as well, so a rewriter always tries to minimize the entire inference cost. Along with DAG rewriting, graph coloring-based register allocation is performed. Finally, code and debugging information emitters are invoked to produce object code or assembler source text.

3 Object-Oriented Design in Compiler Construction

At present, object-oriented design (OOD) is widely used in the software industry. Adherents of OOD assert that it offers better solutions for typical problems arising during software life cycle. In particular, OOD eases program code maintainability and extensibility, increasing the degree of software reuse. Taking the above reasons into account we, however, do not share the opinion that OOD is the panacea for large system design problems. Many requirements that such systems have to meet may be fulfilled with help of the traditional modular design approach. In our opinion, the bias to object-oriented programming and popularity of C++ are to some extent caused by the availability of some modular means in C++ which are not present in pure C. In fact, many C programmers have missed the modular stage of their programming methodology evolution and found themselves right in the object-oriented stage. Really, one should be a strong-will person to write in C according to modular programming principles.

Our design approach is not a conventional OOD, although some of related works recognize it as a preferable way in compiler construction [4]. We strongly believe it would be wrong to use OOD for the whole system being designed without special consideration of which components are worth applying OOD and which are not. Thus, we keep the golden mean in design issues: on the one hand, we remain staunch supporters of the modular design approach which is a good way to achieve the main goal of large system design: *to be able to manage complexity*; on the other hand, we accept the OO approach as a very useful mean to improve reusability and extensibility of particular system components. An outline of the approach that we call *mixed design* looks as follows:

1. Design starts as the traditional modular approach: one defines module data encapsulation and import-export relationships
2. If behavior of some previously designed module should be corrected at runtime to fulfil system requirements, but module interface remains unchangeable, then the module is converted to a class straightforward: module global variables become instance fields and procedures make methods.
3. As a rule, aggregate data types (RECORD types in terms of Oberon-2) are used to represent entities from problem domain. If such a type requires polymorphic processing, it is immediately converted to class. Note that it is usually quite obvious whether a data type is worth using polymorphism: for the lack of OO features polymorphism is usually simulated with a tag field that is checked in implementations of data type operations. The rule is to avoid such implementation technique and use OO mechanisms instead.

The same reasoning concerns extending a RECORD type with new fields: in languages without OO support, it is implemented by casting pointers to different records from within data type operations.

Thus, according to rule 3, we use OO features just to implement data types in a natural way. In other words, *we distinguish the module notion from the data type notion* whereas in OOD they are both merged into the single class notion. We think this design technique may be successfully applied to a broad variety of projects and our own experience shows that it is sufficient to design a compiler construction framework meeting the language and target independence requirement. We suppose this is quite a representative large project. Several significant examples of object-oriented compiler construction are given here.

- The abstract syntax tree has to be designed in OO manner because there is a lot of polymorphic processing involving it: tree traversals for different purposes, control graph markup and analysis, polymorphic containers with HLIR objects for static analysis, IR conversions and so on. Besides, each tree object has specific instance fields for its own that can be implemented by inheritance in a natural way.
- FE and BE components configured on-the-fly in a multi-language retargetable compiler are worth implementing as instance objects of the FE and BE classes, according to rule 2.
- As shown in Fig. 1, the compile-time evaluation block is designed as a distinct component providing its service for both FE and BE. FE usually performs constant propagation on the syntax tree whereas BE requires the capability of constant evaluation when optimizing the SSA form of LLIR. Note that rules of compile-time evaluation vary for different languages. For instance, in Modula- 2/Oberon-2, once integer overflow has happened during constant evaluation, it has to be considered as a compile-time error whereas in Java, it just should be computed as a 2's complement even without issuing a warning. There are many other differences so the constant evaluation module is a good candidate for conversion to class by rule 2.
- Some other components of the XDS frameworks, for example object code and debugging information emitters (see Fig. 1), are also designed as instance objects of some class depending on the system configuration.

Summarizing this section we would like to emphasize that we have profited from the *motivated* usage of OO mechanisms in compiler design and development process.

4   The XDS Evolution

The primary goal of the XDS framework implementation was to bring high optimizing compiler solutions to Modula-2 and Oberon-2 (M2/O2) programmers. Nonetheless, from the very beginning XDS was designed with respect to software reuse so it was not limited to compilation of specific languages. Finished working at the M2/O2 compilers, we were challenged to apply the XDS technology to another language and Java was chosen as the next step. Initially, we supposed that the implementation of a Java compiler requires the development of the respective FE and introducing some minor modifications into native BE. However, we *considerably* underestimated the amount of work involved: many BE optimization algorithms proved to be language-dependent with respect to either correct code generation or performance. In fact, at the sacrifice of performance, we would be able to implement a Java to native code compiler with less efforts, but the usefulness of such a compiler would be doubtful. In this section we describe our experience of extending the XDS framework with the support for Java and implementation of new optimization techniques which are now available in all compilers built on the XDS framework.

4.1   Java Implementation Notes

Despite many similarities between Oberon-2 and Java, implementation of many language features had required significant efforts. It is debatable if they may be considered as advantages of the Oberon-2 facilities or not, but anyway we had to implement them carefully to meet the Java Language Specification.

Cyclic Import. Cyclic import is prohibited in Oberon-2, but not in Java, and it spoiled the separate compilation technique used in XDS compilers before. Apart from smart recompilation of the whole project, every single module was compiled by the simple two-step scheme: firstly, module is parsed to build the syntax tree and then BE is invoked to produce object code. In order to support separate compilation, XDS compiler creates a precompiled version of each module, so-called *symbol file*. All required information on the entities exported from the module is resided in its symbol file: exported types, procedures, variables, etc. Thus, if a module A, being compiled, imports a module B, the compiler just reads $B.sym$ file to complete the syntax tree for A with the entities from B. The acyclic import graph always guarantees that each module may be compiled separately. In Java, the same technique may be applied only if module does not use cyclic import, otherwise all the modules which constitute such a cycle of the import graph have to be compiled at the same time. Fortunately, the XDS architecture did not require significant reengineering, because the modified compilation scheme was easily implemented in the project system — the supervisor responsible for invocation of components as described in Section 3.

Address Arithmetic. Although Modula-2 does not encourage address arithmetic and unrestricted type casting, it still leaves programmer a loophole to write code in such a way. Just opposite to Modula-2, Java imposes "pure type" programming with no low-level operations. In addition, Java does not allow reference variables to point to values of primitive types. Those restrictions may have strong influence on the performance of generating code, especially with respect to pointer aliasing and register allocation algorithms. Thus, implementation of a common Java/Modula-2 BE would result in poorer Java code performance. We have modified the optimization algorithms that can benefit from the absence of address arithmetic.

Bytecode Input Files. It is known that Java applications and class libraries are distributed in the form of .*class* (JVM bytecode) files. This new deployment technology leaves the door open for further optimization of both Java applications and third-party libraries they use. It is a unique opportunity to achieve high degree of optimization because programming languages and deployment technologies used before did not allow libraries to be optimized. Really, C/C++ or Fortran libraries are usually distributed in some form of object code so compilers can not perform global analysis and optimization of entire application including libraries. In order to use that opportunity, Java compilers should be able to compile .*class* files just like they compile other source files. For that purpose, the JVM bytecode front-end component of the XDS framework has been developed. In addition, the XDS project system was extended in order to be able to process bytecode files.

Exception Handling. There are good reasons to implement exception handling for Java in a different way. First of all, according to the ISO Modula-2 standard [3], try-block must (syntactically) coincide with procedure block whereas in Java, it may comprehend an arbitrary set of operators [2]. It has a strong influence on optimization at presence of exceptions, especially with respect to register allocation. The matter is that Java exception handling makes program control graph complicated and requires a redesign of the BE algorithm determining life time of local variables. Otherwise it may result in poor performance or even incorrect generated code. Another point is intensive exploitation of exception handling in fine-grain Java methods. The simple *setjmp/longjmp* technique implemented for Modula-2 has some performance overhead for each try-block and being applied to Java makes performance twice as bad. Instead, we have implemented the other, so-called *frame-to-frame propagation* technique [16] with some modifications that results in no try-block overhead at all in the case of non-exceptional execution. The last solves the performance problem, but the cost is code size increasing, which may be unacceptable for Modula-2 — the language often used in software development for embedded systems.

Floating-Point Arithmetic. According to the IEEE 754/854 standard [17] to which Java complies, no floating-point (FP) operations cause an exception. For instance, 1/0 or even 0/0 are well-defined FP values. It may seem to be curious but they are even typed values, for instance there exists 0/0 of the *double* FP type. The matter is that IEEE 754/854 introduces two new binary-coded values: signed infinity and NaN (not a number). Both of them are supported in Java, so you may find a piece of Java code like this:

```
static final float negInfinity = -1.0/0;
```

As a consequence, some ordinary symbolic computations become incorrect, for instance $0 \cdot x = 0$ because $0 \cdot \infty = NaN$. The required modifications have been made in the constant evaluation component which is language-specific as described in Section 3. But the real Java challenge for the XDS BE optimizer was that the axiom

$$x \leq y \Leftrightarrow \neg(x > y)$$

is no longer valid. No, this is not the three-value logic, just result of comparison between any FP value and NaN is always false. We have modified the optimizer to make it IEEE 754/854 compliant. Thus, it is quite obvious that FP optimizations may not be implemented for Oberon-2 and Java in the same way. The last curious thing is a very suspicious IEEE 754 feature, signed zero(!). In fact, there exist both $+0$ and -0 as distinct binary-coded values such that $+0 = -0$. Only during Java implementation we finally understood what is the difference between them:

$$1/+0 = +\infty$$

$$1/-0 = -\infty$$

Heap Objects. A known disadvantage of Java applications is exhaustive dynamic memory consumption. For the lack of stack objects — class instances put on the stack frame, all objects have to be allocated on the heap by the *new* operator. Presence of Java class libraries makes the situation much worse because any service provided by some library class requires the allocation of its instance object. To overcome the drawback we have implemented a static analysis that allows the compiler to define the life time of dynamically allocated objects and allocate short living objects on the stack. Note that the optimization technique saves both memory and time resources, because stack allocation actually happens at compile-time rather than at run-time and the garbage collector does not have to care about such objects after they die.

Multi-threading. Java has built-in multi-threading support that allows instance methods to be synchronized if they operate on the same object simultaneously from different threads. Many library classes are designed with respect to a possible use in a multi-threaded environment, so even fine-grain methods have the *synchronized* specifier [2]. As a consequence, straightforward implementation of synchronization support results in a dramatic performance degradation. In order to ensure an acceptable performance level, we have designed a special technique, so-called *lightweight synchronization*, that engages the actual synchronization only if several threads actually want to operate on the same object. Note that the implementation of lightweight synchronization is only possible with support from native BE.

The main conclusion we have drawn after development of the Java to native code compiler is that *in order to achieve the high degree of code optimization, some parts of native BE have to be language-specific.*

4.2   Optimizations

It is widely acknowledged that code written in OO programming languages has some performance overhead due to dynamic method dispatch inherent to the languages. Being implemented by VMT (Virtual Method Table), virtual method invocation does not take much processor time itself but it hinders compiler to use the traditional technique of interprocedural optimizations, such as inlining. Type inference [13] is a static type analysis that allows compiler to replace virtual calls with direct ones safely and, thus, to improve performance considerably. The characteristic feature of type inference is so-called *polyvariant* analysis that typically performs repeated traversals of method control graph from within different calling contexts. Note that even with virtual calls replaced we still need to have the syntax trees of all methods at our disposal, for instance, to perform intermodule procedure inlining or analyze the life time of dynamically allocated objects as described above. For that purpose, we have implemented *syntax tree object persistency* allowing an arbitrary IR object graph to be saved to/restored from file. This technique resembles the slim binaries approach [9] used for dynamic compilation although we restrict its use to static code analysis and optimization only. Since real world Java applications use OO features extensively, the implementation of OO optimizations allow us to improve performance of Java code to a great extent. Benchmark results and other information related to the XDS Native Java project may be found at [19].

5   Conclusion

This paper has presented a technique of multi-language, multi-platform compiler construction. The technique has been used to integrate quite different programming languages such as Modula-2, Oberon-2 and Java into a single compiler construction framework. Our results refute the opinion that compiler should be specially designed for certain programming language in order to produce high performance code. The work has shown that language and platform independence and high performance do not contradict, although they require specific architectural decisions. The interesting direction for future works is to investigate a technique of seamless integration between Java and other languages, such as Modula-2, and also probably C. As a rule, some part of a typical Java application called *native methods* is written in other languages so Java programmers are compelled to use several tools including compilers in the development process. It would be interesting to design and implement an integrated compiler environment having all required means of Java application development.

References

1. T. Lindholm, F. Yellin, B. Joy, K. Walrath: *The Java Virtual Machine Specification.* Addison-Wesley, 1996
2. J. Gosling, B. Joy and G.Steele: *The Java Language Specification.* Addison-Wesley, Reading, 1996

3. *The Modula-2 language international standard.* ISO/EEC 10514, 1994
4. J. Holmes: *Object-Oriented Compiler Construction.* Prentice- Hall, 1995
5. *IBM Visual Age family products.*
   http://www-4.ibm.com/software/ad/
6. K J. Gough: *Bottom-up tree rewriting tool MBURG.* SIGPLAN Notices, Volume 31, Number 1, 1996
7. J. Dean, G. DeFouw et al: *Vortex: An Optimizing Compiler for Object-Oriented Languages.* In Proc. of OOPSLA'96, San Jose, CA, October, 1996
8. H. Saito, N. Stravrakos et al: *The Design of the PROMIS Compiler,* In Proc. 8th International Conference, Compiler Construction. Volume 1575 of LNCS, Springer-Verlag, 1999
9. M. Franz, Th. Kistler: *Slim binaries.* Technical report 96-24, Department of Information and Computer Science, UC Irvine, 1996
10. K J. Gough: *Multi-language, Multi-target Compiler Development: Evolution of the Gardens Point Compiler Project.* In Proc. Joint Modular Languages Conference, JMLC'97. Volume 1204 of LNCS, Springer-Verlag, 1997
11. H. Kienle: *j2s: A SUIF Java Compiler.* Technical Report TRCS98-18, Computer Science Department, University of California, Santa Barbara, 1998
12. A. Aho, R. Sethi, J. Ullman: *Compilers: Principles, Techniques and Tools.* Addison-Wesley, 1986
13. O. Agesen: *The Cartesian Product Algorithm: Simple and Precise Type Inference of Parametric Polymorphism.* In Proc. ECOOP'95, Aarhus, Denmark, 1995
14. V. Shelekhov, S. Kuksenko: *On the Practical Static Checker of Semantic Runtime Errors.* In Proc. of the 6th Asia Pacific Software Engineering Conference APSEC'99, Japan. IEEE Computer Society Press, 1999
15. N. Wirth, M. Reiser: *Programming in Oberon. Steps beyond Pascal and Modula.* Addison-Wesley, 1992
16. J. Lajoie: *Exception Handling — supporting the runtime mechanism,* C++ Report, Vol.6, No. 3, 1994.
17. *Pentium Pro Family Developer's Manual. Volume 2: Programmer's Reference Manual, Chapter 7, Floating-Point Unit,* Intel Corporation, 1996
18. *The InterView Source Code Browser.* User's Guide.
    http://www.excelsior-usa.com/intervew.html
19. *D. Leskov. XDS Native Java.* Whitepaper.
    http://www.excelsior-usa.com/jetwp.html

Structuring a Compiler with Active Objects

Patrik Reali

Institut für Computersysteme
ETH Zürich
CH-8092 Zürich
`reali@inf.ethz.ch`

Abstract. We present a concurrent compiler for Active Oberon built itself with active objects. We describe the experience made on parallelizing the Oberon compiler, in particular explaining how concurrency and synchronization are achieved by using active objects, and showing how we achieved ensured deadlock freedom. Based on the implementation, we discuss why we consider active objects beneficial for the implementation of software frameworks and where their limitations are.

1 Introduction

It is almost a tradition to write a compiler in the language it compiles. There are mainly two reasons for this: a compiler is usually a program complex enough to challenge a language and possibly find weaknesses to be removed. The other reason is that in the long range one wants to use only one programming language in a system.

In this paper we show the implementation of a compiler for the Active Oberon language written in Active Oberon. The compiler makes essential use of the concurrency facilities of language. Since active objects are a new concept in the language, we want to use them to gain experience and take advantage of the increased implementation and design potentials they offer. The recent availability of symmetric multiprocessor (SMP) machines at affordable prices is also a motivation to investigate the use of concurrency constructs in the language.

In Section 2 the main features of the language are shortly recapitulated; section 3 introduces the field of concurrent compilation and the previous projects that inspired this work; section 4 discusses the implementation details of the compiler, in particular the concurrent parser and the symbol table, which serves as a common shared data structure; section 5 discusses a new problem introduced in the compiler by the parallelism: deadlock; section 7 then draws the conclusions of this work.

2 Active Objects in Oberon

This section recapitulates the Active Oberon language [7], an extension of the Oberon language [16,18]; it is a homogeneous integrated concurrent programming language that embeds concurrency support in Oberon, by making just

J. Gutknecht and W. Weck (Eds.): JMLC 2000, LNCS 1897, pp. 250–262, 2000.
© Springer-Verlag Berlin Heidelberg 2000

minimal additions to the language and creating a unified framework for concurrent, object-oriented programming. This is done by introducing concurrent activities, protected access and guarded assertions in the language. Figure 1 give an example of an active object.

```
TYPE
  MovieProjector* = POINTER TO RECORD
    frame: ARRAY N OF Frame;  in, out: INTEGER;   window: Window;

    PROCEDURE GetFrame*(): Frame;
    VAR  f: Frame;
    BEGIN {EXCLUSIVE}
      PASSIVATE(in # out);
      f := frame[out];   out := (out+1) MOD N;
      RETURN f
    END GetFrame;

    PROCEDURE PutFrame*(f: Frame);
    BEGIN {EXCLUSIVE}
      PASSIVATE((in+1) MOD N # out);
      frame[in] := f;   in := (in+1) MOD N
    END PutFrame;

    PROCEDURE & Init(window: Window);
    BEGIN
      SELF.window := window;   in := 0;   out := 0
    END Init;

  BEGIN
    LOOP
      time := Timer.Time();
      DrawFrame(window, GetFrame());
      Timer.WaitUntil(time + FrameDelay)
    END
  END MovieProjector;
```

Fig. 1. Example of an Active Object

Compared to Oberon, record types have been upgraded in Active Oberon to have methods (also called type-bound procedures) and an own body. Syntactically, this is done by generalizing the scope concept and applying it to records as well. The methods have privileged access to the record fields, while the body (to be considered itself a method) represents the object's own activity, started asynchronously at the time of object instantiation. The object's activity corresponds to a thread of execution (the two terms will be used here as synonyms).

To protect the objects internal data structure against concurrent access, every object instance acts as a monitor. Methods using the EXCLUSIVE clause make use of protection by ensuring mutual exclusion in the sense that at most one protected method is allowed to be active in an object instance. A module is considered a singleton object instance, its procedures may also be protected.

Any thread of execution can be synchronized with a system or object state by using guarded boolean assertions in a PASSIVATE statement; the thread is preempted until the guarded condition becomes true. Such a thread is said to be *passivated*. It is noteworthy that the operating system itself is in charge of evaluating the conditions and eventually reschedule the passivated threads. When a thread is passivated in an object, it releases its mutual exclusion on that object as long as it remains passivated.

Some other minor adjustments in the language have been made to smoothly integrate the previous changes. First, a symbol named SELF is implicitly defined in every procedure scope, it refers to the current object the procedure is in. Second, it is possible to extend a pointer-based record (a structure with only dynamic instances), but the extending type must also allow only dynamic instances. Third, forward declarations are no longer needed, because they express only redundant information.

Our current system [10] has some implementation restrictions that had to be considered during this work: 1) reentrant locks are not allowed; 2) shared locks are not allowed; 3) global conditions to be passivated on are not allowed; 4) active modules are not allowed. We are conviced that these features should be removed from the language, because they are either redundant or conceptually wrong.

3   Building a Concurrent Compiler

3.1   Classical Compiler Architecture

There is a big experience in building compilers and many textbooks explain this task in detail [15,17,1] (just to cite some). Compilation is divided in phases like lexical analysis, parsing, semantical analysis, data allocation, register allocation, optimization and code emission that may be grouped into passes. The number of phases may vary, depending on the language parsed and the quality and expected complexity of the generated code. The number of passes is a strategic decision in building the compiler; merging all the phases in only one pass can make the compiler very fast, but on the other hand not every language can be parsed in one pass; also many optimizations require a separate pass. In general, more phases allow for more flexibility, but also increase the program complexity [9,15, 8,14].

Many compilers have been developed at ETH under the supervision or inspiration of N. Wirth [17]. All share the common goal of simplicity, compactness, efficiency and the use of single pass top-down parsing. OP2 [2], currently used in many ETH-Oberon systems, is an evolution that divides the compiler in a front-end and a back-end with a shared syntax tree to allow easy re-targeting and more aggressive code optimizations. We based our work on these previous implementations.

3.2 Previous Work

The first multiprocessor machines in the 1970 already challenged the compiler makers to investigate concurrent compilation.

C. Fischer [3] and R. Schell [12] where among the first to investigate the theoretical feasibility of concurrent compilation, by seeking for concurrent parsing techniques. Two approaches are possible: dividing compilation into concurrent phases that execute in a pipelined way or dividing the source code into pieces that are compiled concurrently.

While phase pipelining is limited in its speedup, because the compiler cannot be made faster than the slowest phase, splitting the code in concurrently compiled pieces can result in a good speedup [6,19].

The Toronto Modula-2+ compiler project [19] investigated the implementation of a parallel Modula-2+ compiler on a multiprocessor machine; in that compiler every scope is compiled concurrently and the symbol table is used to synchronize the concurrent parsers. Many of the results can be applied to our compiler on account of the similarities between Active Oberon and Modula-2+.

One obvious problem found in the Toronto compiler is the *doesn't know yet* problem (DKY). It is possible that a visible symbol exists in a scope but has not been processed by its parser and thus is not visible yet. In this case a parser requiring it *doesn't know yet* whether or not a valid declarations exists in the incomplete scope.

Seshadri et al. [13] propose two strategies to handle the problem. *DKY Avoidance* approaches the problem by ensuring that the scopes are complete before their symbols are used; *DKY Handling* treats it by inserting fix-ups to be patched at a later time or by making assumptions on the symbol. They assert that simplest solution is to use DKY Handling in the declaration part of a scope and DKY Avoidance in the implementation part. We will pursue this strategy in our compiler: a parser will be passivated until the desired symbol has been processed by another parser.

4 Implementation of the Compiler

4.1 Parser

The top-down recursive descent paring technology is used. Parsers can be very easily generated by systematically translating the productions into procedures.

Concurrent parsing is implemented by a generic active parser object whose activity is in charge of parsing the definition and implementation parts of a scope, the DeclSeq and StatSeq productions of the language. Figure 2 shows the generic Active Parser.

```
TYPE
  Parser = POINTER TO RECORD
    VAR  scope: Scope;  scanner: Scanner;
    ....
  BEGIN  (*active body*)
    DeclSeq;
    IF sym = begin THEN  scanner.Get(sym);  StatSeq  END
  END Parser;
```

Fig. 2. The generic Active Parser

For parsing modules, procedures and records we define extensions of the generic parser each, in charge of initializing the parser depending on the specific properties of the scope and positioning the scanner at the begin of the declaration section. Figure 3 shows the declaration of the procedure parser object: it prepares itself for the procedure parsing, while the rest of the scope is parsed by the inherited generic parser, which is the same for all the scopes.

```
TYPE
  ProcedureParser = POINTER TO RECORD (Parser)
    PROCEDURE & InitProcedure(scope: Scope;  scanner: Scanner);
    BEGIN SELF.scope := scope;  SELF.scanner := ForkScanner(scanner)
    END InitProcedure
  END ProcedureParser;
```

Fig. 3. The Module Parser

Every time a record or a procedure is encountered by a running, a new parser for it is generated and the scope contents are ignored by the running parser, delegating the parsing to the newly generated parser. Figure 4 shows the parsing of a procedure. Instead of calling directly DeclSeq and StatSeq a new parser is allocated.

4.2   Symbol Table

The symbol table uses three type hierarchies: Object, Struct and Scope. Object models symbols in the table such as variables and procedures; Struct models

```
PROCEDURE ProcDecl;
VAR  parser: ProcedureParser;  procscope: ProcedureScope;
BEGIN
  NEW(procscope);
  CheckToken(Procedure); IdentDef(procscope.name, mark);
  FormalParameters;  CheckToken(semicolon);
  NEW(parser, procscope, scanner);
  SkipScope;
END ProcDecl;
```

Fig. 4. The ProcDecl production implementation

structures such as basic types and composed data types, `Scope` contains a list of symbols and methods to manipulate it.

The symbol table is shared among all the concurrent parsers. It must be protected against concurrent access. We want to hide the concurrency details in the symbol table as much as possible, to minimize the knowledge (and so the troubles) that the synchronization requires.

Scopes are used like state machines. There are three relevant scope states: *filling* means that the scope is not complete and more symbols may still be added; *checking* that all the symbols have been inserted, and are being semantically checked; *complete* that the scope is ready to be used. The way scope operations work, depends on the state a scope is in.

Figure 5 shows the implementation of the `Scope` type. Every scope is owned by a parser; the owner is the only parser allowed to change the state of the scope.

`Insert` appends a symbol to the list. The owner is allowed to insert symbols only while the scope is in the *filling* state.

`Find` is in charge of handling the DKY problem in a way, that hides the details from the parser. In the *filling* state only the owner is allowed to access the scope, because it needs it for completing the definitions; if a symbol cannot be found in the current scope, a fix-up is created which will be resolved when the scope is complete: at this point it is still not possible to tell if the symbol is local to the scope or belongs to a parent scope or is not defined at all. Queries from other parsers are passivated as long as the scope is not complete.

The given implementation already carries out DKY Handling for declarations and DKY avoidance for implementation. The *filling* state correspond to the parsing of the implementations for the current scope: only the current parser is allowed to search for symbols in the scope; if no symbol is found, a fix-up is created because the scope doesn't know whether the symbol will be declared in the same scope or not; the search doesn't need to be propagated to the parent scope (yet) and the fix-up will be patched later (DKY handling). Other parsers, usually in the child scopes, may have to lookup symbols in the current scope too; they are preempted until the scope is complete, thus avoiding the handling of incomplete declarations (DKY avoidance). Note that only parsers in the im-

```
TYPE
  Scope* = POINTER TO RECORD
    VAR  parent: Scope; list: Object; state*: State;
      ....
      PROCEDURE Insert*(p: Object);
      BEGIN
        ASSERT(CalledByOwner() & (state = filling));
        Append(list, p)
      END Insert;

      PROCEDURE Find*(name: ARRAY OF CHAR): Object;
      VAR  p: Object;
      BEGIN
        (* code: DKY Avoidance *)
        IF ~CalledByOwner() THEN PASSIVATE(state = complete) END;

        p := Lookup(list, name);

        (* declarations: DKY Handling *)
        IF (p = NIL) & (state = filling) THEN p := <do fix-up> END;

        IF (p = NIL) & (parent # NIL) THEN p := parent.Find(name) END;
        RETURN p
      END Find;
  END Scope;
```

Fig. 5. The Scope type

plementation section are allowed to lookup symbols in parent scopes. A parser should not perform any semantic check or operations on the symbols during the *filling* state, because they may be a fix-up, thus carrying no information.

The Insert and Find procedures do not need access protection but only synchronization with the scope state, because the design ensures that only one parser will change the scope, and during that time (state = *filling*) no other parser is allowed to access the scope. Only the procedures to change a scope's state need to be protected. This is similar to a simplified readers-writers schema; once the only writer has terminated the writers are free to access the scope and no reader is allowed anymore.

Active Oberon removes forward declarations, hence forward references of symbols must be handled by the compiler. Instead of using a 2-pass parsing algorithm, we choose to take advantage of the concurrent parsers. Forward declarations are just a special case of DKY problem: they are symbols whose declaration come textually later than their use. As the compiler is already prepared to handle DKY cases, this is just one restriction less on the parsing, namely that declarations must come before their use.

4.3   Symbol Checking

The DKY handling for declarations is still not complete: when shall fix-ups be resolved? Only when the scope is complete, the semantic check of its symbols and related structures can be done. We show two approaches to solve this problem.

A first approach is to automatically check all the symbols in the scope after the declarations are completely parsed. A second approach is to do the fixing and checking on demand, when the symbol is first required. The *Find* procedure in the scope can intercept the access to an unchecked symbol and start its checking, which can trigger the checking of the associated structure, and return only after the symbol is completely checked.

To ensure the table consistency, access to the data must be restricted during the check operation. At first sight four lock granularities are possible: the whole symbol table, the scope, the whole hierarchy of the structure or the structure to be checked. Since using the first variant does check all the objects in a scope, it is appropriate to use the scope as lock granularity and forbid access to it during the whole operation. The implementation of the second variant (check on request) can get very complex, depending on the granularity chosen: locking single objects is not enough, since in case of circular structures (with pointers or ill-declared ones) two parsers may start checking two different parts of the structure hierarchy and then run into each other's locks creating a deadlock situation; locking the whole table is too coarse since only the current scope and its parents are visible and thus may be used for the check; locking the scope is exactly what is done in the first variant, with the disadvantage that later the scope should still be traversed for unchecked symbols[1].

Conceptually, the most appropriate lock granularity would be a type hierarchy (e.g. a type and its base types). A first problem is that we don't know a type hierarchy a priori, because we first have to check the single types of the hierarchy; we also don't have an object modeling a type hierarchy nor it is possible to model it (especially in the case of ill-defined structures[2]). Locking would be thus done by locking the single structures, but this is cannot be done as explained before.

We thus choose the first variant on account of its simplicity compared to the minimal efficiency improvement of the second variant at the cost of a much more complicated implementation.

A more subtle problem is caused by the built-in types of Oberon. These types are not defined as keywords; this allows the programmer to redefine their names with a new meanings. The consequence is evident: a parser must traverse all the parent scopes to decide if an INTEGER is the built-in integer type or has a user defined meaning. Since those types are the most heavily used ones and Oberon supports nesting of scopes, this can cause an efficiency problem. The parallel parsing doesn't help either, since a parser can't assume that the parent

---

[1] the fact that a symbol is never used doesn't make its declaration correct

[2] Somebody could object that we don't have to accept ill-defined types; to be able to detect them, the types must first be checked and thus locked. This is a chicken-egg problem.

scopes have already been checked; it may have to wait for their conclusion before being able to access the build-in types, incurring in an even longer delay. We thus implemented the built-in type's names as reserved words and hence do not allow their redefinition. This doesn't change the expressiveness of the language, because type aliasing is always possible. This did not cause any problem, since no single module in the whole Native Oberon release does redefine a basic type.

5   Deadlock Avoidance

Using concurrent processes can create deadlock situations: the parsers may depend on each other for the parsing and thus for making the symbols in their scope available. Whenever a circular dependency between parsers exists, deadlock cannot be excluded.

As described in the previous sections, every scope goes through three stages: filling, checking, complete. The only synchronization in the whole compiler is done in the symbol table, in the **Find** procedure, thus this is the only place where a deadlock situation may occur. The following two rules describe how Find (see Figure 5) works: 1) lookups during the filling and checking phase are allowed only for the parser owning the scope, other parsers lookups' are passivated until the scope reaches the complete state; 2) lookups during the filling phase are local to the scope, otherwise they may be propagated to the parent scopes.

We assume that every parser will always lookup symbols in the own or in a parent scope, never in a child one. To make this assumption hold, we aggregate (conceptually is enough) the interface information of every symbol to the parent scope where the symbol itself is declared. For procedures this means the formal parameters, for records all the fields and methods[3]

We first analyze the case of the parser for the top scope (the one that has no parent scope): in the filling state, Find always terminates, because a symbol is either found or a fix-up for it is created and returned; in the checking and complete states the lookup also always terminates: being the owner of the scope, the thread doesn't get preempted and being the top scope, the search is not propagated to a parent scope, thus always terminating. Since Find always terminates, the parser can process the declarations, check them and eventually reach the complete state.

In the generic case, a scope has a finite number of parent scopes. In the filling state, the lookup always terminates as in the top scope case; in the checking and complete state, when the object is not locally declared, the lookup may have to be done in the parent scopes. Since the top scope eventually reaches the complete state, its children will be allowed to search through it, hence allowing them to eventually reach the complete state themselves. Of course, a scope using only local symbols will reach the complete state without having to wait for the parent scope to be completed. It is possible to inductively show that every scope in the hierarchy will eventually reach the complete state, and thus that the search operation terminates.

---

[3] In Oberon, record fields and methods are always visible in the whole module

6   Discussion

6.1   Data Structures in the Compiler

Using type extension as proposed in [5,4] instead of records with many different meanings made the compiler not only safer but also simpler to understand
and maintain. Invariants are hard-coded in the data structure, and inconsistent
structures can mostly be detected when created and not when first used. We
thus go one step further in using the language facilities to have invariants automatically tested. Using all the language facilities to ensure program correctness
is very important and saves time with debugging. We can only agree with E.
Raymond's quote [11] (paraphrasing F. Brooks): "Smart data structures and
dumb code works a lot better than the other way around".

On the other hand, having a separate type for every kind of object makes
the source code longer, while the program becomes slightly shorter, because less
invariants must be explicitly checked. It's noteworthy that the data structures
don't affect the size of the compiled code and that memory usage is reduced
because the structures are smaller. This also simplifies program documentation,
because the data structures are more expressive and don't need to be interpreted
in terms of a mode field.

We also planned to protect our structures with information hiding, but finally
we did not. To execute efficiently, a compiler needs all the possible informati-
ons available: hiding information would make the compiler slower, because the
same information would have to be recomputed many times or accessed through
procedure calls. On the other hand we realized that there is no need to access
the information through methods: the compiler usually adds information, but
never changes it, thus the data must be only checked when created. Read-only
export of the data in this case would be enough to ensure that the invariant,
once established, will never be broken, while giving a fast and efficient access to
the data. Hence we think that a read-only export option is a necessary addition
to the language.

6.2   Concurrency in the Compiler

We used an active object to model a generic concurrent parser. Making parsing parallel was rather simple and required just to encapsulate all the parsing
procedures and the global variables in the parser object, thus making them a
state of every single parser. Our concurrent parser is very similar to the usual
1-pass parser, but forks a new parser when a scope is encountered. The synchronization is almost completely hidden in the symbol table, thus very local and
simple to understand. Nevertheless it makes the handling of the symbol table
more complex. Deadlock freedom becomes a new complex issue in the compiler.

Concurrent parsing elegantly allows to handle forward references in the implementation section by using synchronization instead of a second parsing pass.
It is rather interesting that this is done by removing an artificial sequentializa-

tion, thus in fact by removing a restriction in the code[4] and an anomaly in the scope rules: in Oberon an identifier can have two meanings in the same scope, depending on the position it is defined:

```
TYPE  BaseDesc = RECORD .... END;
PROCEDURE P;
  TYPE
    Base1 = POINTER TO BaseDesc;
    BaseDesc = ARRAY 5 OF INTEGER;
    Base2 = POINTER TO BaseDesc;
    ....
END P
```

In the previous piece of code, BaseDesc has two meanings in procedure P. This contrast with of the Oberon language report: *"No identifier may denote more than one object within a given scope (i.e. no identifier may be declared twice in a block"* (§4.1). By making the visibility only scope-based, BaseDesc becomes unequivocal in the scope of P.

6.3   Using Active Objects

In our work, we found the protection of objects amazingly simple to use and understand. It is very helpful to declare whole procedures as exclusive and it makes the code readable, because the protected regions can be clearly identified.

Using active objects is simple, as long as the granularity needed to solve the problem is the same as the granularity of the objects; protection and synchronization become straightforward. It is thus convenient to consider the protection granularity when modeling the data structures. In the compiler, the semantic check of types in the symbol table (sec. 4.3) is a good example: granularities ensuring a correct program are table, scope and type-hierarchy granularity. A finer granularity has less collision chances and is thus more efficient. In our design is not possible to lock a type-hierarchy, because we don't have a data structure modeling it, we thus use the scope granularity.

The use of guarded assertions (PASSIVATE) is a step toward better abstract design facilities. A conventional implementation using signals has to disclose its internal state to other threads in order to allow them to decide if and when they should send the signal. Of course the other threads have to know that a signal has to be sent and have to be willing to do the favor. This again is an invariant enforced solely in the documentation! Especially when using software frameworks, it is easy to forget these invariants. Using guarded assertions this potential source of errors is removed, because the system is in charge of restarting passivated threads whenever the condition is established, thus enforcing the invariant automatically without requiring external intervention or even knowledge. We can thus assert that conditional guarded assertions allow an improved

---

[4] the check that a declaration comes before its use

information hiding and safer synchronization for concurrent programs, and that the architecture scales up well in software frameworks.

Proving deadlock freedom of a program is still a burden left to the implementor and the only help that active objects can give, is by making the programs simpler to understand and thus simpler to reason about. In this project we used the hierarchical ordering of the threads to prove that the program is structurally deadlock free.

7 Conclusions

In this paper we reported the experiences made using active objects to implement a concurrent compiler. A concurrent parsing technique allows us to parse forward references by using a slightly modified recursive descent parser technology. The complexity of the synchronization is almost completely hidden in the symbol table.

With this project we challenged Active Oberon's usability. Active objects are a valuable tool that simplifies the implementation of concurrent programs. Data protection from concurrent access is remarkably simple when the locking granularity is the same as that of the designed structure; the synchronization of threads by means of guarded assertions is very elegant and safe. Frameworks can benefit from it, because it minimizes the needed knowledge of the whole framework and ensures a safe resumption of passivated threads without user intervention.

References

1. A. W. Appel. *Modern Compiler Implementation In Java, basic techniques*. Cambridge University Press, 1997.
2. R. Crelier. OP2: A portable oberon compiler (vergriffen). Technical Report 1990TR-125, Swiss Federal Institute of Technology, Zurich, February, 1990.
3. C. N. Fischer. *On parsing Context-Free Languages in Parallel Environments*. PhD thesis, Department of Computer Science, Cornell University, 1975.
4. P. Fröhlich. Projekt froderon: Zur weiteren entwicklung der programmiersprache oberon-2. Master's thesis, Fachhochschule München, 1997.
5. R. Griesemer. *A Programming Language for Vector Computers*. PhD thesis, ETH Zürich, 1993.
6. T. Gross, A. Zobel, and M. Zolg. Parallel compilation for a parallel machine. *ACM SIGPLAN Notices*, 24(7):91–100, July 1989.
7. J. Gutknecht. Do the fish really need remote control? A proposal for self-active objects in oberon. In *Proc. of Joint Modular Languages Conference (JMLC)*. LNCS 1024, Linz, Austria, March 1997. Springer Verlag.
8. Jürg Gutknecht. One-pass compilation at its limits — A Modula-2 compiler for the Xerox Dragon computer. *Software Practice and Experience*, 17(7):469–484, July 1987.
9. D. E. Knuth. A history of writing compilers. *Computers and Automation*, 11(12):8–14, 1962.

10. P. Muller. A multiprocessor kernel for active object-based systems. In *Proc. of Joint Modular Languages Conference (JMLC2000)*, Zürich, Switzerland, September 2000. Springer Verlag.

11. Eric S. Raymond. *The Cathedral & the Bazaar: Musings on Linux and Open Source by an Accidental Revolutionary.* O'Reilly & Associates, Inc., 1999.

12. R. M. Schell, Jr. *Methods for Constructing Parallel Compilers For Use in a Multiprocessor Environment.* PhD thesis, University Of Illinois at Urbana-Champaign, 1979.

13. V. Seshadri, S. Weber, D. B. Wortman, C. P. Yu, and I. Small. Semantic analysis in a concurrent compiler. In *Proceedings of the SIGPLAN '88 Conference on Programming Language Design and Implementation*, pages 233–240, 1988.

14. J. C. Sheperd. Why a two pass front end? *SIGPLAN Notices*, 26(3):88–94, March 1991.

15. Aho; Sethi; Ullman. *Compilers; Principles, Techniques and Tools.* Addison-Wesley, 1986.

16. N. Wirth. The programming language oberon. *Software Practice and Experience*, 18(7):671–690, July 1988.

17. N. Wirth. *Compiler Construction.* Addison-Wesley, 1996.

18. N. Wirth and M. Reiser. *Programming in Oberon - Steps Beyond Pascal and Modula.* Addison-Wesley, first edition, 1992.

19. D. Wortman and M. Junkin. Concurrent compiler for Modula-2+. *ACM SIGPLAN Notices*, 27(7):68–81, 1992.

A Multiprocessor Kernel for Active Object-Based Systems

Pieter Muller

Institut für Computersysteme, ETH Zürich, CH-8092 Zürich

Abstract. A new operating system kernel is being developed based on the Active Oberon language. The kernel is an evolution of the Oberon system and inherits several concepts from it. It is intended to be more generally applicable than Oberon, also in server systems and dedicated systems. The design is based on active objects, which are used to structure concurrent kernel services in an object-oriented way. Applications running on the kernel are also based on active objects. The first application is a version of the Native Oberon operating system that runs as an active object. The kernel is designed for uniprocessors and multiprocessors and it is being implemented for Intel x86-architecture multiprocessor machines.

1 Introduction

The original Oberon operating system[25] was designed for the single-user Ceres workstation developed at the ETH Zürich. It is a lean and transparent language-based system with integrated garbage collection. The system is modular, object-oriented and extensible by end-users.

The ETH Oberon system has evolved with the addition of persistent object support[10], providing the basis for a graphical user interface component framework[16].

Native Oberon[19] is the latest incarnation of the operating system and currently runs on Intel x86-architecture personal computers and DEC DNARD network computers[5] with the Intel StrongARM processor. It is used as a research and teaching vehicle and has also been applied in industrial embedded control systems[21]. Many Oberon applications are available[9].

1.1 Active Objects

The Oberon system uses a simple cooperative multitasking model called *single-process multitasking*. Background tasks are broken up into discrete procedural steps that are executed by the system's main loop while it is otherwise idle. This controversial design decision was justified by its simplifying effects, and the relatively few background tasks required in an isolated single-user system. Although sufficient for the original system's design goals, this model is too restrictive for more general applications like servers, and can not be used for multiprocessors.

In an active object-based system, tasks are executed by *active objects*. Like normal objects, they encapsulate data and have methods for manipulating the

J. Gutknecht and W. Weck (Eds.): JMLC 2000, LNCS 1897, pp. 263–277, 2000.
© Springer-Verlag Berlin Heidelberg 2000

data. In addition, they also have an intrinsic activity, which can call other objects and synchronize with them.

The Active Oberon language[11] is an extension of the Oberon language[23] that supports *active objects* directly. This is done by upgrading record types with an optional body and methods. The body looks like a module body declared inside a record. Methods are procedures declared inside a record. The record scope extends over the body and methods.

An active object is programmed as a pointer to a record, similar to how normal objects are programmed in Oberon. The difference is that the body of an Active Oberon record executes in its own thread, and exclusive methods can be used to coordinate access to shared data encapsulated by an object.

Exclusive methods are declared with an annotation at the beginning of the method, to denote that the caller obtains exclusive access to the object instance. In other words, the object acts as a monitor.

When the body of an active object exits, its thread ceases to exist and the object becomes passive. It can still be used like a normal object, and its methods can still be called by other active objects. It continues to exist until there are no references left to it, and then it is deallocated by the garbage collector.

To synchronize access to an active or passive object by different threads, a special statement is used, taking a boolean guard expression as parameter. The calling object is passivated until the expression becomes true. The guard expression references the variables of the enclosing object. The enclosing method is normally declared exclusive, to ensure that the condition remains true when the calling object is activated again. Typically the variables of the object are only modified inside its own exclusive methods.

The run-time system is responsible for evaluating the guard expressions periodically and re-activating the relevant object.

For an example of an Active Oberon program, see [20].

1.2   Overview

The author is developing a multiprocessor operating system kernel based on Active Oberon – taking the Oberon language and system into the realm of high-performance workstations and servers. The tenets of Oberon are kept in mind: leanness, clarity, modularity and efficiency. The new kernel, called *Aos*, provides an active object infrastructure for building operating systems and concurrent applications. It is attempted to achieve a high level of integration with the original Oberon system, which runs as an application on the kernel.

Figure 1 shows the overall structure of a system based on the new kernel. The bottom layer of the kernel, written mostly in Oberon, provides run-time support for the Active Oberon language. This includes concurrency and active object management. Above this layer, everything is programmed in Active Oberon.

The top layer provides further support for active object-based applications. This includes abstractions for shared devices and services. The device abstractions shield the services and applications from the hardware details. The services shield the applications from details of the device abstractions.

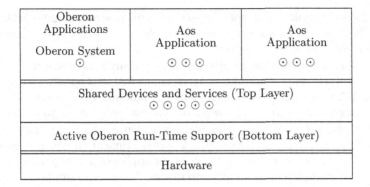

Fig. 1. Structure of a system based on the Aos kernel ($\odot$ = active object)

The kernel is defined as the part of the system common to all possible applications on a specific computer configuration. Possible target configurations include general-purpose workstations, personal computers and servers, but also thin-client network computers and embedded systems. The Aos kernel promises to be easy to adapt to different configurations and port to new machines, because of its layered modular design.

Section 2 describes how active objects are used as a structuring mechanism and section 3 describes the kernel design in more detail. Section 4 highlights some multiprocessor implementation details and presents preliminary results. Related work is referenced in section 5 and concluding remarks are presented in section 6.

2   Structuring Systems Using Active Objects

Active objects are used as a structuring mechanism for concurrency in Aos.

2.1   Processes, Threads, and Active Objects

Orthodox operating systems, like Unix and Windows NT, typically provide two concepts for modeling concurrency: heavy-weight processes with separate address spaces, as well as light-weight processes sharing the same address space (threads). Heavy-weight processes are used to isolate the system and other applications from potentially faulty applications, and as a unit for managing the loading and unloading of programs from memory. Threads are used to structure applications better and improve performance.

In Aos, only one concept is provided to model concurrency: active objects. As in Oberon, the module is used as a loading and program unit.

A language-based system like Aos can use a single shared address space. This simplifies the design and implementation and improves efficiency, because there is no need to create, manage and destroy separate address spaces.

High-level language concepts like strong typing, array bounds checking, garbage collection and nil-pointer reference checking are used to catch faults gracefully and preserve system integrity.

In addition, Oberon encapsulates the potentially unsafe features of the language (like type casting and direct memory access) in a special pseudo-module called SYSTEM. This allows potentially unsafe modules to be identified easily.

Therefore there is no need for separate address spaces in an Aos-based system.

A fine-grained active object takes the role that is usually played by a thread in an orthodox system. For example, a server application can generate a new active object to serve a client request, or an application can generate an active object to perform a long-running computation in the background.

A coarse-grained active object is closer to a process in an orthodox system. For example, a complete single-process system like Oberon can be encapsulated in an active object.

2.2 Modules

Popular object-oriented languages like C++ and Java neglect the role of modules and try to replace them with object classes. In doing so, they deprive the system designer of an important structuring tool.

An Oberon module is a container of procedures, types and variables. Modules are usually used to group closely related objects or functions together with a well-defined interface. The interface is defined by exporting only selected identifiers from the module, hiding irrelevant implementation details. This gives the system designer complete control over the granularity of a module.

A module can import required functionality that is exported from other modules. The system structure can be expressed as a directed import graph showing module interdependencies. Oberon does not allow cyclic import, therefore the module graph is hierarchically ordered.

Modules are loaded into memory dynamically when they are required and because of the hierarchical structure they can also be unloaded easily when no longer in use. This allows flexible configuration of a system, as functional units can be loaded and unloaded as required. In a way, this is similar to how processes are used in orthodox systems, but more structured. For example, in Unix, a special process is responsible for starting other network server processes when client requests arrive for them. When client requests have not arrived for some time, a server process can exit again, freeing resources for other uses. In Aos, the same functionality can be implemented by dynamically loading and unloading server modules, without the overhead of creating a new heavy-weight process.

Like Oberon, Aos is extensible, meaning that new modules re-using existing functionality can be created at any time and loaded into an existing system. With type extension, it is also possible to build heterogeneous data structures that can be extended at any time.

The application programmer interface (API) of a modular system consists of the interfaces of system modules, which are accessed by normal procedure calls, not supervisor calls. In contrast with orthodox systems, there is no overhead of a cross-address-space supervisor call, and all interfaces are strongly type-checked.

Modules are also an important tool for building portable systems, because a module interface can be used to abstract away details of a specific machine or environment. Different implementations of the same module interface can be created for different environments. For example, the Native Oberon system was ported to Linux by replacing a handful of low-level modules with implementations based on Linux system calls and an X Window library.

By replacing selected module implementations, the system can also be optimized for different environments. For example, the the bottom layer of the Aos kernel can be replaced by a streamlined implementation for uniprocessors.

2.3   Active Objects as Resource Managers

An operating system is primarily responsible for managing the resources of a computer system. A resource can be cleanly modeled as an object. In a system with concurrency, access to a shared resource object has to be controlled to protect its integrity.

Active objects can be used to elegantly model shared resources[4]. The data of a resource are encapsulated in the object, and access to the resource is made via protected methods that allow only exclusive access to the data. The synchronization ability of an active object is used to coordinate concurrent access to a shared resource.

An example of a shared resource modeled using an active object is the cache object provided by the abstract block device module of the Aos kernel. The cache object manages a set of fixed-size buffers for a block device like a hard disk. Its functionality is similar to the Unix System V buffer cache[1].

The cache object (see interface definition below) has two main methods: **Acquire** and **Release**, both of which are given exclusive access to the cache's internal data structures (a hash table of all buffers and a least-recently-used list of buffers). Typically a file system based on such a block device will acquire (lock) a buffer from the cache, read or modify it, optionally write it back, and release (unlock) it again. The cache keeps track whether the buffer is dirty (has been modified), and will write all dirty buffers to disk on request (*Synchronize* method). The cache has a body which periodically performs this operation.

```
TYPE
  Cache = POINTER TO RECORD
    PROCEDURE Acquire(dev: Device; block: BlockID; VAR buf: Buffer; VAR valid: BOOLEAN);
    PROCEDURE Release(buf: Buffer; modified, written: BOOLEAN);
    PROCEDURE Synchronize;
  END;
```

The **Acquire** method acquires a buffer for a specific block on a specific device. If the block is already in the cache, its buffer is locked and returned. Otherwise the cache finds an unlocked non-dirty buffer, locks and returns it. There are two situations where this method uses the synchronization statement (called **PASSIVATE**) to synchronize with another active object: when the required buffer is locked it waits for it to be unlocked, and when no non-dirty buffers are available it waits for one to become available. Both these conditions are efficiently expressed in the code as boolean expressions consisting of a simple comparison operation on a basic Oberon type.

The **Release** method releases a buffer after it has been used. The buffer is unlocked and added to the end of the least-recently-used list. This list is used to select the least-recently modified buffer when a buffer has to be re-used.

Several other shared resources in the Aos kernel are modeled using active objects, for example: disk volumes, file directories, files and network connections.

Devices are also shared resources and are therefore modeled using active objects – called *driver objects*. A driver object presents methods that change the state of the underlying device and program it to perform the requested operations. These methods are normally declared exclusive, to serialize access to the underlying device registers. Interrupting devices have to be handled specially (see sec. 3.6).

3   Design of the Aos Kernel

The design of the Aos kernel facilitates uniprocessor and multiprocessor implementations.

3.1   Two-Tier Kernel Structure

As shown in fig. 1, the kernel consists of two layers. The bottom layer provides the run-time environment for the Active Oberon language. It manages the basic resources of the computer: processors and memory, and creates the active object abstraction. It is written in Oberon, with some low-level procedures written using the built-in assembler. This part of the kernel uses only those facets of the language that do not require active object run-time support. The interface it provides to the higher layer is relatively independent of the machine architecture, but its implementation is closely tied to the specific machine architecture.

In multiprocessor implementations of the kernel, spin-locks are used to protect the data structures of the run-time environment from simultaneous update by different processors. These locks are fine-grained, meaning that they are intended to be held only for relatively short periods of time.

The top layer of the kernel provides abstractions for the peripheral devices, and allows them to be shared by concurrent applications. It also builds on these abstractions to provide higher-level shared services like file systems, networking and windowing. This part of the kernel is written in the full Active Oberon language, and uses active objects extensively to model resources and services. It builds on the synchronization facilities provided by the bottom layer. Fine-grained locks are not used here, making the top layer implementation portable to uniprocessor machines.

The configuration of the top layer is intended to be very flexible. Depending on the actual system configuration, specific modules can be included or left out here. For example, on a disk-less network computer no disk device driver module would be used, and the file system could be network-based. In an industrial control application, the networking subsystem might be left out and the file system based on non-volatile RAM. Or in an embedded system the file system and module loader could be left out and all the system modules statically linked together.

3.2   Module Structure

The kernel consists of a hierarchy of modules, with the two layers cleanly separated (see fig. 2). The modules of the bottom layer and their basic functions are (from bottom to top):

AosProcessor* Defines atomic operations, initialization and the processor ID function used to manage per-processor data.

AosLocks Defines fine-grained spin-locks to protect kernel data structures.

AosMemory* Manages the virtual address space, thread stacks and physical memory access for device drivers.

AosStorage Implements the heap, garbage collector and run-time support for the NEW standard procedure call in Oberon.

AosInterrupts* Contains interrupt controller functions and low-level glue code to convert interrupts into Oberon procedure calls.

AosModules* Defines the module abstract data type and the module loader algorithm.

AosTrap Handles processor exceptions.

AosActive* Provides run-time support for active objects, scheduling and condition evaluation.

AosSMP Provides support for the multiprocessor architecture.

AosTicks* Provides a periodic timer facility.

Modules marked with an asterisk define standard interfaces for higher-level modules (bold outline in fig. 2), while the others are mainly implementation-specific.

The acyclic module import structure is used to avoid deadlock in the bottom layer, as in THE[6]. Typically one fine-grained lock is declared per module, and they are ordered according to their level in the module hierarchy. When multiple locks are acquired, this is always done in order, and they are released in the opposite order. As most procedure calls are downward in the module hierarchy, it is relatively simple to show that deadlock can not occur. Upcalls have to be considered specially, and are avoided as far as possible.

To make the kernel adaptable to different configurations a plug-in architecture is used. For example, the module loader does not decode an object file itself, but provides a plug-in interface for a loader module that lives in a higher-level module. This allows different object file formats to be supported, and increases flexibility for booting the system.

Plug-ins are extensively used in the top layer, which has a highly flexible configuration (see sec. 3.1). Typically a service is abstractly defined in a plug-in

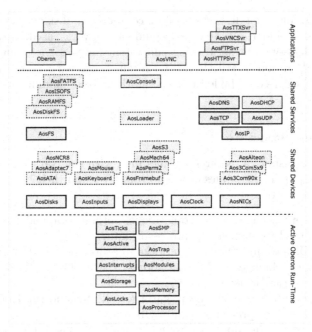

Fig. 2. Aos system module structure (kernel with applications)

base module (e.g., AosFS defines file services). Users of the service import the base module. Implementors of a service (shown with dotted outlines in fig. 2) also import the base module, and register themselves there.

The following modules are typical for the top layer:

AosDisks* Creates an abstraction for disk driver objects and serves as plug-in base for disk drivers.

AosInputs* Creates an abstraction for user-interface input devices.

AosDisplays* Similar to AosDisks, for display drivers.

AosClock* Real-time clock device driver.

AosNICs* Similar to AosDisks, for network interface controllers.

AosATA, AosFramebuf, Aos3Com90x, etc. Plug-in driver modules.

AosFS* Defines abstract file systems and a file system plug-in framework.

AosDiskFS A concrete file system implementation on AosFS and AosDisks.

AosIP, AosTCP, etc. An implementation of TCP/IP on AosNICs.

AosLoader A module loader plug-in for the standard Oberon object file format.

AosConsole A configuration module tying a specific kernel configuration together. Responsible for dynamically loading the rest of the system.

3.3   Active Oberon Run-Time Support

The Active Oberon run-time support is provided by a few procedures in the bottom layer. The compiler generates calls to the relevant kernel procedures when compiling Active Oberon code.

For example, a call to the standard procedure NEW(p), where p is a pointer to a record, is compiled into the following call:

```
AosStorage.NewRec(p, tag)
```

The tag parameter is a pointer to the type descriptor of the record. If p were a record with exclusive methods and a record body, the following calls would be generated instead:

```
AosStorage.NewProtRec(p, tag)
AosActive.NewThread(p, body, flags)
```

The first call allows the kernel to allocate the additional fields required to support object locking. The second call creates a thread to execute the specified body. The flags parameter contains annotations specified on the active object body, e.g., whether the body should be restarted when an exception occurs during its execution, and its priority. The allocation and thread creation calls are separated so that the compiler can also generate a call to the initializer of the active object between them. Thread termination is handled by setting up its stack so that a normal procedure return from the body will jump to the kernel's thread termination procedure.

Kernel calls are also generated when an exclusive method is entered and exited or when the PASSIVATE synchronization statement is used:

```
AosActive.Lock(p)
AosActive.Passivate(p, cond, fp)
AosActive.Unlock(p)
```

The cond parameter specifies a procedure that contains the boolean guard condition. This procedure can be periodically called by the run-time environment to re-evaluate the guard condition. The fp parameter is the frame pointer value of the procedure containing the statement. This is used by the kernel when calling the guard procedure.

3.4   Context Switching

The kernel supports two kinds of context switch: synchronous and asynchronous. A synchronous switch occurs when an active object calls an exclusive method of another active object that is currently locked, or fails the guard expression of a PASSIVATE statement. An asynchronous switch happens when an interrupt occurs (e.g., when a thread's time-slice expires).

Synchronous switches are always made at well-defined places in the generated code, so in cooperation with the compiler, only a reduced number of registers have to be saved by the kernel. Asynchronous switches can happen anywhere, so all registers have to be saved.

The compiler compiles a guard expression as a separate procedure returning a boolean result. This means that the context switch between the evaluation of different conditions is synchronous, and therefore light-weight. In this case there is no need to update the currently running thread, which makes this switch even faster than the normal synchronous case[8].

The execution of a thread is not bound to a specific processor. That means a thread can be suspended on one processor and later resumed on another.

At least three levels of priority are envisioned: interrupt, interactive and background. Interrupt priority is the highest and is intended for device-driver objects. Interrupt-priority threads are not preemptable, for efficient implementation. Interactive priority is the normal level, and background is intended for low-priority tasks.

3.5 Condition Evaluation

Every active object has two queues associated with it: a lock wait queue and a condition wait queue. The former is used to store calling active objects that are waiting on the lock of the object. The latter is used to store calling active objects that are waiting on a guard condition to become true in the object. In addition the object has a lock bit which records whether it is currently locked.

When the guard expression of a PASSIVATE statement evaluates to false, the calling object is suspended and added to the condition wait queue associated with the object containing the statement. If the caller was holding a lock on the object (the normal case), the lock is transferred atomically to another object waiting it, and that object is made ready to run. If no other objects are waiting, the lock is released.

When an exclusive method exits, the objects waiting in the condition queue of the containing object are examined to see if their conditions have become true. The conditions are evaluated in FIFO order, until the first true condition is found. In this case the lock is atomically transferred to the waiting object, and it is readied to run. If the lock is still free after evaluating the conditions, the lock wait queue of the object is examined, and if non-empty, the lock is transferred atomically to the first object waiting for it, which is subsequently readied. Note that the object is still locked while the conditions are being evaluated, providing protection for the guard expression.

3.6 Handling Asynchronous Events

Interrupt-driven devices present a special problem, because the interrupts they generate are asynchronous events. A driver object must act on these interrupts, but without interfering with the user calls to its methods. Therefore, an interrupt is modeled as an exclusive method call, similar to a user call. In this way the driver object simply has to react to a stream of atomic method calls: from the user on the one side and the device on the other side.

The bottom layer of the kernel is responsible for initiating an interrupt method call on behalf of a device. This is done by allocating one special active object – called a *device object* – in the kernel for every enabled interrupt. A kernel call is provided to associate a driver object with a specific interrupt, and its device object. When an interrupt occurs, it is masked temporarily and the associated device object is scheduled by a special low-overhead version of the scheduler. When this object's body runs it performs the interrupt method call on the driver object. This call is usually an exclusive method, and can therefore synchronize with other method calls of the driver object. Once the call returns, the interrupt is unmasked again and the device object is passivated.

A similar mechanism is used to efficiently implement timeouts, which are also asynchronous events. A driver object can arrange to have a special method called whenever a specified amount of time has passed. Only one timing event may be set per driver object, but the time interval can be changed at any time, and the timing event can also be cancelled.

An active object in the kernel – the *timer object* – keeps track of all timing events in a sorted list. It reacts on a periodic timer interrupt, and when the next event is due, the associated driver object's timeout method is called.

4   Multiprocessor Kernel Implementation

The first implementation of the Aos kernel is based on the Intel symmetric multiprocessor architecture[13]. This widely-used architecture supports shared-memory multiprocessor machines with up to 16 x86-based processors[14]. Every processor has an advanced programmable interrupt controller (APIC) unit, which is used to generate interprocessor interrupts and provides other support functions like booting secondary processors. Symmetric interrupt routing is supported in conjunction with a separate IOAPIC unit. The APIC unit is accessed like a memory-mapped I/O device.

The `Acquire` and `Release` operations on spin-locks are implemented in assembler using atomic instructions.

In the cases where per-processor data are required, a static array is declared, with one element per processor. These arrays are indexed with an APIC-supported function that returns a unique ID on every processor.

Under the Intel specification, the machine boots up with just one active processor. This processor executes the boot loader and loads the statically linked part of the Aos kernel. It switches to 32-bit protected mode, and starts to execute the module initialization code. The details of booting other processors are handled in the AosSMP and AosProcessor modules. A standard protocol exists for discovering the machine configuration. The initial processor then sends interprocessor interrupts to the other processors to boot them. Initially the other processors start up in 16-bit real mode, and have to switch themselves to 32-bit protected mode.

The current implementation is still under development. The bottom layer does not yet support priorities or time-slicing. Some of the modules envisioned for the top layer are currently only running as prototypes on Native Oberon.

However, the implementation already has enough functionality to support a version of the Native Oberon system with Gadgets running in a single active object, in parallel with other active objects. The system is in use as a development environment.

Preliminary results of some micro-benchmarks on the implementation are shown in table 1. The tests were run on a Dell OptiPlex GXpro machine with dual Pentium-Pro 180MHz processors. All tests were executed in single-processor and dual-processor mode, and repeated with 1 to 4 active objects. Every test was also repeated with a varying amount of other work between the method calls, to generate a more realistic workload. The results extrapolated from those tests correlate with the figures shown here.

Table 1. Preliminary Aos kernel performance figures (times in μs)

Benchmark	Single-processor				Dual-processor			
	1	2	3	4	1	2	3	4
Context switch (sync)	1.46	2.09	2.25	2.20	1.84	2.28	6.30	4.24
Non-exclusive method	0.12	0.12	0.12	0.12	0.12	0.06	0.08	0.06
Exclusive method (unshared)	2.9	1.7	1.6	1.6	3.7	2.1	1.0	0.98
Exclusive method (shared)	-	1.9	1.6	1.7	-	9.5	14	10

The context switch benchmark measures the time for a synchronous context switch between threads. The results are scaled by the number of active objects in the test, to show the actual context switch time. The surprisingly high value for 3 threads on a dual-processor is presumably because the extra thread always hops to another processor when it is rescheduled. The dual-processor times increase with the number of active objects, because of contention on the fine-grained lock protecting the scheduler queue. A lock-free queue implementation[17] may be used in future to improve this.

The non-exclusive method benchmark measures the time for a normal method call. The single-processor times remain constant as the number of active objects are increased. The dual-processor times decrease, because on average the method calls are executed faster by two processors.

The exclusive method (unshared) benchmark measures the time for an exclusive method call, where the objects are independent. The tests show that the overhead of locking is substantial over a normal method call. This is expected to improve once test code is removed from the kernel and the implementation is optimized. Currently every object has a separate fine-grained lock in addition to its normal lock. By combining the two locks performance can be improved[2].

The exclusive method (shared) benchmark measures the time for an exclusive method call, where all the other objects call the method of the first object. The heavy contention for the lock takes its toll in the dual-processor case.

Table 2 shows the module sizes of the current implementation (including overhead due to test code).

5   Related Work

An Active Oberon uniprocessor run-time system based on Native Oberon, together with some server applications, is described in [7].

Concurrent Oberon[15] addresses the issue of concurrency in the Oberon system by adding a thread library. No attempt is made to integrate concurrency

Table 2. Aos kernel module sizes in bytes

Bottom layer				Top layer				Top layer			
Module	Code	Data	Const	Module	Code	Data	Const	Module	Code	Data	Const
AosProcessor	1364	72	40	AosDisks	5367	8	180	AosIP	5913	180	308
AosLocks	1249	468	16	AosATA	10395	32	636	AosTCP	22669	404	976
AosMemory	4855	612	132	AosKeyboard	4482	32	88	AosUDP	3291	40	28
AosStorage	8497	4208	304	AosMouse	7577	136	272	AosDHCP	1676	0	156
AosModules	3750	64	248	AosDisplays	2438	8	32	AosDNS	7099	120	336
AosInterrupts	3179	1744	24	AosClock	1533	8	52	AosFS	5564	272	32
AosTrap	4834	20	892	AosNICs	2421	40	52	AosDiskFS	22403	148	592
AosActive	6873	152	192	Aos3Com5x9	4925	84	128				
AosTicks	512	28	24	AosLoader	10639	4	292				
AosSMP	4458	52	456	AosConsole	1485	0	96				
	39571	7420	2328		51262	352	1828		68615	1164	2428

in the language, as the goal was to provide preemptive concurrency with as little change to Oberon as possible. The implementation runs on the Ceres machine.

The single-process Oberon tasking model is also addressed in [24], where a modified Oberon system is presented with three levels of tasks: background, interactive and real-time. Tasks at each level must still be programmed cooperatively, and the actions of non-interactive tasks are restricted.

The Aos system relies on high-level language concepts to preserve system integrity, an approach also adopted in SPIN[3] and Inferno[22].

A large body of work on multiprocessor operating system kernels is surveyed in [18].

Active Oberon's synchronization statement is similar to the *await* statement in Brinch-Hansen's shared classes concept[4]. At the time that concept was developed, the general await statement was thought to be too inefficient for practical use[12]. We believe a suitably light-weight implementation enables the effective use of this elegant synchronization construct.

6 Conclusion

The design of a multiprocessor operating system kernel for active object-based systems was presented. The Active Oberon language plays an important part in the design.

Active objects are used as the only concurrency concept, instead of the orthodox approach of having heavy-weight and light-weight processes.

The two-tiered modular design of the kernel facilitates flexible configuration in different environments. Plug-ins are used to keep the kernel lean.

The synchronization mechanism based on arbitrary boolean guard conditions seems sufficiently efficient, but will have to be evaluated with some real-world applications.

The current implementation is still under development, but initial evaluations of the usability and efficiency of the system are promising.

References

1. Maurice J. Bach. *The Design of the Unix Operating System*. Prentice-Hall, 1986.
2. David F. Bacon, Ravi Konuru, Chet Murthy, and Mauricio Serrano. Thin Locks: Featherweight Synchronization for Java. *ACM SIGPLAN Notices*, 33(6), June 1998.
3. Brian N. Bershad, Stefan Savage, Przemyslaw Pardyak, Emin Gün Sirer, Marc E. Fiuczynski, David Becker, Craig Chambers, and Susan Eggers. Extensibility, Safety and Performance in the SPIN Operating System. In *Proceedings of the Fifteenth ACM Symposium on Operating Systems Principles*, December 1995. Operating Systems Review, 29(5).
4. Per Brinch Hansen. *Operating System Principles*. Prentice-Hall, 1973.
5. DEC. The DIGITAL Network Appliance Reference Design. Web Page. http://www.research.digital.com/SRC/iag/.
6. Edsger W. Dijkstra. The Structure of "THE"-Multiprogramming System. *Communications of the ACM*, 11(5):345–346, May 1968.
7. Andreas Disteli. *Integration aktiver Objekte in Oberon am Beispiel eines Serversystems*. PhD thesis, ETH Zürich, 1997.
8. Andreas R. Disteli and Patrik Reali. Combining Oberon with Active Objects. Technical report, ETH Zürich Institut für Computerssyteme, 1997.
9. ETH Zürich Institut für Computersysteme. ETH Oberon. Web Page. http://www.oberon.ethz.ch/.
10. Jürg Gutknecht. Oberon, Gadgets and Some Archetypal Aspects of Persistent Objects. Technical Report 243, ETH Zürich, Institut für Computersysteme, February 1996.
11. Jürg Gutknecht. Do the Fish Really Need Remote Control? A Proposal for Self-Active Objects in Oberon. In Hanspeter Mössenböck, editor, *Lecture Notes in Computer Science 1204: Proceedings of the Joint Modular Languages Conference*, JMLC'97, Linz, Austria, March 1997. Springer.
12. C.A.R. Hoare. Monitors: An Operating System Structuring Concept. *Communications of the ACM*, 17(10):549–557, October 1974.
13. Intel. *MultiProcessor Specification Version 1.4*. Intel Corporation, August 1996.
14. Intel. *Operating System Writer's Guide*, volume 3 of *Pentium Pro Family Developer's Manual*. Intel Corporation, 1996.
15. Spiros Lalis and Beverly A. Sanders. Adding Concurrency to the Oberon System. In Jürg Gutknecht, editor, *Lecture Notes in Computer Science 782: Programming Languages and System Architectures*, pages 328–344. Springer, March 1994. own copy.
16. Johannes Marais. *Design and Implementation of a Component Architecture for Oberon*. PhD thesis, Swiss Federal Institute of Technology Zurich, 1996.
17. Henry Massalin and Calton Pu. A Lock-Free Multiprocessor OS Kernel. Technical Report CUCS-005-91, Department of Computer Science, Columbia University, 1991.
18. Bodhisattwa Mukerjee, Karsten Schwan, and Prabha Gopinath. A Survey of Multiprocessor Operating System Kernels. Technical Report GIT-CC-92/05, College of Computing, Georgia Institute of Technology, 1993.
19. Pieter Muller. Native Oberon Operating System. Web Page. http://www.oberon.ethz.ch/native/.
20. Patrik Reali. Structuring a Compiler with Active Objects. In *Joint Modular Languages Conference*. Springer, September 2000.

21. Josef Sedlacek. Project C2: A Survey of an Industrial Embedded Application with PC Native Oberon. In *Joint Modular Languages Conference*. Springer, September 2000.
22. Lucent Technologies. Inferno. Web Page. http://inferno.lucent.com/inferno/.
23. Niklaus Wirth. The Programming Language Oberon. *Software — Practice and Experience*, 18(7):671–690, July 1988.
24. Niklaus Wirth. Tasks versus Threads: An Alternative Multiprocessing Paradigm. *Software – Concepts and Tools*, 17:6–12, 1996.
25. Niklaus Wirth and Jürg Gutknecht. *Project Oberon: The Design of an Operating System and Compiler*. Addison-Wesley, 1992.

Evaluating the Java Virtual Machine as a Target for Languages Other Than Java

K. John Gough and Diane Corney

Queensland University of Technology, Box 2434 Brisbane 4001, Australia,
j.gough@qut.edu.au, d.corney@qut.edu.au

Abstract. The portability and runtime safety of programs which are executed on the Java Virtual Machine (*JVM*) makes the *JVM* an attractive target for compilers of languages other than Java. Unfortunately, the *JVM* was designed with language Java in mind, and lacks many of the primitives required for a straighforward implementation of other languages.

Here, we discuss how the *JVM* may be used to implement other object-oriented languages. As a practical example of the possibilities, we report on a comprehensive case study.

The open source *Gardens Point Component Pascal* compiler compiles the entire Component Pascal language, a dialect of Oberon-2, to *JVM* byte-codes. This compiler achieves runtime efficiencies which are comparable to native-code implementations of procedural languages.

1 Introduction

1.1 Java and the Java Virtual Machine

The runaway success of the Java programming language[1] in the last few years is a phenomenon arguably without parallel in the short history of programming languages. One of the interesting side-effects of this widespread popularity is the ubiquity of the execution engine of Java, the Java Virtual Machine (*JVM*)[2]. Essentially all computing platforms have at least one *JVM* implementation available for them, and there are an increasing number of lightweight, small footprint *JVM* implementations targetted at embedded devices.

The widespread adoption of Java as an implementation language for mainstream applications has ensured that the typical Java execution environment is endowed with a rich supply of APIs. Thus solutions to issues such as security, network programming, wide character support and so on are suddenly available in a relatively uniform fashion across the spectrum of platforms.

A final factor favouring the availability of the Java execution environment is the elimination of the major argument against the virtual machine approach, that is, the runtime inefficiency of the virtual machine interpreter. As will be quantitatively demonstrated below, the use of the more recent just-in-time compilation systems all but removes the runtime overhead of the traditional, interpretative approach to virtual machine implementation.

J. Gutknecht and W. Weck (Eds.): JMLC 2000, LNCS 1897, pp. 278–290, 2000.

After discounting the effects of fashion, it seems that the popularity of Java is based in two promises: one is the *write-once, run anywhere* claim of universal portability, the other is the runtime type-safety of Java programs. Although it may be observed that both of these claims are subject to some minor quibbles, they hold true to a very large extent.

For many enthusiasts of Java, it may come as a surprise to learn that the two "key advantages" of Java are not properties of Java the programming language. Rather the key advantages are properties of the *JVM*. A consequence of this observation is the claim that programs written in *any* programming language would share all of the advantages of Java, once they were translated into the machine code used by the *JVM*.

1.2   Languages Other Than Java

A number of people, lured by the availability of the *JVM* have written compilers which compile subsets of other languages to the Java bytecode form[3]. In most cases these efforts have been restricted to language subsets, since there is no efficient way of encoding the type-unsafe features of most of the other popular programming languages. This is an intrinsic limitation, since the design philosophy of the *JVM* is based on type safety. Indeed, if an implementor was to find a way of bypassing the type safety guarantees of some implementation of the *JVM*, it seems probable that the exploit could form the basis of a security attack on Java programs. Thus the *JVM* vendor would be obliged to remove the security hole in the next revision, invalidating any programs depending on the flaw.

Leaving aside the issue of type-safety, there is some question as to whether languages of a different design philosophy can be efficiently implemented on the *JVM*. In order to explore the answer to this question, in 1998 a project was begun to provide a complete, efficient implementation of another type-safe language.

The central difficulty standing in the path of languages other than java (*LOTJ*s) is the fact that the *JVM* was designed precisely with language Java in mind. The execution engine does not provide the primitives that are required for the simple implementation of many *LOTJ*s. Common programming language features which require some inventiveness include —

- Reference parameters
- Uplevel addressing (access to non-local variables)
- Procedure variables (function pointers)
- Structural compatibility of types

All of these issues may be solved with more or less difficulty, as is demonstrated by the compiler which forms the main subject of this paper. However, there are other, practical issues which need to be considered as well.

The standard Java runtime environment consist of the *JVM*, together with infrastructure that loads classes as needed. An intrinsic part of this mechanism is the *byte-code-verifier*, which checks the binary form of every class before loading it. JavaSoft describe this tool as a "theorem prover" which refuses verification to any class for which it cannot establish the required properties. As is usual, many of the properties which the verifier attempts to evaluate are undecidable. The analysis is therefore necessarily conservative. This places a novel constraint on the compilers of *LOTJ*s since it is insufficient to generate semantically correct code, instead the code must be generated in such a way that the verifier is able to establish that correctness.

Gardens Point Component Pascal (**gpcp**) is a compiler for the language Component Pascal[4,5]. It implements the complete language. All of the issues listed above needed to be resolved, in order to achieve this outcome.

1.3   Why Component Pascal?

Component Pascal is a dialect of Oberon-2[6,7]. The language was designed by Clemens Szyperski and others for Oberon Microsystems' BlackBox Component Builder framework. Like Oberon-2 it is a small, object oriented language supporting single inheritance based on extensible records.

Compared to Oberon-2, Component Pascal has a number of new features which support programming in the large and component-based programming. The most important change is the use of declarative attributes to control the visibility and heritability of types and methods. Thus, types and methods which are intended to be extended or overridden must be declared **EXTENSIBLE**. Unlike Java, the *default* behaviour corresponds to Java's **final**. Methods must also declare whether they are intended to override inherited methods, or are intended to be **NEW**.

Apart from this richer declarative framework, the base semantics of the language follows that of its predecessors Pascal, Modula-2 and Oberon-2. Thus the language supports nested procedures with block scope, reference parameters, and procedure types and values. Although this is a relatively small language, it has all of the needed functionality to be used as a systems implementation language.

The parameter passing mechanisms of the language are more general than those of its predecessors. Formal parameters may be declared as being of **IN**, **OUT**, or **VAR** (i.e. inout) modes. The default, as with Pascal is value mode. The tighter specification of intended use of parameters allows for stronger static checking by the compiler, but also significantly frees up the use of actual parameters. Recall that for type-safety an **inout** mode formal parameter may have neither a supertype nor a subtype object passed to it as an actual parameter.

As a vehicle for the exploration of the issues involved in compiling *LOTJ*s to the *JVM*, Component Pascal seems an ideal choice. The language poses all of the significant issues that were itemized in the introduction. Furthermore, since the language is completely statically type-safe there was reason to believe that this is one of the few languages for which *the complete language* could be efficiently implemented by the *JVM*.

1.4   Overview

It is the objective of this paper to review the main issues of compilation of *LOTJ*s to the *JVM*, and give some performance figures. A more extensive treatment of the detail of some of the required techniques has been given elsewhere[8].

2   Gardens Point Component Pascal

2.1   The Compiler

Gardens Point Component Pascal (**gpcp**) is a compiler for the language Component Pascal, which targets the *JVM*. It is able to produce either applications or applets, and is able to make use of the Java API to access utilities such as network services and GUI support.

The compiler was initially written in Java, and a new version has been implemented in its own language. Both the current and the future versions of the compiler will be released as open source products. Thus the community may use the compiler directly, or as an example of the techniques of compiling *LOTJ*s to the *JVM*. The current version of the compiler is being fitted with replaceable code emitters which will target other virtual machines, including the *DCode* intermediate form used by other Gardens Point compilers.

2.2   Data Representation and Module Structure

There are only two kinds of data known to the *JVM*. These are the local variables of methods, and dynamically allocated instances of classes and arrays. Local variables are simple scalars or references to objects, and can only be accessed from within their owning method. There is no concept of data address, nor of address arithmetic. It is possible to store and pass references, but these references can only originate from the allocation of objects of known type. In particular, it is not possible to obtain a reference which points to the interior of an object, or points to a local variable of a method.

It follows that all the program data of a *LOTJ* must be mapped onto the available types of the *JVM*. Component Pascal has the usual scalars, arrays, records and has pointers to dynamically allocated arrays and records. Data of all these types may be *static*, that is, allocated at load time, or *automatic*, that is, allocated on procedure invocation.

The mapping of modules onto classes is performed as follows. Each module corresponds to a single class in the *JVM*. Ordinary, that is, non-virtual procedures of the module become static procedures of the class, and module data becomes static data of the class. Each record type of the module becomes a class in the *JVM*, carrying with it all of the type-bound (virtual) procedures of the module. Details are given in Figure 1.

Component Pascal Construct	Java Virtual Machine Construct
module level scalars and pointers	static fields of the class corresponding to the CP module
module level records and arrays	objects referenced by static variables of the module class, and allocated at load time of the class
scalar or pointer local variables of procedures	local variables of corresponding *JVM* method
record and array variables of procedures	objects reference by local variables of the *JVM* method, and allocated during the procedure prolog

Fig. 1. Mapping of data types

2.3   The Java Runtime Environment

At runtime, a *JVM* program may be abstracted as a set of dynamically loaded class "byte-code" files, a stack of method activation records, and an evaluation stack associated with the currently executing method. The class files contain symbolic information in a constant pool, and the executable statements of the methods, encoded as byte-code instructions for the target-independent virtual machine. The virtual machine is an abstract stack machine, with a rich instruction set. The semantics of method invocation and parameter passing are determined by the detailed semantics of the method invocation instructions. These semantics are informally defined in the Java Virtual Machine Specification[2].

Much of the underlying semantics of the Java language is visible in the *JVM* at runtime. For example, the notions of single implementation inheritance, and the implementation of multiple interfaces, are reflected in the operational semantics of the *invokevirtual* and *invokeinterface* instructions.

At runtime, program data consists of primitive data and references to dynamically allocated objects. Primitive data includes various sizes of integers and floating point numbers, unicode characters, and booleans. Every such datum occupies either one or two 32-bit slots in the activation record or evaluation stack. References provide access to instances of class objects and dynamically sized array objects. It is axiomatic that these references provide the only path of access to objects. In particular, there is no notion of "address", and no address arithmetic.

Note that there are no structured data other than the dynamically allocated objects that are accessed by reference.

The language Java passes parameters by value, as illustrated by Figure 2. In the general case if a method requires, say, n parameters, these actual parameters are pushed, in order, onto the evaluation stack. At the call, the n parameter values are transferred into the first n local variable slots of the activation record of the called method.

The only way in which a method can send a value back to its caller is by using the function return-value mechanism. Value returning functions push their return

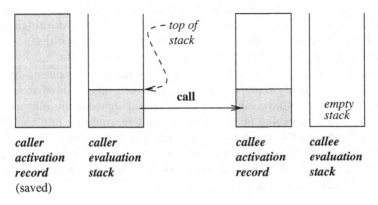

Fig. 2. Method call: parameters are taken from the evaluation stack

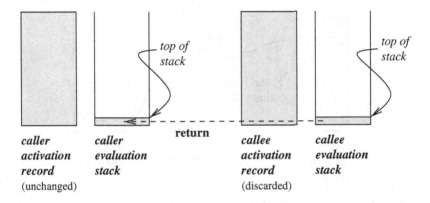

Fig. 3. Function value return: stack value is copied onto the stack of the caller

value onto the evaluation stack. The return instruction, as shown in Figure 3, takes the value on the stack and copies it onto the otherwise empty evaluation stack of the calling method to which control returns.

2.4 Parameter Passing

Parameters are passed in the *JVM* only by value. Since there is no notion of data address, it is not possible to obtain the effect of reference parameters by passing addresses using the language-C idiom.

There are several possiblities which were explored to resolve this problem. Several of these are discussed in a more specialised paper[8] . In summary, precise reference semantics may be obtained by passing a reference to an "accessor" object as the argument, and using that object's *get()* and *set()* methods to access the actual parameter. Note however, that since the local data of inactive stack activation records is inaccessible, local actual parameters still need to be placed on or copied to the runtime heap. A severe consequence of many of the possible solutions to this problem is a proliferation of "junk classes". Junk classes are so-called because they are used for a single purpose only, at a single program point, but clutter the namespace. In the case of the accessor objects, we have a worst case of one junk class per actual parameter per call site.

In the final design, *OUT* and *VAR* (inout) parameters are passed by copying in and out. Since the *JVM* allows only a single return value, this effect is obtained by "boxing" the outgoing value in a unit length, dynamically allocated array. The caller loads the value of the actual parameter variable into the box, and saves a reference to the box through the call. The called procedure updates the boxed value. After the return, the caller uses the saved reference to access the updated value in the box. It finally copies the new value to the actual parameter location. Figure 4 illustrates this concept.

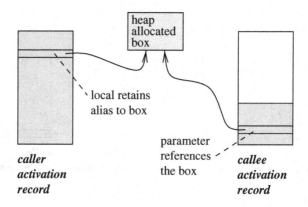

Fig. 4. Passing a boxed value to a procedure

2.5   Uplevel Addressing

Providing access to non-local data in languages with nested procedure scopes poses further challenges for *JVM* implementation. A future technical report will describe the somewhat arcane details. Nevertheless, it suffices here to note that one possible solution is to pass the non-local variables as additional, hidden "quasi-parameters". This is the approach that **gpcp** adopts. In this case, of course, there is no declarative framework to define the mode of such quasi-parameters. In **gpcp** the problem is resolved by using the same dataflow analysis which checks for errors in variable initialization. The analysis discovers the required formal mode for each quasi-parameter. The resulting "mode" information is propagated interprocedurally, so that enclosing procedures will use the correct parameter modes. In this way incorrect initialization of non-locally accessed data is detected, while avoiding spurious error messages.

2.6   Dataflow Analysis

As pointed out in the introduction, it is necessary for any compiler of a *LOTJ* to ensure that the class files which it produces are able to be verified. In particular, the verifier will insist on being able to prove that every local variable is properly initialized before use. This requires conservative dataflow analysis the details of which are implied by the *Definite Assignment* rules of the Java Language Specification. This is a relatively standard *backward-flow, all-paths* dataflow analysis problem.

There is no advantage in performing a more accurate analysis than the verifier, since the verifier has the final say. However, as it turns out the computational framework which is required to perform the analysis may be used for additional helpful compile-time diagnostics. Figure 5 is an example where an interprocedural extension of the dataflow analysis allows **gpcp** to detect an incorrect program construction.

```
PROCEDURE Bar();
   VAR abc,xyz : INTEGER;

   PROCEDURE Fee; BEGIN abc := 0 END Fee;
   PROCEDURE Foo; BEGIN INC(xyz) END Foo;

BEGIN
   Fee; (* this one is ok  *)
   Foo; (* but this is bad *)
**** ^ Non-locally accessed variable may be uninitialised
**** ^ <xyz> not assigned before this call
   ...
END Bar;
```

Fig. 5. Incorrect code requiring interprocedural analysis

There are some interesting consequences of the analysis which is required to guarantee successful verification. Consider the code skeleton in Figure 6 .

```
PROCEDURE FooLoop();
   VAR abc,xyz,ijk : INTEGER;
BEGIN
   xyz := 7;
   FOR abc := 0 TO xyz DO
      <initialise ijk>
   END;
   <use ijk>
END FooLoop;
```

Fig. 6. FOR loop requiring careful code generation

The final use of variable *ijk* in this procedure is correct, as it happens. If the compiler propagates the constant upper bound into the loop it can prove that the loop is entered at least once. Thus the value is always assigned before its use. The question is: how is the byte-code verifier of the *JVM* able to establish this fact, since it does not perform constant propagation and does not understand the semantics of FOR loops?

Clearly it is necessary, in this case, to ensure that the code for this loop is emitted as a post-tested loop in the byte-codes. The verifier will thus see the initialisation of the variable, and pass the code.

Of course, another approach might be applied here: perform the detailed analysis in the compiler so as to produce the detailed, friendly error messages, but then put in default initialisations everywhere to keep the verifier happy. This approach works, but ends up performing unnecessary work at runtime, limiting the achievable efficiency.

2.7   Procedure Variables

Perhaps the most difficult aspect of the whole project turned out to be the implementation of procedure variables (function pointers in language *C*).

The problem is twofold. First, the *JVM* knows of no such construct. Second, procedure variables in those languages which possess them typically are determined to be compatible according to structural equivalence rules. Since the *JVM* knows only of equivalence according to name, the problem follows.

The first issue is easily solved by representing a procedure value as an object with a single "invoke" method. However, when such a value has to be assigned the compiler cannot guarantee that the value is of the same named type as the destination value.

A number of complex schemes were prototyped in an attempt to resolve this issue. In the current version, the solution is simple, but sometimes inefficient. Procedure **types** correspond to *JVM* interface types, while procedure **values** are declared to be of some unique class type. The trick is that the class corresponding to each value implements every conforming interface known to the compiler. There is thus a high probability that any particular invocation of a procedure value will find the value implements the expected interface type. The exceptional cases are trapped at runtime, and the call made using the reflection mechanisms. The compile-time guarantee of structural compatibility guarantees the success of the reflection-mediated invocation.

2.8   Accessing the Java API

The attractiveness of any *LOTJ* is likely to depend critically on the ease with which the Java API is able to be accessed. In particular, for a language such as Component Pascal, it is important that components are able to interwork seamlessly with the Java component framework – Java Beans.

Following previous experience with Gardens Point compiler systems, we defined a *foreign language interface* which allows declaration of Java API access. As it turned out, several problems surfaced with constructs such as interface types, protected methods, and name overloading.

A fundamental issue is that languages such as Component Pascal enforce a strict partial order on compilation order. Java has no such restriction.[1] Rather than write a new compiler especially for interfaces, we have constructed a prototype tool which produces binary symbol files from the metainformation in the corresponding Java .class file. If general, in order to provide access to a particular Java class, it is necessary to process the metainformation for the web of classes that are reachable from the required class. The tool does this automatically.

In response to the other issues, we have enriched the attribute evaluation of the compiler so that it understands some of the semantics of Java as well as Component Pascal. As an example, the compiler understands what it means for a Component Pascal type to extend a Java API class. It also permits Component Pascal types which are extensions of Java classes to contract to implement interfaces. Such obligations are fully enforced.

These choices have certainly added some additional complexity to the compiler. However, they are a necessary addition. Consider for example that the $LOTJ$ classes cannot participate in the Java 1.1+ event handling model unless there is a mechanism for declaring that they implement the necessary event handling interfaces.

3   Performance

Some figures available from preliminary testing suggest that for procedural (i.e. non object-oriented) code the performance of programs is comparable to Modula-2 compiled to native code on the same platform.

Here, we present two rather different synthetic benchmarks, to illustrate the range of possibilities. The first of these benchmarks is a program which discovers all solutions of the *N-queens* problem for all board sizes from 8 to 13. The algorithm is recursive backtracking, so the procedure call and return mechanism is exercised extremely vigorously. Figure 7 shows normalised results for several different platforms.

Platform	Version	Optimised M2	Default M2	CP with JIT	CP interpreted
SPARC/Solaris	JDK 1.2.1	100%	78%	91%	4%
SPARC/Solaris	JDK 1.1.6	100%	84%	72%	6%
Pentium/Win98	JDK 1.2.0	100%	77%	106%	13%
Pentium/Linux	JDK 1.1.7	100%	82%	—	13%

Fig. 7. Relative speeds for NQueens program

---

[1] Consider `java.lang.Object` This class has methods which presume that the properties of `java.lang.String` and `java.lang.Class` are known to the compiler of the interface. But both of these types are extensions of `Object` and presume prior compilation of that class' interface.

In this figure the results have been normalised to factor away the relative speeds of the various platforms, although these all fell within a factor of two in absolute speed. Several factors are worthy of mention here. Firstly it may be seen that for the *SPARC* platform significant improvements have been made to the just in time compiler (JIT) between version 1.1.6 and 1.2.1. Even the interpreter is somewhat faster.

Notice also that Component Pascal, with the aid of the JIT, is faster than native code with the default level of optimisation. Only with the highest level of optimisation turned on does the native code run faster.

For the Intel architecture it is clear that the interpreters are more efficient than on SPARC. In the case of version 1.2 is appears that the JIT produces better code than the GPM compiler with all optimisations turned on. This is a very significant achievment. We did not have access to a JIT for the Linux platform.

The NQueens benchmark is a little unusual, since it involves no object creation at all. A rather different impression is given by the (in)famous *Dhrystone* program. In this case, although this is a purely procedural benchmark, the program requires some object creation for the passing of parameters. Figure 8 shows the comparable performance numbers.

Platform	Version	Optimised M2	Default M2	CP with JIT	CP interpreted
SPARC/Solaris	JDK 1.2.1	100%	82%	25%	4%
SPARC/Solaris	JDK 1.1.6	100%	87%	11%	4%
Pentium/Win98	JDK 1.2.0	100%	82%	11%	3%
Pentium/Linux	JDK 1.1.7	100%	80%	—	3%

Fig. 8. Relative speeds for Dhrystone program

In this figure the results have been normalised to factor away the relative speeds of the various platforms. Taken at face value, these figures are somewhat discouraging. However, further investigation showed that much of the runtime of the program was spent in allocation of objects, and in garbage collection of the parameter boxes.

Some analysis of program behaviour for the third platform in Figure 8 was undertaken, in order to determine the sources of the performance loss. Figure 9 shows elapsed time in seconds for various modified versions of the program in the previous figure.

Apart from the final row of this figure, all of the modifications to the code are ones which the compiler might implement as a result of static analysis[2]. The use of the function return value mechanism to return the first *VAR* or *OUT* parameter is an obvious refinement.

The static allocation of local structures in non-recursive procedures is also amenable to analysis. In practice it should also be combined with enough analysis to ensure that parameter boxes used repeatedly in (say) loops within procedures

---

[2] The current version of the compiler implements these refinements.

Pentium/Win98	Time	Program variation
Optimised M2	1.70	Modula-2 version of *Dhrystone*, compiled with `gpm -O2irts`.
CP with JIT	15.20	Default code generation, including boxed *VAR* parameters.
CP with JIT	10.11	Using function return values to return first *VAR* or *OUT* parameter.
CP with JIT	3.79	Statically allocating local record variable of non-recursive procedure.
CP with JIT	1.90	Subtracting the overhead of the remaining entire, field-by-field record assignment.

Fig. 9. JVM/JIT time spent in Dhrystone program

are allocated during the procedure prolog. Some subtle profitability analysis is probably warranted here.

The final overhead, subtracted in the final row of the figure, shows that almost half of the total runtime of the previous line is being spent in a single assignment statement. Since the *JVM* provides no "block copy" operation, entire assignments are performed by calls to a special method which for each class defines a field-by-field copy. Experiments are ongoing in this area.

In any case, the analysis of this example suggests that some care in code generation, can remove most of the residual overheads of our current, naive code generation techniques.

4   Conclusions

The compiler **gpcp** convincingly demonstrates that it is possible to execute at least suitable *LOTJ*s using the *JVM* as an execution platform. As indicated here, the whole of the language may be successfully translated with reasonable efficiency. The advantages of the *JVM* as an execution mechanism are thus available to a wider range of languages.

It is interesting to consider which other languages might be candidates for complete translation. Certainly languages with a high degree of type safety are candidates, with perhaps Ada, Sather and Eiffel springing to mind. The situation with other languages is not so clear. There are certainly useful subsets of many other languages which might be successfully translated. However, the chance of capturing large quantities of legacy code by this mechanism seem dubious. The problem is that many unnecessary but prevalent idioms in programming praxis use non type-safe mechanisms. For example, almost all uses of union types are intractable to the *JVM*.

There is another language dimension which needs consideration, that of immediate translation languages. These languages occur, for example, whenever a command language is translated on-the-fly to some intermediate form and then immediately executed. Given the amount of technological advancement in JIT compilation sparked by the Java revolution, the use of *JVM* byte-codes as an intermediate form for such dynamic compilation systems seems without parallel. It may transpire that the most important application of this research into compiling *LOTJ*s is for such dynamic compilation languages.

Acknowledgements. The work reported here was partially supported by ARC grant A49700626. Useful discussions with Clemens Szyperski, Nam Tran, Wayne Kelly and Paul Roe are acknowledged. The work on the interface to the Java API depends heavily on the Java Tools project of DSTC, particularly the work of Ken Baker.

References

1. J. Gosling, B. Joy and G. Steele, *The Java Language Specification*, Addison-Wesley, Reading MA, 1997.
2. T. Lindholm and F. Yellin, *The Java Virtual Machine Specification*, Addison-Wesley, Reading MA, 1997.
3. R. Tolksdorf, *Programming Languages for the Java Virtual Machine* (Web bibliography) `http://grunge.cs.tu-berlin.de/~tolk/vmlanguages.html`
4. Oberon Microsystems, 'Component Pascal Language Report' available at — `http://www.oberon.ch/resources`
5. Cuno Pfister, 'The Evolution of Oberon-2 to Component Pascal'. Oberon Microsystems (technical report), available at — `http://www.oberon.ch/resources`
6. N. Wirth, 'The Programming Language Oberon'; *Software Practice and Experience* 18:7, 671–690; 1988.
7. H Mössenböck and N. Wirth, 'The Programming Language Oberon-2'; *Structured Programming* 12, 179–195.
8. K John Gough, 'Parameter Passing for the Java Virtual Machine' *Australian Computer Science Conference* ACSC2000, Canberra, February 2000, IEEE Press.

Building Your Own Tools:
An Oberon Industrial Case-Study

Paul Reed

Padded Cell Software Ltd, PO Box 1880, London NW6 1BQ, United Kingdom
paulreed@paddedcell.com, http://www.paddedcell.com

Summary: Our experience creating custom application software has taught us that total control over our development tools is a necessity. Project Oberon provided an excellent starting point for us to build our own cross-platform application programming environment. Our adaptation of Wirth's compiler is re-targetable at run-time via a small set of installable up-calls, enabling a single machine-specific code-generation module of typically less than a thousand lines of code. The only significant additions to the original Oberon language are floating-point binary-coded decimals and open-array variables with string concatenation (e.g. s := "Error: " + t). Accompanying run-time libraries, written in Oberon, for operating systems such as Microsoft Windows (32-bit) and MS-DOS have been developed. Several systems created using the new tools have been in use by customers for some time.

1. Introduction

We present an industrial application of Niklaus Wirth's and Jürg Gutknecht's research project [1], the programming language [2] and operating system Oberon, which aims to retain the original's simplicity, clarity and reliability. First the motivation for developing the software is explained, and the occasionally roundabout route which led to it is described in some detail. The particular design aspects of our version of the Oberon compiler and its target run-time environment are summarised, and finally we outline the steps involved in writing a new code generator for a given machine. In publishing these experiences, we hope that others may be encouraged to take Wirth's blunt attitude to 'bells and whistles', and enjoy reliable software as a natural result.

2. Motivation

Providing working software for real customers is in most cases hard work, yet despite warnings [3] the complexity involved continues to be underestimated by the industry's practitioners. Many large, high-profile software projects fail completely - and 'small' software is often unreliable. Critics often contrast this with civil engineering, where (on the whole) bridges do not tend to collapse during construction. Considering that in software we have far more control over the properties of our tools and materials than in other branches of engineering, the phenomenon is all the more surprising.

We reject the argument that computing is still in its infancy and therefore that such failures are only to be expected - consider aviation, where through great effort and the will to create a safety culture, passenger flights were made acceptably safe by the

J. Gutknecht and W. Weck (Eds.): JMLC 2000, LNCS 1897, pp. 291-298, 2000.
© Springer-Verlag Berlin Heidelberg 2000

1930's and fatality rates were improved again by an order of magnitude by the late 1950's.

In our experience, the biggest obstacle to providing finished software is finding the time to write it. Analysing our past projects, which used the complex development tools available commercially, it dawned on us that a frightening proportion of intellectual effort and time was being wasted on installation, configuration and debugging of these tools - we estimated in one extreme case as much as eighty percent of the entire project time.

We feel that it is partly *because* software offers the freedom to design ridiculously over-featured compilers and other development tools (most of which are far from bug-free) that the complexity of projects can get out of hand. Wrestling with the unpredictable properties of a fault-ridden programmer's tool may be stimulating, but it is distracting, and leaves less of our mental capacity available to solve the problems in the customers' domain.

Creating simple, single-purpose tools is unfashionable because it restricts scope and flexibility; but this can sometimes actually be beneficial, reducing the sheer number of decisions to be made along the way. An example of this is the software running the tiny computer fitted to the Voyager 2 space probe, whose outstandingly successful mission inspired Wirth to begin the original Oberon project [1].

The concept of providing just enough is expounded repeatedly in Project Oberon. But what makes it unique is the presentation of the entire source code of the operating system and compiler, and extremely lucid descriptions of their design and construction, all in a single compact volume. Many excellent expositions of compiler design and compiler-writing toolkits exist, for example [4], [5]; but the emphasis is often on a general approach. Attention in the literature tends to be focused on writing a 'front-end', where statements formulated in the source language are parsed, whereas actual code-generation (the 'back end') is sometimes even left as an exercise to the reader.

Knowing that we could fall back on the source code and explanations in the book, at the beginning of 1997 we decided to start a project to build some new in-house development tools based around the hand-crafted, single-pass, recursive-descent Oberon compiler designed by Wirth.

3. Objectives

The goal of our project was a simple, portable application programming environment gained in a reasonably short time scale.

Simplicity was essential in order to ensure a complete understanding of the tool on which we were totally reliant. This avoids being in the position, when developing software systems for customers, of blaming tools like bad workmen. There is also usually a need to maintain and adapt software long after it has been created, and our compiler tool would not be exempt from this.

Several different machines and operating systems, including at least Microsoft Windows (32-bit) and Apple Macintosh, would need to be supported. So the compiler would need to be portable, generating code for more than one processor chip (at least Intel 80386 and Motorola 68000 respectively).

The third requirement was that the programming of the tools should not be an undue distraction - either during their construction or afterwards. We had no intention of becoming a development tools company, spending large amounts of time on the maintenance of our compiler for each machine platform - we wished actually to *use* the tools.

4. Getting Started

The initial plan was to take the (1996) standard ETH distribution of Oberon System 3 with a view to using it as-is, modifying it only slightly for our needs. Ports existed for many different processors, including the Intel and Motorola code generators which we required. Our idea was for one person to spend a year (part-time) building a usable integrated development environment (program source code editor, compiler, and linker) for the two platforms, Windows and Macintosh. We had learned from previous cross-platform projects that developing for more than one platform *at the same time* leads to better software: when it is discovered that a bug is either platform-specific or application-specific, this becomes the first step in the divide-and-conquer approach to correcting the error.

Unfortunately, although Regis Crelier's portable OP2 compiler [6] on which the System 3 Oberon distributions are based is an elegant and simple design, we found the actual implementations on each machine platform to be rather inscrutable. This is partly due to the vagaries of each machine's instruction set and run-time environment (particularly Intel) but also born from the desire to 'optimise' code-generation to produce high-performance machine code as the result. We were more concerned with maintainability and reliability of the tools - we had been 'bitten' in the past by optimising compilers which, when optimisation was turned on, generated the *wrong* code.

Reluctantly, we embarked on the one-man development of our own Oberon compiler version, using Project Oberon and Wirth's little Compiler Construction book [7] as our guides. A 'throw-away' MS-DOS compiler for Oberon-0 (a subset of the Oberon language) was developed, based on the Oberon-0 compiler described in Compiler Construction. This had the dual role of allowing us to see whether we were up to the task, and also gave us a rudimentary estimate of how long a full project might take. A compiler capable of compiling a demonstration of the Syracuse or "3x + 1" problem [8] was finished after three months. It was realised that one man-year had been somewhat optimistic, and the time-scale was re-set to three years (part-time). This meant that completion neatly coincided with the end of the century, a useful psychological deadline.

After the completion of our Oberon-0 compiler, we made what in hindsight we consider to be our biggest mistake of the project. The decision was made to define a subset of the language, which we called 'Oberon Enough', which was enough to implement the compiler. The thinking behind this was that we could reduce the amount of the compiler that we needed to get working, before the compiler would compile both itself and the final compiler. The problem was, what we were able to leave out (for example LONGINTs and REALs) did not really decrease the complexity of the compiler. The result was a six-month-long detour while we implemented another compiler which we have now discarded. Nevertheless, the experience gained certainly helped us implement the final compiler.

The Oberon Enough compiler, based heavily on the Project Oberon design, compiled itself successfully and reliably in MS-DOS by the end of October 1997, the ten-month mark. This meant that we were now self-sufficient in the tools we were using to create our tools - indeed Oberon Enough was also used for some minor customer projects. In the two years before it was eventually replaced by our final portable compiler, we discovered only three or four bugs, each of which was fixed in a matter of minutes. The benefits of building our own tools were already becoming clear.

5. Building a Portable Compiler

Having gained experience with Oberon-0 and Oberon Enough, we now embarked on the design of our ultimate, portable compiler.

The central idea became clear - to keep it simple we would not attempt to output optimal code. Twenty- to fifty-fold improvements in the speed of semiconductor technology between 1987 and 1997 had released us from the obligation to squeeze every ounce of performance out of a target machine. We even discovered, for example, that choosing a simpler register-allocation and spilling scheme than in Oberon Enough actually generated smaller and faster code in all but the most complex expressions. Wirth reports similar discoveries [1] - where a far less complex design turns out in practice to perform almost as well as a 'clever' one.

As a result, we made many machine-independent decisions about how code was to be generated. This enabled us, starting again with the Project Oberon design, to migrate all of the machine-specific parts of the compiler into a single module, of around a thousand lines of source code. A few machine-dependent variables (pointer size, stack alignment size) persist, which are set initially and are accessible by the rest of the compiler where necessary.

We then realised that by having the machine-dependent code generation module install itself into the rest of the compiler via a small set of up-calls, or procedure variables (function pointers in other languages), we could make the compiler re-targetable at run time. These up-calls (e.g. Move, Addr, BinOp etc.) are precisely the procedures which need to be written for a new processor. By constraining the interface of the code generator, it had become much easier and quicker to port the compiler to new architectures.

It is often tempting when developing a compiler to add features to the language. We kept these to a minimum, implementing only two significant extensions which were absolutely essential to us: a floating-point binary-coded decimal type for quantities such as money, and open-array variables supporting string concatenation. String handling in the original Oberon language was not sufficient for us efficiently to develop commercial applications, where character strings are extensively manipulated. A way was found to expand on Oberon's idea of an open-array parameter, and also provide an infix "+" operator for strings, without radically changing the Project Oberon design.

Complementary to the compiler code generator is the run-time environment provided, around which application software can be created. In the Oberon system, this includes a kernel, containing low-level functions such as memory-allocation, and also higher-level libraries like user-interface operations. Conversely, in the case of application software like ours, the run-time library provides a machine-independent layer, which in turn calls on the services of the target operating system such as Microsoft Windows.

The Windows 32-bit environment was targeted as the first test of our portable compiler, and a simple kernel and user-interface library was written. This allowed us to create new versions of some of the data-entry applications which we had previously provided to our customers as MS-DOS programs. It was even possible to postpone the implementation of run-time garbage-collection (reclamation of unused dynamic or 'heap' memory); our first few programs simply terminated and restarted themselves with a clean heap at key points transparent to the user.

One of the first applications completed with our new tools was a Windows-based library management system for the National Gallery in London. This has already proved extremely reliable in use over more than eighteen months, and a version is now also used at the Tate Gallery. Development and maintenance of these systems has been straightforward, and the impact (on our application) of major systems changes at both sites has been slight. We believe that all this is due in no small part to the simplicity of the tools used to construct the application software itself.

Once a nearly feature-complete compiler was being used in-house to generate programs for customers, the next step was to complete the 16-bit code generator in order to compile the compiler, obviating the need for our separate Oberon Enough compiler. This was completed by coincidence on the second anniversary of our finishing Oberon Enough, at month thirty-four.

Finally a Motorola 68000 code generator module was added to the compiler. This was written by one person in 52 hours (in 15 days over one month). Around five bugs in other parts of the compiler were uncovered, but no changes to the working design were necessary.

6. Compiler Design Summary

Most design decisions concerning our implementation of the compiler were influenced by simplicity and reliability, rather than performance. First, for example, taking a lead from Java [9], we too 'stick a stake in the ground' and force all basic types to be the same size on each machine. This reduces the number of machine-dependent variables needed by parts of the compiler other than the code generator module; and it also avoids the irritating experience (found for example in the C language) where the numeric range handled by an integer variable differs from machine to machine.

The run-time memory layout is standardised across all machines, using a fixed *arena pointer* (sometimes called static base) for each module, which is usually loaded into an address register and is saved and restored when calling across module boundaries. Module variables and type tags are accessed at negative offsets from this pointer, and other data, such as the arena pointers of imported modules, are accessed at positive offsets.

As explained above, no attempt is made to make the very best use of the resources on any particular processor: controversially, for example, we do not always use all available machine registers, instead providing standard 'spill' locations reserved in each module's arena for use in complex expressions.

Unsupported operations on particular processors, such as long integer division, as well as certain other library routines (some type conversions, floating-point decimal arithmetic, string concatenation) are called through a *trap vector* stored at offset zero in the arena. Constant data, such as strings, are accessed through a *constant pointer* located in each module's arena immediately after the trap vector.

Encapsulating the interface to the code generator using procedure variables as described above means that the compiler can contain code generators for several machines, selectable by a command-line option or other method. In addition to the convenience of having only one compiler to use, this enhances the maintainability across all platforms.

The approximate size of each module of the compiler is indicated by the figures given below, for a particular platform (MS-DOS, 16-bit Intel 8086):

```
Module                    source lines      object file (bytes)
Scanner                       402                 5955
Symbol table                  671                14111
Object file writer            529                 9765
Expressions                   983                26025
Statements                    404                 9276
Main parser                   979                19838
Command-line reader           199                 4248
Code generators:
  16- and 32-bit Intel       1644                25935
  Motorola                    825                13324
                            -----               ------
Total:                       6636               128477
```

7. Writing a New Code Generator

The general method which we found extremely helpful when developing a new code generator is the same as that explained in Project Oberon [1]. Before describing his compiler in detail, Wirth first lists fifteen sample 'code patterns' (we added a sixteenth for our open-array operations), showing what machine code should be output for a particular set of sample Oberon statements and expressions.

These patterns are far from working programs, but as Wirth points out, the discipline of deciding *which* code should be output (usually with a paper and pencil in our case) is a prerequisite, before discovering *how* best to design the generator. Working our way through the patterns kept the complexity of the task in check.

Each code-generation procedure has a standardised interface, and there are 14 procedures in all:

```
Released()  Move()  Addr()  Index()  MonOp()  BinOp()  Branch()
Jump()  Trap()  Case()  PrepCall()  Call()  Enter()  Return()
```

The procedures usually take as parameters one or more variables of type *Item*, a data structure (described in Project Oberon and Compiler Construction) containing information used by the code generator to select addressing modes and sizes of operands:

```
Item = RECORD
  mode, lev: INTEGER; (*addressing mode and scope*)
  a0, a1, a2: INTEGER; (*various*)
  typ: Struct; (*type, e.g. Integer, Record*)
  ...
END;
```

For example, when compiling code for a procedure call, a variable may need to be pushed onto the stack as a parameter. The procedure

```
Move(VAR x, y: Item)
```

will in this case be called with

$x.mode = Stk$ (stack), $y.mode = Var$ (a static or local variable).

If the variable is a static LONGINT, at offset -4 from the arena pointer, then

$y.a0 = -4$, $y.lev = 0$, $y.typ.size = 4$ (and $x.typ.size = y.typ.size$).

Note that type checking has already been performed by the machine-independent parts of the compiler.   The Move() procedure uses the information from the x-Item to select the addressing mode for the stack, and from the y-Item the addressing mode for the LONGINT variable. These are then combined into one or more instructions to be output as machine code.

We illustrate first how the above Item information is used when generating code for the Intel 80386 processor. On this machine, the stack addressing mode dictates a specialised push instruction which has a binary op-code value of 11111111 aa110aaa; the aa-aaa bits represent the addressing mode of the data to be pushed onto the stack.

In the case of the 80386, where we choose to store the arena pointer in the EBX register, the addressing mode selected by the y-Item will be "EBX register indirect with 8-bit displacement", 01---011. This is combined with the op-code and an 8-bit displacement argument, -4 (FC hex), so that the final result is the issue of the 3-byte instruction

```
FF 73 FC          push    dword ptr [ebx-04].
```

When targeting the Macintosh, the same Move() call will instead select a general 68000 "long move" op-code, 0010dddDDDSSSsss, where dddDDD is the destination addressing mode selected by the x-Item, and SSSsss is the source mode from the y-Item (capitals are used here to denote the addressing mode, lower case the register number involved).

The code generator uses the 68000 "address register indirect with predecrement" mode for the destination, using the A7 address register (stack pointer); the binary code for this is DDD=100, ddd=111. For the source (y-Item), where the arena pointer on this machine is held in address register A3, the "address register indirect with displacement" is selected: SSS=101, sss=011.

The op-code word with both sets of addressing mode bits is combined with the 16-bit displacement argument -4 (FFFC hex), culminating in the issue of the two-word instruction

```
2F2B FFFC         move.L  (-4,a3), -(a7).
```

8. Conclusion

Rather than continue to tolerate the complexity and unreliability of available commercial application development tools, we decided to build our own, based around the Project Oberon compiler [1].

We have isolated and simplified the code generator interface within the compiler, reducing the amount of work required when targeting a new processor instruction set. This has been brought about by supporting the generation of good, but not 'optimal' code for each target processor, and by standardising the run-time memory layout across different machines and operating systems. Additions to the Oberon language to better support application programming have been kept to a minimum.

A satisfactory portable compiler for application development was the result of three years' part-time work by one person, which we consider to be a reasonable timescale even for a small company. However, we wish to point out that this has been achieved only by adhering to the essentials required, keeping the tools *as simple as possible*.

Acknowledgements

The author wishes to thank in particular Dr. J. M. Benson and also Dr. S. M. Ginn for their encouragement and invaluable suggestions.

References

[1] Wirth, N. and Gutknecht, J. (1992). Project Oberon: The Design of an Operating System and Compiler. Addison Wesley
[2] Reiser, M. and Wirth, N. (1992). Programming in Oberon: Steps Beyond Pascal and Modula. Addison Wesley
[3] Wirth, N. (1995). A Plea for Lean Software. IEEE Computer, vol. 28, no. 2
[4] Fischer, C. and Leblanc, R. (1988). Crafting a Compiler (1st Ed). Benjamin Cummings
[5] Tanenbaum, A. S., van Staveren, H., Keizer, E. G., and Stevenson, J. W. (1983). A Practical Tool Kit for Making Portable Compilers. Communications of the ACM, vol. 26, no. 9
[6] Crelier, R. (1991). OP2: A Portable Oberon-2 Compiler. Proceedings of the Second International Modula-2 Conference, Loughborough University of Technology (ftp://ftp.inf.ethz.ch/pub/software/Oberon/OberonV4/Docu/OP2.Paper.ps.gz)
[7] Wirth, N. (1996). Compiler Construction. Addison Wesley
[8] Lagarias, J. C. (1985). The 3x+1 Problem and its Generalizations. American Mathematical Monthly, vol. 92, no. 1 (http://www.cecm.sfu.ca/organics/papers/lagarias/)
[9] Gosling, J. and McGilton, H. (1996). The Java Language Environment: A White Paper. Sun Microsystems, Inc. (http://java.sun.com/docs/white/langenv/)

Author Index